THE WASHINGTON MONUMENT,

Mount Vernon Place.

THE MONUMENTAL CITY,

ITS

Past History and Present Resources,

BY

GEORGE W. HOWARD.

BALTIMORE:
J. D. EHLERS & CO., ENGRAVERS AND STEAM BOOK PRINTERS,
87 Second Street,
1873.

TO

CHAUNCEY BROOKS, Esq.

This volume is dedicated by its author, as an humble testimony of the personal esteem he has entertained for him through a long series of years, and as, in some measure, a memorial of the proud position that gentleman to-day occupies in the city of Baltimore. Time in its cycles works many changes. Some men are unable to stem the current of adverse fortune, and pass away with naught left to embalm their memories, save the sad thought that their efforts were honest but unavailing; while others live to see the realization of their hopes and the glorious fruition that accompanies a well-spent and successful life. To the latter class Mr. Brooks belongs, and it seems peculiarly appropriate that a volume professing to give a sketch of Baltimore, with a succinct recital of the vast resources she at present possesses, should be dedicated to one who is so thoroughly identified with her history through a period of more than fifty years. Mr. Brooks, at a ripe old age, can look with pleasure upon gigantic corporations, great business enterprises, and mechanical forces, the birth of which he favored, and whose feeble infancy he strengthened by timely, judicious and unostentatious aid. That He who knoweth the good deeds of men may bountifully lengthen out his life, and that his future may be as peaceful and serene as his past has been useful and honored, is the prayer of the

AUTHOR.

PREFACE.

It is proposed in the present volume to give a sketch of the past of Baltimore, with brief allusions to those crises which marked her history and exercised an important bearing upon her progress as a city, also a running essay upon the useful and æsthetic features which make her to-day the most desirable location in America for those in search of *homes*, or contemplating a change of residence; together with short but comprehensive articles upon the various corporations at present in existence or soon to be organized, and the different departments of trade, commerce, and manufactures, which centre in our city.

If readers at a distance are disposed to regard critically, the spirit which induces a citizen of Baltimore to sound her praises more than perhaps the most guarded taste might suggest, let them consider that the same course has been pursued by all the larger cities in America, and that the great spirit of competition more thoroughly developed in this country than elsewhere, will not suffer her to remain silent at a time when her sisters have inundated the United States with the most fulsome accounts of their respective advantages. Let them bear in mind also, that already have travellers, not only from different sections of the Union but from the great centres of Europe, placed on record the most ample and possibly exaggerated accounts of the various features which endear her to her own citizens, and render the city peculiarly inviting to strangers; and lastly, let them remember that a pardonable pride is the greatest incentive to development and progress in the future. We ask at the hands of the public a generous criticism, inasmuch as this is a novel enterprise in Baltimore, and the means of securing information are exceedingly limited. With this brief preface we launch our little vessel, trusting that it may bring to our port the treasures which our merchants and business men so richly deserve.

BALTIMORE.

HISTORICAL SKETCH.

MR. McMAHON has remarked, in his Historical View of the Government of Maryland, that "the colonial history of Maryland is distinguished more by results than by incidents;" and he has further pointed out that "the gradual accessions to a nation's wealth, power and liberty, which she derives from a peaceful devotion to her own interests, are perceived only in their general results." If this be true of a nation, more especially is it true of a city; and therefore especially devoid of incident must be a historical sketch of a city, the principal object of which is to note the rise and progress of its commercial importance. In the following pages it is sought to set forth such facts as will best illustrate the growth and development of Baltimore, and the causes which most directly contributed to those results,—noting events of general or national character only where the history of Baltimore is intimately connected with them, in the relation of a part to the whole; and while the annals of Baltimore have at different times been marked by events of striking character and of considerable local interest, they have, for the most part, been such as belong to a political, rather than a commercial history.*

As introductory to the history of the city, it may be found useful to give some preliminary account of the Province in which it was founded, and the causes which led to its establishment.

The Province of Maryland had been settled for nearly a century before the first foundations were laid of the city that was destined to become the commercial metropolis of the State, and one of the leading cities of the American continent.

George Calvert, the first Lord Baltimore, having found that his efforts to establish a colony at Avalon, in Newfoundland, were attended with but little success, determined to seek a more favorable region in which to carry out his plans of colonization. With this view he visited, in the year 1628, the colony of Virginia. Of the favorable situation and flourishing condition of that colony he was well aware, having himself been a member of the Virginia

* *E.g.*—The outbreak of the war with England in 1812, the bank failures in 1835, and the outbreak of the civil war in 1861, were occasions of great excitement in the history of Baltimore.

Company before it had been deprived of its charter, in 1624, by a judgment of the Court of King's Bench. During his visit to Virginia, it is probable that Lord Baltimore personally explored the Chesapeake Bay; at all events his experienced judgment readily detected the advantages that would be secured to a colony upon its shores. Accordingly, upon his return to England, he procured from his royal master, Charles I., the promise of a grant of territory in the region which he had just visited.

The Virginia colonists were not unmindful of the facilities for traffic afforded by the Chesapeake, which stretches inland for a distance of two hundred miles from the ocean, with rivers emptying into it whose head-waters are far back in the interior. In the years 1626, 1627 and 1628, William Clayborne, Secretary of State for the colony of Virginia, obtained from the English government authority "to discover the source of the Chesapeake, and to make other explorations within the government of Virginia." Vested with this authority Mr. Clayborne appears to have improved the opportunities it gave him for establishing and conducting a trade with the natives upon the shores of the upper part of the bay; and for the furtherance of this object he probably erected some trading houses upon the Isle of Kent, which thus became the first place within the limits of Maryland in which any European settlements were made. The value which the Virginians placed upon the bay and the adjacent country, is further shown by the violent opposition they manifested to the establishment of Lord Baltimore's colony; and in a petition preferred to the King shortly after the grant had been made to Lord Baltimore, they particularly complain "that grants had lately been made of a great portion of the lands and territory of their colony, *being the places of their traffic.*"

The advantages for trade, together with the attractions of a fertile soil and a grateful climate, determined Lord Baltimore in the selection of the site for his future colony; but in consequence of his death, which occurred early in 1632, the charter promised to him, but which did not pass the seals until June 20th of the same year, was issued to his son Cecilius, second Lord Baltimore, upon whom devolved, together with his father's title and estates, the work of carrying out his wise and beneficent plans of colonization.

The territory embraced in Lord Baltimore's grant is described in the charter as follows: "all that part of the Peninsula, or *Chersonese,* lying in the parts of America between the ocean on the east, and the bay of Chesapeake on the west; divided from the residue thereof by a right line drawn from the promontory, or headland called Watkin's Point, situate upon the bay aforesaid, near the river Wighco, on the west unto the main ocean on the east; and between that boundary on the south, unto that part of the bay of Delaware on the north, which lieth under the fortieth degree of north latitude from the equinoctial; and passing from the said bay, called Delaware Bay, in a right line, by the degree aforesaid, unto the true meridian of the first fountain of the river of Potomac, thence verging towards the south, unto the farther bank of the same river, and following the same on the west and south, unto a certain place called Cinquack, situate near the mouth of the said river, where it disembogues into the aforesaid bay of Chesapeake, and thence by the shortest line unto the aforesaid promontory or place, called Watkin's Point." All the waters comprehended within these boundaries, and the islands lying in them, together with all islands off the coast, within ten leagues of the shore, were expressly mentioned as included in the grant. And in order that this region might "be eminently distinguished above all other regions in that territory, [America,] and decorated with more ample titles," it was erected into a Province and nominated Maryland.* Of this Province Lord Baltimore was made Absolute Lord and Proprietary, yielding only unto the crown of England, as pledge of his allegiance, two Indian arrows annually, and the fifth part of all gold and silver ore which should be found within the limits of the Province. To the Proprietary were given by the charter, the same rights, jurisdictions, prerogatives, royalties, &c., as appertained to the Bishop of Durham, within the bishopric or county palatine of Durham; with power to enact laws with the advice and assent of the freemen of the Province or their delegates; to appoint judges, administer the laws, and exercise jurisdiction over the persons resident in the Province even to the extent of depriving them of life or liberty; to impose taxes; to raise and command an army, either to defend the Province from invasion or to quell insurrection. At the same time, it was provided that persons emigrating to this Province should retain their rights as English subjects, both for themselves and their children; and the privilege was granted to them of trading with England, or in default of finding a market there, of conveying their merchandise thence to "any other countries they should think proper" which were in amity with England.

The boundaries prescribed for the Province of Maryland, as given above, became at different times the occasion for dispute on all sides, and as a consequence thereof, the present limits of the State are considerably less than those assigned to the Province. On the northeast, the State of Delaware has been erected within the limits of Maryland. On the north, the location of the boundary between Maryland and Pennsylvania was a matter of dispute until 1763, when it was determined by Messrs. Mason and Dixon, who, acting under a joint commission of the two Provinces appointed for the purpose of settling the difficulty, surveyed the line which now constitutes the boundary between the two States, and which, as the recognized boundary between the Northern and Southern States, has acquired a notoriety far beyond that which belongs to its local and original purposes. On the part of Virginia, a dispute arose as to whether the north or south fork of the Potomac was its "first fountain," by which the location of the western boundary of Maryland was to be deter-

*England's first Province. It was at first intended to call the Province *Crescentia;* but when the charter was presented to Charles I. for his signature, he struck out that name and substituted Maryland, in honor of his Queen, Henrietta Maria of France.

mined; and although the south fork is sixty miles the longer, and the territory lying between the forks is estimated at half a million of acres, Maryland has been compelled to establish her boundary upon the north fork. Upon the eastern shore of the Chesapeake, the precise location of the boundary between Maryland and Virginia is unsettled to the present day.*

Provided with a charter upon such favorable conditions, Lord Baltimore immediately commenced preparations for sending a colony to his new possessions. He at first intended to accompany the expedition in person, but abandoning this plan, he confided the leadership to his brother, Leonard Calvert, whom he appointed Governor of the Province, with the title of Lieutenant-General. On the 22d November, 1633, the colonists, to the number of about two hundred, many of them gentlemen of fortune, and most of them Roman Catholics, set sail from Cowes in the Isle of Wight. Taking the old route by the Azores and West Indies, and having stopped for some time at the Island of St. Christopher's and Barbadoes, they arrived off Point Comfort in Virginia on the 24th February, 1634. Letters which Governor Calvert brought from the King of England, secured for the colonists a favorable reception by the government of Virginia, and on the 3d of March they proceeded up the bay to the Potomac. Entering the river, they effected a landing and made their first settlements upon its banks. On the 25th of March, having erected a cross and celebrated mass, they took formal possession of the country "for our Saviour, and for our sovereign lord, the King of England." On the 27th the whole company landed and occupied an Indian town that had been ceded to them by the natives, and which, under the name of *St. Mary's*, continued to be the capital of the Province until 1692.

Thus the colony was first established almost at the southern extremity of the Province, and for some time after, the settlements upon the western shore of the bay were chiefly confined to that portion of the country. Various causes contributed to hinder the extension of settlements into the interior, in places remote from the more thickly settled portions of the Province. Wars occurred, both with the Indians and the Dutch settlements in the north-eastern portion of the Province, upon the Delaware Bay, and the Province itself was not exempt from internal commotions. In 1644 occurred the formidable insurrection known, from the name of its leader, as the "Ingle rebellion," the effects of which are felt to the present day by reason of the loss of many of the early records of the Province, which were carried away from St. Mary's by the insurgents and destroyed. The Proprietary government too was twice interrupted from without during the first hundred years of its existence. During the time of the Commonwealth in England, the government of the Province was usurped by commissioners appointed by Cromwell. And after the revolution which resulted in the establishment of William

* There is now a joint commission appointed from the two States, for the purpose of adjusting the boundary line between them.

and Mary upon the throne of England, the government of the Province was assumed by the crown. The royal government continued from 1692 until 1715, when the Proprietary's rightful authority was restored to him by George I.

The interval between the suppression of the Ingle insurrection and the arrival of Cromwell's Commissioners, (1651,) short as it was, was long enough to be signalized by an event that has made illustrious the colonial history of Maryland, and which to this day is looked back upon with pride. In 1648 Lord Baltimore prescribed a new oath of office to be taken by the Lieutenant-General of the Province; and in that age, when religious toleration, as now understood, was unknown in Europe, that officer was made to bind himself by this oath that he would not "directly or indirectly trouble, molest or discountenance any person whatsoever in the Province professing to believe in Jesus Christ, for or in respect of his or her religion," or the free exercise thereof; and that he would not "make any difference of persons in conferring of offices, rewards or favors for or in respect of their said religion;" and further that if any officer or person should molest or disturb any person within this Province on account of his religion, he would protect the person molested and punish the offender. At the session of the Assembly the same year, "an act concerning religion" was passed, by which these principles were embodied in the statute law, and their observance enforced under penalties.

In consequence of this wise and liberal policy of religious toleration, Maryland, under the auspices of a Roman Catholic Proprietary, became the common refuge for all who were suffering religious persecution. Members of the Church of England, Quakers and others, resorted thither from among the Puritans of New England, and Puritans came from Virginia to escape the requirements of the Established Church there; while Protestants from France and Portugal and the Netherlands, fled thither from the persecutions in those countries. So that this policy was in its effect as beneficial to the Province, by the valuable additions secured to the population, as in its conception, it was honorable to the Proprietary.*

As the population gradually increased, new and more extended settlement began to be made. Baltimore County was created in 1659, and in 1683, at a session of the Assembly held at the Ridge in Anne Arundel County, among several new towns that were created, two were situated in that county. Indeed there seems to have existed at that time a mania for making towns, no less than thirty-three having been created by the Assembly in the space of

* Of the Proprietary who thus stands before us as a man far in advance of the ideas of the age in which he lived, it may be said, that his life which lasted until 1675, was continually devoted to the best interests of the Province. Of him it was written, "never did a people enjoy more happiness than the inhabitants of Maryland under Cecilius, the founder of the Province." (Ramsay—Hist. Rev. War.)

The condition of religious equality which he established continued until 1692, when under the royal government which temporarily supplanted the Proprietary, there was for the first time an ecclesiastical establishment in Maryland.

four years. But for the most part they were but tentative, being intended only for places of landing and shipment, having but little territory assigned to them, and being as easily unmade as made. The excessive number of the towns was however for a long time a great hindrance to their growth and development, on account of the division of interests it occasioned, and the rivalries and jealousies which consequently arose.

As the settlements extended northward it was impossible that the advantages to be derived from the establishment of a port near the head of the bay could long escape the consideration of the colonists; and in looking for a place adapted for that purpose, their attention would naturally be drawn to the Patapsco River, in which, at a distance of only about fourteen miles from the bay, they found, at tide water, a safe and commodious harbor, easy of access, and navigable by the largest vessels. Accordingly, in 1729, an act was passed by the Assembly "for erecting a town on the north side of Patapsco in Baltimore County, and for laying out into lots sixty acres of land in and about the place where one John Flemming now lives." The "sixty acres" which were thus assigned as the dimensions of the town, were purchased by the Commissioners appointed for that purpose, at forty shillings per acre, or about ten dollars of our present money.

The metes and bounds of the town as originally laid out are thus described in Griffith's Annals, viz: "Commencing at a point near the northwest intersection of what are now called Pratt and Light streets, and running northwesterly along or near Uhler's alley towards the great eastern road, and a great gully, or drain, at or near Sharpe street, then across Baltimore street east of the gully northeasterly with the same road afterwards called the Church Road, and now McClellan's alley, to the precipice which overhung the falls at or near the southwest corner of St. Paul street [now Saratoga] and St. Paul's lane, then with the bank of that stream, southerly and easterly, various courses unto the low grounds ten perches west of Gay street, then due south along the margin of those low grounds to the bank on the north side of the river, and then by that bank various courses, nearly as Water street runs, westerly and southerly, to the first mentioned point." Although the position selected for Baltimore indicates that its founders had in view the facilities for trade which it enjoyed, the small amount of land originally taken, and the nature of the ground selected, surrounded as it was by hills, water courses and marshes, clearly show that they had no anticipation of what were actually to be the size and importance of the city they were founding. The hills with which the city abounds, and which at this day contribute so much to its picturesqueness, have rendered the work of extending and grading streets in many instances both difficult and expensive. "The precipice overhanging the falls"* alluded to, has either entirely disappeared, or been converted into graded declivities. Through the city of to-day flow no less than three streams, known as Jones' Falls, Harford Run and Chatsworth Run, (but of these only

* Jones' Falls, a stream that flows through the midst of the city.

the first named is now uncovered,) while a fourth, Gwynn's Falls, forms a portion of the city's boundary upon the west. A marsh which extended along the border of Jones' Falls, and formed the eastern boundary of the town as first laid out, has long since been filled up and built upon.

Notwithstanding these disadvantages, the unusual facilities for direct communication with the interior, the great security of the harbor, the remarkable healthfulness of the situation, (probably greatly contributed to by the excellent natural drainage,) the fertility of the surrounding country, the abundance of stone, lime, iron and timber in the immediate vicinity, and the many mill seats obtainable upon the neighboring streams, amply justify the sagacity shown in the selection of the site.

The town having been duly surveyed, and divided into sixty lots of about one acre each, an office was opened for purchasers on the 14th of January, 1730. It was stipulated in the terms of purchase that a house "covering at least four hundred square feet" should be erected within eighteen months; and no person was permitted to take up more than one lot during the first four months. The buyers appear to have been very few, and the lots went off but slowly;—so slowly indeed that some of them having remained untaken for seven years, reverted to the original owners of the land, according to the terms of the law under which the town was erected.

When the town was first laid out, there was scarcely a house standing upon the whole sixty acres; some few settlements had however been made in the neighborhood, and lands had been taken up as early as 1662. The first actual settler is said to have been Mr. David Jones, who, about the year 1680, having purchased some land, erected a house upon the north [or east] side of the falls, which bear his name. Other houses were built in that neighborhood, and in 1732 the settlement was erected into a town by the name of Jones-Town, comprising ten acres of land, and separated from Baltimore-Town by the falls and the marsh, of which mention has already been made. In 1743 the two towns were united, and the name of Baltimore given to both, and in 1747 the intermediate territory, comprising eighteen acres, was added to the town. On account of the older settlement in that locality, Jones-Town was generally called "Old-Town," and the name is still applied to that portion of the city which occupies the site of the ancient town. In 1730, William Fell, a ship-carpenter, settled upon the point one mile southeast from the town upon the outer basin. In 1773, although at that time a long stretch of vacant country lay between, the point, which had then become a flourishing settlement, was added to the town. Like "Old-Town," it has retained its ancient name, being still called, after its first settler, "Fell's Point." Whetstone Point, on the south side of the basin, upon the extreme end of which Fort McHenry is situated, and which now forms a part of the city, was made a town as early as 1706. From these separate towns and settlements the city has grown up. They have for many years been united, not only in name, but by unbroken lines of buildings which cover all the spaces by which they were once separated; so that only the traditionary names are left to distinguish the old localities.

For some years after its foundation, Baltimore gave little promise of its future greatness. In 1752 a rough sketch of the town, as it appeared from Federal Hill, was made by Mr. John Moale. A reduced cut of this sketch as corrected and completed by Mr. Daniel Bowly, is given on the opposite page. Though twenty-two years had elapsed since its foundation, the town then numbered but twenty-five houses, including a school-house and a church. The church (St. Paul's) which is represented in the sketch upon the highest point in the town, was begun by the members of the Church of England in 1731, but was not completed until 1744. Its successor, the present church at the corner of Charles and Saratoga streets, occupies a site very near that upon which the original building stood. But four of the houses in the town at that time were built of brick, and for these the bricks were imported from England; as the inhabitants had not yet discovered that directly under their feet was the clay for making the finest bricks in the world. Judging from the number of houses, the population of the town could not then have been more than 200; but in the Gentlemen's Magazine the population of the *county* for the same year is given as 17,233.

The only two sea-going vessels then owned in the town, are represented in the sketch. They were the sloop "Baltimore," belonging to Mr. William Lux, and the brig "Philip and Charles," belonging to Mr. Nicholas Rogers. The latter was the first square-rigged vessel owned here. To the right of the picture appears the first Tobacco Inspection Warehouse, the importance of that product of the Province, which at that time was its principal article of export, having already given occasion for the inspection system which prevails to this day.

The effect of the war, which raged shortly after this period between the English and French settlements in this country, tended to promote the growth of Baltimore by disposing the inhabitants to remain at the old settlements rather than penetrate into the sparsely inhabited regions in the interior. After the defeat of the English forces under General Braddock at Fort Du Quesne, in 1755, the Indian allies of the French, having passed Forts Cumberland and Frederick, penetrated to within eighty miles of Baltimore. So great was the consternation created in the town by raids in the neighborhood, that the women and children were put, for greater safety, upon the vessels lying in the harbor, and a strong fence of palisades was ordered to be constructed, encircling the town. The successful issue of the campaign of 1758 and the capture of Fort Du Quesne having caused the fears excited by these incursions to be allayed, the defences soon fell a prey to the more needy portion of the community, who found in the palisades a convenient supply of fire-wood.

In the year 1756 a considerable addition was made to the population of the town by the arrival of a band of French refugees from Nova Scotia, (then called Acadia,) of which the English had obtained possession.

BALTIMORE IN 1752.

1 & 2. Two Houses near Forrest lane and Baltimore st.
3. Near the corner of Sharp and Baltimore streets.
4. Brewery, Hanover street opposite Indian Queen.
5. House opposite Indian Queen Stables, German lane.
6. A House which stood in Baltimore street.
7. The first Tobacco Inspection House, Charles street.
8. On or near Vulcan alley.
9. Capt. Darby Lux's, opp'e Bank and west of Light st.
10. Near corner Chatham street and St. Paul's lane.
11. St. Paul's Church, the first built.
12. Mr. W. Rogers', N. E. cor. Balto. st. and St. Paul's la.
13. Kamineskey's Tavern, Bank near Light street.
14. N. W. corner of Bank and Calvert streets.
15. The first Brick House built in Baltimore, erected about 40 feet south of New Court-House; bricks and corner stones imported.
16. Mr. N. Rogers', on ground of back building of No. 108 Baltimore street.
17. Ward, the Barber's, on ground 99 Baltimore street.
18. Opposite Maryland Insurance Office.
19. Near corner of South and Water streets.
20. Southeast corner South and Baltimore streets.
21. On or near Holliday street, opposite Theatre.
22. Part of Old or Jones-Town, up the Falls.
23. The Cool Spring, generally used by the Town, at the head of the Basin, a few feet west of Charles street.
24. Deep point, where the second wharf was built.
25. Skeleton of Sloop Dove, first vessel belonging to Baltimore.
26. Sloop Baltimore, the second vessel.
27. Brig of Mr. N. Rogers; the first square-built vessel, and the only one at that time.
28. Jones' Falls, as they appeared at that day from Federal Hill, whence Mr. Moale made his Draft.
29. Calvert Street Wharf. 30. Philadelphia Road.
31. Site of Battle Monument.

From about this time seems to date the growth of Baltimore. Fell's Point, which, as has been already remarked, was not added to the town until 1773, became a busy seat of industry. Ship-yards were established there, and on account of its greater accessibility for the shipping, many merchants made their residence there, so that for a long time it was doubtful whether town or point was to be the nucleus of the future city. A disposition for internal improvements manifested itself at this time. In 1763, the first market-house was built, situated at the corner of Baltimore and Gay streets. In 1766, the marsh between Frederick street and the falls was ordered to be filled, and in 1768, Baltimore had risen so much in importance as to justify the removal of the court-house from Joppa, (now an inconsiderable village in the northwestern portion of the county, on the Gunpowder River,) to this place. Baltimore continued to be the county seat until 1851, when the city and county jurisdictions were separated and the county courts established at Towsontown. In 1769, the first fire-engine, which was bought by a few public spirited men at a cost of £99, was introduced, and the same year, the first Roman Catholic Church was erected. The site of it is now occupied by Calvert Hall, a school of the Redemptorists, on Saratoga street. In 1773, a workhouse was established, a small theatre erected, and a Methodist congregation organized. The members of the Methodist Society (which was yet in its infancy) built a church for their use in Strawberry alley, and the next year, one in Lovely lane.

The general prosperity of the Province since the foundation of Baltimore appears from the rapid increase in the population. In 1733, the *taxable inhabitants*, (*i. e.* all males above the age of sixteen and all negro or mulatto females,) numbered 31,470. In 1748, the *entire population* was 130,000, (94,000 whites and 36,000 blacks.) In 1756, it had increased to 154,188, (107,963 whites and 46,225 blacks.) In 1761, it amounted to 164,007, (114,332 whites and 49,675 blacks.) A valuable addition to the population during this period, (but one which was greatly deplored at the time by the good people of the Province,) was the number of convicts imported, which is estimated to have been no less than fifteen or twenty thousand. They were brought over by private shippers, who made a contract with the government of England for the purpose, and sold them into servitude in the Province for their term of transportation. Hazardous as it was to introduce into a community such great numbers of persons whose past record was that of crime, the experiment worked well. The lack of labor, which, as in all new countries, had been felt as a serious inconvenience in the colony, was by this means supplied, and the convicts, becoming identified with the ordinary population, when their term of servitude expired, many of them were transformed into useful and reputable citizens, and some of them rose to honorable distinction.*

The exports of tobacco from Maryland to England were estimated in 1761 to be about 28,000 hhds. annually, valued at £140,000. The other exports at

* McMahon, p. 314.

this period were wheat, lumber, corn, flour, pig and bar iron in small quantities, skins and furs; but the total value of all these commodities was estimated in 1761 at only £80.000.*

The policy of England was to stifle all manufacturing industry in her colonies, so as to preserve in them a market for her own productions. In pursuance of this system, manufactures were prohibited, and notwithstanding the guaranty given in the charter of Maryland to the contrary,† the trade of the colonies was restricted to England and her possessions. Thus thwarted and repressed, Maryland made but little progress in commerce during this period. Beyond the coarse homespun manufactured in private families for their own use, there was nothing deserving the name of manufacture in the Province, excepting the production of iron; and so great was the jealousy with which England looked upon even this enterprise, that in order to discourage it, a bounty was offered upon English iron imported into the colonies.‡ The Assembly of Maryland, in 1719, attempted to counteract this influence by offering a free grant of one hundred acres of land to any one who would put up a furnace or forge. As early as 1749, eight furnaces and nine forges were in operation in the Province; § but for the materials for clothing and all the appliances of civilized life, the colonists were kept entirely dependent upon England. In the condition of the shipping, the same state of dependence existed; in restricting the trade of the colonies to English ports, England took care to see that that trade was carried in English bottoms. So that, while in 1761 there were employed in the trade between England and Maryland, one hundred and twenty vessels of 18,000 tons burthen, the entire shipping of the colony, (which indeed had suffered considerable diminution during the war with the French settlements,) amounted to but thirty vessels of 1,300 tons, chiefly employed in the trade with the English possessions in the West Indies.|| Notwithstanding that these conditions of commercial dependence upon England were for a long period quietly acquiesced in, the Province gradually grew in strength and population, and in the development of those internal resources which are a necessary condition to the independent existence of every State.

Affairs were in this condition when there came the first mutterings of that storm which was about to break over the American colonies, and amid the

* McMahon, p. 315. † See page 9.

‡ McSherry's History of Maryland, page 116. In 1750 an act was passed by the English Parliament, taking the duty off of American iron, but at the same time prohibiting the erection of slitting or rolling mills in the colonies. The object of this measure was the preservation of the English forests from consumption as fuel for furnaces.

§ An interesting relic of the iron manufactories of those days recently came into the possession of the Stickney Iron Company, consisting of two or three pigs of iron discovered at the bed of the Patapsco River, just below the city, at a point between Fort McHenry and the wharf of the Stickney Company's Furnace. These pigs are corroded and covered with barnacles, but distinctly bear the mark "Principio * 1751," showing that they have probably lain at the bottom of the river for more than a century. The Principio Furnace was erected in Cecil County, about 1715-20

|| McMahon, p 316

struggles and hardships of which, the bands which bound them to England were to be finally severed, and the foundations laid of their future greatness.

The restrictions and encroachments which had been made by England, under the plea of regulating commerce, upon the trade of the colonies, although giving rise to occasional manifestations of dissatisfaction, had for the most part been quietly submitted to. But notwithstanding this, the colonies with one consent stoutly maintained their exclusive and indefeasible rights to regulate all matters relating to their own internal government, and the imposition of taxes. In no colony was this feeling more deeply rooted than in Maryland. Proud of their charter government, and the rights it assured them, the freemen of this Province viewed any encroachment upon their liberties with peculiar jealousy. England on the other hand was as persistently determined to abrogate all chartered rights, and take the matter of taxation into her own hands, so as to derive a revenue from the colonies by this means. When, at length, the war with France having been brought to a successful termination, the French possessions in America were ceded to England by the Treaty of Paris, (1763,) and England was thus left to deal with only her own colonies, without the possibility of foreign intervention, the time seemed to have come when the long cherished plans of taxation might be put into successful operation. Well aware of the difficulties of the undertaking, and the opposition which it would excite on the part of the colonists, the English government proceeded slowly towards its accomplishment, cautiously feeling the temper of the colonists, and seeking to adopt, as the entering wedge of the odious measures, some plan of taxation which should be as little onerous as possible. The history of the "Stamp Act," by which it was hoped that a tax—free from all the annoyances of collection—might be successfully imposed upon the colonies, belongs to the history of the whole country. The act was passed by the English Parliament in March, 1765. Perceiving the necessity for united and concerted action on their part, the colonies had recourse in this emergency to a *Continental Congress.* The Congress assembled at New York in October of the same year, and in its firm but temperate tone, the colonies gave unmistakable evidence that they were arrayed with an unbroken front against the aggressions of the mother country.

The sturdy opposition to the tax which was maintained by all the colonies, and which led to the repeal of the act by the English Parliament the very next year after its passage, manifested itself in Maryland by the prompt expulsion of the Stamp distributor from the Province, with every mark of indignation and contempt, immediately upon his arrival from England; and a quantity of stamped paper which arrived here was not suffered to be taken from the ship in which it was brought over.

Although from the impossibility of enforcing it, the English Parliament was thus obliged to repeal the Stamp Act, the long cherished purpose of taxing the colonies was not abandoned. The next method resorted to for accomplishing this object, was the imposition of a duty on certain articles—especially tea—imported into the colonies. This duty, it was thought, might be successfully imposed under cover of the right to regulate commerce, which had been already conceded to the English government. But public feeling in this country was now too thoroughly aroused for any plan of taxation to be submitted to. "Non-importation Societies" were formed for the purpose of excluding English merchandise from the colonies. The American market being thus closed, a large quantity of tea accumulated in the warehouses of the East India Company. It then became the interest of that Company to co-operate with Parliament in attempting to force the tea into the American colonies; and in order to facilitate that Company in its efforts, in May, 1773, Parliament allowed a drawback upon tea exported to America, so that the duty might be imposed without enhancing the price of the article. Under this arrangement, several cargoes of tea were shipped with the hope that now they would be admitted into the country. But the colonies were contending for a principle; they claimed that they could not be taxed by a Parliament in which they had no representation, and they would agree to nothing that involved a surrender of that principle. The vessels consigned to New York and Philadelphia were forced to return without unloading; that consigned to Boston was boarded at night by a party of citizens in disguise, and its contents thrown overboard. Several packages of tea that were brought over by a vessel that came into the St. Mary's River, Maryland, in August, 1774, were sent back without being unloaded; while a vessel which arrived in the October following, at Annapolis, (then the principal city, and still the capital of Maryland,) with eighteen packages of tea on board, was not allowed to come up to the landing; and the consignee, who had paid the duty on the tea, in the hope of being permitted to land it, could only allay the popular indignation by burning the vessel and its contents, setting fire to it with his own hand. As a consequence of the destruction of the tea at Boston, a bill, depriving that city of its privileges as a port of entry and discharge, was passed by Parliament, and received the royal sanction March 31, 1774.

A Continental Congress, which had proved so successful against the Stamp Act, was in the present emergency again resorted to. It assembled in Philadelphia, September 5th, 1774. The unanimous and determined resolution exhibited by this Congress to maintain the colonial rights and liberties, showed plainly that the English government had aroused a bold and free-spirited people. A system of non-importation, which had already been very generally adopted, was now formally recommended, excluding from the country not only the taxed articles, but all articles whatsoever which came either directly or indirectly from Great Britain or Ireland. Corresponding restrictions were laid upon exportations; so that the system recommended was really one of non-intercourse with the mother country. The object which the colonies sought to accomplish by these means, was the repeal of the obnoxious measures of taxation. They still hoped that the English government would recede from its position, as it had done in the case of the Stamp Act. A strong feeling yet existed, on the part of many, against hostilities with the country they still called "home." But the course of the English government showed that there was nothing to be hoped for from that quarter. "The petitions" of the colonies "were spurned, their assemblies declared rebellious, their persons and property made objects of plunder, and those bloodhounds of war, foreign mercenaries, were to be let loose upon them to pillage and desolate their country."* All hope of reconciliation was now removed, and the American people were ready to sever the last ties that bound them to England. On both sides the preparations for hostilities began. The decisive step was at last taken. On the 4th of July, 1776, the Continental Congress, then assembled in Philadelphia, published to the world the Declaration of Independence. The news was received in Baltimore with great enthusiasm. On the 22d of the month, the Declaration was publicly read from the Court-House, amid the acclamations of the people, the firing of salutes, and cries for the prosperity of the United States. At night the town was illuminated.

The Proprietary government of Maryland was at this time held by Henry Harford, Esq., an illegitimate son of the last Lord Baltimore, who had died in 1771, and with whom the title had become extinct. Towards the government of the Lords Baltimore, who, for the most part, had ruled the Province with a beneficent sway, the people of Maryland entertained feelings of loyal attachment; but towards the present Proprietary, a stranger in person and in name, none of these feelings existed. His government was promptly overthrown, and a Convention called to frame a constitutional government for the new "State of Maryland." In this Convention, which assembled at Annapolis, on the 14th of August, 1776, Baltimore-Town, (which could now boast of 564 houses and 5,934 inhabitants, with 821 more at the point,) for the first time had representation separate from the county, being permitted to send two delegates in addition to the four returned from the county.

From the very commencement of the war, and throughout its continuance, Maryland entered into it with spirit and energy. The nearness of the battle-fields caused constant demands to be made upon this State, for supplies of both troops and provisions. The demands were promptly met; and the troops themselves, by their gallant conduct in many a hard-fought field, have made famous the name of the Maryland Line. At the battle of Long Island, (Brooklyn Heights) August 27, 1776, when the Maryland troops were for the first time brought into action, a part of a battalion shook, with repeated *bayonet charges*, a whole brigade of British regulars. The reputation which they then won, as being the first American troops to use the bayonet, was well maintained. On more than one occasion thereafter, Maryland troops charged and repulsed the enemy with unloaded muskets. In addition to her troops in the field, Maryland had, during a part of the war, to maintain a separate

* McMahon, p. 429.

marine service, for the protection of her shores from the English cruisers, which, until the arrival of a French fleet in 1779, continually infested the Chesapeake Bay.

The demand for money for the public service, far beyond what could be raised by taxation, which the necessities of the war occasioned, led to immense issues of State and Continental paper currency. This currency, without credit, and with a compulsory circulation, very soon became greatly depreciated. Perceiving the ruinous tendency of a superabundant and depreciated currency, Congress sought to correct the evils inseparable from such a condition of affairs, by calling upon the States to contribute their respective shares for redeeming the greater part of the circulation. The portion for which Maryland was thus called upon to provide, was more than $20,000,000. Finding it quite impossible to raise this sum by taxation, it was finally determined by the Assembly of Maryland, in March, 1781, to redeem it, by a new issue, (called the *black* money,) at the rate of forty of the old for one of the new. The next year the black currency was replaced by a new issue, called the *red* money. The credit of this issue was better sustained than that of former issues, as the proceeds of the sales of the confiscated property of persons disaffected to the cause of American liberties, was pledged for its redemption.

The privations and necessities of the Revolutionary War, called for the exercise in the American people of the very qualities which formed the best guaranty of the stability of that independence for which they fought; namely, a dependence on themselves and their own resources. Various branches of manufacture which had been prohibited under British rule, were established during this period, to supply the place of the foreign products, which could no longer be obtained. As early as 1778, there were established in Baltimore-Town a linen factory, a bleach yard, a paper mill, a woollen and linen factory, a slitting mill, a card factory and two nail factories. And notwithstanding the difficulties which had to be encountered, a very considerable foreign trade was carried on—chiefly with the West Indies—in the swift-sailing craft of the Chesapeake. The progress made in commerce at this time, was sufficiently great to lead to the establishment of a custom-house at Baltimore, in 1780; thus relieving the merchants of this place from the delays and inconvenience to which they had hitherto been subjected, in entering and clearing their vessels at the custom-house at Annapolis.

During the years intervening between the cessation of hostilities (1782) and the adoption of the Federal Constitution, (1788) there was a temporary suspension of even that commercial activity that had been able to exist during the war. With a depreciated currency, inadequate shipping, an unpaid war debt of $44,000,000, and the future condition of the country, and even its national existence, enveloped in uncertainty, there was cause enough to paralyze for a while even the most determined energy. The commercial difficulties at this time were very much increased by an over-importation of foreign goods. The low prices of tobacco and flour, which still formed the principal articles of export from Maryland, added to the distress in this part of the country. But this state of things was not destined to continue long. The establishment of the Federal Government, and the funding of the public debt, restored a feeling of confidence, and there soon followed a period of remarkable commercial activity and prosperity.

A new avenue that was opened for the tobacco trade, tended directly to secure for Baltimore that pre-eminence to which it was justly entitled, but for which it had long to struggle with several other towns, which in those days were formidable rivals. Under England's colonial system, the tobacco trade before the Revolution, had been carried on exclusively with English merchants, who had their agencies at some of the older towns, situated at convenient places of landing and shipment upon the rivers. Among the principal seats of this trade were Annapolis, Bladensburg, Upper Marlboro', and Elk Ridge Landing. To these places, the tobacco, securely packed in hogsheads, was conveyed from the plantations by being *rolled* along roads that were constructed for the purpose. Several of these primitive roads still exist in the State. One of them, which leads through a part of Baltimore County to Elk Ridge Landing, still bears the name of the "Rolling Road."

After the war, the English merchants sought to regain their lucrative traffic, and for this purpose re-established their agencies at the former places of trade; but in the meanwhile a Dutch house had settled at Baltimore, and entered largely into the tobacco business, purchasing for direct shipment to Holland. By the acquisition of capital, the Baltimore merchants were soon enabled to make shipments in their own vessels, and for their own account. In this manner, the tobacco trade became entirely diverted to Baltimore, and the agencies of the English houses at other places were discontinued.

With the advancement of commerce, the condition of the harbor of Baltimore began to attract attention. In 1783, a board of nine port-wardens was appointed, with authority to make a survey and chart of the basin, harbor and Patapsco River, to ascertain the depth and course of the channel, and provide for the cleaning of the same. In order to defray the expense of this undertaking, an impost of one penny per ton, (afterwards increased to two-pence,) was laid upon all vessels entering or clearing.

The water at that time reached up to Exchange Place and Water street on the north, and nearly to Charles street on the west; the space occupied by water being estimated as equal to double the surface of the present basin and docks. While the means of intercourse with foreign countries were being thus improved, domestic and inland connections were not overlooked. In 1782 a line of stages was established between Philadelphia and Baltimore, and the following year lines to Frederick-Town and Annapolis. A company was organized to make a canal on the Susquehanna, and shortly after the Potomac Canal Company was formed. The Chesapeake and Delaware Canal Company was not organized until 1799, but the project had been contemplated, and the surveys made, as early as 1769. As the first indication in this vicinity of the revolution which steam was about to introduce in the commercial world, James Rumsey, of Cecil County, procured, in 1784, the exclusive privilege for this State for making and vending "vessels to be propelled by steam with or against the current."

In the general spirit of progress manifested at this time, the internal improvement of the town was not neglected. The streets were extended, and for the first time paved; and the various bridges across the falls were put in a more substantial condition. The single market-house which had hitherto been used, being found inadequate to the wants of the growing population, (which in 1782 was estimated at 8,000, an increase of one-third since 1775,) it was abandoned in 1783 and three new ones erected, in which market was held on different days of the week. The three new markets established were the Centre Market, on land given by Mr. Thomas Harrison; the Fell's Point Market, for the benefit of the residents at the Point, which was built on land given by Mr. William Fell; and the Hanover Market, for the accommodation of persons in what was then the extreme western portion of the town.

The ground upon which the Centre Market was erected was a part of the marsh which has been hitherto spoken of as lying along the western border of the falls. It was at first intended to dredge, out and make a long dock of the lower portion of this marsh; but this plan was in part abandoned when the erection of the market-house was determined on. From the nature of its site, the Centre Market is still popularly called the "Marsh Market," and the dock that comes up to its lower end, bears, and well merits, the name of "Long Dock." In 1785, the wharves of the town were much extended and improved. Among the improvements of this year, may be especially mentioned the construction of Bowly's Wharf.

In 1784, the first Sugar Refinery was established in the town, and the same year some Glass Works were erected on the Monocacy River, in Frederick County, by some German manufacturers. These works were removed to Baltimore in 1788, and located upon the south side of the basin, where they still continue.

The revolution in France, and the subsequent wars upon the continent of Europe, gave the occasion for that period of commercial enterprise and activity to which allusion has already been made. The opportunity was grasped by the merchants of Baltimore with promptness and energy; and from 1790 until the outbreak of the war with Great Britain in 1812, this city was distinguished for its rapid growth in population and commercial importance.

The interruption to agriculture occasioned by the wars, caused an increased demand in Europe for American wheat and flour. The colonies too of European nations, which, under the prevailing colonial system, were permitted in time of peace to have intercourse with the parent countries only, being cut off by hostile cruisers from their accustomed avenues of trade, were compelled to seek in America a market for the sale of their produce and the purchase of their necessary supplies. An active foreign trade, both with

Europe and the West Indies, was thus created; and the sailing qualities of the craft of the Chesapeake, which had already acquired a high reputation, before the invention of steam, for fast sailing, secured for Baltimore the greater portion of that trade. The sailing qualities of these vessels, which have made the name of "Baltimore Clippers" familiar throughout the world, were at that time unequalled by any vessels built in this country, and unapproached by any built in Europe. Indeed, it was long before the art of constructing them was practised anywhere outside of the Chesapeake Bay. They were schooner-rigged, and the great secret of their excellence lay in the fact that they were built so as to sail within four or four and a half points of the wind. The advantage that this peculiarity gave them, enabled them in most cases successfully to elude the pursuit of any vessels belonging to the blockading squadrons of the belligerent powers that might offer to give them chase; for if they could but get to windward of their pursuers, it was useless for vessels of any other construction to attempt to follow them.

Such was the success of the "Baltimore Clippers," that this city enjoyed during the period of which we are speaking, the chief part of the European and West Indian trades of this country, besides doing a large carrying trade between the nations of Europe and the West Indies. For the latter, this was one of the principal markets in the world, whether for selling or purchasing; and those West India goods that found their way to Europe, were for the most part shipped first to Baltimore, and reshipped from here to their place of final destination. The quantity of these goods brought to this port was so great, that sales of them were chiefly made at auction, in entire cargoes. These auction sales were at that time a special feature of the Baltimore market.

Upon the restoration of peace in 1801, the nations of Europe immediately enforced their colonial systems, (by which the trade of the colonies was restricted to their parent countries,) and thus that portion of the foreign and carrying trade of Baltimore, that had arisen in consequence of the suspension of those systems, was for a time interrupted. But the interruption was of short duration. Upon the resumption of hostilities, in 1803, occasion was again given for the exercise of that adventurous spirit of enterprise that had before been so successful; and notwithstanding the *Orders in Council* and *Decrees* wherewith the belligerent powers of Europe sought to close each other's ports against the commerce of the world, the adventurous merchants and daring seamen of Baltimore succeeded in maintaining their commerce until the close of the year 1807, when, as a retaliatory measure to the restrictions imposed upon trade by the nations of Europe, a general embargo was proclaimed by the government of the United States.

Although the hazardous trade of this period was for the most part successfully and profitably prosecuted, heavy losses were occasionally incurred by the capture of some of the blockade-runners, while attempting to elude the vigilance of the squadrons which were everywhere on the lookout for them. Prior to the year 1795, when the first Marine Insurance Companies were established here, the merchants either took the risk of these losses themselves, or else effected an insurance with private capitalists, who, for a consideration, would guarantee them against loss. This was, during the last century, the usual method of marine insurance practised both in this country and in England, where the custom which long prevailed, of exposing the name and description of vessels upon which insurance was asked, at *Lloyd's* Coffee House, for the capitalists who congregated there to *write under* their names and the amounts they were willing to venture, has caused the terms "Lloyds" and "underwriting" to be permanently identified with the business of marine insurance.

Upon the removal of the embargo in 1809, besides the reopening of the old channels of trade, the neutral shipping of America was largely occupied, from that time until the outbreak of the war with Great Britain in 1812, in supplying the English army in Spain, which it was found necessary to provision chiefly from this country.

The prosperity of Baltimore at this time was not maintained solely by a foreign and carrying trade. The imports, which were far beyond the requirements for home consumption, could not have been disposed of, if a market had not been found for them beyond the limits of the town, nor could the demands for export have been met, if produce and cereals had not been drawn from the agricultural regions of the interior. Its central position, its accessibility as an inland seaport, and the direction of the water-courses, made Baltimore the first, as it is still, the natural market for the West.

The western trade, which, before the Revolution, had been conveyed on the backs of pack-horses, walking in single file through the narrow paths which led across the mountains, now required for its transportation the huge canvass-covered "Conestoga" wagons, which, with their teams of six or eight horses, and jingling bells, used to traverse the old Braddock's road and the turnpikes that had been constructed as far as the navigable waters of the West. The relics of this old method of transportation may yet be discerned in the immense yards, made for the accommodation of these wagons and teams, attached to a few of the old inns in Baltimore that have yet escaped the march of improvement.

The actual growth of Baltimore during this period is best indicated by the increase in the population, which, from the United States census reports, we are now able to observe by decades. In 1790, the population numbered 13,503. In 1800, it had increased to 31,514, and in 1810, to 46,555. A considerable accession had been made, in 1793, by the arrival of French refugees, to the number of about 3,000, from Cape François. Besides the increase in the population, which this arrival made, it was of benefit to Baltimore as the means of stimulating that West Indian trade, which contributed so greatly to the prosperity of the city during this period. The tonnage of the town, which, soon after the adoption of the Federal Constitution, was reported as 36,305 tons registered vessels, and 7,976 licensed and enrolled, had increased in 1795, to 48,007 of the former, and 24,470 of the latter. The same year there were counted in passing to Baltimore 109 ships, 162 brigs, 350 sloops and schooners, and 5,464 bay craft and small coasters. On the 31st December, 1796, sixty-seven years after its foundation, "Baltimore-Town" was at last promoted to the dignity of a city, incorporated by the State Legislature under the name of the "Mayor and City Council of Baltimore."

Among the public buildings and internal improvements which deserve mention, Fort McHenry, on the extreme end of Whetstone Point, was built in 1794. In 1795, a number of flouring mills were established in and about the city. The Baltimore Library Company was established the same year. In 1805, the present court-house was begun, and occupied in 1809. The corner-stone of the Roman Catholic Cathedral was laid in 1806, but this building was not completed sufficiently for consecration until 1821. In 1808 the water company, for supplying the city with water was incorporated, and the same year, the manufacturing interests of the city were increased by the erection of several new factories upon Gwynn's and Jones' Falls.

The arrogant claims made by England to a "right of search," that is, a right of overhauling on the high-seas and searching the vessels of foreign nations, with the purpose of taking therefrom any seamen that might be claimed as British subjects, added to the restrictions with which she constantly sought to embarrass the trade of this country, led to a declaration of war by the United States government on 18th January, 1812. While some portions of the country were violently opposed to that measure, Maryland, though from her position and the nature of her trade, necessarily one of the chief sufferers by the war, was forward and determined in supporting the policy of the general government.

From the commencement of the war, the Chesapeake Bay was vigorously blockaded by the British fleet. Its position, affording an approach to the interior and the National Capital, and the reputation its craft had acquired in the commerce abroad, made it an important place to occupy and close. Occasionally a Baltimore vessel was able to elude the blockading squadron and get to sea, but a return to port was quite impossible. In this extremity the merchants of Baltimore resorted to the expedient of ordering their vessels to return to other ports less vigorously blockaded, and there deliver and receive their cargoes. By availing in this way of other ports, and conveying their merchandise inland by means of wagons, the merchants of Baltimore were able to retain possession, in large measure, of their foreign commerce.

During the war a number of privateers were fitted out at Baltimore, some of which performed very gallant and distinguished service. In 1814, the war was brought directly home to our people. Hitherto, descents had been made by the enemy's fleet only at comparatively undefended points along the bay shore; but in August of this year, a force of 5,000 men, under General Ross, was landed on the Patuxent River, and began their march towards Washington. Having overcome, on 24th August, a force which had been gathered at Bladensburg to resist them, they proceeded to Washington and burned the National Capitol, the President's Mansion, Government offices, public records, the Library, and much private property.

After this success, General Ross next turned his attention towards Baltimore. On the 12th September a force of 5,000 men was landed upon North Point, at the mouth of the Patapsco River. They were met by an inferior force of Maryland and Pennsylvania militia, and a sharp engagement ensued, at the close of which the militia fell back to a position nearer the city, but not until they had inflicted such a loss upon the enemy as deterred them from following. The commander of the invading force, General Ross, was killed early in the engagement. On the evening of the next day an unsuccessful attack was made by the fleet upon Fort McHenry, and during the night a force, which, under cover of the fleet, had passed by the fort in barges, was met with such a destructive fire from the batteries which had been erected on the point, above the fort, that one of the barges was sunk, and the others retreated precipitately to the fleet. Thus gallantly resisted by land and water, the invading force abandoned the attack upon Baltimore, and made no similar attempt upon other cities. The war was brought to a close about the end of the year by the Treaty of Ghent, signed 14th of December, and ratified by the United States the 17th of February following.

After the close of the war, commerce began to resume its former channels. But the wars with which the Continent of Europe had been so long convulsed were about drawing to their close. And upon the final overthrow of the Empire in France, in 1815, and the return of peace, the nations of Europe resumed their own carrying trade, and the American merchants were thus deprived of a trade of which they had had almost a monopoly. In the years 1817, 1818 and 1819, short wheat crops in England caused a demand in that country for Maryland wheat; and in consequence of the removal of the Portuguese Court to Brazil, and the revolutions which resulted in the overthrow of Spanish rule in South America, new avenues of trade were opened to the enterprise of our merchants in that quarter.

But a greater evil than the curtailment of foreign trade had to be contended with at this time. The Bank of the United States had expired by limitation in 1811. Immediately there sprang up a host of local banks subject to no restrictions whatever in their operations. Upon the closing of the ports upon the Chesapeake Bay during the war with England, and the consequent diversion of the trade of the Middle States to places which were less molested, it soon appeared that the specie of the Middle States would be attracted to places of greater activity. To prevent this drain, the banks resorted to the suspension of specie payment and the issue of a paper currency. And when the demand for money occasioned by the exigencies of the war arose, it was met by large issues of this money. This method of manufacturing capital was found so easy and attractive, that it was indulged in recklessly and without limit. A dangerous spirit of speculation was engendered. Every one rushed into the arena, borrowing the easily obtained money upon almost any species of property, with little thought bestowed upon the day of reckoning by either borrowers or lenders. The result of this system soon appeared in a rapid depreciation of the money, (which had at best a fictitious value,) and wide-spread financial distress and embarrassment; for these evils, though falling most heavily upon the Middle States, were felt throughout the country. It was finally determined that the means for curing all these evils, and establishing a uniform currency throughout the country, would be secured by the re-establishment of a national bank. Accordingly, in 1816, the new Bank of the United States was inaugurated. The enterprise was eagerly entered into, and of the capital of $28,000,000, $4,014,100 were subscribed in Baltimore.

The principles upon which this bank was established made it necessary that the local banks should prepare for specie payment. This at once placed a check upon the accommodations which they had been extending to their customers, and upon which the latter had become dependent. Everywhere the creditor pressed the debtor, and the financial difficulties increased. Added to this, it soon became evident that it was quite impossible for the Bank of the United States to redeem the promises that had been made for it, and a fall in the price of its stock occurred to such an extent as to plunge in absolute ruin many of the subscribers.

Although thus beset with difficulties, their characteristic spirit of enterprise did not forsake the people of Baltimore. Since the critical period of which we have been speaking, and which reached its climax in 1819, the history of Baltimore for forty years, is a history of steady growth, interrupted only by the financial crises of 1837 and 1857, which shook to their base the commercial interests of the entire country. The foreign commerce during this period was not what it had been during the continuance of the peculiar circumstances amid which it took its rise; and though the spirit of adventure and excitement which had been fostered by the former conditions of trade, had to accommodate itself to a slower motion, the latter is probably the more healthful condition, and more truly indicative of steady and permanent growth.

Among the public buildings, etc., erected between the time of the war with Great Britain and the year 1820, may be mentioned the School of Medicine on Lombard Street, (part of the University of Maryland,) completed and occupied in 1812; the Washington Monument, and the one known as the Battle Monument, both begun in 1815; the Merchants' Exchange, undertaken in 1815 and completed and occupied in 1820. This building is now occupied by the United States Government as a Custom-House and Post-Office. In 1816 Gas Works were established here, which were the first in the country to afford a general supply for the use of citizens, and for lighting the streets. The corporate limits of the city were extended the same year to the present size, embracing an area of about 10,000 acres.

The comparative sizes of the original town and the present city, are accurately shown in the accompanying cut. The original water-line on the side of the basin is carefully marked, and the original course of Jones' Falls, which once reached, in a deep horse-shoe bend, as far as to the corner of Calvert and Lexington Streets. On the eastern side of the Falls, the location of "Old Town"* is indicated, and north and south of the harbor, appear Fell's and Whetstone Points, with Fort McHenry upon the extreme end of the latter.

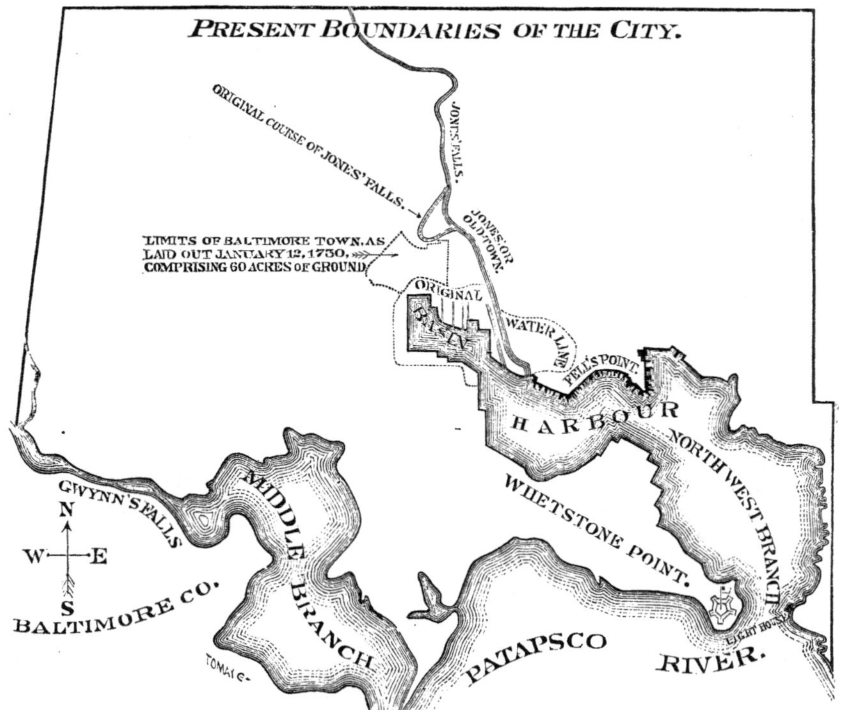

In 1813, the first steamboat was introduced here, to run between Baltimore and Frenchtown, as a part of the line between this city and Philadelphia. The application of the newly discovered power of steam, which was then deemed little better than experimental, soon began to exercise a powerful influence upon the business relations of Baltimore.

The introduction of steamboats upon the Ohio and Mississippi Rivers opened to the people of the West a new and cheaper mode of communication

* See page 13.

with the seaboard than was afforded by the wagons and turnpikes upon which they had hitherto depended. The establishment of steam communication with New York, also attracted in that direction the trade which had hitherto come to Baltimore. The people of Baltimore were not, however, of a temper to permit the resources, which their natural advantages gave them, to slip from them by reason of the superior artificial advantages of other cities. In December, 1823, a public meeting was held in the Merchants' Exchange, to take the sense of the people on the subject of canals, or rather, (as their utility was recognized,) to ascertain whether it would be most acceptable to the citizens to undertake, first, a canal to the Susquehanna, or one to the Ohio. The great majority preferred the former. An act of the Legislature was therefore procured, authorizing the city to make a canal to the head of tide-water on the Susquehanna, and further, if permitted by the State of Pennsylvania. Another act was passed, incorporating the Potomac Canal Company, for the purpose of constructing a canal from tide-water on the Potomac, to the Ohio River. The next year, this latter was merged into the Chesapeake and Ohio Canal Company, which was incorporated by the Legislature of Virginia for the same purpose. In 1826, upon the publication of estimates, showing the immense expense that would be incurred, and the great difficulties that would have to be overcome, in constructing a canal across the mountains to the Ohio, it was at once perceived that this cherished plan would not yield all the advantages that had been anticipated by its projectors. This discovery only led the citizens of Baltimore to devise some new means by which to secure their western communications. Their deliberations resulted in the determination to accomplish their purpose by the construction of a railroad. Accordingly, in February, 1827, an Act was passed by the Legislature, chartering the Baltimore and Ohio Railroad Company, which was the first railroad chartered in the United States. The canal was not abandoned in consequence of this rival enterprise, but the corner-stones of each were laid July 4th, 1828, Charles Carroll of Carrollton officiating for the railroad, and President Adams for the canal. On the 9th of August, 1829, the hundredth anniversary of the passage of the act creating Baltimore-Town, the Susquehanna Railroad was begun. In 1837 the Philadelphia, Wilmington and Baltimore Railroad was opened for travel. In 1853 the Baltimore and Ohio Railroad was completed to the Ohio River, and in 1857 its continuation to St. Louis was perfected. In 1854 the Susquehanna Road was consolidated with other roads extending through the State of Pennsylvania, under the name of the Northern Central Railway. In 1829 the Chesapeake and Delaware Canal was undertaken.

As in 1816 Baltimore had the distinction of being the first city in this country that was lit by gas, and in 1827 of being the first to inaugurate a railroad, so, in 1844, it was again distinguished by the erection, by Professor Morse, between Baltimore and Washington, of the first electric telegraph in the world.

The growth of the city during a period of forty years, is indicated by the United States census returns of the population:

In 1820 the population was			62,738
" 1830	"	"	80,625
" 1840	"	"	102,313
" 1850	"	"	169,054
" 1860	"	"	212,418

The trade of Baltimore, which first rose to importance during the Revolutionary struggle, and flourished amid the dangers incident to subsequent wars, both at home and abroad, was at length destined to be seriously crippled by a war that came to our very doors. In the civil war of 1861-5, between the Northern and Southern States, Maryland occupied the position of a border State between the contending sections. Although herself the field of battle on but two occasions, her frontier position, the constant presence of large bodies of troops within her borders, the severance of all communication with her Southern customers, and the risk attending the communications with the West, from the liability of the railroads to interruption, and the freights to capture or seizure, caused the loss to Baltimore, for the time, of her Southern trade, and on account of the impoverishment of the Southern people, the permanent loss of much that was owing from that section; whilst the Western trade became temporarily and partially diverted to other cities.

Since that period of enforced inaction, a reviving spirit of life and energy has been manifested. The railway communications extend, by the Northern Central Road, north and west to the lakes and Canada; by the Philadelphia, Wilmington and Baltimore Road, to all parts of the Northern and Eastern States. The Baltimore and Ohio spreads its constantly increasing connections over the whole of the western country, and as far as San Francisco; while its southern branch through Washington connects throughout the Southern States and as far as New Orleans. Of local roads, there are the Western Maryland, extending through the rich farm-lands of Carroll, Frederick and Washington Counties to Hagerstown, and projected to Williamsport, upon the Potomac River; and the Baltimore and Potomac, opening up a fertile country hitherto inaccessible by rail, and affording a southern connection for the Northern Central Road, and the Pennsylvania Central with its connecting lines. Now in course of construction, there are the Baltimore and Drum Point Railroad, which will extend from the city, south, through the entire length of Anne Arundel and Calvert Counties; and the Union Railroad, which, making almost the entire circuit of the city of Baltimore, will afford the means for prompt connection between the various railways that enter the city. These various roads secure to Baltimore by steam communications, its natural advantages as the seaboard depot, indicated by the geographical formation of the country, for the West. Domestic lines of steamers communicate with Boston, New York, Philadelphia, Richmond, Norfolk, and all the lesser places on the Chesapeake Bay and its tributaries, Wimington and New Berne, N. C., Charleston, Savannah, Key West, New Orleans, Havana and Galveston; while two prospering lines of steamers to Europe, the North German Lloyd to Bremen via Southampton, and the Allan line to Liverpool via Halifax, demonstrate the fact that the foreign commerce that was once enjoyed by Baltimore needed but the opportunity to return.

The imports at the port of Baltimore, which in 1860, amounted to $9,784,773, and in 1862, in consequence of the war, had fallen to $3,696,620, rose in 1870, to $21,017,313; in 1871, to $26,770,181; and in 1872 to $29,429,439. The exports of domestic merchandise for the same years were, in 1860, $8,804,606; in 1862, $8,375,303; in 1870, $12,396,518; in 1871, $18,236,166, and in 1872, $17,381,591. The industrial products of the city and county of Baltimore amounted, according to the census of 1870, to the sum of $59,219,993 annually, in which was employed capital amounting to $26,040,040. The population of the city had increased from 212,418 in 1860, to 267,599 in 1870.* The property in the city and county was estimated in the census at $401,634,738. The tonnage of the port is 150,086.

Thus rapidly and in the merest outline, we have endeavored to trace the growth of Baltimore, from the straggling village of 1730, to the prosperous city of 1872. Whatever its growth has been hitherto, it is but the earnest of its capabilities for development. Its geographical position as regards the interior has been spoken of; as regards Europe, its position at the head of a bay, which was formerly considered a disadvantage to it as a seaport, enables the shipping to come *that much nearer the interior*, and by conveying freight further by water, and in bulk, causes a corresponding reduction in the cost of transportation; while the proximity of Baltimore to the coal regions, and the direct communication with them, which enables the steamers to take in their coal at $2.50 per ton less than it costs in New York, gives a direct saving of $2,000 upon the 800 tons consumed by steamers in each voyage across the Atlantic. The neighboring mines of anthracite and bituminous coal; the marble quarries of Baltimore County; the iron beds with which the State abounds; the lavish wealth of the Chesapeake Bay, with its world-renowned game and oysters and fish, afford in themselves a ready-made and apparently inexhaustible store of riches.

* An enumeration made the same year by the City Police, put the population at 283,375

TO-DAY.

BALTIMORE, as a home, is one of the most delightful cities in the world. It possesses more solid advantages than any other city on the Atlantic seaboard for those desirous of establishing themselves in a great metropolis, for purposes of trade, commerce, or business of any description. Situated about the centre of the Atlantic coast, at the head of the great Mediterranean Sea of America, it is equally removed from the intense cold of northern latitudes, and the blinding heat of our more tropical sisters of the South. An equable climate, soft, balmy, salubrious, and almost entirely free from the

NEW CITY HALL.

dense fogs which are the horror of the generality of cities adjacent to the seaboard, gives to it that healthy mean, which is seldom present along any of the water courses of this country or Europe. Its mild winters usually furnish ice enough for home consumption, gathered during the *cold snaps* that occasionally occur; while the pleasant bracing weather, which prevails during many weeks of that season, gives abundant opportunities for outdoor labor, the use of hydraulic power and navigable water, and demands far less fuel than is required in cities further north. Located upon a small but beautiful river Baltimore extends back over a succession of gently sloping hills, whose substratum is a sandy marl, and through which no mephitic vapors arise, no dampness injurious to health or life. In the original construction of the city, these hills probably presented serious obstacles to our worthy forefathers. Some were steep and unsightly, and required much grading, but the gradual expansion of the town enabled its builders to trim the rough edges, and cut down only so much as would relieve their precipitous character, without impairing their beauty and picturesqueness. These hills rise one above another step by step, until, on the outer boundaries of the city as now constituted, at almost any point, magnificent views of Baltimore, its harbor and the Chesapeake Bay, can be obtained. It may be also added that

THE CATHEDRAL.

because of its peculiar topography a person walking in any direction for three or four hundred yards, can obtain panoramic views of different sections of the city, such as can be had in few other places in the world. The Patapsco River with its inlets indents the land upon which Baltimore is built to a very considerable extent, forming natural extensions for wharf-fronts, and at the same time adding greatly to the beauty of the harbor, and the general landscape. Perhaps at some early period in the history of our city the marshes which formed at the head of these inlets, by their malaria may have produced those bilious diseases so frequent along the water courses of the Chesapeake, and a citizen of to-day feels doubtless a sensation of compassion, not unmixed however with self-congratulation, when he thinks of his ancestor, racked and tortured with the *shaking-ague* as he hurried from his morning meal to attend to the wants of his palsied customers. The marshes have long since been drained, the shores about the inlets converted into substantial wharves for the accomodation of our rapidly increasing commerce, and the miasma no longer rises from the lowlands, to disconcert the calculations of our citizens. Whether he dwells upon the heights where he can view the broad expanse of water, the spreading woods and well tilled fields of the surrounding country, or lives in a lowly hut on the river's bank, the inhabitant of Baltimore is to-day in either case exempt from any of the diseases popularly supposed to be generated in that element. In fact, Baltimore is one of the *most healthful cities* in the world. Its location would make it so necessarily. "Cleanliness is next to godliness" and certainly very conducive to health. The City, from every point, converges by gentle slopes to the river. It matters not what may be the condition of the streets, a heavy rain will thoroughly cleanse them of all impurities, and in case of a drought it is only necessary to turn on the water by means of the plugs, to secure this result. Baltimore was built gradually; obstacles of no common magnitude were to be surmounted, and though these were regarded as disadvantages at the moment, they have since proved its most attractive and healthful features. Their presence has given to us broad and well ventilated streets, and a pleasing variety of surface, the absence of which is so oppressively felt in other cities. In some instances irregularities have resulted from the many hills encountered, but these without imparing their usefulness, have added greatly to the beauty of the city. But there are other reasons why Baltimore is delightful *as a home*.

There is a subtle something, hard to describe, *bon-homie*, good fellowship, good breeding, refinement, perhaps a combination of many excellent qualities, which seems to pervade the very atmosphere of the City, and to penetrate all the avenues of life. From time immemorial the reputation of our State and City for hospitality has been national. Recent events—the opening of lines of railway, and the concentering of business and commercial interests in Baltimore, through their representatives—have given a practical turn to this feature of the people, and have spread its fame throughout the length and breadth of the United States. Indeed, the numerous great assemblages that have taken place in our midst during the past few years have borne such ample testimony to this quality, that any further reference might savor of egotism. Society in Baltimore is delightful, and this remark is intended to apply to all grades and classes. The lines of demarcation between the different strata are finely drawn. The most severe and exclusive circles, refined, intelligent and educated, exist side by side with less ostentatious, but not less cultivated coteries; and in the humblest ranks of the community there is an independence of thought and action which beget manhood in the higher sense of the term. That our citizens fully appreciate this is attested by the fact, that Baltimoreans, in whatsoever section of the globe they may be, like the Swiss for their native Alps, long for the City that gave them birth, and never lose their pride in its beauty and delights.

A stranger from any of the large cities in this country or Europe, upon his entrance into the City of Monuments, is struck by the utter absence of *tenement-houses*—those fearful scourges, the hot-beds of crime and pestilence in so many of the larger communities throughout the civilized world. There are none here. Baltimore does not need them. Her unlimited capacity for extension in any direction is a practical barrier to the fabulous prices obtained for land in other cities; and rents are so reasonable, and the rates of living so much less expensive than elsewhere, that the humblest mechanic or laborer can ensconce his family in a modest dwelling and surround them with the pleasures and comforts of home. Instead of the indiscriminate herding of the industrious and the slothful, the sober and the drunken, the upright and the criminal, the healthy and diseased, and the promiscuous mingling of the sexes, so destructive both to morality and life itself, the struggling man with small means can gather his household about him, in a commodious dwelling, absolutely removed from impure contagion, and amenable only to those influences which emanate from himself or his associations. He and his family acquire an individuality and manliness which are apt to display themselves for the right, in their careers through life. Home-influence, the strongest, the purest, and most precious that can surround man, either in his relations to society, or the family circle, is offered here in all its freshness and luxuriance; and other cities should not be surprised when we claim superiority in this regard.

For many years Baltimore has fostered a Public School system, of which her citizens have learned to speak with pride. Through all the dissensions of politics, and we have not been exempt from them, this "stable bulwark" of good government and free institutions has never been suffered to languish. We would not consider it illustrative of our progress

BETHANY INDEPENDENT METHODIST CHURCH.

in this respect to exhibit a model school-house at a World's Exposition, and yet our Public School edifices will compare favorably, in point of architecture, internal adornment, and personal comfort, with those of any city in the world. Further—by zealous and persistent efforts on the part of our legislators, and careful study of the systems of the most advanced states in America, and the most enlightened nations of Europe, our School

System has been perfected as far as it is possible to do so with our present experience. The useful features of other plans have been incorporated with our own, and their blemishes unhesitatingly rejected. The Public Schools are open to all—from the pitiful gamin who cries the news through the day, and painfully ekes out his nightly slumbers on cellar doors or market stands, to the fastidious scions of our most aristocratic families, all are equally entitled to the benefits which our schools vouchsafe, and, what is more to the point, they avail themselves of these advantages. Experience has led our citizens, without sectarian or class distinctions, to send their children to the public schools of the city, and perhaps this commingling of the various elements that form the community has done much to produce that fellowship which binds the different classes to each other. When a boy has passed successfully through the various established grades—the Primary Department, the Grammar School, and the City College—he has received as thorough and comprehensive an education as can be obtained in many of the Colleges or Universities in this country. This is plainly exemplified by the number of prominent merchants, successful bankers, skillful physicians, learned lawyers and shrewd politicians in our midst who can claim no other *Alma Mater*. There are other schools and colleges in Baltimore, and thickly strewn through the State, of high repute, and supplied with corps of Professors, whose names are a guarantee of the advantages they claim. The education of the female portion of our population has been an especial care of those who have been intrusted with the supervision of our schools. Wise and virtuous mothers naturally lead to upright, manly and useful sons. Nowhere has this truth been more fully appreciated than in Baltimore; and the Female Department of our Public Schools bears ample testimony to its practical adoption. While the æsthetic and showy features of the more fashionable finishing institutions for ladies have not been overlooked, the solid and substantial training which leads to perfect womanhood is made to assume its proper place in the system. Thus the women of our city are imbued with accomplishments which fit them to adorn whatever station they may be called to fill, and at the same time are taught those durable branches of knowledge which place them above the fickleness of fortune and the vicissitudes of life.

We give a summary of the number of Schools, Teachers, Pay Scholars, Free Scholars, and the number on the roll October 31st, 1872, with the average attendance and number of different pupils in the various Public Schools of Baltimore City during the year.

GRADES.	No. of Schools.	No. of Teachers.	No. of Pay Pupils.	No. of Free Pupils.	On Roll October 31, 1872.	Average Attendance.	No. of Pupils in School during the year.
Baltimore City College, ...	1	10	317	23	340	314	502
Eastern Female High School, . .	1	11	297	67	364	320	486
Western " " " . .	1	12	379	49	428	384	565
Male Grammar, ...	18	98	2,378	1,467	3,845	3,194	5,918
Female "	19	102	2,535	1,711	4,246	3,437	6,390
Male, (unclassified)	1	5	169	63	232	184	351
Female, "	1	6	187	110	297	232	404
Male Primary, ...	28	142	2,081	4,387	6,468	4,840	9,756
Female "	31	146	2,312	4,390	6,702	5,042	10,286
Evening Schools, Male, ...	6	20	12	712	724	445	724
" " Female, . . .	1	1		29	29	18	29
Day Schools, (Colored)	10	41	603	1,567	2,170	1,487	3,977
Evening Schools, "	4	12	316	214	530	362	530
Music Teachers, ...		4					
Drawing "		4					
	122	614	11,586	14,789	26,375	20,259	39,918

The promotions during the year were to the Grammar Schools 486, and to Primary Schools 2,401; making a total of 2,887. Total number in School during the year 37,031.

Besides the Public Schools, there are "Institutes" for the education of females, supervised and conducted by ladies whose very names are synonymes for all that is lovely and refined in private life, where girls are taught by precept and example the beauties and delights of the home-circle, and are fitted for that condition which has been so aptly styled "unspotted faith and comely womanhood."

The "Normal School," for the education of teachers, is a branch of our Public School system, and has been found very advantageous in the production of proficient instructors. We would like to dwell more circumstantially upon the really admirable features of this system, but our space is limited.

PEABODY INSTITUTE.

As a natural auxiliary to the above, we come to those institutions which have been founded through the munificence of some, and the public spirit of others of our citizens. Among these "The Peabody Institute" stands pre-eminent, both because of the bountiful nature of the benefaction, and the truly sublime character of the Donor. The aim of Mr. Peabody in the construction of the Peabody Institute has been but partially understood by many of our citizens. He was as wise as he was munificent. He had arisen from the humblest walks of life to affluence, and almost princely power. The sordidness usually begotten of wealth, and the arrogance which attends the acquisition of power, found no lodging place in his great soul. His love for mankind, which was circumscribed neither by race nor nationality,and his sound judgment,springing from a series of successful commercial transactions, in which neither avarice nor dishonesty played a part, taught him that there were strata in the human race which must be separately treated—that "what was one man's meat was another's poison"—that efforts to contribute to the advancement of all classes of people by the same means, were likely to result in the rending of the ties which bind classes to each other, and would ultimately convert what was intended as a blessing into an occasion of dissension and strife. Such certainly were the sentiments which actuated him in bestowing upon Baltimore the munificent Institute which now crowns the summit of her most beautiful thoroughfare. He never intended it to be *popular*. The directions given by Mr. Peabody for the selection of a Library, for the creation of the Academy of Music, for the interior governance of the Institute, all point conclusively to the fact that he had in his mind's eye the elevation of the great middle class of people, the safeguard of every enlightened government on earth. Aristocracy was as far removed from his thoughts as was its antipode. The former is supposed, through its wealth and influence, to be able to take care of itself, and if at all desirous of soaring to the empyrean in art, science, or literature, a visit to foreign lands will quickly assure the gratification of such a taste; the latter class, except in extreme cases, develops no such inclination. Abject poverty, undisciplined tastes and passions, and utterly uncultivated minds, do not prepare people to wrestle with the higher branches of education, any more than does preaching fit a man for soldiering, or ploughing qualify him for the judicial ermine.

The poorest classes of the people are provided with ample instruction for whatever course in life they propose to follow, and generally, they seek just so much as will enable them to pursue it. Occasionally some youth more ambitious than the rest, or more richly endowed with qualities which win, breaks through all obstacles, and outstrips his fellows in the race of life. There is nothing in this country to stay his progress. It is as republican in tone, as democratic in form. Class distinctions are of the slightest character—a helping hand is immediately extended to such an one, and he at once passed from the lowest stratum, to a higher place in society. Then can he avail himself of the advantages which "The Peabody" holds out to every citizen of Baltimore. Mr. Peabody had experienced just such a transmutation. From humble life, by regular gradations he had reached the highest social and financial position. His mind closely analytic with reference to his fellow-creatures, and wonderfully clear-sighted, wrought out for their benefit, schemes in different portions of the world perfectly consistent with their wants in those localities.

In London, where thousands of the poor perish annually from starvation, he devoted a princely fortune to the amelioration of their condition. In America, where it was required, he bestowed a similar amount; but as has been said above Mr. Peabody was as far-seeing as he was benevolent. America was the land of his nativity. He loved her, as only her sons can love who have spent many of their days in a foreign land—when he returned to her shores, after a lengthened absence, he saw many things to admire; but one element was lacking which he had learned during his European experience, to consider essential to a nation's advancement. That solid system of education fostered by a thousand years of aristocratic and kingly rule in England, and on the continent, was nowhere to be discerned. With scarcely an exception, the institutions of learning in the United States actually left off where the Universities of Great Britain and Europe commenced. The whole American people were subject to a system of semi-education, which might serve for the present the spirit of money-making inordinately developed among us, but which would in the future, totally unfit men for grappling with the great problems that might arise when teeming millions would swarm where thousands now imagined themselves crowded. Imagination too, ideality, what was known to the Greeks as "the beautiful," which makes up one-half, and far the better half of human life, was in danger of being forgotten. No school of Art that deserved the name existed. To provide for such an anomalous state of society, and to direct the American mind to the contemplation of all that is grand and beautiful in life, he determined to found institutions in different parts of America, through which, by libraries of the first excellence, the diffusion of the principles of science, the illustration of the nobler efforts of art, and the gradual education of the popular taste for the sublimer masters in music, the Americans would ultimately come to learn and appreciate the advantages of thorough, solid education as well as their neighbors across the water. His own declarations, his own instructions, and the institutions which have arisen under his far-seeing beneficence, tell us that such must have been his idea, and can there be a grander?

Mr. Peabody amid the multitudinous cares of a splendid mercantile and financial career, ever turned to Baltimore his adopted home and the scene of his early business successes. When released from the restraints and anxieties of commercial life he repaired hither, and selecting men of the most exalted tone in our city, he placed in their hands his princely donation, with the most ample instructions for its disposal. A massive marble structure has arisen near the base of the Washington Monument. A more appropriate place could

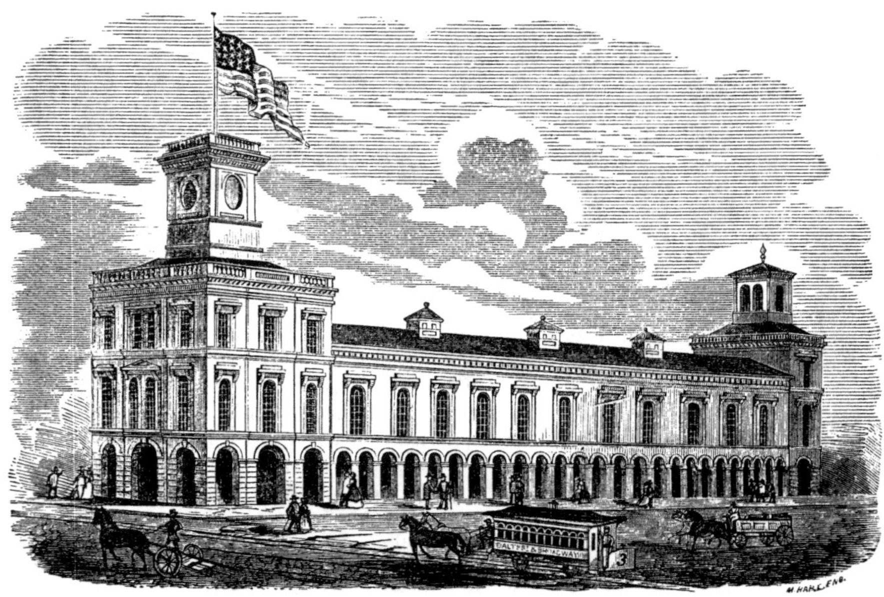

MARYLAND INSTITUTE.

scarcely have been selected. Both structures commemorate men who towered above their generations, and who alike conferred incalculable benefits upon the American people. Mr. Peabody lived to see the completion of a portion of the Institute, and its practical operation. Already have those, whose education and tastes were sufficiently advanced, received great and enduring benefits from the Peabody Institute, and its influence is being rapidly extended through our city. All institutions must grow, but more especially is this the case with one whose noble aim peers so far into the future. To cultivate and elevate the tastes and understandings of the people of Baltimore, was not the only object of George Peabody—his prophetic soul looked far beyond that—he knew that Baltimore was destined to become a great city, about which would radiate thousands of satellites. It was to extend to all these dependencies of the future, the benefits which Baltimoreans may at present derive from his splendid donations. That his hopes will be realized there can be no doubt.

We now come to the "Maryland Institute for the promotion of the Mechanic Arts." About twenty-five years ago a number of public-spirited citizens perceiving the want of some institution for the instruction and improvement of the masses in our city secured from the Legislature a charter. The institution was immediately organized under the name

EUTAW PLACE BAPTIST CHURCH.

given above. Its subsequent success is a matter of notoriety to our citizens. It is essentially a popular Institute, and supplies exactly the need in our city for which the Peabody was not designed. Its course of popular and scientific lectures, meets just such longings as the great masses of the people are likely to feel, while the lectures at the Peabody are intended for those much further advanced on the road to knowledge; in fact, for the few who have the energy and will to penetrate the arcana of nature, and pluck from her all that man has yet been able to unearth of her secrets. The course of lectures at the Maryland Institute has been for years, one of the most attractive features of our city. The greatest care is exercised in the selection of the lecturers, and no expense spared to make the course entertaining and instructive. The Institute contains a large circulating library with quite a number of valuable books, and very excellent selections from the popular literature of the day. Here again we see the contrast between the two institutions, and how admirably, in their respective spheres, they minister to the necessities of our city. The Library of the Peabody is for reference. It was so intended by its founder. The most costly volumes, compiled by the great Academies of Europe through royal bounty, are to be found on its shelves. When the student has exhausted the resourses of the Maryland Institute and acquired a fondness for study, and a thirst for knowledge through the avenues it so generously creates, he can betake himself to the Peabody, and he will find the one the complement of the other. The various schools of the Maryland Institute, conducted upon a scale of liberality which places them within the reach of the poorest and most humble student, are provided with a corps of competent professors. Pupils are well-grounded in all the elements of education, and fitted to strive for that higher sphere of intellectual cultivation which Mr. Peabody so eagerly hoped our countrymen would reach in the near future. In addition to these features, an annual Exhibition is opened in the Institute Hall generally in October. These Exhibitions are very attractive, collecting as they do specimens of the handi-work and ingenuity of the inhabitants of different sections of the United States; and there are usually offered to the inspection of the public, choice and varied specimens of the Fine and Useful Arts. Many thousands of our citizens, young and old, have availed themselves of its advantages, and the benefits that Baltimore has derived from its establishment are inestimable.

About thirty years ago a number of gentlemen met together in the old Postoffice Building to organize an association for the purpose of "collecting, preserving and diffusing information relating to the Civil, Natural and Literary History of the State of Maryland, and American History and Biography generally." A charter was obtained from the State Legislature in 1845, and the association organized under the title of the "Maryland Historical Society." The Athenæum, a substantial building at the corner of St. Paul and Saratoga streets, was completed in 1848 at an expense of $45,000, and presented to this Society by the citizens of Baltimore. The progress of the Association has been slow but steady. The nucleus of seventeen, has enlarged to upwards of four hundred members, embracing many of the most prominent and distinguished merchants and professional men of the city.

The library of the society has increased to sixteen thousand volumes, many of them rare and valuable; while the collection of Maps, Coins, Medals, Manuscripts, Charts &c. is very large, and in point of excellence not inferior to any similar accumulation in this country.

The Mercantile Library Association was organized in 1839, by the merchants' clerks of Baltimore. In 1848, the Association obtained a perpetual lease of the lower floor of the Athenæum building, and since that time the success of the enterprise has not been debateable. The Library has rapidly increased and has become a feature in our city. It is circulating in its character, and all classes of our citizens, ladies as well as gentlemen are permitted to enjoy its privileges upon payment of the necessary dues. Proper care is exercised in the selection of books, and only those are placed upon the shelves which are likely to elevate the tone, or encourage the literary taste of the reader. A reading-room is attached to the library, which is always abundantly supplied with the latest journals, and most popular periodicals.

John McDonogh, a native of Baltimore, but for many years a resident of New Orleans, died in 1850 in the latter city, leaving a very large fortune to Baltimore and New Orleans

YOUNG MEN'S CHRISTIAN ASSOCIATION BUILDING.

for the education of poor children. The will of Mr. McDonogh was contested and for a number of years a legal war was waged which threatened to engulph the whole estate, and which did consume a large portion of the money intended for charitable purposes. The contest was at length decided in favor of the two cities, and in the division of the property Baltimore received about $800,000. The intention of the donor was to establish a School-Farm, where children were to be instructed in the Christian religion, a plain English education, music, and the art of husbandry or farming. The Trustees, who have charge of the fund have purchased a farm of eight hundred and thirty-three acres of land in Baltimore County, about ten miles from the city, and purpose erecting thereon an institution with all the necessary improvements to carry out the views of Mr. McDonogh. The school will begin with one hundred pupils, and with a fund of $700,000 the interest from which will be amply sufficient to cover all expenses.

We now propose to notice briefly the Societies and Associations in our city that are devoted to the relief of suffering humanity.

"God loves a cheerful giver"—so do the poor. We know of nothing more refreshing than the genial smile of benevolence playing over the countenance of a silver-haired grandfather who has battled with the world for three-quarters of a century. If after contemplating all the meannesses, the frauds, the deceptions, the disappointments of his own life, he can smilingly put his hand in his pocket and draw forth from its recesses with real pleasure the wherewithal for the comfort of those less fortunate, that man is simply sublime, and his name is written in letters more lasting than bronze. Charity, which vaunteth itself and is puffed up, the noisy demonstrative counterfeit of the genuine article, is as abundant in Baltimore as elsewhere, but for true beneficence our city has no superior.

We will premise first that a street beggar is a rarity in Baltimore. Many things have conduced to this result,—the utter absence of tenement-houses, with their squalid wretchedness,—the fact that prior to the war the bulk of the poorer classes consisted of negroes, and these were cared for by their masters,—the ample provision made by the city for this class of our population,—but above all, the genuine spirit of benevolence which pervades every avenue of our city, and gushes out regardless of race, sect or condition of life. Almost every church in Baltimore has attached to it an eleemosynary association of some description, and the vast majority of well to do and reputable citizens are connected with one or more of the organizations for the relief of suffering humanity. Among those that deserve special mention is the "Association for the Improvement of the Condition of the Poor." Enrolled on its books are the names of the most prominent of our citizens. Its system, as far as we know, is peculiar to Baltimore. No imposing structure arises ostentatiously to point to the spot from whence the good works spring, but a back office in a building on a by no means conspicuous street, is all that the Society can call their own. The object of the Association is not to assist paupers, but to discourage vagrancy and street begging as much as possible. As was said above, the city provides abundant refuge for those who are unable to care for themselves, and however much the Association might desire to give aid in this way, their limited resources would render it impossible. Their aim is to help worthy persons to help themselves. Large communities swarm with individuals, and even families, thoroughly worthy, whose daily lives are martyrdoms. They struggle honestly, earnestly and industriously, but either owing to misdirected efforts, or causes that neither economists nor philosophers have yet been able to explain, they go down in the strife.

Frequently the heads of families are stricken down in the midst of their usefulness, and helpless women and children are thrown upon the community without the means of obtaining bread, or the worldly wisdom necessary to acquire those means,—business men by a series of luckless operations are overwhelmed and paralyzed for the time being by the very force of their misfortunes,—young men with situations which give them a bare support are overtaken by disease,—a disastrous fire may sweep away the accumulations of years,—in all of these cases the parties would be too proud or too manly to become a burden on the city, but a little help, the slightest in the world, extended at the proper moment, will bridge over the chasm in their lives, and enable them to continue honorable and useful members of society. To this portion of our population the services of the Association have been unremitting. Quietly, on the principle that the right-hand should not know what the left is doing, have the officers and agents moved through the city on their errand of mercy,

> "To the alleys and lanes, where misfortune and guilt,
> "Their children have gathered, their city have built,
> "Where hunger and vice, like twin beasts of prey,
> "Have hunted their victims to gloom and despair.
> * * * * *
> "To the garret, where wretches, the young and the old,
> "Half-starved and half-naked, lie crouched from the cold."
> * * * * *

No portion of the city has been neglected in their visitations, and an especial feature we think of our community, ladies refined, delicate, daintily dressed, as ministering angels, follow in the footsteps of these Good Samaritans, and the dark dens of wretchedness—for such there must be in every large city—are not seldom illumined by their gentle presence. As we have dwelt at considerable length upon the above organization, we are compelled to enumerate the other minor charitable institutions without comment. They are as follows: "Henry Watson Children's Aid Society," "Boys' Home," "Manual Labor School," "House of Industry," "Home for Girls," "St. Paul's Boys' Home," "Industrial School for Girls," "St. Mary's Industrial School," "German Orphan Asylum," "Union Orphan Asylum," "Baltimore Orphan Asylum," "Colored Orphan Asylum," "Christ Church Orphan Asylum," "St. Mary's Orphan Asylum," "St. Vincent's Orphan Asylum,"

"THE HOMELESS BOY."

"St. Patrick's Orphan Asylum," "Hebrew Orphan Asylum," "St. Peter's Orphan Asylum," "St. Francis Orphan Asylum," "St. Anthony's Orphan Asylum," "St. Paul's Orphan Asylum," "Aged Men's Home," "Aged Women's Home," "Home of the Friendless," "House of the Good Shepherd," "Church Home," "Protestant Infirmary," "Lombard Street Infirmary," "Washington University Hospital," "The Home,"

THE OLD FIRST PRESBYTERIAN CHURCH, BUILT IN 1791.

"St. Joseph's German Hospital," "Young Catholic Friends' Society," "Sabbath Association," "St. Joseph's School of Industry," "St. Vincent's Infant Asylum," "St. Agnes' Hospital," "Asylum of the Little Sisters of the Poor," "Conferences of St. Vincent de Paul," "Confraternity of St. Peter," "McKim Free School," "Colvin Institute," "Prisoners Aid Association," "Young Men's Christian Association," "Young Women's Christian Association," and eight Dispensaries which distribute medicines gratuitously to the poor. The above are all imbued with the same spirit of homely charity as that association of which we have spoken at length. They realize the truth of the adage, that "charity begins at home," and they find an inexhaustible field for the display of their energies. To say that Baltimore has reaped incalculable benefits from their exertions, and that the conspicuous lack of real poverty in our midst is mainly due to them, is but a feeble expression of the work they have accomplished.

THE NEW FIRST PRESBYTERIAN CHURCH.*

A magnificent edifice has been dedicated to the poor by our City Fathers on the eastern limits of the city. The building entitled "Bay View" because of the expansive view it affords of the Chesapeake Bay and the surrounding country, is spacious, commodious, and from its inner comforts, and the adoption of all modern improvements more suggestive of the ample means of some nabob who has retired from the cares of life upon a princely income, than of the home of the forlorn and helpless vagabonds which the seething cauldron of city life casts to the surface. It was built at a cost of $500,000 and is surrounded by grounds containing forty-six acres of land, from whence all the vegetables indigenous to this portion of the globe, can be had in quantities to insure an unfailing supply to the occupants.

* Height of Towers, 78, 128 and 268 feet.

Immediately outside of the western boundaries of our city is located another monument of the energy of some of our citizens, and those who administered the affairs of the corporation in times agone. This is the House of Refuge, for the reformation of boys who, like Topsy, "never had no mother, but growed," or whose parents after a series of years of unsuccessful training have pronounced them *incorrigible*, and have turned them over to the tender mercies of those who recognize no such word in their vocabulary. For years this asylum was tolerably well supplied with inmates, but the establishment of the "Boys' Home," and kindred institutions, has materially retarded the growth of these embryotic felons, and it is to be hoped that the rapid enlargement in the future of their sphere of usefulness will leave the House of Refuge without occupants.

The nations of antiquity were divided as to their policy for disposing of those afflicted with constitutional infirmities. While some maintained the doctrine that those who, by reason of the loss of one or more of the senses, or because of physical deformity, could not contribute towards the support of the State, should be summarily slaughtered; others upheld the less revolting but almost equally absurd theory, that this class were divinities or demi-gods, and should be worshipped accordingly. The insane, the idiotic, the blind, the deaf and dumb, were in some communities immediately put to death, while in others their mad prattle or incoherent mutterings were unhesitatingly adopted as oracles upon which depended the fate of empires. Though perhaps it is quite as impossible now to "minister to a mind diseased" as in the days of yore, it must be confessed that the moderns in their appreciation of this unfortunate class are far ahead of the ancients.

Every enlightened community regards them as the wards of the nation, an outgrowth it may be of the sins of the people, but nevertheless irresponsible for their misfortunes, and to be cared for with the utmost kindness and tenderness, as does a parent for an afflicted child. Some of the finest edifices in our country, imposing in design, artistic in structure and splendidly finished, attest the consideration which our people evince toward this phase of suffering humanity.

The State of Maryland has vied with private benevolence in her efforts to provide for the afflicted, and the result has been the erection of Asylums magnificent in point of architectural finish, and embracing in their management all the best features that the extensive experience of the nineteenth century can furnish. Nineteen years ago a project was set on foot which had for its object the erection of an Insane Asylum. A number of citizens banded together and raised an amount sufficient to purchase one hundred and thirty-six acres of land on the road leading from Baltimore to Catonsville. This property was donated to the State, on condition that an Asylum should be erected for the insane.

Successive legislatures appropriated about $750,000 for this purpose and the result has been the "Spring Grove Asylum," an institution complete in all its appointments, with capacity for three hundred patients, and which is equal in every respect to any similar establishment in this or any other country.

Moses Sheppard, descended from a Quaker family and a member of that persuasion himself, died in this city in 1857, after having amassed by industry and frugality, a very considerable fortune. Mr. Sheppard, early in life was horrified at sight of the treatment extended to insane paupers in our almshouses and jails. Men and women were crowded into narrow cells, stripped of every comfort, chained to the floor or braced to the miserable apologies for beds and literally suffered to wallow in filth. Their coarse and insufficient food was grudgingly meted out to them, and scantily clad they were exhibited like wild beasts to the morbid gaze of those whose gorge did not revolt at the spectacle. Many whose mild maladies might have been cured by timely and proper treatment, were transformed into raving maniacs, and instances were not rare of patients tortured to death by the use of the scourge or the lack of decent food. They were treated as though they were incarcerated for heinous crimes rather than confined as a security to themselves, with the hope of ameliorating their condition. This system was long in vogue in many sections of this country. Custom had deadened the sensibilities of the public, and its very antiquity was a sufficient excuse for its brutality.

That we have been emancipated from this frightful incubus, that we have awakened to a proper appreciation of this unfortunate class of people, and that the insane from all parts of our State can now, within a stone's throw of Baltimore, receive the best attention and treatment that skill or experience can suggest, is due to the munificence and energy of such men as Moses Sheppard. For many years this subject was the leading idea of his life. He surrounded himself with plans, examined carefully the designs of the most prominent Asylums in the country, and studied the various systems adopted for the

HEBREW HOSPITAL.

treatment of lunatics. Before his death he had matured a scheme for an Insane Asylum somewhat novel in its character, and it is to be presumed, from the care bestowed upon its creation, the best that has yet been devised.

Six hundred thousand dollars were donated by Mr. Sheppard for the erection and maintenance of the institution. The money was prudently invested, and has since that time with the property acquired increased to $1,000,000.

Three hundred and seventy-seven acres of land have been purchased within six miles of Baltimore, with an outlet both upon Charles Street Avenue and the York

Road. The land is beautifully located in one of the most picturesque sections of our State, and in the hands of the landscape-gardener is destined to become a most exquisite addition to the natural ornaments which surround our city. The building is in course of erection, the annual income from the endowment furnishing the funds for its construction. The style of architecture is Elizabethan. When completed it will have no superior on this continent for beauty of design, or substantial comfort to those who will be its occupants.

The patients are to be selected by the Trustees, according to their best judgment,—and as the establishment is mainly designed for a curative Hospital, care must necessarily be taken to open its doors principally to those whose types of insanity are such as hold out hopes of ultimate recovery. The charges for maintenance of patients are to be regulated by the ability of themselves or their relatives to pay their expenses; if utterly unable, the charges will be remitted altogether.

"Mount Hope," in the Northwestern suburbs of the City, has long been celebrated for its treatment of insane patients. The accommodations of the institution are ample, while the beautiful grounds by which it is surrounded must, if anything can, produce a soothing effect upon the terrible maladies of those who saunter through its avenues or rest under the peaceful shadows of the foliage, so near to the whirl and bustle of the busy city, and yet so entirely separated from its life and passions.

It will thus be seen that through State aid and private charity and enterprise, those bereft of reason in our midst have been most lavishly provided with homes.

Closely allied to the above, are the institutions for the cure of inebriates. The opinion has rapidly gained ground during the past few years that drunkenness, like insanity, consumption and a host of other maladies is constitutional or inheritable. Whether this be so or not it is unnecessary here to inquire. Philanthropists have been awakened to the necessity of placing a check upon this frightful scourge. Whether proceeding from the painful weakness of human nature, or the reckless carelessness which has almost become a feature of modern life, the results of drunkenness are the same upon the public weal, and society to save itself has been forced to seek the best method of preventing it. Inebriate Asylums have been established in different parts of the country, and Baltimore has not been behindhand. A number of benevolent persons founded a few years ago, an Asylum in the Western part of Baltimore, and Mount Hope Retreat, about six miles from the City, has a distinct department reserved for the restoration of inebriates. It may seem quixotic to direct benevolence to this channel, but when we consider that the majority of diseases are directly or indirectly the result of violations of the plainest principles of nature, and that by far the greater number of crimes may be traced to the improper use of spirituous liquors, the question assumes another aspect. Instances are not rare of poor besotted wretches rescued from the gutter and taken to these retreats, limp, quivering with horror and bearing about them but the semblance of manhood with its noble attributes, its god-like qualities nearly dead. Kind words, gentle nursing, soothing remedies have restored the relaxed muscles, and given tone to the broken spirit, and a few weeks have sufficed to effect a radical cure. Many a valuable life has been saved, many a useful citizen restored to society through their influence.

The maimed, the halt, and the blind have been equally the objects of solicitude in our City and State. The "Deaf and Dumb Asylum" established by the State in the city of Frederick, is an enduring memorial of her consideration for all classes of her citizens. In addition to the substantial and handsome edifice erected for their comfort, the institution has been supplied with a corps of competent instructors, who educate the unfortunate children confided to their care as far as their sad deprivations will permit, and the proficiency attained by the pupils in all branches of knowledge is truly wonderful when we consider the obstacles against which they have to contend. An Asylum has been established on Broadway, in this City, for the care and education of colored deaf mutes.

The Maryland Institution for the Instruction of the Blind, located on North Avenue, in this City, was incorporated in 1853, through the efforts of several benevolent citizens. The present building, constructed of Baltimore County Marble at a cost of $145,000—is beautifully located and can accomodate all who are likely to apply for admission for years to come. Those who are able to pay are expected to do so, but the indigent are received and educated at the expense of the State.

Mr. Thomas Kelso, a native of Ireland, but for eighty-two years a citizen of Baltimore, has been long known in our city as a benevolent and philanthropic gentleman. His many donations to charitable purposes, and the princely aid he has given to churches would of themselves entitle him to special notice. Age has not dimmed that spark of humanity which shone with such lustre in days of yore, nor has experience tempered its brightness. Eighty-nine years of life have but intensified his love for his fellow beings. Within a few weeks he has purchased a house and lot for a Methodist Episcopal Orphan Asylum, and

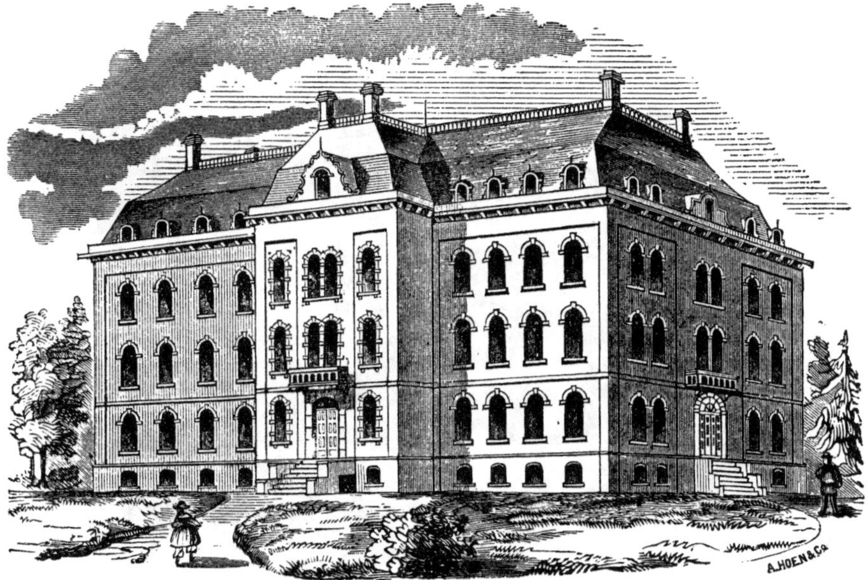

BLIND ASYLUM.

has endowed it with one hundred thousand dollars. Thus in the evening of his days he is enabled to contemplate the practical workings of his many charities, and to behold this crowning memorial which will number him among the benefactors of mankind.

Samuel Ready, a native of Baltimore County, but for many years a lumber-dealer in our City, left at his death $400,000, for the establishment of an Asylum for Female Orphans. Early in life his attention was attracted to those pitiful waifs who stray into lumber-yards, and earn a precarious livelihood by the pickings and frequently, stealings they may gather thence.

He was painfully aware of the manifold temptations to which they are exposed and the aim of his existence appears to have been, by rigid economy and close application to business, to set apart a sufficient sum to provide these little creatures with a shelter and home.

Mr. Johns Hopkins, a gentleman thoroughly identified with the interests of Baltimore, and one of her wealthiest and most influential citizens, has determined to establish a series of charities which for munificence and scope, will exceed any heretofore instituted by any one person in America. Mr. Hopkins is of an old and highly respectable Quaker family from the adjoining county of Anne Arundel, and came to Baltimore in 1812, and entered upon a mercantile career which by his sagacity, frugality and energy, has developed into a success unexampled in the history of the City. While amassing a fortune, colossal in its dimensions, he has kept steadily in view the prosperity and advancement of Baltimore, and has contributed greatly to the improvement of the City by fostering her commercial interests, erecting solid and substantial edifices for her increasing trade, and extending timely and judicious aid to her young and enterprising merchants and manufacturers.

The material assistance which he granted to the Baltimore and Ohio Railroad in the hours of darkness which shrouded that corporation prior to 1857, is deserving of special mention. Mr. Hopkins endorsed the paper of the corporation to a large amount, and pledged his private fortune in support of the Company's interests. The present condition of that great work fully attests his sagacity, and to the judgment which led him to embark

BOYS' HOME.

his capital in the fortunes of this company, is due much of the success which has attended his subsequent business career. He now proposes to crown a useful life by conferring upon the community in which he made it the perpetual benefit of much the larger portion of his great fortune.

The "Johns Hopkins University" has been organized by the appointment of trustees. They have been carefully selected by Mr. Hopkins from among the business men of the highest standing and character in Baltimore. It will be a University in fact and not merely in name—embracing in its functions the various branches necessary to thorough education, to which will be added a Botanical School on an extended scale. His magnificent and beautiful estate on the outskirts of the City, "Clifton," containing nearly four hundred acres of land, has been set apart for this purpose, and the trustees have been clothed with ample powers for the maintenance of the University in a manner which will be creditable to the City and an honor to the memory of the donor. Its endowment will be four millions of dollars.

The site of the old Maryland Hospital, fourteen acres within the City, has been purchased by Mr. Hopkins for the erection of a Hospital for the reception of all persons

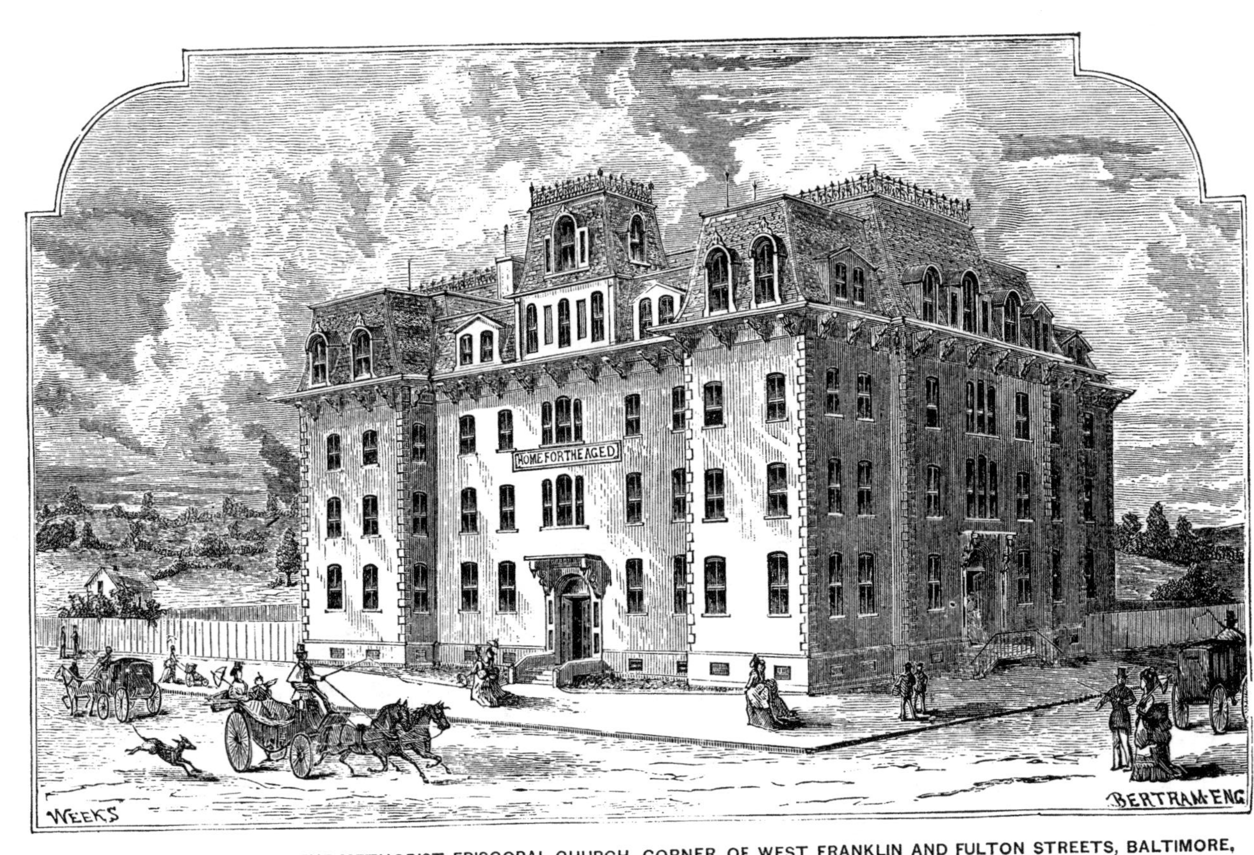

HOME OF THE AGED OF THE METHODIST EPISCOPAL CHURCH, CORNER OF WEST FRANKLIN AND FULTON STREETS, BALTIMORE,

afflicted with bodily injuries or non-contagious disorders. Separate buildings will be provided for the sexes, and also for the unfortunate of different races. The services of the most skillful surgeons and physicians will be secured, and an endowment of over two millions will provide ample means for its support.

In addition to the above, Mr. Hopkins has made liberal arrangements for the erection of an asylum for the education and maintenance of about four hundred colored orphan children, which will be under the supervision of the trustees of the "Johns Hopkins Hospital."

"THE PRESS" of Baltimore is peculiar. In these days when journalism may be said to be paramount, when it directs public opinion, frames legislation, prescribes the code of morality, and at the same time furnishes highly seasoned and meretricious food to palates vitiated by excess of sensation, the Press of our City is almost original. Its aim thus far has been "to hold up the mirror to nature," faithfully to portray current events as they actually occur, to exaggerate nothing, "nor set down aught in malice."

The example set by several of the great dailies of New York, of transforming the most trivial events into matters of excitement through the magic of a vivid imagination, or of relying entirely upon that wonderful faculty for striking impressions, has been extensively imitated in many of the large cities of America. Public taste thus perverted reacts upon public journals, and a morbid appetite is engendered which newspapers find it difficult to satisfy. The Press of our City has happily avoided this snare, and the public of Baltimore, by its appreciation, endorses what it considers the true vocation of journalism.

Our journalists are men of culture, education and ability, and what is of infinitely more importance, incapable of prostituting the censorship they exercise, for personal considerations. The *entente cordiale* is strictly observed between those engaged in rival enterprises, and rarely forgotten even in the ardor of a political campaign.

The history of the Press of Baltimore would be exceedingly curious and interesting, but our space will only permit a brief reference to those newspapers at present in existence, and wielding a potent influence in the community. *The Baltimore American and Commercial Advertiser* naturally heads the list, both because of its antiquity and its importance as a public journal. Away back in the annals of the City, when Baltimore was little more than a country village, and Annapolis a commercial emporium, we find mention of a Mr. William Goddard, a printer of Rhode Island, who, with the acuteness and enterprise so characteristic of his section, moved from Philadelphia, where he had for sometime resided, and on the 20th of August, 1773, established a paper in this City, entitled the *Maryland Journal and Baltimore Advertiser*. Prior to this date it was customary to receive the paper from and send advertisements to either Annapolis or Philadelphia.

It is difficult to conceive at this day that Baltimore could have been at any time so helplessly dependent upon Annapolis, that venerable connecting link between the present and the past. Goddard's paper was at first issued in weekly instalments from a house on South street, near the main thoroughfare of the City. The smouldering fires of the Revolution were being rapidly fanned into a blaze, and a feverish excitement had taken possession of the public. A better moment for beginning a newspaper enterprise could scarcely have been selected, and the old files of the paper give convincing proof of the proprietor's appreciation of the crisis. Mr. Goddard more than once during "the times that tried men's souls" displayed an indomitable perseverence in the acquisition of news so characteristic of modern journalists, but not viewed in a friendly light by our Revolutionary fathers. On several occasions he was called to account for inopportune publications, or for the freedom with which he criticised the actions of those in power, and the ardor with which he espoused the cause of Gen. Charles Lee, when that officer was suspended by the fiat of a court-martial, brought about his ears the indignant protests of a number of patriotic citizens, and but for a timely recantation, which he subsequently disclaimed,

THE BALTIMORE AMERICAN BUILDING,
126 & 128 West Baltimore Street.

he would have received the coat of tar and feathers which was administered by the populace to several of his less fortunate supporters.

After the war, and during the suspension of Benjamin Franklin from the Postoffice Department, Mr. Goddard resigned the editorial chair to his sister, Miss Mary K. Goddard, and undertook the establishment of post-routes in different parts of the country. Miss Goddard was perhaps the first of her sex in America to assume the arduous duties of a journalist, but with the assistance of several gentlemen of talent and public spirit, she more than maintained the high character the paper had acquired under the management of her brother. She afterwares took charge of the local postoffice, and discharged the duties of both positions with credit to herself, and to the entire satisfaction of the great public of Baltimore, which at this period consisted of some seven or eight thousand persons.

The early files of the paper, a number of which are still preserved at the *American* office, exhibited signs of business energy and enterprise which compare very favorably with like manifestations in our city to-day. The advertising columns were well filled, and the accuracy and celerity apparent in the collection of news seem marvellous when we consider the impossibility of easy and regular communication.

These old files give a very fair picture of the customs which prevailed at that period. The announcement of a combat to take place on Laudenslager's hill, between a royal Bengal tiger and four well trained dogs, sounds rather primitive to modern readers of newspapers, and the result of the terrific struggle, the dying agonies of the royal brute, and the subsequent exhibition of his stuffed skin to the public at a shilling a head, and half price for those of tender years, is really refreshing in the light of these degenerate days, when the *fancy* are confined to the tamer amusements of cock-fighting, rat-killing and punching each others heads.

In 1798 the name of the *Maryland Journal and Baltimore Advertiser* was changed to the *American and Daily Advertiser*, and in the year 1820 to the BALTIMORE AMERICAN AND COMMERCIAL ADVERTISER, the title under which it is issued at present. The *American* during the hundred years of its life has not been exempt from the vicisitudes of fortune.—Like other papers its lines have sometimes been cast in pleasant places, and at others the reverse has been the case. Its course however has always been consistent. Bold and outspoken in its sentiments and generally enlisted on the side of good government and the true interests of Baltimore, it has become a power in the community and has aided very materially in the development and progress of our City.

In 1855, Mr. Charles C. Fulton, its present proprietor, took charge of the paper. A practical newspaper man himself he fully appreciated the fact that a public Journal to be successful must give the *news* to its readers in an attractive form and with as near an approach to accuracy as circumstances will permit. Since that time the success of the *American* has been uninterrupted As its name imports, it is an admirable commercial paper and relied upon by our merchants and business men for its able and thorough market reports and monetary articles.

The tone of the paper is temperate and the impartial bearing it has maintained upon all questions affecting the growth and development of our City and its internal management, has established for it a reputation for good sense and sound judgment, and its advice has been repeatedly sought and acted upon by the municipal authorities, even though opposed to its political teachings. The financial management of the paper since 1869 has been marked by great ability and enterprise, and has contributed measurably to its prosperity.

The publication of THE SUN, of which Mr. A. S. Abell, the original founder, is the proprietor, was begun May 17th, 1837. It was the first attempt made in this city to establish a penny-paper, and its success during the first nine months of its existence far exceeded the most sanguine hopes of its projectors. The breaking out of the Mexican war and the energy displayed by the proprietors of *The Sun* in securing the earliest intelligence from the seat of war by means of a *pony express* gave the paper an impetus which it has since then maintained, in fact, its subsequent career has been an uninterrupted success.

As a public journal, giving the news in a concise but readable form, *The Sun* has no superior in the country. Sagacity and enterprise are exhibited in its management, and its editorial columns are marked by ability and sound sense. The *Sun Iron Building*, on the southeast corner of South and Baltimore streets, from whence the paper is at present issued, was the first edifice of that character erected in America. It was built entirely of iron at a time when business men generally were unwilling to try the experiment, and its usefulness and beauty have abundantly attested the discernment of Mr. Abell.

The publication of THE DAILY EXCHANGE was begun in this City on the 22d of February, 1858. The paper because of the bold stand it assumed with reference to local disorders and its manly and vigorous leaders, immediately attracted attention.

It was mainly instrumental in restoring a healthy tone to local politics, and during the first year of its existence became a power in the community.

The Exchange was suppressed by the strong arm of the military in 1861, but promptly reappeared as the MARYLAND NEWS SHEET, under which title it was published until the cessation of hostilities in 1865, when it was issued under its present name, THE BALTIMORE GAZETTE. On the 3d of May of the present year *The Gazette* partially changed hands.

Mr. CHARLES J. BAKER, a prominent merchant and manufacturer of this City, and a gentleman of no ordinary enterprise, united himself with Messrs. Welsh & Carpenter in the conduct of the paper—the latter having been connected with it from its origin. The name of Mr. Baker must be a tower of strength to any journal issued in Baltimore City. With rare business tact, large experience and ample means, he unites sterling integrity and a lofty and generous nature, whose impulses are ever enlisted for the advancement of the City and the good of the people.

The Gazette will be published hereafter in the quarto form, after the manner of the leading New York dailies. Its prospectus is admirable. "It will maintain fully and fearlessly an independent position; but whilst it will be free from all partizan trammels, it will consistently advocate and maintain Democratic principles.

It will be under the control of no cliques It will not admit the right of any one to dictate its policy. It will utter its own opinions.

It will defend the right. It will denounce wrong. It will strive to be worthy of public confidence, by correct accounts of current events, and fair discussion of public measures; by withholding scandal, as well as exposing public vices. It is pledged not to screen wrong doing in any one. Political and commercial friends will be sustained, so far as they are right. If they wish wrong palliated, or schemes of plunder and mismanagement in public affairs defended, they must seek other helpers.

Considering the growth and wealth and resources of this city, its extending commerce, its many avenues of trade, * * * *; considering its position and capability of becoming one of the largest centres of commercial and manufacturing activity in the country; considering the number and increase of its public charities, and plans of public education, we have room among its growing activities for more public journals, and especially for one of the very highest class.

In carrying out its plans it will scrutinize the management of public institutions and faithfully comment on their administration, and the capacity and uprightness of their managers. It will advocate a liberal policy for public schools; and whilst it will be a cherished aim to watch these nurseries of thought and morals for evidences of successful and conscientious administration, it will not hesitate to oppose promptly partisanship or incapacity in school boards or teachers."

With the enlargement of the size of the paper there will be a corresponding increase in the amount of reading matter, and no pains will be spared to obtain the earliest and most trustworthy news and the most interesting correspondence.

GERMAN CORRESPONDENT BUILDING,

CORNER BALTIMORE STREET AND POST OFFICE AVENUE.

The above is the programme of *The Gazette* under its new auspices. The names of the gentlemen who have charge of the paper are a sufficient guarantee that it will be complied with in every respect.

This journal already wields a potent influence in the City of Baltimore and many sections of Maryland and the Southern States. That this will be measurably increased under its new direction admits of no doubt.

The emigration of Germans to our city has aided materially in its development. As a class they have been industrious, energetic and enterprising, and many of the interests, detailed minutely in another portion of this volume, owe their rise and subsequent success to their sagacity and skill. A large number of them upon reaching our shores find it dfficult to master our language, and in consequence several newspapers have been established in this city which are published in the German language.

The most prominent is the GERMAN CORRESPONDENT, founded in 1840 by Col. Frederick Raine, who has been since that time, a period of nearly thirty-three years, its proprietor and chief editor. The paper began its career as a weekly journal, with a list of eighty subscribers, but, through the prudence and energy of its proprietor, in 1848 it became one of the leading dailies of our city. In 1869, the Marble Building at the southwest corner of Baltimore street and Post Office avenue, was built by Colonel Raine at a cost of $200,000, and since that time the *Correspondent* has been regularly issued from that handsome and substantial edifice. Its success is sufficient evidence of the admirable management of the paper and the ability displayed in the editorial columus has made it an influential organ among the Germans of Maryland and the neighboring States.

A number of weekly papers are published in this City, prominent among which is the BALTIMORE BULLETIN, of which *W. Mackay Laffan and S. S. Early* are proprietors.—This paper was established in 1870, and by its sprightliness, wit and common sense, soon earned for itself a popularity surpassing that of any weekly in Baltimore. It is not likely to lose its prestige in the hands of its present publishers.

Among the periodicals published the SOUTHERN MAGAZINE occupies perhaps the most conspicuous place. Its selected matter evinces taste and judgment, and the original articles which appear in its pages give evidence of ability and cultivation.

Among the weeklies and monthlies there are a number of journals devoted exclusively to religion. These are under the auspices of the different denominations and are well supported by the respective Churches, both in this City and the rural districts of this and other States.

THE MERCHANTS EXCHANGE AND NEWS ROOM has been organized for more than a half century. For the past thirty years it has been under the management and proprietorship of *Mr. George U. Porter*. Prior to the purchase by the general Government of the old Exchange Building, the reading rooms were located therein, but in 1857, they were removed to the adjoining building where they have since been located. A careful record is preserved at the Exchange News Rooms, of the marine and commercial news; telegraphic advices of the New York and Liverpool markets are received; together with files of papers from all the principal points in our own and foreign countries. The rooms are maintained at considerable expense and for support are dependent upon the annual subscriptions of the members.

The MARINE OBSERVATORY is situated on Federal Hill, overlooking the river and Chesapeake Bay to a distance of twenty miles and signaling vessels as they approach the harbor. Though entirely independent of the Exchange, it is nevertheless a valuable auxiliary.

THE BOARD OF TRADE of Baltimore, with the single exception of the New York Chamber of Commerce, is the oldest in the United States. It was organized in 1820, and in 1849 a reorganization was effected which proved highly beneficial, the Board since that time having proved itself thoroughly active and efficient. Recently, similar organizations have been formed in nearly all the cities on the seaboard, from Portland to New Orleans, and every prominent city in the West to the Pacific coast has its Board of Trade or Chamber of Commerce, designed more especially to promote the interests of its immediate locality, but by united representation in the National Board, destined to wield much influence in shaping the commercial policy of the country. The high character of the men who compose the Board in this City have given to it a tone and strength almost peculiar to Baltimore.

The members elect annually a President, four Vice Presidents, Secretary, Treasurer, and twenty-four Directors. Stated monthly meetings are held in their rooms at the Exchange Reading Rooms for the transaction of business. The first President under the reorganization in 1849 was John C. Brune, who filled that position with credit to himself and to the satisfaction of the Board until 1862, when he was succeeded by Thomas C. Jenkins, who served three years. The lamented Albert Schumacher was then chosen President, which position he occupied until his death, on the 26th of June, 1871. Horatio L. Whitridge was selected as the successor of Mr. Schumacher and still occupies the position with B. M. Hodges, Jr., J. Hall Pleasants, Laurence Thomsen and Israel M. Parr, Vice Presidents, Edward B. Dallam, Treasurer, and George U. Porter, Secretary. Mr. Port has filled the position of Secretary to the Board since 1849, the date of its reorganization, with great acceptability to the members.

THE BALTIMORE PRICE CURRENT AND WEEKLY JOURNAL OF COMMERCE was first issued on 29th June, 1849, by George U. Porter and Thomas W. Tobin. Prior to that period and for some years thereafter but little attention was bestowed by the daily newspapers upon commercial reports, and the need of such a publication was keenly felt by our merchants. Since the death of Mr. Tobin, in April, 1862, Mr. Porter has edited and conducted this journal, and is at present its sole proprietor.

The Price Current is a faithful index of the Baltimore markets. It is conducted with marked ability, and is accepted by our merchants and business men as the highest authority in all matters pertaining to the trade and commerce of our City.

No city in America offers a broader field than Baltimore for the development of journalistic enterprise. Those papers already established are eminently worthy of the patronage they receive, but in a city of 300,000 inhabitants there must necessarily be room for at least twice the number of journals which now occupy the field.

The moral and religious tone of our community is excellent. Though the city is not exempt from the nameless evils incident to all localities where human beings dwell together in masses, immorality does not rear its brazen front with impunity, nor does the law by its inaction encourage vice or embolden its votaries. Purity from time immemorial has been claimed as an especial virtue of the inhabitants, and our citizens have not soiled the fair fame which has come down to them as a priceless legacy from their ancestors. Baltimoreans are eminently a church-going people.

There are two hundred and four churches within the limits of the City divided among the different denominations as follows: Methodist Episcopal 46; Protestant Episcopal 30; Catholic 24; Presbyterian 18; Evangelical Lutheran 13; Baptist 10; Jewish Synagogues 9; Methodist Episcopal (South) 9; Methodist Protestant 8; United Brethren 8; African Methodists 7; Reform Church 6; Independent Methodists 2; Friends 3; Swedenborgian 3; Evangelical Association 2; Independent Church 2; and the Christian, Seamen's Union Bethel, Unitarian, and Universalists each one. Of the two hundred and four churches, seventeen are maintained by the colored population of the City. In this summary of churches none save those within the boundaries of the corporation are enumerated.

Immediately outside of the jurisdiction of the city are numerous churches and chapels, many of them constructed and maintained largely through the liberality of our citizens, which would swell the aggregate considerably. There are two hundred and thirty-seven ecclesiastics actively engaged in ministerial duties who may be classified as follows:

Catholics 61; Methodist Episcopal 43; Protestant Episcopal 44; Presbyterian 18; Evangelical Lutheran 12; Baptist 9; Methodist Protestant 9; Methodist Episcopal (South) 9; United Brethren 6; Reformed Church 6; African Methodist 5; Independent Methodist 2; Evangelical Association and Independent Church, two each; and the Christian Church,

ST. PAUL'S P. E. CHURCH.

Seamen's Union Bethel, Universalist and Unitarian, each one. The Province of Baltimore being at the head of the Catholic Hierachy in this country, the Primate of that Church in America, Archbishop Bayley, with his council, resides in this City. Bishop Whittingham, the Senior Bishop of the P. E. Diocese of Maryland, Bishop Ames of the

M. E. Church; Bishop Weaver of the United Brethren and Bishop Wayman of the African M. E. Church, also live in Baltimore.

Sunday is emphatically a day of rest in our City. Under the law, business of every description is suspended, and the citizens willingly co-operate with the authorities in the enforcement of its provisions. A stillness unbroken, save by the tinkle of the car-bells or the voices of the people as they move to and from the houses of worship, reigns through the city during the morning hours, and upon pleasant afternoons the promenades and thoroughfares are fairly alive with happy faces eager to bathe in the soft Sabbath sunlight and breathe the invigorating air which rolls up from the Chesapeake.

A large amount of capital has been invested in the construction of Church edifices, and many of them furnish evidences of cultivation and taste. This brings us to the consideration of another feature of our City.

The effect of its buildings upon the character of a city is not always properly appreciated. Sombreness or gaiety, lights or shadows, depend oftener than is generally supposed upon the style of ornamentation adopted in the construction of our houses; and the tastes and habits of a people may be sometimes accurately inferred from the style of ARCHITECTURE prevalent among them. Not many years ago the popular mind was completely fettered in this regard by arbitrary rules. The most tyrannical despot could not have more thoroughly bound his subjects hand and foot. The severity of Grecian models or the almost equally simple outlines of Roman architecture, formed the framework upon which were designed all public buildings, while private dwellings, with few exceptions, were constructed solely with a view to their inner convenience and comfort, and without a thought to their external adornment. Wherever these heavy styles obtained exclusively, a corresponding gravity was noticeable among the people.

The attention of Ruskin was attracted to this phase of the subject, and the efforts of that practical but exquisite thinker, coupled with the exertions of his co-workers, have effected a complete revolution in the science of architecture abroad, while the fresh and vigorous impulses of Americans have done much to emancipate them from the master they learned to serve in provincial times. The spirit which held us in Grecian and Roman bonds is rapidly giving way before the ambitious efforts of our energetic architects, and a system has grown up not referable to any particular style, but a combination of many which may be described as distinctively American.

The steady and substantial development of Baltimore has been favorable to the construction of stable and handsome public edifices. While no recognized style of architecture has been rigidly enforced, the beauties and advantages of the Grecian, Roman, Corinthian and Gothic have been adopted by our architects, and blended with more modern ideas, varied occasionally by suggestions originating with themselves. As an illustration of the advances since made in this direction we subjoin a cut of the old Light Street Methodist Episcopal Church, built in 1797. The Roman outlines of its windows scarcely relieve the primitive aspect of the building, and we turn with pride and somewhat of enthusiasm to the magnificent Gothic structure known as the Mount Vernon Place M. E. Church, and completed in 1872.

But the desire for architectural adornment manifested itself at an early period in the history of Baltimore. In 1806 the foundations of the Cathedral, the metropolitan Church of the Catholics in this country, were laid, and in 1821 it was consecrated. In thoroughness of design and substantial workmanship it has no superior in the United States. It is located at the corner of Cathedral and Mulberry Streets, an elevated portion of the City, and is an unfailing source of admiration to all who visit Baltimore. It approaches nearer the Roman style of architecture than any other, in its construction, though the architect did not permit himself to be circumscribed by the limits of a particular school. It is built in the form of a cross. The immense Dome suggesting grandeur, while the massive

THE OLD LIGHT STREET M. E. CHURCH.

pillars and towering arches are indicative of a strength and durability, calculated to defy the insidious ravages of time for many generations. The interior of the Cathedral is profusely decorated with paintings of rare merit, and its vaulted recesses by the manifold vibrations they create, have given it a national reputation for acoustic properties.

MOUNT VERNON PLACE METHODIST EPISCOPAL CHURCH.

DIXON & CARSON, ARCHITECTS, BALTIMORE.

St. Paul's Church, at the corner of Charles and Saratoga streets, a fair specimen of the Romanesque or Lombardic, by its uniqueness of design gives variety to our church architecture.

In point of beauty, exquisite finish and faithful adherence to scientific principles the First Presbyterian Church, at the corner of Madison and Park streets, stands alone. It is built in the Pointed Gothic Style, of a very richly colored freestone from the quarries of New Brunswick. The ornamentation though simple is highly wrought and the perfect symmetry and grace of its numerous spires, and in fact of every portion of the edifice will challenge comparison with any similar effort at home or abroad. The eye dwells upon its bold but comely outlines with ever increasing delight, and the citizen evinces a legitimate pride in a structure which is at once a triumph in architecture, and a memorial of the taste of Baltimoreans.

Among the churches possessing claims to notice for architectural finish may be mentioned the Independent Methodist Church at the corner of Lexington and Calhoun Streets, and the Eutaw Place Baptist Church—both of them modified specimens of Gothic Architecture.

But the spirit of improvement in the science of architecture, has not been confined to the embellishment of churches. Many of our public buildings give evidences of marked progress in this respect. The City Hall, now approaching completion in the heart of the City is a magnificent marble structure, the design of which is in accordance with the Roman style, very materially modified by modern innovations, of which the French roof is a prominent feature. The marble was obtained from the quarries near the City, and dressed in the vicinity of the building by Baltimore stone cutters. The City Hall, when finished, will be one of the handsomest and most imposing edifices in this country, and will reflect credit on our City, the materials for its construction, to the minutest item, having been obtained within the limits of the State, and the work upon it, having been done altogether by the artisans of Baltimore.

The Baltimore City Jail, a massive granite structure, Romanesque in its outlines, combines with usefulness and durability all the most attractive features of that impressive style of architecture, and may be cited as a model for the erection of prison buildings, an experience of fifteen years having demonstrated as well its security as its thorough sanitary properties.

The Masonic Temple, on Charles street, and the Young Men's Christian Association Building, to be constructed at the corner of Charles and Saratoga streets, the one of white marble, the other of pressed brick, with freestone dressings, are distinctive types of what may be termed American Architecture. Their outlines are referable to no received schools, but embrace features which resemble in some respects the leading characteristics both of Grecian and Romanesque styles, so blended with modern principles of construction and originality of design, as to puzzle the student pertinaciously bent upon adding to his classical knowledge, but none the less interesting and attractive to the general public on that account. The United States Custom House and Court House are both substantial buildings, the one located for convenience at the corner of Gay and Second streets, in the business heart of the city, and the other at the corner of Fayette and North streets, in close proximity to the offices of the members of the Bar and the State Courts of Justice.

In addition to the above there are many other public buildings of prominence, a very large number of which are built entirely of white marble, inexhaustible supplies of this material lying within easy access of the city and procurable at rates which make it specially desirable for building purposes.

Any reference to the architecture of Baltimore would be incomplete, without an allusion to the dwelling houses of her citizens. In traversing some cities, a feeling of oppressiveness steals over the traveller which he strives in vain to overcome. The streets are methodically laid out, the houses neat, regularly built, and uniform in appearance, and the stranger instinctively looks within himself for an explanation of his dullness. This feeling is easily accounted for. Nature abhors equality and similitude. This very uniformity produces a sensation of weariness. A street may be lined on either side for miles with handsome residences, but if they are of the same size, built exactly alike, with similar door-heads, windows, shutters, cornices, and roofs, the effect is necessarily monotonous, and when to this is added an indefinite number of streets, counterparts of the one described above, we cease to wonder at the tiresome impression created. Baltimore is certainly as free from this fault as any city in the United States. While the streets in many portions of the city are lined with costly and elegant dwellings, there is generally sufficient variety in the mode of construction, and external adornment to attract attention and insure interest, and the numerous cottages which dot the sides of our thoroughfares especially in the sections recently built, impart a charm to the landscape which must be seen to be appreciated.

It is proverbially said that Republics are ungrateful, and the adage earns confirmation from the spectacle presented to-day in the Capital of the Country. A huge mass of marble rises out of the mud-flats on the Potomac river. Misshapen, unfinished and gradually settling in the ooze upon which its foundations are laid, it is rather a monument to the bad taste of the American people, or their representatives, and the lukewarmness with which they regard their great benefactors, than a memorial of him who was "first in peace, first in war, and first in the hearts of his countrymen." For more than twenty years the most strenuous efforts have been made by the patriotic people of the United States of both sexes to complete this marble column in honor of him whom *the world* calls great, but the shaft has scarcely risen above the foundations.

The vividness of the contrast presented by the action of our own people fairly entitles Baltimore to be styled "The Monumental City," a name by which she is known both at home and abroad, and of which she is justly proud. In 1809, while the City was yet in swaddling clothes, a number of well-known citizens were empowered by the Legislature of Maryland to erect in Baltimore a Monument to GEORGE WASHINGTON. It was to have been built upon the spot where the Battle Monument now stands, but the breaking out of the war between this country and Great Britain soon absorbed public attention, and the project was held in abeyance until hostilities had ceased. In the meantime the City had been saved from destruction by the Battle of North Point, and the heroism of those who had fallen in that memorable action was fresh in the minds of the citizens. To honor their memories appeared as natural as commendable to Baltimoreans, and the echoes of the guns had scarcely died away ere a petition was circulated by the Committee of Safety soliciting subscriptions for this purpose. All classes contributed freely, and in 1815 the "Battle Monument" was reared in the centre of the space now known as Monument Square.

This necessitated a change of location for the Washington Monument, and Col. John Eager Howard, distinguished as an officer in the Revolutionary war, and subsequently Governor of Maryland, offered the Commissioners as much land as was needed about the crest of the hill now known as Mount Vernon Place, but which was at that time covered with forest trees. In those days it was customary to make use of lotteries to secure the necessary funds for the prosecution of public enterprises, a rather questionable expedient in the light of modern ideas of morality. Churches and buildings for secular purposes were alike indebted to the blind goddess. It was thus that much of the money was raised for the completion of the Washington Monument.

The corner-stone was laid with appropriate ceremonies on the 4th of July, 1815, and the statue, representing Washington resigning his commission, was placed in position October 19th, 1829. The Monument is a graceful Doric column built of white marble. The base is 50 feet square and 24 feet high, and the column is 164 feet in height. The whole structure rises to an elevation of over 280 feet above tide-water, and from its top can be obtained a view which for beauty, variety and extent is seldom equalled.

At the base of this memorial lies the MONUMENTAL CITY, a picture, the inequalities of which are softened by the distance of the spectator, and whose attractive features are beautifully blended by its subtle enchantment,—to the south, the Patapsco rolls on to the

WASHINGTON MONUMENT.

stately Chesapeake, land-locked and obstructed by many a rudely jutting point from the adjacent County of Anne Arundel, or the low-browed shores on the opposite side,—to the west, the hills, gathering strength as they recede, rise one above another until a lofty spur of the Blue Ridge marks the horizon, and its azure lines shut out the scene beyond,—to the north and east the beautiful villas and smiling valleys of Baltimore County are seen in numbers—the whole forming a gorgeous panorama which the visitor once contemplating will not easily forget.

WILDEY MONUMENT, BROADWAY.

Baltimore has other claims to the title mentioned above. On the 26th of April, 1865, the Odd Fellows' Monument, an unique structure surmounted by a Grecian Doric column, the whole 52 feet in height, was dedicated to Thomas Wildey, the founder of the Order of

Odd Fellows in America. The Monument is on Broadway, above Baltimore Street, and is a very handsome ornament to the eastern section of the City.

The Wells and McComas Monument has been erected in Ashland Square to the memory of the two young men who are popularly supposed to have slain General Ross, the commander of the British troops in the battle of North Point, contributing thereby very greatly to the defeat of the invaders, though neither of them lived to learn the service they had rendered to their native City.

In America the taste for Painting and Sculpture has not proportionately developed with her material advancement. While in the number, variety and usefulness of her discoveries and inventions, the United States has surpassed every other enlightened nation, she has never ceased to pay tribute to Europeans in the matter of the FINE ARTS. This does not arise so much from the want of talent among our people as from the morbid national tendency to sacrifice the ideal to the desire of gain, and the absence of that higher class in our midst upon whose patronage and wealth, Art has always been completely dependent. Thus in almost every instance where native artists have attained eminence it has been secured under the fostering influence of a more congenial clime and accompanied by the aid and countenance of persons other than Americans.

In matters of art Baltimore has made much unostentatious progress, and to day there are collections of pictures, growing little by little, in the possession of some of her citizens, which promise within the near future to assume proportions of national interest. Mr. William T. Walters is the owner of one which is conceded to be the finest in the United States. Colonel J. Stricker Jenkins comes next, with a large and extremely valuable collection, a majority of the pictures in which were painted upon direct commissions from the owner and not purchased when already finished and in the market. The most distinguished names in contemporary art are to be found in it. There are several other prominent collectors, foremost among whom may be mentioned Mr. John King, Jr., Vice President of the Baltimore and Ohio Railroad; Mr. George R. Vickers, a retired merchant; Mr. Samuel S. Early, a Baltimore editor, formerly of Terra Haute, Indiana; Mr. B. F. Newcomer, Mr. D. L. Bartlett, Dr. George Reuling, and others.

Mr. Walters' collection is a remarkable one in many respects—in the pictures that it contains, the history of their acquisition, and the extreme beauty of the gallery, which for graceful design, appropriateness to its purpose and costliness of material, is not anywhere equalled in this country. It is situated in the rear of Mr. Walter's elegant city residence on Mount Vernon Place, and the several years occupied in its construction have been amply repaid. Nothing could be more charming than the beautiful spectacle that it presents or the effect conveyed by the warm neutrality of its tapestry, fresco, woodwork, and carpeting in contrast with the brilliant kaleidoscope of art treasures that hang on its walls. Among the artists represented the following are noted at random from the different schools: Delaroche, Meissonnier, Gerome, Frere (Edouard), Jalabert, Rousseau, Breton, Vibert, Plassan, Calame, Corot, Willems, Gallait, Jaique, Zeim, Bonheur, Bida, Hamon, Gleyre, Lasalle, Dargelas, Des Goffes, Odier, St. Jean, Tissot, Chavet, Landelle, Breton (E.), Merle, Duverger, Prever, Hubner, Troyon, Van Marcke, Weber, Muller Bischoff, Leutze, Achenbach, Hiddeman, Heilbuth, Fichel, Kensett, Hart, Durand, Woodville, Stevens, Johnston, Richards, Church, Lambert, Trayer, Jacovacci, Herring, &c.

In Colonel Jenkins' collection must be noted several remarkable pictures by such artists as Jalabert, Jourdan, Bouguereau, Schreyer, Delort, Plassan, Brillouin, Piot, Beranger, Castres, Caille, Escosura, Baugniet, Grandchamps, Boulanger, Bakalowicz, Arnold, Chavet, Fichel, Castan, Toulmouche, Pecrus, Herbsthoffer, Coomas, Comte-Calix, Seignac, Antigua, Billotte, Baron, Van Schendel, Hamon, Lemmens, Robbe, Coutourier, Frere, Kensett, Hart, Gray, Baker, Huntingdon, Elliott, Rossiter, Benson, Gifford, Casilear, Richards, Boughton, Lambdin, Durand, Church, &c. All these are of the highest order of merit and have, many of them, a reputation that extends not only to all American art collectors, but also to those of European capitals.

Among native artists who, by reason of the reputation universally accorded them, deserve special notice may be mentioned the sculptor, William H. Rinehart. Mr. Rinehart was born in Carroll County, Maryland, and began life as a stone cutter. He soon developed an extraordinary talent for sculpture, and through the kindness of friends was

MASONIC TEMPLE.

enabled to pursue his studies in Italy, "the cradle of the Muses." His early promise has been more than realized. He has won for himself a proud place among living sculptors, and as has been justly said, "the State owes him much for the reflected honor of his well earned reputation." His works are numerous and many of them adorn the dwellings and grounds of Baltimore's wealthy citizens. Among them may be mentioned the statue of

"Clytie,"—regarded by the artist himself as his *chef-d'œuvre*—which was purchased recently by our public spirited townsman, Mr. John W. McCoy, and presented by him to the Peabody Institute, where it is placed in an elegant and appropriate setting, and by the terms of the gift is accessible to the public, at all times, without charge; the statue of Chief Justice Taney, lately unveiled in Annapolis, the capital of the State; the Woman of Samaria, in possession of Mr. Wm. T. Walters; the Bronze Door to the Capitol at Washington; the Monumental Female Figure, in bronze, in Greenmount Cemetery; a beautiful group of Sleeping Babes, in marble, in the same Cemetery; "Christ—I am the Resurrection and the Life"—with the Angel of the Resurrection, in Loudon Park Cemetery; and a host of minor productions which display as well the fertility of his genius as his perfect taste and marked merit.

An annual exhibition and sale of paintings in this City, begun in 1871 and continued since that time, has brought to light a number of artists, evidencing that if Painting has not reached its highest development, a talent for it has at least been very generally diffused in our community. These exhibitions bear testimony both to the ability and versatility of Baltimore artists. Among those who deserve mention for a creditable degree of talent may be cited Mrs. S. Schwing, her "Marguerite" and "Hero and Leander" having received the commendations of the critics and press generally; A. Quartley, whose Coast Scenes are very much admired: A. J. H. Way, a very able and painstaking painter of Still-Life Studies; and H. Bolton Jones, some of whose Landscapes are an earnest what the public may anticipate in the future.

The rare opportunities offered by the extension of the Peabody Institute and the enlargement of its sphere of usefulness will make Baltimore, at no distant period, a very desirable location for artists who are pursuing their studies, while the encouragement given by one of the Clubs, the Allston, has also a most beneficial tendency.

Already the example set by Mr. McCoy has borne fruits. Mr. George S. Brown, a prominent banker of Baltimore, presented to the Peabody recently two statues, Pocahontas and Venus, possessing great merit, and the prospect is that before long the Institute will be able to form an Art Gallery of no mean pretensions.

The BAR OF MARYLAND has ever been renowned for the standing and ability of its members. When Baltimore was but an overgrown village the adjacent counties of Anne Arundel and Harford were known all over the country through the prominence of their lawyers—in fact, the revolutionary struggle was barely at an end when Luther Martin, towering over his fellows by his massive intellect and legal acumen, became the leader of his profession in the young but vigorous Republic, and maintained this proud position against all competitors, until disease prostrated those powers which had been the admiration of the thirteen colonies. In those early days the names of Dulany, Chase and Johnson were household words in our State. They were as noted for their sterling integrity, as for their standing at the Bar.

William Pinkney, whom Chief Justice Marshall styled the greatest of American lawyers was a contemporary of Luther Martin. His great talents were publicly recognized by his appointment as Minister to the Court of St. James, and his efforts subsequently in the Senate of the United States made it matter of profound national regret that his taking off in the flower of his life so abruptly terminated his services to his country.

During the professional career of Pinkney, Baltimore began to lose somewhat of its provincial character, and with its growth came gradually the concentration in our city of the legal talent of the State. William Wirt, a native of Maryland, but by adoption a Virginian, sought here a wider field for the display of his wonderful genius as did also Robert Goodloe Harper, and the encounters between these intellectual athletes have furnished rich material for the essayists and biographers of the present day.

But the line of distinguished lawyers did not stop with Pinkney and his contemporaries. Their mantle fell upon the shoulders of such men as Chief Justice Taney, the great Christian jurist, and John Nelson, the fiery Templar of modern jurisprudence; the one a beautiful exemplar of that justice which the storms of passion, prejudice and unreasoning malice were powerless to change, the other the advocate, whose eloquence like a torrent, swept everything before it, and whose versatility of genius made him equally at home in the Cabinet of the Nation or the Courts of Princes. Nor must the name of John V. L. McMahon be omitted. His herculean efforts in behalf of the Baltimore and Ohio Railroad have forever linked his name with that corporation, while many of the gems which adorned his popular speeches are unwittingly used at the present day to round a period or give force to an otherwise pointless speech.

REVERDY JOHNSON, a native of the City of Annapolis, is to-day confessedly the leader of the Baltimore Bar, and without a peer in the United States. His knowledge is profound, his reason singularly analytic and his conclusions marked by a clearness and accuracy which give to them the force of judicial decisions. The reputation of Mr. Johnson is not circumscribed by national boundaries. He is well and favorably known in Europe as in America. He has held in turn the offices of Cabinet Minister, United States Senator and Minister Plenipotentiary and Envoy Extraordinary to Great Britain, and in each of these capacities has demonstrated his right to the proud eminence he has attained as the great expounder of constitutional law. Mr. Johnson to-day, at an advanced age, is as vigorous in mind and body as when in the prime of life, and is justly revered by his fellow-citizens, who feel themselves to a certain extent sharers in the honor he has reflected upon his native State and the City of Baltimore.

We have simply spoken of those members of the Bar whom the world has known, and each one of whom was *princeps inter pares* in his day and generation. There were many others who added lustre to the galaxy named above, and who aided materially in building up the reputation of the Baltimore Bar and giving to it that high tone which is at this present writing its most cherished feature. That there is no likelihood of degeneration in the future, might be shown by the number of gentlemen whose names are already well known to the country. The Library of the Baltimore Bar is one of the largest and most carefully selected in America, containing in addition to the reports from the different States in the Union, reports of all the leading cases adjudicated in Great Britain and on the continent of Europe.

The Law Department of the University of Maryland is furnished with an excellent corps of Professors and its influence and efficiency are becoming more apparent every year.

The Science of MEDICINE has made decided advances in the last half century. A corps of tireless workers have watched, noted and compared results in the squalid huts of poverty and amid the poisoned air of the pest-house. With dauntless courage they have stood between the pestilence and humanity and though not always victorious they have faithfully used all the weapons which scientific research could furnish, and if nothing more, like true sentinels have fallen in their armor and at their posts. Statistics have been compiled from which reliable inferences can be drawn, and a hospital system perfected that has gone far to alleviate the sufferings of the sick and has saved many lives which would have been sacrificed heretofore by neglect or inexperience.

The Medical men of this State have not been behind their brethren elsewhere in their contributions to the common cause. The names of Littlejohn, Brown, Mackenzie, Donaldson and Buckler, are household words and their memories are revered by the descendants of those whom they so well and truly served.

Appreciating the importance of united effort for the public good, as early as 1799, they organized the "Medical and Chirurgical Faculty of Maryland," and by an act of incorporation were made examiners of all who desired to practice the healing art, thus showing their recognition of the need of the highest intelligence and most careful preparation as prerequisites for the successful physician. This Society is still in existence, and the suggestions thrown out at its semi-annual meetings through the medium of scientific discussions and essays are of value to the profession.

The University of Maryland was incorporated in 1812. A handsome building was erected and a full corps of Professors secured. Like similar institutions in this country, it had its early struggles, and not until 1827 were its advantages generally recognized by the public. Among many eminent men who have taught within its walls some have acquired a world-wide reputation, as for instance Granville Sharpe Pattison and Robley Dunglison, but to no one is the school more indebted for its standing than to NATHAN RYNO SMITH. Professor Smith, son of the celebrated surgeon of that name at Yale College, was elected to the Chair of Surgery in the Maryland University in 1827. Possessed of abilities which

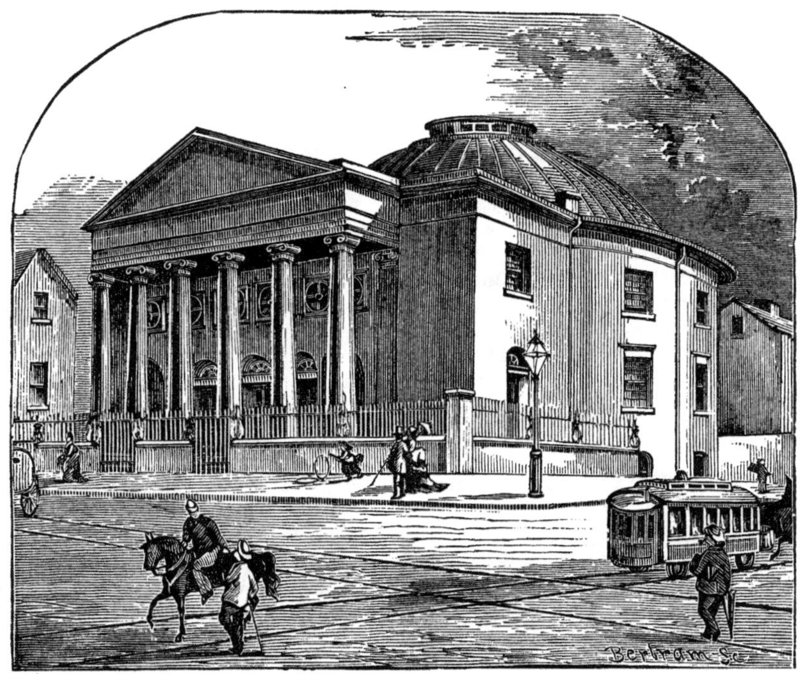

FIRST BAPTIST CHURCH.

would have distinguished him in any path of life, it may be regarded as fortunate for the world that he selected medicine as his profession. His acceptance of a chair in the University infused new energy into the institution and the reputation which he soon earned as one of the most daring and skillful Surgeons in the country, attracted students from all parts of the South and West, and frequently from States lying North of Maryland. Dr. Smith, combined with wonderful energy and great experience, unusual originality and the world is indebted to him for the invention of instruments for lithotomy and fracture by means of which much suffering has been prevented and many lives saved. For more than forty years he has pursued his professional career with unwearied steps and constantly increasing usefulness. In 1867 he visited Europe and was the recipient of the most flattering attentions from Physicians and Scientists of distinction. It rarely happens to the lot of professional men to receive such honors while yet alive, but Dr. Smith, at a ripe old age, has universally accorded to him the proud title, the Chief of American Surgeons.* Although he has retired from the University his example and influence still stimulate his younger brethren who are so successfully sustaining the reputation of the School.

The success of the Maryland University encouraged our enterprising physicians to undertake an institution of similar character. In 1867, a favorable moment for the establishment of a second Medical College, the Medical Department of Washington University was reorganized in this city. The zeal and ability displayed by the Faculty in the inculcation of "the mysteries of the healing art" have been rewarded with unusual success. The reputation of the Institution has kept pace with their efforts, and is now national. The course of instruction is thorough and comprehensive, embracing all the branches commonly taught in such Colleges. Adjoining the School is a large Hospital, under the exclusive control of the Faculty, where students may witness at the bed-side the practical illustration of what is theoretically taught in the lecture-room.

Within a recent period another competitor in the race for professional honors has been added to the list—the College of Physicians and Surgeons. Its Professors are young men of high culture, who are determined by earnest work to make up for any advantage that age may have given its rivals. Latterly, a number of diseases particularly belonging to the domain of Surgery have been so developed by the discoveries of the Microscope, Opthalmoscope, &c., that specialists have devoted themselves exclusively to their study and treatment. In addition to the medical schools proper, these correlative institutions have been established in our City, and are presided over by as distinguished and capable Occulists and Aurists as can be found elsewhere.

Chemistry and Pharmacy are so nearly allied to Medicine that wherever the one Department is found in healthy growth the advance of the other may be safely predicted. The Maryland College of Pharmacy was established in 1841, under the presidency of the veteran pharmaceutist, George W. Andrews. This institution has an excellent reputation. Its diplomas are as valuable as those granted by any similar institution in the country.

It will thus be seen that in all that enters into the practical value, scientific resources and efficient teaching of Medicine and its sister sciences, Baltimore offers superior advantages.

In one sense DENTISTRY is a modern science. That it was known and practiced in ancient Egypt, is evident from the discoveries in the Pyramids; and that a measure of skill was attained, is apparent from the remnants of workmanship still preserved, but its disappearance was as complete as the passing away of the Lost Arts, and in the eighteenth century practical Dentistry had no existence. During that period public attention was attracted to the subject, and a number of theoretical treatises were written by enthusiastic physicians. It was not however until the early part of the present century, that the views of its votaries assumed a practical direction sufficient to elevate it into a distinct science. America had the honor of nursing it through its infant struggles, and Baltimore may with propriety be called the birthplace of modern Dentistry.

In 1826, the "Principles of Dental Surgery" appeared in London, a work written by Leonard Koecker, a Baltimore physician. This was followed, in 1839, by the establishment in Baltimore of the "American Journal and Library of Dental Science," and in 1840 the "Baltimore College of Dental Surgery" was organized under a charter granted by the Legislature of Maryland. Shortly afterwards the great standard work of Dr. Chapin A. Harris, the "Principles and Practice of Dental Surgery," made its appearance. The Baltimore College of Dental Surgery, in which Dr. Harris was for a number of years a leading Professor, is not only the oldest, but if we may judge by results, one of the best in the world. Seven hundred and nine students have been graduated by this institution since its foundation. They are distributed pretty generally through the civilized por-

*Since writing the above, Professor N. R. Smith has been called to the Presidency of the Medical Faculty of the Maryland University, with the title of "Emeritus Professor of Surgery."

tions of the globe, and wherever they have located the fame of their *Alma Mater* has accompanied them. Every Dental College in this country contains in its faculty some graduate of this institution, and a large majority of the Court Dentists of Europe acknowledge their obligations to the same source. The Museum of the College is, without doubt, among the most complete in the United States, possessing a large and rare collection of pathological specimens, while the course marked out for the students is very comprehen-

SHARP ST. M. E. CHURCH, (COLORED,) BETWEEN LOMBARD AND PRATT STREETS.

sive, embracing anatomy, physiology and chemistry, the lectures upon these subjects being very full and minute.

Baltimore took the lead in this department of science from the first, and has steadily maintained her position. The students matriculating in this city, are not confined to the United States, but many come from the enlightened centres of Europe to avail themselves of the advantages which Baltimore extends to those desirous of acquiring a knowledge of

Dentistry. The great advances made latterly in this science would seem to suggest the propriety of pursuing a similar course with reference to other parts of the human body. By separating the science of Medicine into distinct branches perhaps the same beneficial results might ensue.

There is a Dental College organized here, (to be opened in the fall,) the faculty of which embraces some of the most prominent and distinguished *Practitioners* of Dentistry in the city.

Club-life, an almost universal feature of London society, and extensively imitated in some American cities, has received but little encouragement in Baltimore. This is due possibly to the superior attractiveness of domestic life in our City. There is small need for Clubs where cultivated and refined society, divested of artificiality, offers such tempting inducements. Clubs have been organized here, however, and they will compare very favorably with those in other places.

The Maryland Club, the oldest in the City, was founded by a number of the most cultivated gentlemen in the State for the purpose of keeping alive a civilization in some respects peculiar, and which was endangered by the rude but vigorous strides of Young America. It at present numbers among its members gentlemen from all portions of Maryland, and the close communion thus established has resulted in the perpetuation of that traditional hospitality of which every true Marylander is proud. Gentlemen from all parts of the United States and from the centres of civilization in Europe have referred with pleasure and somewhat of enthusiasm to the courtesies received from its members.—The Allston Association is more ambitious. In addition to the amenities of social life it designs to inspire a taste for the beautiful, and with this end in view a series of entertainments are given annually which combine the æsthetic with pleasurable features. It differs from "The Maryland" also in the fact that ladies may become honorary members of the Association, and a number of the most gifted in Baltimore have availed themselves of this privilege.

The Baltimore Club, recently organized, is a worthy competitor of the above, and already embraces within its membership many of the leading gentlemen in the City.

Our citizens of foreign birth or ancestry, the Germans, Irish, Scotch and English have organized Clubs which, aside from their social characteristics, have been the means of relieving much suffering and materially benefiting their brethren newly arrived upon our shores.

Baltimore has always been more remarkable for the social qualities of its people than for any decided *penchant* on their part for public amusements. In the past, the full development of the one has measurably done away with the necessity for the other. But with the enlargement of trade and commerce and the consequent addition to the transient population of the City the taste for popular entertainments has greatly increased. Ford's Grand Opera House, at the corner of Fayette and Eutaw Streets, will compare favorably with any similar place of amusement in the country. Its external finish is tasteful, while the appointments of the interior are luxurious and elegant. The drawing-room or parlor on the second floor is decorated by the genius of the best portrait and landscape painters in Baltimore. The advantages of the auditorium are ample room, great height of ceiling, and perfect optical and acoustic properties. The roomy stage, numerous modes of exit, and massive strength of the entire building, make it one of the pleasantest and safest theatres to visit in the United States.

Mr. JOHN T. FORD, to whose enterprise our City is indebted for this creditable Temple of the Muses, has further exerted himself to offer to the public, entertainments, both operatic and dramatic, the best to be had. Holliday Street Theatre, the Old Drury of

Baltimore, under the management of the same gentleman, is a cosy and pleasant retreat where the citizen or the stranger within our gates, may be entertained for an evening by the latest novelty in the dramatic line. Mr. Ford has shown himself to be a public-spirited citizen, by the decided and progressive views he has entertained and oftentimes enforced with reference to the government of the City, and by his bountiful charities during periods of great public distress. His Theatres have been surrendered repeatedly to the little ones in our midst, and the wonders of the Arabian Nights revealed to their astonished and delighted gaze, thereby setting an example which has been followed in some of the cities along the Atlantic seaboard with great benefit to the needy innocents.

Front Street Theatre, under the management of its present proprietor, has catered with commendable success to the public taste, offering what is known in dramatic parlance as a variety entertainment, which justifies the name, and the ever-recurring novelties of which, have won for Colonel Sinn no small reputation as a theatrical manager.

The above are the most prominent places of entertainment in our City. An Academy of Music is now being erected on Howard Street, under the auspices of a stock company, composed of our most eminent and influential citizens. The location is central and admirably suited for the enterprise. It will be built under the direction of a committee selected because of their peculiar fitness, and will doubtless prove a powerful auxiliary in the future progress of Baltimore.

The MARYLAND STATE AGRICULTURAL AND MECHANICAL ASSOCIATION was incorporated in 1867. It was simply the revival of a Society which had existed for many years prior to the civil war and which numbered among its members many of the first men in Maryland. Appropriations were made both by the State and City, and the grounds at Pimlico on the outskirts of the City were purchased for the use of the Association. Situated in the heart of a beautiful country and accessible to the public through the railways and delightful county roads, perhaps a better location could not have been selected in the vicinity of Baltimore. The grounds were carefully laid out and proper buildings erected for the convenience of exhibitors and the purposes of the Society. The Annual Exhibitions which take place usually in October, have steadily increased in popularity and excellence, and have begotten a very decided improvement in husbandry throughout the State The leading farmers, and merchants, are thus brought together and the community of intercourse established, produces a reciprocity of sentiment which cannot fail to be advantageous to both classes of our citizens.

Marylanders from a very early date have evidenced a decided taste for out-of-doors sports. The State was among the first to import the race horse from England, and fox-hunting, racing and field sports generally, were almost as familiar to those who became distinguished in olden times as were the means whereby they raised themselves to eminence. For many years Maryland horses bore off their full share of honors from the numerous contests which took place in different parts of the country and care was exercised by the farmers and planters in rearing the best specimens of this noble animal.

For some unexplained reason, racing fell into disrepute, and at the close of the war no organized Jockey Club existed in the State. Mr. Sanford, the winner of the Saratoga Cup at the Saratoga race meeting in 1868, gave a dinner immediately thereafter to eight persons. Among the invited guests was GOVERNOR ODEN BOWIE, of Maryland. The conversation at table drifted to the establishment of races on a firm and reputable basis, to be presided over by gentlemen and from which, fraud and rascality, so often in the past unpleasant concomitants of the course, should be banished. It was proposed during the dinner that each of those present should subscribe $1,000 to make up a stake for the Fall of 1870. The proposition was enthusiastically adopted and the subscriptions closed. In a subsequent conversation as to where the race should take place, Governor Bowie assured the gentlemen that if it was run at Baltimore he would pledge a club and a course. This was the origin of the celebrated "Dinner Stakes" of 1870, and also of the Maryland Jockey Club which already numbers among its members many of the most influential and distinguished gentlemen in the State, and which, though as yet in its infancy is favorably known through the country.

An arrangement was effected with the Agricultural Society by which Pimlico was secured and a charter was obtained from the Legislature for the organization. Stables were built upon the grounds, the track, a mile in length, put in perfect order and a Grand Stand constructed which for strength, amplitude and the expansiveness of view it affords, is probably superior to any in the United States. The meetings of the Maryland Jockey Club which have taken place annually since 1870, in the autumn, have been eminently successful. The Course over which the races are run has steadily improved until at present it will compare favorably with any race-track in the country, and the great influx of strangers drawn hither during the annual meetings, tempted by the reputation of our citizens for hospitality and the æsthetic features for which our city is remarkable, together with the patronage extended by all classes of our own people have encouraged the Club to greater exertions, and hereafter two race-meetings, in the spring and fall respectively, will be held at Pimlico. The object contemplated in the organization of the Club, the purification of the Turf and its freedom from debasing influences has been kept steadily in view and the meetings are marked by the presence of the beauty, wealth and fashion of Baltimore.

If the history of each large city was traced it would be found that its progress had been marked by the springing up of towns and villages within reach of its influence. That these towns as soon as they had attained a sufficient degree of importance had been absorbed by the parent city and the intermediate space filled up with a hardy and industrious population—that perhaps to these offshoots is due in great measure the health of some cities and to their paucity the unwholesome atmosphere of others.

Villages or towns built at a distance are laid out with a latitude of which the costly ground in cities proper will not admit. The land lying between the villages and cities is comparatively speaking cheap, and persons are somewhat more careful of the æsthetic features when laying it off into towns and townships, just as the farmer with time and space will have an eye to the beautiful and picturesque, while his poorer neighbor is compelled to make every foot of ground minister to the wants of himself and family.

Some of the largest cities in America owe their present importance and much of their beauty and healthfulness to these accessories. Boston, with its dozen satellites is a city of much grander proportions than the simple town embraced within the corporate limits. Philadelphia, with Germantown, Kensington, the Northern Liberties and Philadelphia County, presents a more imposing array of inhabitants than would that same city divested of these important adjuncts. Baltimore is encompassed by a number of these surburban towns and villages which add greatly to the attractiveness and prosperity of the city.

Waverley, formerly known as Huntingdon, lies immediately outside of the city limits to the north of Baltimore. It contains a population of about 5,000 inhabitants and is well supplied with churches, public buildings and school houses. It is interesting as embracing the former seats of some of our older families, together with "Friendship" originally owned by the Quakers, "The Homestead" and Peabody Heights. The inhabitants are largely operatives, but many engaged in business in the City, have established their homes and have erected handsome dwellings within its limits. Two lines of horse-cars afford easy and constant communication with the City, its incorporation with Baltimore is a matter that cannot be much longer delayed.

In these latter days when fact has usurped the place of fancy and nothing which does not minister to the material advancement of the community can secure a lodgment within its limits, Mr. Horatio N. Gambrill, a gentleman of unsurpassed business capacity and energy deserves at least a passing notice.

A more perfect representative of the practical side of the American character could scarcely be instanced, and the town of Woodberry, on the very verge of our City, is likely to prove an enduring monument to his sagacity and enterprise. In 1839, Mr. Gambrill leased the property then known as the Old Whitehall Flouring Mill, and in company with others, commenced the manufacture of Cotton Duck on a very limited scale. Trained from early youth in a cotton factory, he brought to the undertaking a thorough knowledge of his business, and his adventurous spirit cared little for the overgrown monopoly which had its seat in Patterson, New Jersey. The enterprise prospered—the original factory was enlarged and others erected until a thriving and beautiful town sprang into existence. Woodberry has at present a population of from 5,000 to 6,000 inhabitants. Situated under the shadow of Baltimore's handsomest ornament, Druid Hill Park, not the least attractive portion of which, "Tempest Hill," was contributed by the town itself, Woodberry is one of the most promising villages around the City of Baltimore. In addition to the cotton duck factories, Pool & Hunt's mammoth machine shops are located here. The inhabitants are mostly operatives and their families.

The town is noted for its high moral tone which has been fostered and encouraged by those who have thus far controlled its destinies. No intoxicating drinks are allowed to be sold within its precints, and it is abundantly supplied with churches and school houses.

Mount Washington is perhaps the most picturesque of the small towns which encompass Baltimore. It is located upon lofty hills about five miles from the City. Elevated and healthy, with pure water and cultivated society, the village has of late years grown very rapidly and its eminences are now studded with the residences of merchants and business men from Baltimore. Both Woodberry and Mount Washington are situated on the Northern Central Railroad, within a few minutes ride of the city, and the trains of that railway and the Western Maryland are constantly passing backwards and forwards.

Brooklyn, southeast of Baltimore, and connected by a commodious bridge over the middle branch of the Patapsco, was settled by the Patapsco Company in 1857. It is a flourishing village, regularly laid out, healthily located, and increasing rapidly in population and importance. Brooklyn has been selected as the terminus of the Baltimore and Drum Point Railroad, a work designed to penetrate the lower counties of the Western Shore of the State. It has a land-locked harbor and a water front of one and a half miles with a depth of water greater than can be found elsewhere in the vicinity of the City, and as the trade and commerce of Baltimore expand, doubtless the development of Brooklyn will be proportionate.

Towsontown, the county seat of Baltimore County, is situated on the York road, about seven miles from the City. It is delightfully located near the most elevated point on the road between Baltimore and York, and is being rapidly improved. It connects with our City by means of a horse railway, and the completion of a steam railroad now in process of construction will bring the town within a few minutes ride of Baltimore.

Govanstown, located on the same road, about midway between Baltimore and Towsontown, is a flourishing village, and has of late increased longitudinally to such an extent as to render it difficult to fix accurately its boundaries, in fact, the York road from Baltimore to within a short distance of Towsontown is a continuous street, lined on either side with houses. The adjacent lands are in many instances laid off in town lots, with broad avenues and thoroughfares, awaiting only the touch of capital to turn them into thriving towns and cities.

Pikesville, about seven miles from the City, on the Reisterstown road, is a beautiful village, and notable as the location of the United States Arsenal, established prior to the war of 1812. There are many other towns and villages in the immediate vicinity of Baltimore in addition to those mentioned above, which are destined to great development in the near future, and which will add vastly to the importance of the City.

The growing tendency on the part of merchants and business men to reside in the country during the summer months, or to make their homes permanently in those towns within easy communication of the City, has assisted wonderfully in the development of the district contiguous to Baltimore, and it is estimated that the population of these towns will aggregate at least fifty thousand at the present moment, with a ratio of increase which leaves it matter of easy conjecture what the number of inhabitants will be in a few years.

When the early settlers of Maryland founded the town of Baltimore they little supposed it was destined to become one of the leading ports of entry on the Atlantic coast. Its inland position, almost at the head of navigation, seemed to be an effectual barrier against

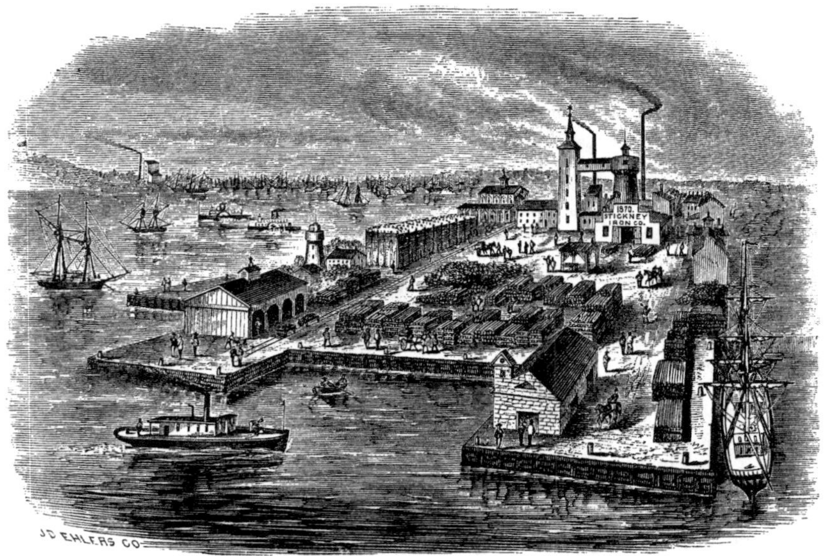

foreign commerce, which it was thought would seek those cities lying more immediately along the Atlantic. The location of Baltimore however conduced more perhaps than any other cause to her advancement in this regard. In addition to the safe and commodious harbor furnished to shipping, freight was brought that much nearer to the interior by water, the cheapest mode of conveyance.

The introduction of steam as a motive power on water led to the construction of vessels of much heavier draught than were used in the old merchant service, and our shippers had to contend against a real bugbear in the shape of a defective channel. The channel of the Patapsco was neither deep enough nor sufficiently wide for the safe passage of first-class steamers when heavily laden. Fifteen years ago the attention both of our own citizens and the national authorities was attracted to this difficulty and lukewarm and desultory measures undertaken for its removal. From time to time small sums were appropriated by Congress and the city, and an officer of engineers in the United States Army was assigned to this post, for the purpose of deepening the channel. But little progress was made in the work until 1871, when the advent of several lines of foreign steamers awakened both the community and the general Government to the paramount importance of securing to the rapidly increasing foreign trade of the city easy access.

The City appropriated $200,000 for the improvement of the harbor and the national legislature $40,000 additional. Congress, in 1872, supplemented its appropriation with another of $100,000, and at the session of 1873 voted an additional $200,000, which the municipal authorities of Baltimore gracefully acknowledged by voting a similar amount for the same purpose. Since 1871 the work upon the channel has progressed rapidly under the direction of Colonel Craighill, of the United States Army. The money in hand at present amounts to $450,000, a sum amply sufficient for the completion of the improvement. It is proposed to clear the channel to a depth of 24½ feet at low tide, and to give it an uniform width of 300 feet. It will be finished in 1874, and the harbor of Baltimore will possess a channel equal in all respects to the best approaches to ports of entry in this country, and will be accessible for the largest vessels employed in the merchant marine of any nation on the globe.

Baltimore, like other cities, has had its periods of misrule, when anarchy usurped the place of order, and the lowest, most disreputable elements of the community rose to the surface, and for a time defied the honest efforts of law-abiding citizens. Such a state of affairs undoubtedly existed during the years 1858, 1859 and 1860. The Roughs obtained control of the City and inaugurated a reign of terror similar to that which at present disgraces one of the largest cities in the country. This saturnalia of rowdyism was short-lived. Good citizens, irrespective of party, combined for the protection of society, and during the winter of 1860 the State Legislature enacted the famous "Metropolitan Police Bill." THE POLICE FORCE was organized in accordance with its provisions on the 7th of May of the same year. The features of the bill were simple. Its main characteristic was the separation of the local government and *that* organization which must be manipulated with impartiality to make it honest and efficient. Its workings were magical.

The transition from a state of rowdyism to perfect order was instantaneous. The Bowie-knife and the Bludgeon were laid aside, and the law suffered to interpose its protecting arms for the good of the community. The Roughs either abandoned their infamous mode of living, or betook themselves to other cities.

From this period onward, with a brief interruption during the continuance of the civil war, Baltimore has been emphatically an order loving city. With little modification, and that of a serviceable nature, the Police System of 1860 is at present in operation, and our City can challenge comparison with any other in the country for the security of the lives, liberties and property of her citizens.

The perfect order preserved in every portion of this great metropolis is really a subject for admiration, when taken in connection with the numerical force by which it is accomplished. As at present constituted, the organization consists of three Commissioners, styled the Board of Police, a Marshal, Deputy Marshal, 4 Captains, 8 Lieutenants, 43 Sergeants and 489 men. The officers are appointed by the Commissioners, and are usually selected from among the men for meritorious conduct. No man is placed upon the Force because of his political opinions, or for any other reason than general efficiency; nor are any dismissed therefrom, save for misconduct, demonstrated to the satisfaction of the Board. While the duties of the police of Baltimore are more numerous and onerous than those of the same class in other cities, their numerical strength is much smaller than that of similar organizations in any of the cities of America of approximate size or importance. We have dwelt at some length upon the merits of our Police System, because they have been freely recognized by all classes in the community regardless of political affiliation.

Baltimore was among the first cities in America to avail herself of the great improvements in the apparatus for subduing fires. In 1858, the old volunteer **FIRE DEPARTMENT,**

6

with its hand engines and internal dissensions, was abolished and an organization formed under the pay and control of the City. The new Department was furnished with improved Steam Fire Engines, and it very soon demonstrated both the superiority of the system and the utility of steam as a means of overcoming conflagrations Since that time the Department has been strengthened and enlarged. Under the management of a Board of Commissioners, selected from our most estimable citizens, and whose services are given to the city gratuitously, it has become the most perfect organization in the country, a subject of pride to Baltimoreans and of admiration to visitors from other cities.

The apparatus of the Department consists at this time of ten engines in service, and two reserve engines, with the necessary hose-carriages, and three hook and ladder trucks. The entire force numbers one hundred and sixty men. Since the institution of the Steam Fire Department there have been but few fires of magnitude in our City. Indeed, Baltimore has enjoyed an exemption from the ravages of this terrible scourge that cannot be altogether attributed to the efficiency of the Fire Department, ably managed as it undoubtedly is, and a further reason for which may be found in the construction of the city, the broad streets and well-built houses.

As an exhibit both of the usefulness of the Department and the marked immunity of the City from fires, we append the following table, giving the number of fires, losses, number of Companies, and expenses of Departments in seven of the leading cities of the United States, from November 1st, 1871, to October 31st, 1872:

CITY.	NO. FIRES	LOSS.	NO. COMPANIES.	EXPENSE OF DEPARTMENT.
New York	1,647	$2,725,000	52	$1,000,000
Philadelphia	523	1,275,000	27	250,000
Chicago	489	973,000	26	328,000
Boston	549	704,000	38	331,000
Cincinnati	213	453,000	23	281,000
San Francisco	300	1,411,000	25	180,000
Baltimore	172	300,000	13	145,672

Of course the losses by the great fire in Boston have been omitted in the above estimate. It will be seen from this table that Baltimore, with a Department scarcely half the size of the smallest of these cities, has suffered a loss by fire of $300,000, a sum less by $153,000 than that acknowledged by the most fortunate of those enumerated.

The WATER-SUPPLY has already become a question of paramount importance in large cities. Those along the Atlantic coast are prone to pride themselves upon the efforts they have made in this regard, and not without reason, though it may be doubted whether any of the works established in modern times would compare in magnitude and completeness with some of the magnificent structures of the ancients, the remains of which are still in existence. The Croton Aqueduct in New York and the Fairmount Water-works in Philadelphia, are monuments of modern engineering skill, and constitute exceedingly attractive features of the cities to which they respectively belong.

The attention of our citizens was directed many years ago to the necessity of securing an abundant supply of Water, and in 1804 the old Water Company was established. This corporation served its purpose for a number of years, but in 1854, the rapid development of Baltimore made it evident that this source of supply could not much longer be relied upon, accordingly the City bought out the Company, and in 1858 commenced the construction of the works which now supply the inhabitants. An exquisitely beautiful artificial lake, with a capacity of 500,000,000 gallons, known as Lake Roland, was formed at the Relay House, the intersection of the Western Maryland and Northern Central Railroads, about eight miles from Baltimore. Hampden Resorvoir, a smaller basin constructed near the village of Hampden, with a capacity of 50,000,000 gallons, and Mount Royal Reservoir, on North Avenue, with a capacity of 30,000,000 gallons, both of the latter supplied by means of an aqueduct from Lake Roland, were considered amply sufficient for the requirements of the City for years to come. Subsequently Druid Lake, with a capacity of 493,000,000 gallons was formed in Druid Hill Park, more with a view to ornamentation and as a storage reservoir, than with any actual expectation that the increasing needs of the City would require its services during the lives of its projectors.

Twenty years had scarcely elapsed after the commencement of these works ere the City Fathers were admonished, by the rapid increase in population and the equally speedy multiplication of industries requiring the free use of water, that the demand would soon exceed the supply, and a plan is now matured by which an unlimited quantity of this indispensable element will be brought into the City from the Gunpowder River, a stream of fresh and pure water, which passes through the centre of Baltimore County, and empties into the Chesapeake Bay. This great undertaking cannot be completed for at least three years, and in the meantime a temporary method has been devised by which the immediate wants of the City will be abundantly supplied. When finished, the Gunpowder Water-works will exceed any similar enterprize in this country, and perhaps in Europe. A conduit through which may be passed 170,000,000 gallons of water daily, will convey the supply from the Gunpowder to the City, a distance of about eight miles. The elevation of the water above tide will be 163 feet, sufficient for present necessities or for any likely to occur in the future of our City

It has been said with truth that its PARKS and SQUARES are the lungs of a city. Baltimore is bountifully provided with these adjuncts to healthfulness. Druid Hill Park, in the northwestern portion of the City, contains seven hundred acres of land, and for varied natural scenery is perhaps unequalled in this country.

For more than a century and a half prior to its purchase by the city, the Park was the homestead of a Maryland family. Some older member of the house had displayed exquisite taste in the preparation of the grounds, and succeeding generations had the good sense to perpetuate his ideas with simply a touch here and there to heal the blows of time and preserve the design in its original purity.

During the year 1860 the City obtained possession of Druid Hill, at a cost of $500,000, and since then it has been enlarged by purchases of contiguous tracts of land. Its management as a Park has been characterized by wisdom and enlightened policy. Immediately after its acquisition by the City it was placed under the government of a Commission consisting of a number of gentlemen of intelligence and high standing in the community, selected because of their peculiar fitness for the undertakiug. This Commission, with enlarged powers, has been continued to the present time. The main effort appears to have been to preserve, as far as possible, the natural beauties of Druid Hill, and only to interpose art when needed by the poverty of the landscape or the wants of the City. In this the Commission has been eminently successful.

A broad expanse of land is spread out before the spectator, rolling in great waves of verdure, forming at some points gentle undulations intertwined with pretty little glens, and at others rising in terraces, one above another, until lofty hills disclose the City, the river, the bay, and the territory of Maryland as far as the eye can reach. Majestic primeval forest trees, hickory, oak, chesnut, and walnut, of immense size, are succeeded by impenetrable thickets where the greenbrier and the laurel strive for the mastery. Spreading groves invite the citizen, weary and worn with the turmoil of busy life, and joyous fountains gush forth at his feet to moisten the parched lips or cool the heated brow. Pleasure boats play over the silvery bosom of the lake, and swan move gracefully through the waters of the numerous natural basins which intersperse the grounds, while fallow deer in groups roam through the woods and groves. Beautiful drives traverse the Park

ENTRANCE TO DRUID HILL PARK.

in every direction, many of them adorned with antique vases filled with flowers and covered with creeping vines, and rustic retreats are so judiciously distributed as often to beguile the visitor with their perfect semblance to nature.

Nor has the Commission been unmindful of the convenience of those whose modest means forbid the use of showy equipages. Walks, with the truest regard to taste, have been arranged through the grounds, and the valetudinarian, when once the Park is reached, may fairly revel in the ever changing pictures and invigorating atmosphere he is permitted to enjoy through the foresight of the City's former guardians.

Druid Hill is at present the most beautiful Park in America, and with the ample revenue derived from the tax on City Passenger Railways, it is impossible to fix any limit to its improvement in the future. The influence of the Park upon adjacent property has been wonderful. Its value has been greatly enhanced, streets have been opened, avenues created, long lines of elegant and costly residences have been built, and the time is probably not

EDMOND'S WELL—DRUID HILL PARK.

remote, when the Park will form a centre around which will cluster the fashion and wealth of the City of Baltimore.

Seventeen acres have been set apart within the enclosure for the erection of a Botanical Garden. A Conservatory 300 feet long and 30 feet high is about to be erected, and a Nursery established for the purpose of supplying the other Parks and Public Squares with trees. The Botanical Gardens will be enlarged to forty acres as soon as circumstances will permit, and a Zoological Department added, which will contribute much to the attractiveness of this truly beautiful spot. The project was originated by the Maryland Academy of Sciences, but will be under the supervision and control of the Park Commission.

Patterson Park, in the eastern section of the City, contains 76 acres of land. Already it has been handsomely adorned, and the contemplated improvements will make it a delightful place of resort for the citizens of this portion of our City. From any part of the grounds a magnificent view can be obtained of the harbor and Chesapeake Bay, and the neighboring counties of Baltimore and Anne Arundel.

In addition to the Parks, Baltimore has a number of Public Squares judiciously distributed in different portions of the City. In the western section are Union Square, Franklin Square and Harlem Square; in the north-west, La Fayette Square; in the centre, Monument Square and the City Spring; in the north-east, Madison Square; in the east, Jackson Square, and the eastern City Spring, and in the south, Battery Square. With the exception of Monument Square, they are all sodded down with turf and beautifully decorated with shade trees, forming reservoirs of health for the citizens enervated by the fierce heat of summer and unable to betake themselves to the fashionable places of resort.

It is proposed to establish another Park in the southern section of the City, with Battery Square as a nucleus. This Square is located in the immediate vicinity of the middle branch of the Patapsco, and when its limits are extended so as to embrace the intervening property, it will become, because of its water view, one of the most attractive spots in the City.

FOREST TREES—DRUID HILL PARK.

From the Parks of Baltimore to her CEMETERIES is a natural transition. Tender love for the memory of the dead is a distinctive feature of some nationalities. With the French it is a passion. Poets, Warriors, Statesmen and Philosophers, severed in life, are all brought together within the narrow confines of PERE LA CHAISE. The tomb of Abelard and Eloise blooms perennially with fresh flowers, while the immortelles never die on the graves of such men as Ney, Moliere, and a host of others.

Though Americans do not exhibit the intense pathos displayed by the French, Mount Auburn, Greenwood, Laurel Hill, Greenmount and Bona Ventura, all Cemeteries on the Atlantic coast bear ample testimony to the care displayed by the American people for the repose of their dead. Greenmount Cemetery, formerly the country seat of a citizen, is situated on the York road, just within the City limits. It contains about sixty acres of land, handsomely embellished. Its natural beauty is very great. The land is rolling in character and very thickly studded with shade trees and evergreens. The hand of the landscape gardener has added much to its attractions. It is intersected by graceful avenues and promenades, and many of the memorials to the departed, so beautifully distributed within the enclosure, evidence taste and a high order of merit in the artist, among which may be mentioned the bronze statue of a female, sprinkling flowers upon a tomb, and several other pieces of statuary by Rinehart, a native of the State.

At an elevated point in Greenmount a monument has been erected by the City of Baltimore, to the memory of John McDonogh. A massive granite base supports a marble pedestal which is surmounted by a statue of the great philanthropist.

This city of the dead is often visited by our citizens, both because of its exquisite beauty and the tender associations which cluster about its "quiet places," and the flowers and

SILVER LAKE—DRUID HILL PARK.

freshly planted evergreens upon many of the mounds are an assurance that those who are gone are *not* so soon forgotten. In addition to the above, there are a number of Cemeteries in and around our City, some extending over a greater area than Greenmount, and several highly ornamented and possessing considerable natural attractiveness.

Upon opening this volume the reader will find a very comprehensive MAP OF BALTIMORE and its environs. The present boundaries of the city are clearly indicated, as also those portions lying beyond the corporate limits, together with the straggling villages located within one and a half miles of the City proper. By reference to the Map it will be seen that much of what *should* constitute the City of Baltimore lies in the county. The City itself covers an area of but 10,000 acres. The boundaries established in 1816 by legislative enactment have never been changed. Efforts, oft repeated, have been made by our citizens but for reasons presently stated the enlargement of the City limits has been deferred until hope has well nigh sickened and died. The census of 1870 places the population of the City proper at 267,354. The unfairness of this estimate, not to characterize it by a harsher term, is glaring to every resident of Baltimore, and its palpable absurdity would provoke a smile were it not so serious in its consequences to the welfare of our City and State. A subsequent enumeration under the direction of the City government, hurried in its character, and hence liable to many errors against the City, made the population of Baltimore 283,375. We must not be understood as accepting either of these sets of figures as a correct exhibit of our numerical strength; on the contrary a census taken by a thoroughly reliable citizen of Baltimore, and taken under circumstances from which accuracy may be reasonably inferred, has placed the population far beyond either of these enumerations. But assuming 283,375, the number ascertained by the municipal authorities, as the population of Baltimore in 1870, that portion of the City which lies outside of the corporate limits, and which probably will soon be brought under the control of the corporation, would have swelled the number of inhabitants to 350,000, and would have made Baltimore in this respect the fourth city in the United States.

That the extension of the City limits cannot be much longer delayed is apparent to the opponents as well as to the friends of the measure. Baltimore County has heretofore claimed, and with some show of reason, that by wresting from her this large and valuable slice of her domain, the City will so diminish the basis of taxation as to embarrass the county government. The City on the other hand desires room for expansion, and the people who live on the debateable ground are crying out for the protection and benefits that will accrue to them from annexation. The requirements of our rapidly increasing population and the advantages which the middle and poorer classes, residing on the outskirts of Baltimore, will reap from the enlargement of her boundaries, constant supplies of gas, water and the like, with the security afforded by a well regulated police force, must in a brief space override any minor considerations.

The people of the county feel that the blow is inevitable, and already many are favoring the annexation of Baltimore County in its entirety in imitation of the example set by Philadelphia and New York, while others are beginning to realize that the decrease in the revenues of the county would be temporary, as the prosperity of Baltimore must eventually inure to the advantage of the territory which surrounds her.

The enlargement of the City limits once determined, the ægis of the municipal government extended over this region would produce that feeling of security which is certainly lacking now, and which would lead mechanics and operatives to lease lots and erect for their families houses where their close proximity to the agricultural districts would insure the very cheapest rates of living. The intermediate spaces between Baltimore and the towns within the circle of expansion would rapidly fill up with a thrifty population, while satellites would multiply about the parent city.

This has been the experience of all great cities in the past, and, when similar influences are working with ten-fold force in our midst, can we doubt that the analogy will be complete?

In concluding an article which has for its object the exposition of the resources of Baltimore, it may be well to summarize the forces that have ministered to her importance. The great natural necessities in these days of steam-power are *iron* and *fuel;* iron to be worked into the multitudinous forms of which it is susceptible, and which the ingenuity of man has discovered, and fuel to supply the motive-power for its manipulation. Wood in this country, where it was supposed it would be abundant for many generations, is actually becoming a scarce commodity before one hundred years of the national life have transpired, and in some places the system, so long in vogue in Great Britain and on the continent of Europe, the plan of setting out groves of trees as a farmer would a crop of corn, has already been adopted.

A substitute, under the circumstances, becomes a matter of the first importance, and wherever this can be found, trade and commerce will necessarily gravitate towards that point rather than to a locality unfortunately bereft of this wonderful auxiliary in the the march of Progress.

Baltimore is *absolutely* independent of her sister cities in these respects. The bituminous coal beds of Alleghany, West Virginia and portions of Pennsylvania have been barely opened; in fact, several of those in the vicinity of Cumberland have never been tapped, and, though it is known that the supply is vast beyond computation, its real richness is as yet only conjectural.

The Baltimore and Ohio Railroad, a mammoth corporation, and the Chesapeake and Ohio Canal, almost equally extensive in its operations, with their combined strength have been utterly unable to develop these beds of wealth beyond the threshold, and two more railroads are now projected for the purpose of bringing the coals to our city. In addition, the various species of this mineral, such as gas, cannel and anthracite coal, are supplied by the numerous roads leading to Baltimore, in unlimited quantities. Iron is so plentifully imbedded in the soil of Maryland as almost to constitute the State a great bed of this ore. In Alleghany, Anne Arundel, Baltimore, Cecil, Frederick, Garrett, Harford, Howard, Prince George's, Queen Anne's, Washington and Worcester Counties the beds of ore, inexhaustible and of the finest description, are being worked with profit to their owners and to the rapid advancement of our City, into whose lap the most of this metal is poured. Besides the coal and iron of Alleghany, lime stone, sand stone, hydraulic cement, and wonderful water-powers abound, and the city of Cumberland, the county seat, is rapidly becoming the centre of a very important trade, the enterprise of her citizens expediting this result and exhibiting an example that might be followed with a happy issue by others.

Anne Arundel County, in addition to the supply of iron ore, possesses a wide stretch of fertile territory where tobacco and grain are grown in large quantities, and truck-gardens are located sufficient in themselves to supply the demand in Baltimore for fresh and wholesome vegetables. Annapolis, the county seat, and capital of the State, is one of the oldest cities in America, and notable as being the place where the illustrious Washington resigned his sword after the completion of his labors in the War of Independence, and as still possessing the building (State House) in which the deed was done, and where Congress met immediately after the same war. This city is remarkable also as having produced a number of the most distinguished lawyers that have ever graced the Bar in this country.

Baltimore County, in addition to her great beds of iron ore, has fine water-powers, and is noted for her extensive milling operations, carpet, cotton and woollen factories, furnaces, foundries, paper and flouring mills. The finest and strongest cotton-duck and flour equal to any manufactured in the world are made here. This county contains also valuable copper mines and chrome ore, a large proportion of the latter article used in the State being obtained from Baltimore County. Exhaustless quarries of marble, lime stone and building stone are found here, from the latter of which gneiss and granite are taken in large quantities.

Calvert County produces the best tobacco grown in the State, as well as boundless supplies of fish, oysters and wild fowl, and tripoli is found in many localities.

Caroline County, on the Eastern Shore of Maryland, is celebrated for its fine peaches and fruits of all descriptions, and this remark will apply with equal force to Dorchester, Kent, Queen Anne's, Somerset, Talbot, Wicomico and Worcester, all located on the same side of the Chesapeake. Their mild climate, rich soil and proximity to the Bay and Ocean enable them to produce the earliest and most superior fruits and vegetables, which are sent in large quantities to the Northern cities, where they find a ready sale at fancy prices. Large supplies of shell-marl, green sand and marl are found in this section, the latter furnishing an excellent manure, by means of which the strength of the land can be regularly renewed.

Carroll County possesses first-class water-powers, cotton and woollen factories, merchant and paper mills, also a great number of tanneries, copper mines and extensive quarries of granite, marble, lime stone, soap stone and slate.

Cecil County has quarries of granite and soap stone, the most valuable chrome mines in the world, clay for fire-bricks, fine water-powers, great shad and herring fisheries, kaolin or porcelain clay, and a tremendous trade at Port Deposit, on the Susquehanna river, in lumber and logs.

Frederick County has an abundance of water-power, a large number of mills, tanneries and various domestic manufactures, quarries of lime stone and slate, copper mines, a species of stone similar to Italian marble, and a quarry resembling *verde-antique*, together with marble of variegated colors, the light and dark red prevailing. Frederick City, the county seat, is a large and thriving town, with an intelligent and energetic population.

Harford County contains extensive water-power, furnaces, factories, foundries, flour mills, quarries of building stone, gneiss or granite, iron ore and valuable chrome beds, quarries of slate and kaolin or porcelain clay.

Howard County has factories, mills, furnaces, quarries of lime stone, also a stone that resembles very much Quincy granite, and Porphyritic granite.

Montgomery County possesses quarries of sand stone and marble, excellent roofing slate, other building stone, also chrome ore and fine water-powers.

Prince George's County, in addition to iron ore, sulphuret of iron, bole, tripoli and large shad and herring fisheries, produces the largest quantity of tobacco grown by any single county in the United States, and contains large cotton factories.

Saint Mary's County is the oldest in the State, and the first government of the Province had its seat there for many years. Marl is abundant and tobacco the principal crop.

Washington County produces lime stone, slate of a very superior quality, emery or corundum, and is a great grain growing section of the State, containing extensive flouring mills. Hagerstown, the county seat, is a prosperous and growing city.*

Of course the resources of the counties would advance but little the interests of Baltimore City were there not convenient methods of reaching them. Let us see what they are. Through Baltimore County the lines of four extensive railroad corporations already pass at such favorable distances that nearly all the wealth to which we have just alluded may be poured into our City in quantities to suit the demand of the market. Shorter lines of railroad stretch their arms into the richest portions of her territory in all directions, while county roads of the first excellence offer the strongest inducements to producers. Another very useful railroad, the Maryland Central, is about to be put under contract. It will pass through the most fertile sections of Baltimore and Harford Counties, fixing its terminus at the Pennsylvania line. The northwestern tier of counties, Montgomery, Frederick, Washington and Alleghany are pierced in all directions by the Baltimore and Ohio Railroad and its branches, and bounded on the south by the Chesapeake and Ohio Canal, while Carroll, Frederick and Washington Counties are almost bisected by the Western Maryland Railroad. Harford and Cecil are crossed by the Philadelphia, Wilmington and Baltimore Railroad, and the latter is intersected at various points by the Philadelphia and Baltimore Central Railroad, and the Columbia and Port Deposit Railroad.

The Baltimore and Ohio, and its branches, pass through Howard County in several places. This County is also tapped by a number of short lines.

The lower tier of counties on the Western Shore consisting of Prince George's, Anne Arundel, Calvert, Charles and St. Mary's, much the larger portions of which have been heretofore without railroad communication with Baltimore, are about to be abundantly supplied. Already the Baltimore and Ohio through its branches strikes Anne Arundel and Prince George's, and brings the former into easy communication with our City by

*NOTE.—The author desires to express his obligations for facts relating to the Counties to a volume entitled "The Atlas of Maryland, District of Columbia, and the United States," by S. J. Martenet, H. F. Walling and O. W. Gray. G. W. H.

means of the Annapolis and Elkridge Railroad, while the Baltimore and Potomac Railroad passes directly through Anne Arundel, Prince George's and Charles to the Potomac River. The Drum Point Railroad, at present under contract, bisects Anne Arundel and Calvert through their entire length and strikes the Patuxent at its mouth. The Washington City and Point Lookout Railroad, which is also under contract, will run from Washington City down through Prince George's, Charles and St. Mary's to Point Lookout, the extreme southern end of the Peninsula and intersecting the Baltimore and Potomac at a point in Prince George's, will bring the produce of these counties directly to Baltimore. Already the Baltimore and Potomac Railroad connects with the great Union Railroad, a road incorporated to unite all the lines of Railway running into Baltimore, and arrangements are now being perfected by which the Drum Point Railroad will leave its terminus at Brooklyn, on the Patapsco, and passing round the City, will enter the same road at the tunnel.

It must also be borne in mind that these lower counties are intersected in all directions by navigable rivers and streams which furnish by far the cheapest mode of transportation.

We have reserved the Eastern Shore Counties until the last. They have never heretofore had railroad communication with our City save by long and circuitous routes which were practically, barriers to commercial intercourse, and the Bay and its tributaries have been relied upon as a means for securing the produce of that wealthy section of Maryland. Much of the valuable traffic which should have found its way to Baltimore, the great metropolis of the State, was on this account diverted to Philadelphia by the extensive railroad connections with that city through Delaware. The surface of the land on the Eastern Shore is admirably adapted to railroad construction, and unusual energy has been displayed in the location of those wonderful adjuncts to civilization. Besides the great facilities they possess for water communication, each county can boast its railroad, all of which connect with the Delaware Railroad, which meets the Philadelphia, Wilmington and Baltimore Railroad, 71 miles from Baltimore and 28 miles from Philadelphia, thus naturally urging trade to the latter city.

All this is about to be changed and by a means so simple as to cause amazement that the project has never been seriously entertained before. The Baltimore, Chesapeake and Delaware Bay Railroad Company has been organized and the money necessary for the construction of the road subscribed. It is to be built from Love Point, the northern extremity of Kent Island, on the Chesapeake Bay, (18 miles from Baltimore) immediately across the Eastern Shore, through the counties of Queen Anne's and Caroline, to Harrington in Delaware, a distance of 40 miles, where it connects with the Delaware and the Junction and Breakwater Railroads. The connection with the latter road unites by an air-line the Chesapeake and Delaware Bays. The results to Baltimore will be, first, communication with New York by the cheapest and pleasantest route yet projected, the Company having contracted with the Lorillard Steamship Company to take freight and passengers from the Delaware Breakwater to New York immediately upon the arrival of the train, while several Baltimore corporations are at present striving to secure the contract for their conveyance between Baltimore and the railroad depot at Love Point on the Eastern Shore of the Chesapeake. This will constitute during much the larger portion of the year the most agreeable line of travel between Baltimore and New York, and by all odds the cheapest route for freight at all seasons. There will be but one change on the line, as the cars will be carried across the Chesapeake on very heavy steamers. But this is the least of the advantages likely to accrue to Baltimore from the building of this railroad. It will run within a stone's throw of Queenstown, the western terminus of the Queen Anne's and Kent Railroad, with which, of course, connection will be made and which intersects the Kent County Railroad at Massey's Junction. It will intersect the Maryland and Delaware Railroad at Hillsborough, and thus the productions of Kent, Queen Anne's, Talbot and Caroline, will be immediately diverted to Baltimore. At Harrington, it will tap the

Delaware Railroad, the real main-stem of all the railroads south of that point, and thus the productions of Dorchester County, through the Dorchester and Delaware Railroad; of Wicomico, through the Delaware and the Wicomico and Pocomoke Railroads; of Worcester through the latter and the Worcester Railroad, and of Somerset through the Eastern Shore Railroad, will all be poured into Baltimore, while much of the produce of Delaware will follow the same channel; trade always chosing for itself the most natural and expeditious routes. It will thus be seen that through this little railroad only forty miles in length, and which will be constructed at comparatively insignificant cost, all the trade of the purely Eastern Shore Counties, and much of the State of Delaware, will be attracted to our City, the route to Baltimore being shorter by one half than that which now draws a large portion of this trade to Philadelphia.

It is proposed to construct another line of railroad between this City and New York. The New Jersey Southern Railroad, which has recently changed hands it is said, proposes to build a road across the Delaware River, somewhere in the neighborhood of Fort Penn, which will strike the Delaware Railroad at Townsend, and from thence using the Townsend Branch Railroad, and the Kent County Railroad, will reach a point on the Chesapeake Bay near Rock Hall. Here passengers and freight will be shipped direct to Baltimore in steamers constructed for the purpose.

If carried out, this route will prove as effectual in diverting to Baltimore the trade of the Eastern Shore and Delaware as the road mentioned above.

The City by its admirable location, situated in the very heart of the country, at the head of a bay which is superior to the ocean because of the protection it affords to shipping, gives access to a broad reach of territory on either side, from which stores can be drained by water communication, and the receipts of our foreign and domestic commerce distributed at the smallest possible cost to producers.

The great grain fields of the far West are made tributary to her through gigantic lines of railway; the Valley of Virginia, teeming with cereals, mineral wealth and forests of inestimable value, through the same source pours into the City its varied productions; the South, with its inexhaustible resources, lumber, cotton, rice, tar, pitch, turpentine, rosin and tobacco is linked with her by splendid lines of steamers; competing railroad corporations are already struggling for the mastery in their efforts to empty into her lap the riches of the Central West, and the great Mississippi Valley; her enterprising merchants, business men and railroad companies have established, in connection with foreign corporations, magnificent lines of steamers which connect the City with the prominent ports of Europe, and the cheapness of these modes of communication are being practically demonstrated to the satisfaction of the South and West; her inner attractions, her beautiful parks, public squares, refined society, handsome and well ventilated thoroughfares, the high moral tone of her citizens, healthfulness, cheapness of living within her limits, her institutions, and the hospitality which has distinguished her in every period of her history, her iron works, cotton factories, sugar refineries, machine shops, glass works, flour mills, and her other great and important interests, have all been elaborated with care in the progress of this volume.

To predicate the future of Baltimore, with such a combination of resources as a basis, requires neither the use of isothermal lines, nor analytic deduction extending through long cycles of ages. Theories may be true and useful, but facts are stubborn and indisputable. The future of Baltimore depends upon but one hypothesis. The elements of her present and prospective greatness stare us in the face and need only utilization by a proportionate amount of energy on the part of our people to realize a prosperity scarcely exampled in the history of the world.

UNIVERSITY OF MARYLAND
SCHOOL OF MEDICINE.

Hon. SEVERN TEACKLE WALLIS, LL. D., Provost.

FACULTY.

NATHAN R. SMITH, M. D.
Emeritus Professor of Surgery and President of the Faculty.

WILLIAM E. A. AIKIN, M. D., LL. D.
Professor of Chemistry and Pharmacy.

GEORGE W. MILTENBERGER, M. D
Professor of Obstetrics.

RICHARD McSHERRY, M. D.
Prof. of Principles and Practice of Medicine.

CHRISTOPHER JOHNSTON, M. D.
Professor of Surgery.

FRANK DONALDSON, M. D.
Professor of Physiology and Hygiene, and Clinical Professor of Diseases of the Throat, Lungs and Heart.

SAMUEL C. CHEW, M. D.
Professor of Materia Medica and Therapeutics, and Clinical Medicine.

WILLIAM T. HOWARD, M. D.
Professor of Diseases of Women and Children and Clinical Medicine.

JULIAN J. CHISOLM, M. D.
Professor of the Diseases of the Eye and Ear.

FRANCIS T. MILES, M. D.
Professor of Anatomy, and Clinical Professor of Diseases of the Nervous System.

ALAN P. SMITH, M. D.
Professor of Operative Surgery.

L. McLANE TIFFANY, M. D.
Demonstrator of Anatomy.

THE regular course of Lectures commences on the 1st of October, and terminates on the last day of February. For further information apply to any member of the Faculty for an annual Circular.

NOTE.—See pages 74, 75 and 76 for further information in regard to the University of Maryland.

BALTIMORE
College of Dental Surgery

No. 2 NORTH GREENE STREET.

The Baltimore College of Dental Surgery, the oldest Dental College in the world, was incorporated by an act of the Legislature of the State of Maryland in the year 1839.

Six hundred and sixty-four students have had conferred upon them the degree of "Doctor of Dental Surgery" by this institution since its organization, and its diploma is recognized in all civilized countries as a testimonial of proficiency in the science of Dentistry.

The majority of the eminent practitioners of Dentistry in Europe are graduates of this College, and there are but few Dental Colleges in this country in whose Faculties are not found graduates of the Baltimore College.

PHILIP H. AUSTEN, A. M., M. D., D. D. S.
Professor of Dental Science and Mechanism,

FERDINAND J. S. GORGAS, A. M., M. D., D. D. S.
Professor of Dental Surgery and Therapeutics.

HENRY REGINAL NOEL, M. D.
Professor of Physiology and Pathology.

E. LLOYD HOWARD, A. M., M. D.
Professor of Anatomy.

M. J. DEROSSET, A. M., M. D.
Professor of Chemistry and Materia Medica.

JAMES H. HARRIS, M. D., D. D. S.
Professor of Clinical Dentistry.

WILLIAM FARMER, M. D., D. D. S.
Demonstrator of Operative Dentistry.

B. M. WILKERSON, M. D., D. D. S.
Demonstrator of Mechanical Dentistry.

THOMAS S. LATIMER, M. D.
Demonstrator of Anatomy.

The regular sessions commence in October of each year, and continue until March.

FOR FURTHER INFORMATION ADDRESS,

F. J. S. GORGAS, M. D., D. D. S.
DEAN OF THE FACULTY,
259 N. EUTAW STREET, BALTIMORE, MD.

NOTE.—See pages 76, 77 and 78 for further information in regard to Dentistry.

BALTIMORE EYE AND EAR INSTITUTE,

55 FRANKLIN STREET,

BALTIMORE.

JULIAN J. CHISOLM, M.D.

PROFESSOR OF EYE AND EAR DISEASES IN THE UNIVERSITY OF MARYLAND,

SURGEON IN CHARGE.

One of the largest and finest Residences in the City of Baltimore has been purchased, and fitted up with every convenience as a "HOME" for persons suffering from Eye and Ear Diseases who come to Baltimore for Surgical treatment. The SURGEON IN CHARGE RESIDES IN THE INSTITUTION, so that he can visit his Patients frequently, and at all hours.

For further information apply to

JULIAN J. CHISOLM, M. D.,
55 Franklin Street,
BALTIMORE.

MARYLAND EYE AND EAR INSTITUTE,

66 N. CHARLES ST. and 77 SARATOGA ST.

BALTIMORE.

OFFICERS.

PRESIDENT—JOHN B. MORRIS, ESQ.
VICE PRESIDENTS—B. F. NEWCOMER, ESQ., CHRISTIAN AX, ESQ.
SECRETARY—J. J. STEWART, ESQ.
TREASURER—WILLIAM WILKENS, ESQ.

BOARD OF DIRECTORS.

JOHNS HOPKINS, Esq.	CHRISTIAN AX, Esq.	JOHN H. B. LATROBE, Esq.	H. H. GRAUE, Esq.
JOHN B. MORRIS, Esq.	J. HARMANUS FISHER, Esq.	C. MORTON STEWART, Esq.	Dr. W. CHEW VAN BIBBER,
Hon. G. W. DOBBIN,	JACOB TRUST Esq.	CHARLES G. KERR, Esq.	Dr. JAMES CARY THOMAS,
B. F. NEWCOMER, Esq.	G. W. GAIL, Esq.	JOHN STELLMAN, Esq.	Dr. JOHN MORRIS,
SAM'L M. SHOEMAKER, Esq.	JOHN A. NICHOLS, Esq.	WILLIAM WILKENS, Esq.	Dr. J. L. WARFIELD,
WILLIAM F. FRICK, Esq.	Col. S. M. HESS,	J. J. STEWART, Esq.	Dr. GEORGE REULING.

Surgeon in Charge, GEORGE REULING, M. D.

We respectfully announce to the Medical Profession and Public generally, that this Institute, incorporated April 3d, 1869, and now located at No. 66 N. Charles Street, and No. 77 Saratoga Street, has been lately enlarged and improved, and offers increased facilities for the treatment of those suffering from

DISEASES OF THE EYE AND EAR.

Application should be made to GEO. REULING, M. D., Surgeon in Charge.

CORNER OF SECOND & HOLLIDAY STS.

BALTIMORE

CORNER OF SECOND & HOLLIDAY STS.

The largest and most complete Establishment South of New York.

A call and Examination of Specimens is solicited.

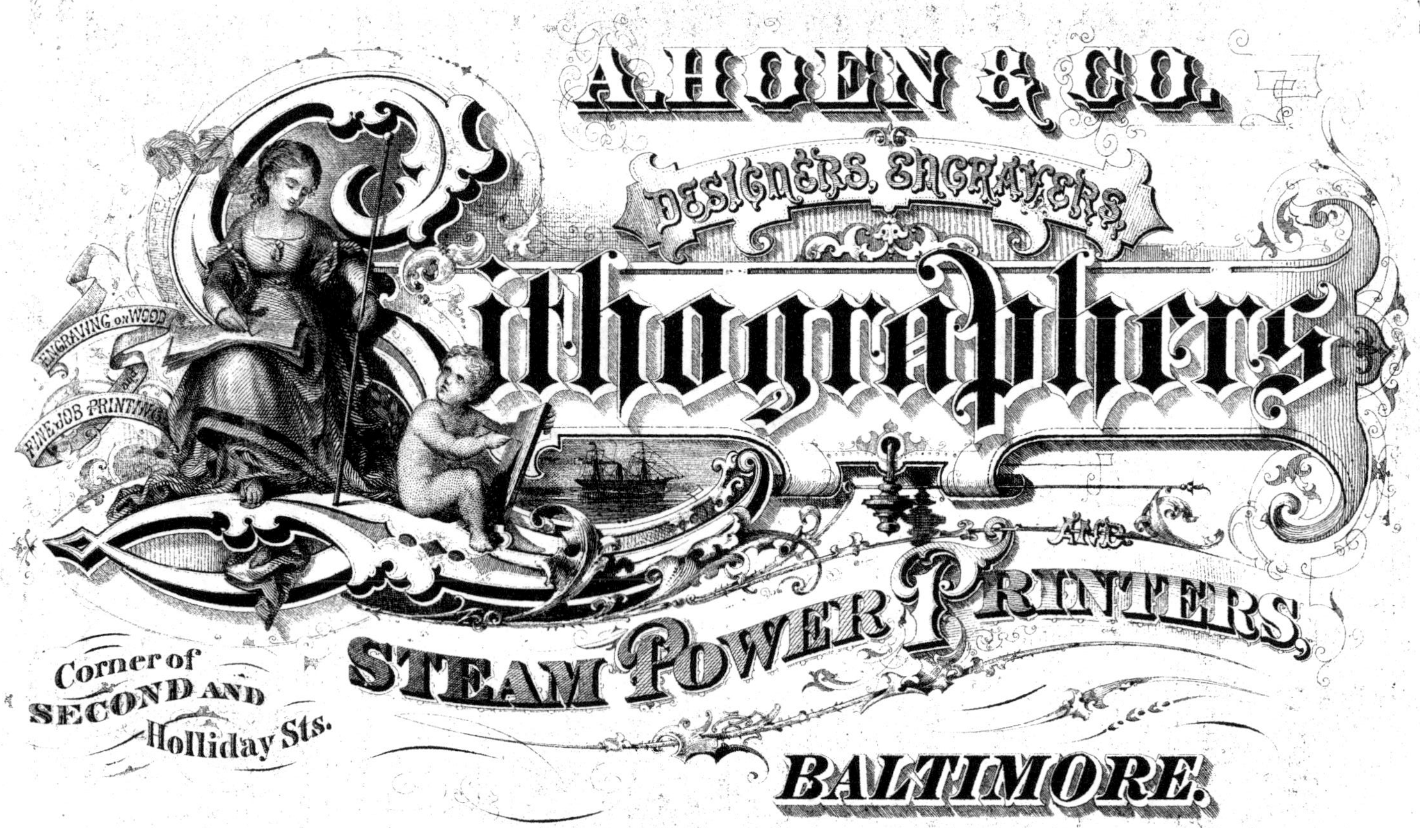
A. HOEN & CO.
DESIGNERS, ENGRAVERS
Lithographers
AND
STEAM POWER PRINTERS,
ENGRAVING ON WOOD
AND
FINE JOB PRINTING
Corner of
SECOND AND
Holliday Sts.
BALTIMORE.

Oyster, Fruit and Vegetable Packing.

THE Oyster Trade of Baltimore City, in its various branches, constitutes a most important industry, and one which has no rival in the other cities of the United States. The unlimited supply afforded by the Chesapeake Bay and its tributaries, and the superiority and delicate flavor of the Oysters, make it impossible for any other city in the world to compete with Baltimore in this regard. About thirty years ago a single house was established on Federal Hill, for the canning of cooked Oysters; its owner had discovered the secret of sealing the cans, and vainly imagined that it could be confined within his own brain. He wore his life away in his efforts to amass a fortune, and his secret was soon discovered, which, in course of time was to convey to sections that had scarcely heard by name of the delicious bivalves, bountiful supplies as fresh and as pure as those to be found on our tables. At present there are more than one hundred packing establishments engaged in the business, some of which employ as many as six hundred hands; upwards of twenty thousand persons are identified with the trade from first to last, in some form. A failure of the Oyster supply would bring distress to hundreds of households. Our space does not permit a detailed statement of the *modus operandi* of packing. Eight hundred pungies or small schooners and fully three thousand smaller boats are engaged in gathering Oysters. They commence work about the middle of September. The pungies separate the Oysters from the beds by means of dredges, while from the smaller boats tongs or rakes are plied by hand. The Oysters brought to the packing establishments are shucked, and if intended for shipment raw, are washed, and packed in the cans until every particle of air is excluded, and hermetically sealed; or they are first cooked and then packed in the same manner. As an exhibit of the amount of packing done, fifty thousand cans of raw are put up daily by a single house, and thirty thousand cans of cooked Oysters by another. The trade is kept up without intermission until the warm days of spring warn the proprietors that the Oysters will soon be unfit for use. There is then a short intermission; the hands are suffered to take a holiday and the pungies lie idly at the wharves. In a very few weeks fleets of these small vessels line the waters of the bay, and the streams which flow into it. The orchards and market-gardens adjacent to the streams are stripped of their fruits and vegetables, the packing-houses are transformed into huge bee-hives, the operatives go to work with renewed vigor, countless thousands of boxes of these perishable productions of the soil are poured into their insatiable reservoirs, and by a process somewhat similar to that made use of in Oyster packing, are stored away in cans and sent to all sections of the world to be kept pure and fresh until demanded by the ever increasing requirements of modern palates. Pickles, Sauces, Preserves, are all canned in large quantities by the packers and find a rapid sale in the market. These canned Oysters, Fruits and Vegetables are sent to all portions of the United States, and are exported to all sections of the civilized world. The Hindoos, the Chinese, the Japanese, and all European markets are largely supplied with canned goods from the packing-houses of the city of Baltimore. An industry so extensive necessarily tends to the development of other branches of trade intimately connected with it; among these is the manufacture of tin-cans.

A few of the packing-houses find it convenient to import their own tin and make their own cans. The machinery for this and the hands employed form no inconsiderable portion of the whole establishment, but by far the larger number rely upon the houses which have been established in the city exclusively for that purpose. The increase in the importation and manufacture of tin has kept pace with the development of the packing trade, and at this writing it is estimated that between twenty and thirty million cans are manufactured yearly for this market.

The trade is increasing and the resources for conducting the packing business are inexhaustible. It is impossible to fix any limits to this branch of the trade of Baltimore in the future. Another business connected with the packing trade deserves notice. The cans of Oysters, Fruits or Vegetables, after they are sealed, are supplied with labels denoting the character of their contents. Great competition has arisen between the firms engaged in the business, and they have sought to secure the most unique and beautiful designs, with which to advertise their wares to the world. Large printing-houses now exist in the city whose sole occupation is the printing of these labels. Much capital has been employed and great pains taken to reduce their designs to perfection. The result is that many of these designs at first glance can scarcely be distinguished from wood engravings. Where so many Oysters are shucked the question will naturally be asked, what becomes of the shells.

Many of the larger packing-houses have extensive lime-kilns, with a capacity of one thousand to twelve hundred bushels each. One firm alone burns twenty thousand bushels into lime every four days, and has made as much as six hundred thousand bushels of pure white lime in a year. Even this immense quantity does not dispose of the accumulations, and in many instances farmers and others are paid to haul away the shells for the construction of roads, or the improvement of the lands adjacent to the city. It will be seen from the above that the packing trade is already of paramount importance in Baltimore, and is rapidly increasing in extent and the number of substantial citizens engaged in it.

The Oyster laws of the State form no inconsiderable portion of the Code, and the efforts of legislators have latterly been directed to the regulation of the manner of taking the Oysters, that the beds may not be permanently injured by this traffic. An Oyster-navy has been established with this view, and efficient officers selected to command it; and during the season the vessels composing this water-police are constantly in motion for the purpose of enforcing the Oyster laws.

Shot.

AMONG the most prominent objects in a distant view of Baltimore, towering far above the loftiest building, and, although situated near the water level, rivalling in height the summit of the Washington Monument, is the Merchants' Shot Tower. This immense piece of masonry was erected in 1828, and is said to be the finest specimen of brick work on this continent, and perhaps in the world. It is two hundred and twenty feet high, above the pavement, and has a foundation seventeen feet in depth, resting upon solid rock. This gives the tower the rare and important advantage of being absolutely free from vibration, except during the heaviest gales of wind, when the maximum vibration at the highest floor does not exceed four inches. This absence of vibration is essential to the perfectness of the Shot. The walls were built entirely from within, no outside scaffolding having been used; they are six feet thick at the base of the tower, tapering off to eighteen inches at the top. The circumference at the base is one hundred and twenty-nine feet. The top is reached by a spiral stairway of three hundred and ten steps.

With regard to the manufacture of the Shot, it is sufficient to say that the large sizes of Shot, from B to 3 T inclusive, are dropped from the highest floor, while the smaller numbers are dropped from the middle floor. The company which works this tower claims to make the most perfect Drop Shot in the world, in consequence of the firm foundation and substantial structure of the tower, which secures it against vibratory motion. The sizes of their Shot, moreover, are carefully graded by fixed standards, and are mathematically perfect. The manufacturing capacity of the tower is now 100,000 bags in a season; it can readily be increased to 200,000 every six months, or indeed if necessary to half a million annually.

Provisions.

THE immediate connection of Baltimore with the West, renders it the chief point for distribution southward, of the great Provision supplies from that important and rapidly growing section of our country. It has long been known as one of the cheapest ports for this purpose on the entire seaboard; but the Provision trade with the States of Georgia and South Carolina was in some measure diminished by the establishment of direct lines of railway to the Mississippi valley. The trade with the Southern Atlantic States has however been largely augmented of late years, both through a disposition to purchase in Baltimore, and because the consumption in those States has greatly increased. In view of this fact, the railways and lines of steamers communicating directly or indirectly with the South, have become much more active than formerly. During 1872 Baltimore distributed 70,000 hhds. of bacon and bulk meats; 20,000 casks of hams; 50,000 tierces of lard; 30,000 bbls. of pork. A large proportion of these articles is sent to the West Indies and points further South; while to Great Britain and Germany great quantities of lard are shipped annually. The aggregate export of lard to Liverpool and Bremen alone, in 1871, was about half the total amount of 4,877,470 lbs. The demand for this article has become so great, that the refining of the cruder grades has risen within a short period into a very important branch of manufacture, of which we treat in the succeeding article.

GEORGE & JENKINS
Dealers in
HAMS
SIDES
SHOULDERS
BEEF
PORK
& LARD
PROVISIONS
GEORGE & JENKINS
MANUFACTURERS OF
REFINED LARD & LARD OIL,
No. 48 SOUTH ST.
LARD OIL
REFINED LARD
BALTIMORE.
J.D.EHLERS & CO. SC

HENRY W. DRAKELEY. AARON FENTON. JOEL HINMAN.

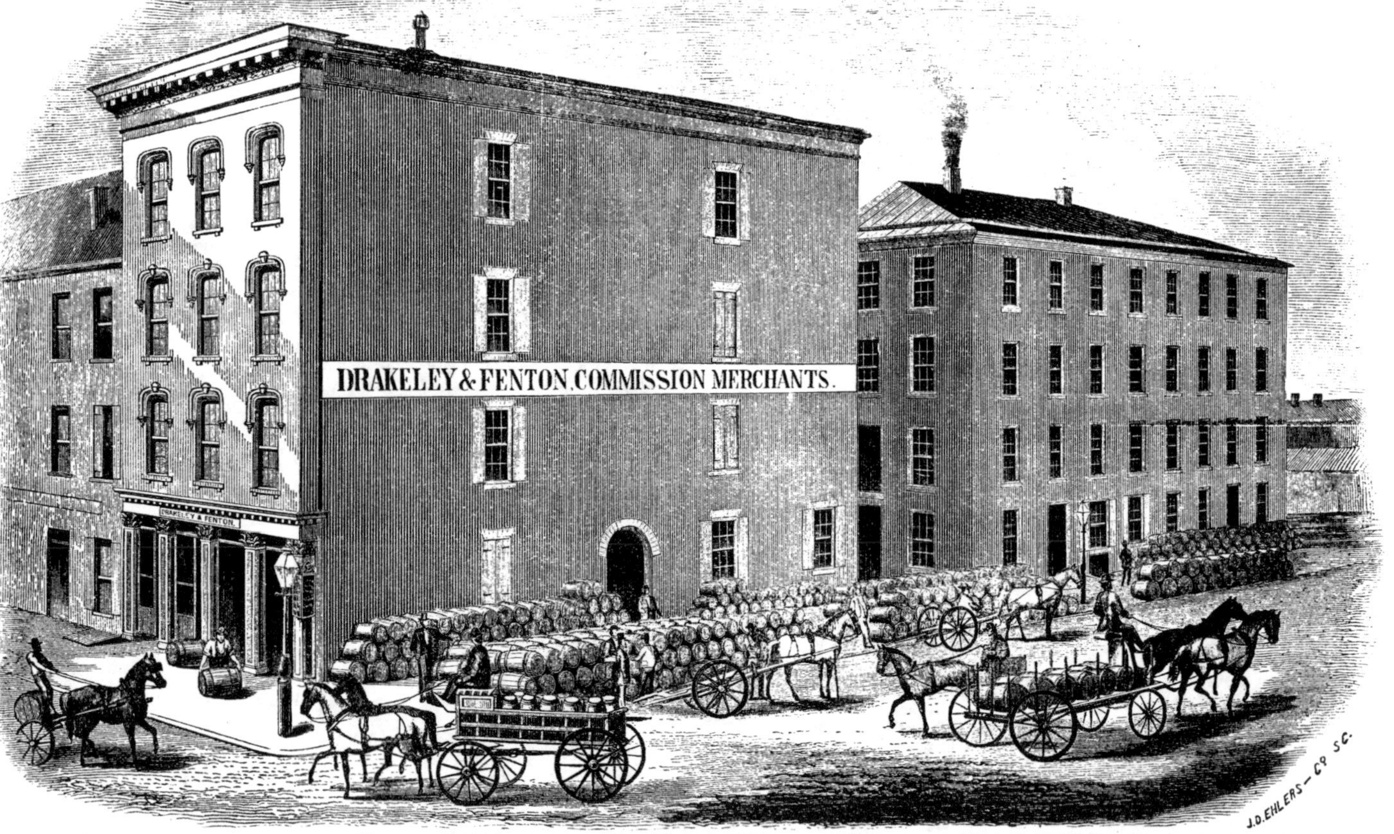

PROVISIONS AND PRODUCE. *(Established 1837)* 387 W. BALTIMORE STREET.

Refined Lard.

WITHIN three or four years past a new branch of the Provision trade has arisen in Baltimore, and, growing with astonishing rapidity, has already become one of the important departments of manufacture and commerce. This is the preparation and exportation of Refined Lard. The crude article, formerly exported as received from Western markets, is now cleansed of impurities, in establishments conducted on a very large scale, and being thus rendered easier to handle, as well as fitter for use, is sent in immense lots to Europe and elsewhere. There are four refineries now engaged in this business, which, only three or four years ago, was almost unknown; and of these four, two are also occupied in the preparation of Lard Oil.

The shipments for the last three years have been as follows:

1870	1,791,360 lbs.
1871	4,876,760 "
1872	12,622,649 "

Butter and Cheese.

AS a market for Butter and Cheese, produced in the great pasture lands of the country, Baltimore now fairly rivals New York City. The trade was formerly quite inconsiderable, in the days when each farmer made into Cheese the products of his own dairy; but since the establishment of large factories, the supply now of refined quality and vast quantity, is an important branch of commerce in both of the cities named. The transportation facilities of our own market for these articles are now fully as cheap, as rapid, and as convenient as those of New York, while we are nearer to the large Cheese and Butter consuming Southern country. As a consequence of this point in our favor, so large a proportion of the annual production comes to Baltimore, that occasionally New York merchants have found it to their advantage to purchase in this city; and the daily sales here are now several hundred per centum greater than they were a few years ago. These remarks, though made especially in reference to Cheese, are equally true in regard to Butter, of which the best article is received in very large quantities as cheaply as in New York.

The trade in Butter has increased largely during the year 1872, the receipts for that period being 10,000,000 pounds, and the receipts of Cheese during the same time have aggregated fully as much as during any former year.

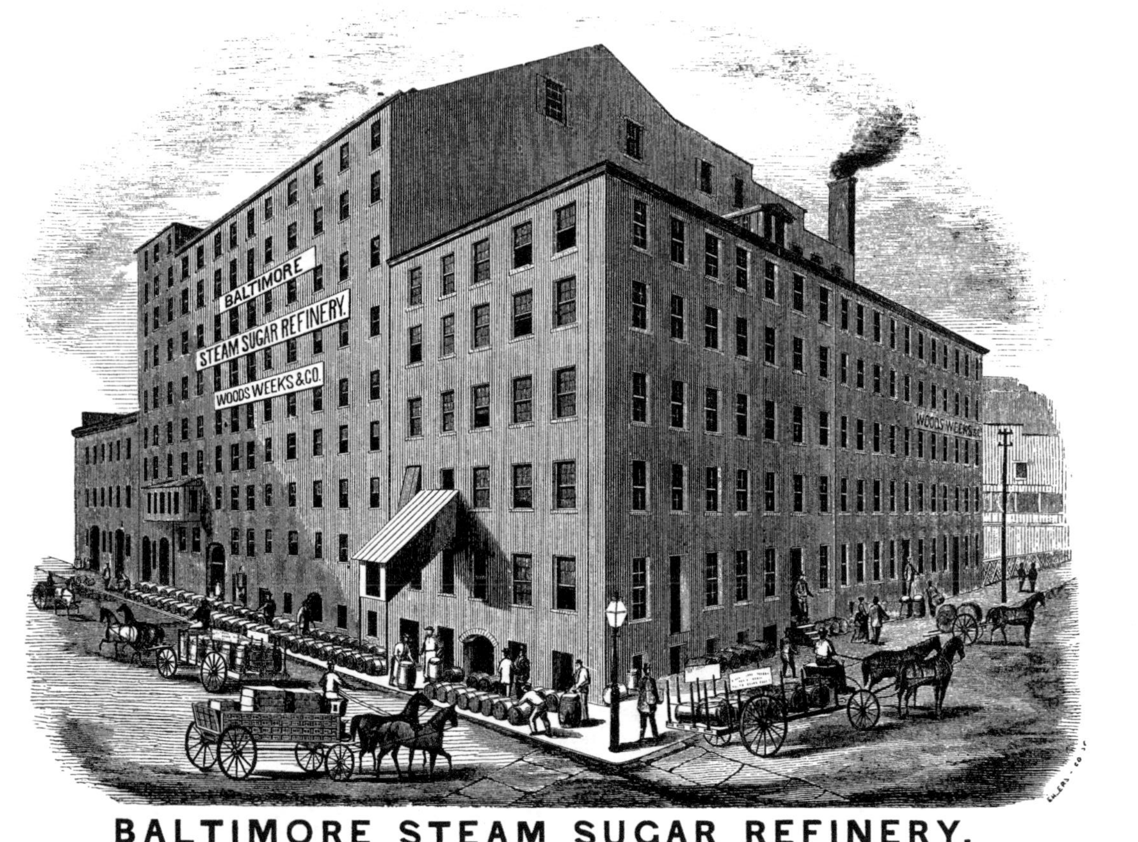

BALTIMORE STEAM SUGAR REFINERY,

WOODS, WEEKS & CO., Proprietors.

MANUFACTURERS OF ALL GRADES OF REFINED SUGARS AND SYRUPS.

THE CALVERT SUGAR REFINERY

STIRLING, AHRENS & CO., AGENTS, BALTIMORE.

Sugar.

IN the importation of Sugar, as well as of Coffee, the business of Baltimore has increased surprisingly within three years past. In 1870, New York alone could show larger receipts; but in Sugar especially, Boston reported almost an equal amount, and Philadelphia was not far behind. In 1871, the receipts at Baltimore were nearly two-thirds as great as the aggregate of Boston, Philadelphia and New Orleans; and the current year shows thus far a still heavier augmentation of the receipts. At the close of the first six months of 1872, the aggregate of imports for those months, as compared with the corresponding period of the previous year, were as follows:

	HHDS.	BOXES.	BAGS.	TIERCES.	BBLS.
1872, . .	76,024	39,193	33,000	3,170	6,671
1871, . .	69,601	23,895	21,233	1,421	9,597
	Inc. 6,423	Inc. 15,298	Inc. 11,767	Inc. 2,769	Dec. 2,908

The rapid growth of the trade in the past four years is displayed in the following table of receipts:

1872..................	122,402 hhds.	70,180 boxes,	41,100 bags.
1871..................	122,075 "	53,945 "	44,620 "
1870..................	87,598 "	57,444 "	29,678 "
1869..................	81,461 "	57,761 "	10,930 "

These large cargoes of raw Sugars are of course brought to Baltimore not merely for local consumption; and this introduces another extensive manufacturing interest of our city—the work of the Sugar Refineries. These factories are of great importance, inasmuch as their influence upon the prosperity of the city reaches far beyond the mere employment of a given number of laborers, or the production of a certain value in merchantable wares. By them importation is promoted, and our port is made to assume a high position as the great medium of traffic in one of the principal articles of necessity in the civilized world; while every means of transportation is called into activity by the requirements for distribution of the immense product.

In the Baltimore, Maryland, Calvert and Chesapeake Refineries the aggregate amount of the crude material worked up during the year 1871 was 109,686,000 pounds, from which were produced 91,000,000 pounds refined Sugar, and 1,929,272 gallons Syrup. Two other companies, the Canton and Merchants', which are employed in preparing Sugar from Molasses, boiled in 1871, 23,000

MARYLAND SUGAR REFINING COMPANY,
A. SCHUMACHER & CO., AGENTS, O'DONNELL'S WHARF, BALTIMORE.

hogsheads of Molasses, producing 11,300,000 pounds of yellow Sugar, and 440,000 gallons of Syrup. During that year, the receipts of Molasses, though so largely in excess of the previous years, were inadequate to the needs of the several establishments, and work was suspended much earlier in the season than is usual, in consequence of the deficiency of material. The Canton company, which worked up during the season 8,000 hogsheads, with a capacity of 15,000 hogsheads, was compelled to draw half even of this reduced amount from Northern markets. This deficiency of course suggested the necessity of heavier importations, and the receipts of the current year, as shown above, have been much larger.

Baltimore is undoubtedly destined to become a great market for both crude and refined Sugars and Molasses, and the character of the gentlemen who control the trade should be a sufficient inducement for purchasers to seek our city, when the other inducements offered compare so favorably with other places.

Coffee.

COFFEE is an article of importation in which Baltimore stands second among the ports of the United States; more prominently so, indeed, than in the case of Sugar, as here the receipts are more than twice the aggregate entries at the three other chief ports, of Boston, Philadelphia and New Orleans. The amount recorded for 1871, at Baltimore, was 92,892,904 pounds, principally Brazil, (or Rio,) while the receipts at Philadelphia, 5,792,915, at Boston, 6,398,256, and at New Orleans, 33,072,914, make a total of 45,264,085 pounds—less than half that of Baltimore, notwithstanding the great importance of New Orleans as the port of distribution to the valley of the lower Mississippi. The large supply given above is yet below the real amount, as large cargoes are shipped westward under bond without showing to the credit of Baltimore on the books of the Custom-House.

The following average of monthly sales during five years will give an idea of the rapid progress of the trade:

(160 lbs. to the bag.)

For 1867	20,810	bags,	or 3,329,600	lbs.
" 1868	20,919	"	" 3,347,040	"
" 1869	29,534	"	" 4,724,440	"
" 1870	42,213	"	" 6,754,080	"
" 1871	45,900	"	" 7,344,000	"
" 1872	32,922	"	" 5,267,520	"

The crop of 1872 was short; Baltimore importing its full share.

Baltimore, indeed, has become a port of entry in coffee, even for New York merchants, in consequence of the facilities offered for economical handling, and for cheap and speedy transportation to various points in the West.

Salt.

THE three great markets for Salt in this country are New Orleans, New York and Baltimore. We name them in point of prominence. The article itself is such an absolute necessity that the wonder has often been expressed from where does it all come. Liverpool, Turk's Island and some of the local wells, situated principally in the States of New York, Michigan, Ohio and West Virginia, furnish the bulk of the article consumed in this country. There have been brought from the West Indies to this port during the past year about 150,000 more bushels of Salt than at any similar period of our history. The importation from Liverpool has somewhat slackened during the same time, owing to the strikes at Liverpool, and high prices and scarcity only; but the figures made up by one of the largest Salt dealers in America, very clearly indicate that Baltimore is to become the greatest market on the Atlantic seaboard for the importation and sale of that commodity. The fact that gentlemen of undoubted probity and substantial resources have control of the Salt market in Baltimore, should be an inducement to all buyers in the South and West to come to this city for their supplies. The facilities for importation are unequalled and the prices correspondingly low. The rates of freight and railroad transportation are not surpassed in this country for cheapness, dispatch and security to the buyer.

W. WILSON, Jr. F. BURNS, Jr. F. H. BURNS.

30 S. HOWARD STREET.

Teas.

THE Tea trade of Baltimore is a large and growing interest. Prior to the establishment of the Pacific Mail Steamship Company, Teas were brought direct from the East to New York. This Line to some extent changed the direction of Eastern goods; but the completion of the Central Pacific Railroad, and the low rates for freight established by that corporation, have effected a complete revolution in the Tea trade. Tea is now brought by water to the Pacific coast, and shipped overland to the Eastern Cities of America.

The geographical position of our City, and the energy of her Merchants, have secured for her much of the trade, which was formerly monopolized by New York. At least, one of the largest Houses in Baltimore has a member of the firm in the East, as special agent for the selection and purchase of Teas; and all those engaged in the business are very careful of the character of the goods offered to the market. Large quantities of Tea are shipped from Baltimore to the South, and South-West; and from present indications our City at no distant day will compare favorably with her sister Cities on the Atlantic coast, in this very extensive branch of commerce.

Rice.

THE Rice Market of Baltimore, without very great variation in the total amount of its business, has changed considerably in its character during the years of which we take especial note in this sketch. Domestic crops are now consumed wholly within the United States, and fall considerably below the needs of the country; and in consequence of this, and the cheap rates of through shipment, much of the business in home-grown Rice is done in Charleston and New Orleans. On the other hand, and in consequence of this insufficiency, the receipts of foreign Rice have greatly increased, and the report of the current year shows an aggregate at least fifty per cent in excess of last or any previous year—say 25,000 bags as compared with 15,000 for the entire receipts of 1871. In exact figures, there were received last year 25,618 bags, in 1871, 15,873 bags, and in 1870, 8,980 bags. The report of domestic Rice, for the same years, shows also a slight excess in favor of 1871, over 1870, notwithstanding the short crops in the South.

Of the foreign cargoes received, fully three-fourths are sold for home consumption, but the sales for exportation to the West Indies and elsewhere abroad, are steadily increasing. Among the kinds of Rice brought from the East Indies, that called Patna Rice, said to be produced from American seed, and which has a fine, bright, slender grain, is a favorite article. Rangoon Rice is received in large quantities for shipment to the West Indies, and when of very good quality, often goes largely into consumption in the United States.

Spices.

FEW articles are more generally used than manufactured Spices. They appear upon the table of every household in the city, and enter into the preparation of nearly all the dishes that are served for human consumption, and yet but few are aware of the extent of their manufacture, or the vast amount consumed. In Baltimore there are five extensive establishments engaged in their production, besides a number of smaller houses, which do a flourishing business. Pepper, Ginger, Cloves, Nutmegs, Mace, Cassia, Cayenne, &c., &c., are manufactured in immense quantities, and of a character certainly equal to the productions of the factories in any other sections of the country. The very best materials are used by the manufacturers, and our market in this regard is entirely independent of all others. Jobbers complete their stocks from the home factories, and their experience is decidedly favorable to a continuance of this system. Large capital is invested in the business, and the gentlemen engaged in it are among our most reliable and sterling merchants. This fact gives confidence that in a trade where probity and fair dealing are absolutely essential, dealers can purchase with the utmost security. The manufacture of Spices in Baltimore has already assumed large proportions, and the demand increasing every day, will doubtless lead to an indefinite expansion of the trade in the future. The manufactured goods are sent from this city in immense quantities to the South, West and North-West, and to the neighboring States.

Fish.

AMONG the many advantages offered by the location of the City of Baltimore, are the products of the Chesapeake Bay, whose waters teem with Fish suited to the table of the most fastidious epicure, as well as adapted to the requirements of trade. In almost every season the markets are supplied with its offerings, and the Bay Mackerel, Potomac and Susquehanna Shad, Sheepshead, Drum, Taylor, Rock, white and yellow Perch, and other numerous varieties are supplied in greater quantities and more decided excellence than can be found in any port of this or any other country. In addition to these, large quantities of Shad and Herring are yearly caught at the fisheries on the shores of the bay and its tributaries, which find their way to this mart, and form an important article of trade and commerce. Owing to the geographical position of Baltimore it is also a centre for the distribution over its various railroads of the Fish from the British Provinces and the New England States, and the Carolinas; the Western country being almost entirely supplied from this Port with these commodities.

Soap and Candles.

THE manufacture of Soap and Candles has been carried on in Baltimore for many years past, and there are now in the City five large factories, with quite a number of smaller establishments. At two of the larger Houses, Candles are manufactured on a considerable scale. Large shipments are made to the West Indies, and also to other foreign regions, especially Cape of Good Hope. Notwithstanding the influences exerted against this trade by the general use of coal oil in various forms, and the extensive introduction of gas, the exportation from Baltimore has been at least quadrupled during the past twenty years.

Matches.

THE manufacture of Matches was commenced in this City in 1865, under favorable auspices. Experienced and skillful workmen were employed; and the interest has steadily increased in importance. At present upwards of one hundred hands are employed, and from two hundred and fifty to three hundred gross are daily manufactured. Both Sulphur and Parlor Matches are made which compare favorably in quality, with those manufactured elsewhere in the country. Baltimore is the only city south of Wilmington, Delaware, where these very necessary articles are manufactured; and hence the demand is very great. Besides supplying the home market, large quantities are sent to the South, at rates certainly as favorable as are offered in any other localities. The superiority of Baltimore Matches has created for them a popularity in some localities, which has materially enlarged the business. This branch of industry is growing in importance, and the fact that all the materials necessary in the manufacture can be purchased here, makes it specially remunerative.

Imported Wines and Liquors.

IN addition to the Whiskey trade of our city, quite a large business is done in Imported Wines and Liquors. Before the civil war, in this country, large quantities of Brandies and superior Wines were imported into this market. But the excessive duties afterwards imposed, caused a falling off in the consumption. The establishment of the Bremen and Allan Lines of Steamers, together with partial reduction in duties, have very materially revived this branch of our commerce; and to-day Baltimore can compare favorably with other cities both in the stock offered to buyers, and the character of the gentlemen engaged in the business. The fashions have somewhat changed in this branch of industry of late years. The introduction of Lager-Beer and the cheapness of Whiskey as compared with foreign Brandies, &c., and the finer classes of Wines, have altered to a very considerable extent the public taste, and at present large quantities of the cheaper French and German Wines, together with heavy invoices of "Brown Stout," India Ales, and fermented Liquors are brought to this Port. Gin, too, is imported in considerable quantities; and the wholesale dealers in this City have always on hand choice selections of the finest Foreign Wines and Liquors, and offer inducements to customers certainly not inferior to those extended by other cities.

Whiskey.

FOR many years, Baltimore has borne a reputation deservedly high for the manufacture of fine Rye Whiskies, and at this writing controls the markets of the United States in these grades. The manufacture of Whiskies of all kinds and qualities is extensively carried on in and around the city; and the sales foot up an aggregate in barrels, which mark it as one of our most important industries. Five Houses are at present engaged in its production, with a capacity in the aggregate of 4,500 bushels of grain, or from 450 to 500 barrels of the raw material daily. Fully two hundred Houses, large and small, are engaged in the Liquor trade. Six of the larger sell 50,000 barrels annually, while the business transacted by the others, placing it at 50,000 barrrels, a moderate estimate, will bring the sum total of sales, to 100,000 barrels annually. The capital invested in the Whiskey business in this city is about $3,000,000, while the receipts from sales, allowing an average price of $1.50 per gallon, would aggregate $6,000,000. Of course the large amount of Whiskey manufactured and sold here is not all intended for home consumption. To the extreme South, heavy shipments of the very best grades of Rye Whiskey are made; while with the neighboring States, the trade consists principally of inferior grades. Massachusetts, New York and northern Pennsylvania, also consume large quantities manufactured here. In the West, where the people have heretofore used exclusively the Bourbon or Corn Whiskey, manufactured in the vicinity of Louisville and Cincinnati, a taste is developing for the better grades of Baltimore "Old Rye." The increase since the war in the manufacture and sale of Whiskey in this city has been very decided, and the evidences furnished by the transactions of the last two years, lead to the conclusion that its expansion will be more rapid in the future.

W. T. WALTERS & CO.

68 EXCHANGE PLACE,

BALTIMORE.

WHOLESALE DEALERS IN

LIQUORS.

SOLE PROPRIETORS OF THE CELEBRATED

BAKER'S PURE RYE WHISKEY.

ESTABLISHED 1825.

THOS. J. FLACK & SONS,

WINES AND LIQUORS,

52 SOUTH STREET, BALTIMORE.

FLACK BROTHERS,

Distillers of Rye and Bourbon Whiskies, Rum, Gin and Brandy,

OFFICE, 52 SOUTH STREET, BALTIMORE, MD.

Distillery, bounded by Clinton and First Streets and Fifth and Sixth Avenues.

Grain.

BALTIMORE, the commercial centre of a large and wonderfully rich agricultural region, has long been one of the leading Grain markets of this country. The soil and climate of the sections naturally tributary to our city, are peculiarly adapted to the growth of cereals. Prior to the development of the gigantic West, and the introduction and extension of railroads, a short or full crop of Grain on the "Chesapeake" established the value of Breadstuffs along the entire Atlantic coast. The portions of our country which more immediately feed the Baltimore market, comprise the State of Maryland, a large part of Virginia, with sections of Delaware, Pennsylvania, and North Carolina.

Those divisions which lie more directly on the Chesapeake, produce the very finest varieties of Wheat; unsurpassed, and probably not equalled in quality by that grown in any other part of the world; being of a bright color, thin skin, plump berry, and rich in gluten. The Baltimore milling demand for this high grade Wheat, absorbs nearly the whole crop at high prices; leaving but little or none for export, or for neighboring markets. The Corn produced in this favored section, is also of superior quality. "Baltimore White Corn" is well-known, and sought after by the trade of the Atlantic States and Great Britain whenever a high grade article for human food is wanted. The waters of the Chesapeake furnish a rapid and cheap mode of transportation to farmers, in vessels whose tonnage is from two to five thousand bushels. The cargoes are taken immediately from their farms, at a cost of five to seven cents per bushel, and reach market in one to five days.

With the radical change in the labor system, and the sub-division of farms, this rich section of country is destined to rapid development, and great increase of crops. It offers to capable and industrious farmers with moderate means, the finest opportunity for location and settlement, that can now be presented.

The completion of the Baltimore and Ohio Railroad, and the extension of its Western connections, together with the facilities granted by its great competitor, the Pennsylvania Company, have caused a large increase in the Grain trade of Baltimore during the past few years. With a wise policy, and proper facilities extended by the management of these Roads, we hope soon to recover our former paramount importance; or at least to become a close competitor with the present leading market on the coast.

An extensive Grain Elevator established by the Baltimore and Ohio Railroad Company, facilitating the handling of Western Grain, has greatly increased the receipts of Corn; so that Baltimore has already become a considerable exporting Corn Port. The success attending this enterprise has led to the projection of several others of a similar character. The Baltimore and Ohio Railroad Company we learn will immediately build additional Elevators, and the Pennsylvania Company having obtained desirable property on deep water, at Canton, will soon erect another; thus enabling our Merchants eager for the trade, to handle our portion of the ever increasing surplus of the West.

The extension of the Baltimore and Ohio Railroad to Chicago, must add largely to the receipts of our Port, and enable Northwestern Wheat to reach foreign markets through Baltimore, at cheaper rates, and in better condition than by any other route.

The rigid inspection of Grain established by the Corn and Flour Exchange, together with the great care exercised by shippers, have already given to cargoes shipped from Baltimore, a very high reputation abroad; thereby maintaining the boasted supremacy of our market for quality. Since the establishment of the Baltimore and Ohio Elevator, the receipts of Corn have largely increased. For the first six months of 1872, 5,908,000 bushels were received, against 2,398,000 for the same period of the previous year; and 5,735,000 bushels for the entire year 1871. The extensive improvements and additions to our Railroad facilities, and other causes, will in the near future magnify our Grain trade to such proportions, as the most sanguine amongst us can now scarcely appreciate.

We append a table showing the comparative receipts of Grain at this market for four years:

	1872.	1871.	1870.	1869.
Wheat	2,456,100	4,076,017	3,039,357	3,249,995
Corn	9,045,465	5,735,921	3,831,676	3,923,563
Oats	1,959,161	1,833,409	1,243,720	1,171,424
Rye	90,938	88,956	77,778	177,246
Peas	10,000	10,000	10,000	10,000
Beans	35,000	30,000	30,000	30,000
Total	13,596,664	11,774,303	8,232,531	8,562,228

Lith by A. Hoen & Co. Balto.

Flour.

A REVIEW of the Flour and Meal trade naturally follows that of Grain. The requirements of merchants engaged in the Breadstuffs trade, led to the establishment of the Corn and Flour Exchange, where this business is exclusively transacted.

The high character and position of the merchants engaged in this trade in Baltimore, is proverbial, and excelled nowhere in America. Baltimore situated in the centre of a great Wheat growing country, has always maintained the first-class reputation as a Flour market. The Grain is obtained principally from Pennsylvania, Virginia, Maryland, and the West. The manufacturing capacity of our city is extensive. Large and substantial Mills, with all modern improvements, are located upon powerful streams within and contiguous to the city; and several large Steam Mills of great power are favorably located. The great drought of the past few years, the consequent diminution of water, and its interference with milling operations, have caused some proprietors of Mills to add to their water-power, steam engines to supply the constantly increasing demands. The Flour manufactured in Baltimore, from the high grade and fancy Maryland and Virginia Wheat, is of well-known superior quality, and wherever introduced maintains this reputation. The highest grade for family use, such as the famous "Patapsco" brand and others well-known, are unsurpassed, if ever equalled in the world, and have become the standard in markets, for the best grades.

A very high grade of "Strong Flour," a quality well-known to the trade and to bakers, is also manufactured with great care in this city for shipment to Brazil and other South American ports. This Flour is capable of standing long voyages to the tropics. Its quality is due to the peculiarity of the

Wheat grown in this section, in addition to judicious selection and careful attention bestowed on its milling. The proprietors of the celebrated "Rio" brands, such as the "Mount Vernon" and others, are very jealous and deservedly proud of their reputation, which is equal to that of any Flour ground and shipped from the States. The Country and Western Flour received here for sale is generally of high or good grade, and is exported to Europe and the West Indies, or goes into domestic consumption. Inferior or very low grades are not received in any quantities, as they are not suitable to the market; and merchants will not take them to the profit of the shippers.

After continued effort by the trade, the compulsory State inspection laws with regard to Flour, were abolished by the Legislature, and expired on the first day of May, 1872. These laws were always an incubus upon trade, and resulted in giving us incompetent inspectors, (whose sole recommendation was party fidelity,) to examine and report the quality of goods submitted to them. We have done with them. The only inspection of Flour now with us is voluntary. The merits of the article itself, the judgment of the buyer, and above all, the character and reputation of the miller or seller, are the safeguards against imposition and fraud, and these are sufficient without the dictum of an ignoramus to "brand" the goods according to his bad judgment, prejudice or partiality.

Our market has been singularly free from any of the disreputable practices said to prevail elsewhere. In fact the trade "wont stand it." *We* look to reputation as a guarantee of the goods.

With the opening and extension of the various arteries of trade, we confidently look forward to a rapid development of the Flour Trade of this Port, together with an increase of receipts of Western Wheat, and a large addition to our milling capacity.

The following table will show the receipts of Flour at this market for the last four years:

1872	1,175,967	bbls.
1871	1,123,028	"
1870	1,117,314	"
1869	1,051,251	"

In addition to the trade of Flour, large quantities of White Corn are ground in and around the city for domestic consumption, and for the contiguous country. Yellow Corn, kiln-dried, ground and packed in barrels for shipment to the West Indies, and British Provinces, is an important article of manufacture and commerce. Hominy, prepared from a peculiar variety of Maryland white Corn of superior quality, is manufactured on a large scale, and meets with a great domestic and export demand.

The Baltimore Corn and Flour Exchange,

SOUTH ST., WOOD ST. and BOWLY'S WHARF,

MAIN ENTRANCE ON SOUTH STREET.

S. SPRIGG BELT, - - - - - - - - - - - - - - - - - *President.*
J. M. GIRVIN and GEO. F. ANDERSON, - - - - - - *Vice Presidents.*
R. M. WYLIE, - - - *Treasurer.* | *WM. F. WHEATLEY,* - *Secretary*

EXECUTIVE COMMITTEE:

H. F. TURNER, JOHN GILL, A. W. GOLDSBOROUGH.

BOARD OF DIRECTORS FOR 1873.

JAS. E. TYSON,	HERMAN WILLIAMS,	ALLEN DORSEY,	THOS. I. DAIL,
FRANK HERSCH,	EDWIN HEWES,	HARRY MCCOY,	GEO. P. WILLIAR,
J. M. GIRVIN,	GEO. F. ANDERSON,	R. M. WYLIE,	H. F. TURNER.
JOHN GILL,	A.W.GOLDSBOROUGH,	S. SPRIGG BELT,	

The Corn and Flour Exchange, of Baltimore, was established in 1853, for the promotion of the general business of the city, but more particularly for the facilitation of trade in Breadstuffs, and the convenience of parties engaged therein. Since its establishment, having grown in the confidence and esteem of the community, it has of necessity attracted many associate interests, and has thus become the leading and most influential commercial organization in the city. Its usefulness and influence are being constantly extended. Inaugurated in 1853. incorporated under general laws in 1855, its charter amended several times, as the wants and experience of the trade demanded, it finally received from the State in 1870, an ample charter, giving the Directors more complete control, with power to establish and maintain the highest tone of commercial morality.

The Exchange is governed by a Board of fifteen Directors, elected annually. The President, Vice Presidents and Treasurer are elected by and from the Board.

Qualification for membership requires the applicant to be a citizen of the State, engaged in business in Baltimore, and election by the Executive Committee.

The charge for Membership is $50 initiation fee, and $20 yearly subscription. Firms cannot become members as such. Each and every individual doing business on the floor, must become a member. Clerks are admitted, to transact business only for their employers paying the yearly subscription.

Strangers are admitted by card, upon the introduction of a member.

The main Hall in the Exchange Building is furnished with tables for the exposition of samples, the yearly rental of which is one, two and three dollars, according to size. The occupancy of these tables for the grain is sold at public auction; premiums for the choice ranging from $25 to $150. Much excitement prevails at these Annual Sales.

The roll of membership for the year 1872 contained 464 names.

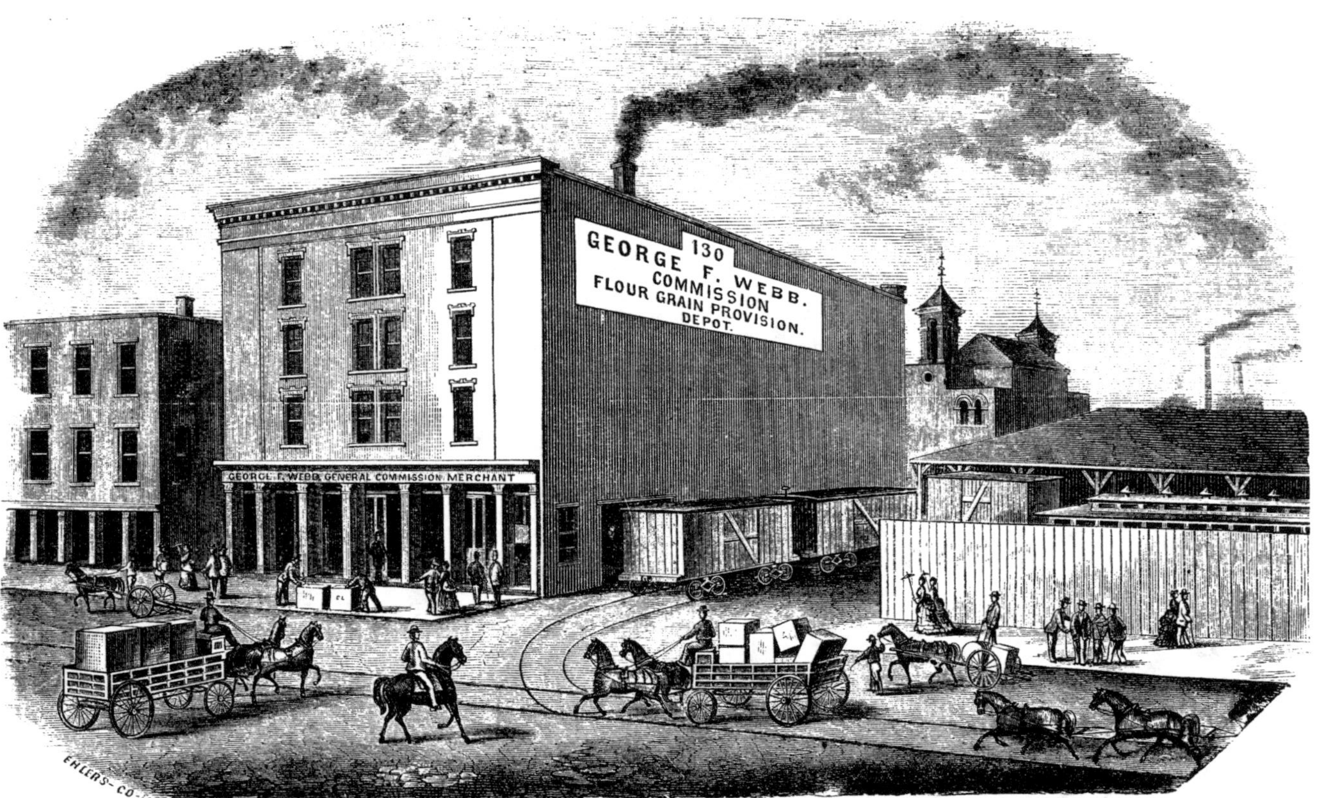

GEORGE F. WEBB, FLOUR, GRAIN AND GENERAL COMMISSION MERCHANT, 130 NORTH ST., BALTIMORE.

Liberal Advances made on Consignments. *Adjoining the Northern Central Railroad Depot.*

Pearl Hominy.

AMONG the novel and interesting business features of Baltimore, may be mentioned a large Mill for the preparation of Pearl Hominy. But recently established, it has rapidly extended its capacity until at present 2,500 bushels of Corn are daily consumed in its operations. Kiln-Dried Pearl Hominy, Grits, Pearl Maizene, Corn Flour, &c., &c., are prepared in immense quantities. Corn Flour, a new article when mixed with bread made of Wheat Flour, gives to it additional whiteness, and causes it to retain its freshness much longer than that made exclusively of Wheat Flour. The articles prepared at this establishment are shipped to different sections of the United States; and of late a foreign trade has grown up, orders having been received from Paris, Liverpool, London and Glasgow. The most flattering inducements are offered to purchasers in this market.

Malt.

IN connection with the extensive manufacture of Lager-Beer in our city, there are several large establishments for the production of Malt, an ingredient which enters largely into the composition of Beer. Six Malt Houses are now in operation, with an aggregate capital of $1,500,000, employing three hundred hands. The principal element used in the manufacture of Malt is barley. This grain is grown upon an extensive scale only in Western New York, the Western States, and Canada.

The establishment of these large Malt Houses, and the consequent demand for the grain, has led to efforts on the part of our enterprising agriculturalists to produce barley, and the experiments of several have resulted so favorably, that they have been encouraged to make other and more persistent efforts. The demand for Beer is not likely to decrease. The numerous Breweries already established are in a flourishing condition, and others are constantly being started. The sales from the Malt establishments sum up probably $5,000,000, with a tendency to increase. Some of our capitalists are engaged in the business, and the flourishing condition of the trade invites money from abroad.

Candies and Foreign Fruits.

AMONG the branches of trade which have given impetus to the growth of our city, and have decidedly ministered to its importance as a commercial centre, may be mentioned the trade in Candies and Foreign Fruits. The two are so thoroughly joined, that separate consideration of them would perhaps be out of place. In New York City, specialties seem to be the tendency of the trade. One house will import Mediterranean Fruits; another will deal entirely in West Indian goods; while a third will expose for sale only the products of the Canton trade. In Baltimore this is not the case. Quite a number of large and imposing buildings have been erected by our Candy and Fruit dealers, which stand out as conspicuous monuments of the enterprise of the firms which constructed them, as well as handsome additions to the æsthetic features of our city. Candy, French or American, Mediterranean Fruits, such as Oranges and Lemons from Sicily, Almonds and Raisins from Malaga, Raisins from Valencia, Currants, Citron, Figs, Dates, Prunes, Sardines, Canton Ginger, Fire-Crackers, &c., &c., can be purchased at any of these Houses upon terms as advantageous as are offered by any market in the country, with the additional facility to buyers of being able to fill their entire order in one large establishment, instead of being compelled to go from one House to another, as in other cities, with the cost of drayage, &c. Baltimore is entirely independent of any other city in the Candy and Fruit trade. The business has increased fourfold within twenty years. Five hundred hands are employed, and a capital of more than one million dollars is invested in the business. The facilities which her geographical position and varied industries give her in this regard, are such, that the merchants can offer their goods at the lowest market prices. Refined Sugar, which is the ingredient in the manufacture of Candies, can be secured at our great Sugar Refineries; and this is the only article used in the production of Candy in Baltimore, as no adulteration has ever yet been practiced or detected upon home goods in the market. In regard to the Mediterranean Fruit trade, much could be said, but our space is limited. The enterprising gentlemen who are connected with it, by a series of successful operations, have gradually enlarged their business until at present Baltimore can boast of one of the most extensive Mediterranean Fruit importing houses in the country. In addition to their regular trade in the articles already enumerated, these parties are now importing large quantities of Brimstone from Sicily to supply the extensive manufactories of Chemicals, Acids and Phosphates in this city. The annual consumption of Brimstone for the above purposes in Baltimore, is about five thousand tons, all of which it is designed to import direct to this market.

John G. Clarke. **William H. Jones.**

CLARKE & JONES,

CANDY MANUFACTURERS,

AND WHOLESALE DEALERS IN

FOREIGN FRUITS, NUTS, &c.

No. 15 Light St., Cor. German,

BALTIMORE.

The Jobbing Trade.

THE Jobbing Trade of Baltimore has kept pace with her increasing importance as a commercial and manufacturing city. Its various departments, such as Dry Goods, Groceries, Hardware, Notions, Boots and Shoes, Hats and Caps, Clothing, Books and Stationery, Queensware, Straw Goods and Millinery, Drugs, &c., &c., are fully up to the standard, and will compare favorably with those of any other city in this country. As a general rule these departments are in the hands of old and established Houses, whose proprietors are among our most highly esteemed and responsible citizens, who have been educated to their calling, and whose natural tastes and judgment have been strengthened by the experience of a lifetime, and a thorough rational application to business. Many branches of the Jobbing Trade not enumerated above are successfully conducted in this city: and the number of new establishments and branches of old ones, is a clear indication of the prosperity of the Trade, as well as the growth of the City. The stock carried by these Houses embraces full supplies from all the best factories in the United States, and the choicest selections of goods from foreign countries. The Lines of Steamers between this City and the Ports of Europe, furnish facilities for the importation of the most desirable goods at lower rates than at any other Port. The port charges are lighter, ship supplies cheaper, and the difficulties in the way of shipping comparatively trifling. Since the establishment of steam communication between Baltimore and Europe, our merchants engaged in the Jobbing Trade have displayed an energy and enterprise which command admiration. They make regular trips to Great Britain, and the continent of Europe for the purchase of goods; and the articles imported are selected under their own inspection. Baltimore is largely independent of the Eastern Cities, in her Wholesale Jobbing Trade; and bids fair in a short time to compare favorably with New York, as a distributing market. In each department there are Houses contending for business, and making of course the most active competition, thus reducing prices to minimum rates. Her proximity to the South and West, offers inducements to merchants from those sections, which cannot be lightly estimated. The trade in Dry Goods, Groceries, Hardware, Clothing, Boots and Shoes, Hats and Caps, Millinery Goods and Notions is particularly active; and the rival Houses engaged spare no pains to make their stock as full and complete as possible; so that the taste of every section may be gratified, and favorable prices assured. The Jobbing Trade, comprehending a large number of important interests, necessitates the employment of a vast capital, which in this city aggregates many millions of dollars. It is not unreasonable to infer, that in the near future Baltimore will become the great reservoir of supplies for the entire South, South-West, and many portions of the Central-West. Many of the great manufactories of the country have agencies here, selling at factory prices.

The attractions of Baltimore as a Jobbing centre, are so well-known to the local Retail Trade, embracing within itself some of the most intelligent dealers in the country, that they are content to buy at home. The closest buyers have tried rival markets time and again, without advantage of prices or terms. Capital, competition, and a thorough knowledge of business, have accomplished for Baltimore quite as much as for the more northern Cities. Our City for the quality and variety of goods, is fully equal to New York; and the market will be found always adequate to the demand.

Although Baltimore is not so large a market as New York, it is yet larger than New York formerly was, when it commanded the entire trade of the country; and sufficiently so, for the general demands of its present trade. The merchants, in view of the rapidly augmenting trade, have increased their facilities; and to-day extend all the inducements which can be offered by any other city in the country.

William Devries. Christian Devries, of S. William R. Devries. Solomon Kimmell.

Wm. Devries & Co., Wholesale Dealers in **Foreign & Domestic Dry Goods & Notions,**
312 W. BALTIMORE ST., (Between Howard and Liberty,) **BALTIMORE.**

ESTABLISHED IN 1846.

HODGES BROTHERS

23 Hanover Street,

BALTIMORE,

Direct Importers of British and Continental

Dress Goods

Irish Linens,

And every description of

ALSO,

White Goods, Handkerchiefs, Shawls, Laces, Hosiery, Underwear, Gloves, Umbrellas and Parasols,

Together with a large and well assorted stock of

Gentlemen's Furnishing Goods

AND NOTIONS GENERALLY.

One of our firm, having made purchasing trips to Europe, semi-annually for nineteen years, and buying all our domestic goods for cash, we have great confidence in assuring the Trade that our Foreign and American business is on a footing that defies competition. Merchants, not dealing with us, are invited to make our acquaintance when they next visit Baltimore. Our stock can be examined without much labor, as the use of steam elevators renders the ascent of staircases unnecessary.

L. Passano & Sons

IMPORTERS AND DEALERS IN

WHITE GOODS, NOTIONS,
TRIMMINGS, HOSIERY,
GLOVES and SMALL WARES,

268 W. Baltimore Street,

BALTIMORE.

Brosius & Co.

MANUFACTURERS AGENTS FOR AND IMPORTERS OF

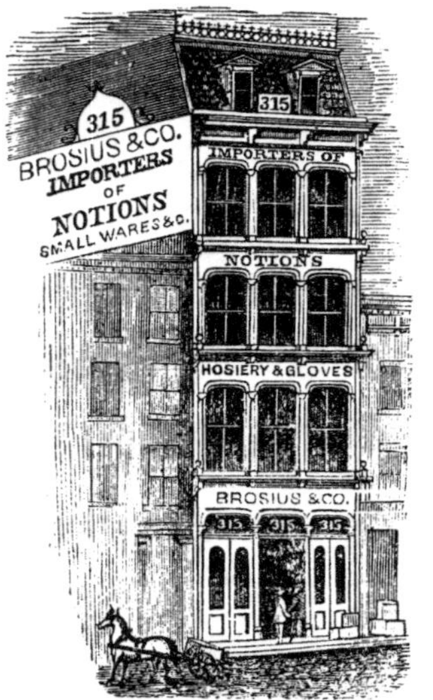

NOTIONS
White Goods,
Ribbons,
Shawls, Etc.

315 BALTIMORE STREET,
BALTIMORE.

S. H. BROSIUS. SILAS BROSIUS. A. W. FITZHUGH. S. B. HOOPMAN.

ESTABLISHED - - - - - - - - - - - - 1841.

IMPORTERS,

W. MALLINCKRODT & SON,

22 GERMAN STREET,

BALTIMORE,

OF

Cloths, Doeskins and Cassimeres.

Robert Moore & Bro.

IMPORTERS AND JOBBERS OF

AND VESTINGS,

No. 233 BALTIMORE STREET,

BALTIMORE.

JOHN A. GRIFFITH & CO.

Importers and Manufacturers of

TAILORS' TRIMMINGS

Baltimore, 249 W. Baltimore Street.

Cincinnati, cor. Fourth and Walnut Sts.

Henry Bogue. Robt. H. Bogue.

HENRY BOGUE & SON

N. E. cor. Charles & Baltimore Sts. 54 Sixth Street,

BALTIMORE, PITTSBURGH,

IMPORTERS OF

Cloths, Doeskins, Worsted Serges, Drapd' Etes,

SILK SERGES & SATINS DE CHINES, VELVETS, ITALIANS,

And all Kinds of Tailors' Trimmings.

Millinery.

THE Millinery business of Baltimore is one of her leading industries. In addition to the domestic goods manufactured in this city, and other sections of the United States, large quantities of the choicest goods are imported from abroad for this market. The largest House in the country, and perhaps the oldest, is located in this city. It was established in 1813, and by enterprise and prudence, has developed into its present proportions. The Firm occupies four buildings, two as warehouses and two for the transaction of its daily business. The clerical force of the establishment numbers seventy-two persons, in addition to which, seventy females are employed (in the Work Rooms) in the manufacture of Millinery. White Goods, an interest which is largely represented in many of our leading Jobbing Houses, has been made an especial feature of their business. In connection with this Establishment, is a Firm, engaged Extensively in the manufacture of Ladies' Hats, &c. These hats are made exclusively for the Millinery Establishment mentioned above, and during the months of March, April, May, June, September, and October, one hundred females are constantly engaged in their manufacture. It will thus be seen that a single establishment in our city for the manufacture and sale of Millinery, and the sale of White Goods, gives employment during the greater portion of the year to two hundred and fifty persons. Their importations are very large; two Buyers, one for the White Goods Department, and the other for the Millinery, being employed for the selection and purchase of foreign goods; and only such as are superior in quality and design to those manufactured in our own country are offered to the Trade in this city. The Southern trade with Baltimore in this branch of industry is very great; while of late years, extensive connections have been formed with the West, and a heavy business is done in the States of Ohio, Indiana, Kentucky, Kansas, and Missouri.

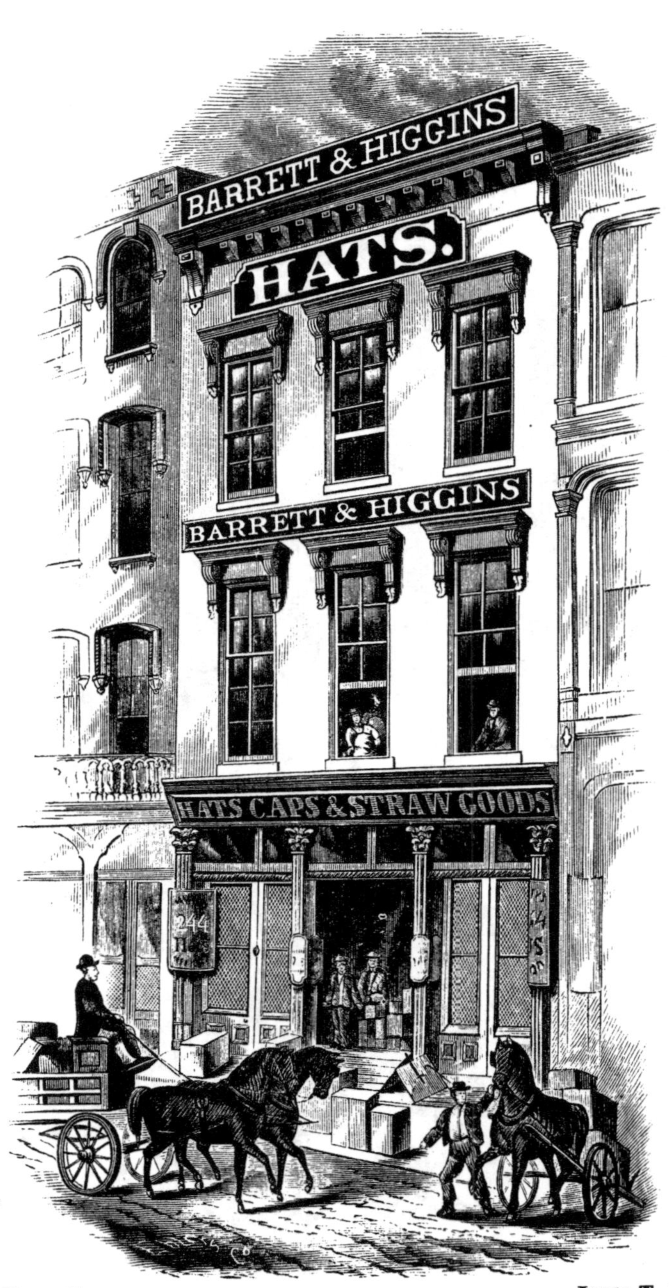
BARRETT & HIGGINS
HATS.
BARRETT & HIGGINS
HATS CAPS & STRAW GOODS
244

The Shoe and Leather Trade.

THE Shoe and Leather Trade of Baltimore is one of immense and daily increasing importance. Few persons in our midst are aware of its magnitude. It is authoritatively stated, that this interest is the largest after that of Agriculture, in America; the exhibit of official statistics placing it thirty-three per centum above those of cotton and wool combined. For many years New England, comparatively speaking, monopolized the trade in this country, and of late years Philadelphia acquired quite a reputation for fine work, in so much, that Southern and Western buyers were attracted to that city, to make their purchases of fancy goods. The Trade has recently undergone a very decided change in this regard. Tanneries have multiplied rapidly in Maryland, and factories for the manipulation of their products, have increased in corresponding ratio in our city. The Line of Steamers established between this Port and Boston, and known as the "Boston and Baltimore Steamship Company," has had much to do with this rapid increase in the trade; but the sagacity and energy of the gentlemen who have embraced this branch of business, have been the main springs of its prosperity. There are at present in Baltimore twenty-six wholesale Manufactories, working thirty-one McKay machines, each machine making from two hundred and fifty to three hundred pairs of Shoes per day, and arrangements are now being made to organize several new factories on a large scale. During the past year, great improvements have been made in the style and quality of the goods manufactured here. Southern and Western buyers need no longer go to Philadelphia, to obtain their supplies. As fine and stylish Shoes are made in Baltimore, as can be produced anywhere in the country; and this fact has come to the knowledge of the trade throughout the South and West, who are already displaying an appreciation of it, by resorting to this market to make their purchases. The terms obtained here, are as favorable as can be secured anywhere else in America. As an evidence of the solid growth of the trade, it may be as well to mention, that not a single failure has ever occurred among the manufacturers, and those who have begun with small capital, and very meagre stock, have been encouraged to enlarge their sphere of operations, and enter into competition with old and established Houses. About three years ago the Baltimore Shoe and Leather Board of Trade was established, and its influence has been very beneficial to the growth of this branch of industry. It has endeavored to bring about a proper state of feeling between the laborer and capitalist, and ward off the strikes, so destructive to the true interests of any business, and in the main it has been successful. The officers of the Shoe and Leather Association are as follows: President, Henry C. Smith; Vice Presidents, Jas Carey, Geo. J. Appold, T. J. Magruder, Wm. F. Larrabee; Recording Secretary, E. S. Allnutt; Corresponding Secretary, Arthur P. Baer; Treasurer, Wm. T. Dixon.

The manufacture of Boots and Shoes gives employment to at least four thousand persons, the average weekly salary being $22 for men, and $12 for women and girls. The Rubber trade, a branch of the Shoe business, has assumed large proportions. From a statement of the President of the Shoe and Leather Board of Trade, we give the following statistics for 1872:

Sales of boots and shoes by jobbers and retailers......	$8,500,000
Rubbers sold..	500,000
Manufacturers..	6,600,000
Auction sales..	500,000
	$16,100,000
Sales of leather about..............................	3,000,000
Sales of hides..	1,256,000
	$20,356,000

Most of the Leather (over two-thirds of the hides) is tanned in Maryland, and one-third is consumed by the factories of Baltimore, while a very large amount is exported to New York city, Philadelphia, Rochester and other places.

The rapid growth of the trade, made necessary about two years ago the addition by the Baltimore and Boston Steamship Company, of another first-class Steamer to their Line, making in all six fine Steamers plying between this Port and Boston; and these having been found insufficient to accomodate the rapidly increasing trade between these two Ports, another splendid Steamer has been ordered, and will be ready for the line by the first of September, 1873. As was said above, the gentlemen engaged in this branch of business by their high character, and substantial position in the community, are a sufficient guarantee to purchasers from abroad, that they will receive *here*, what they buy, and at prices which compare favorably with those elsewhere offered.

GEO. APPOLD & SONS, Hide and Leather Dealers, 8 and 10 Water Street, Tannery, North and W. Madison Streets.

CASH ADVANCED ON CONSIGNMENTS.

LARRABEE'S BLOCK.

E. LARRABEE & SONS,

WHOLESALE

LEATHER

AND

SHOE FINDINGS,

NO. 20 S. CALVERT STREET,

BALTIMORE.

Paper.

AMONG the many interests that have rapidly developed of late years in our city, may be mentioned the manufacture and sale of Paper. Fifteen years ago but one or two paper-mills were in operation in the State, while $200,000 would probably have covered the capital invested in its production and sale. To-day the capital employed in this branch of industry, will not fall far short of $4,000,000, and the gentlemen engaged in it are among our most substantial and reliable citizens. Numbers of mills have been established along the streams accessible from Baltimore. Large numbers of operatives are employed, and nearly all the different varieties of paper known to the Trade, are manufactured as cheaply and of as good quality as at any similar establishments in the country. In fact, with the exception of the finest kinds of writing paper, paper of any grade manufactured in our own State, can be bought in Balimore at as low prices as in any city in America, and the large wholesale dealers are ready to guarantee the statement. Straw wrapping Paper that originally came exclusively from New York is now manufactured in such quantities by our wholesale dealers, as to render the home market entirely independent. Straw-Print, Rag-Print, No. 2 Book, No. 1 Super, are all staple productions of the mills; and several large establishments are now engaged in the manufacture of bogus Manilla and No. 1 Manilla. In the single article of Printing-paper, upwards of 50,000 pounds are manufactured daily in this State. Indeed in the manufacture of Book and Printing paper, New York is made to pay tribute to our city. The mills engaged in supplying the wholesale dealers in Baltimore, are extensive, and fitted with the most costly and thoroughly improved modern machinery. They are located upon streams immediately adjacent to the different lines of Railroad leading to the city. The location of Baltimore is favorable to an indefinite expansion of their numbers, as the demands of the trade increase. For the finer grades of Writing-paper, agencies are established in this city by the manufacturers, and such goods can be purchased here at factory prices. Paper is now sent from Baltimore to all parts of the country, and the limits of the trade are enlarging every day.

In addition to the above, the finest classes of French and German Paper are imported to this city, and distributed to all sections of the United States.

11

Monograms, Crests and Coats-of-Arms.

161 W. BALTIMORE ST., BALTIMORE.

SOUTHERN DEPOT FOR
BANK, RAILROAD AND OFFICE STATIONERY.

We have Our Own Steam Printing Office, AND BLANK BOOK BINDERY.

And Initial Stamping AND COPPER-PLATE PRESSES

All in One Building,

Under Our Personal Supervision.

Employ the best workmen, use the best material; and can compete successfully with any house in the country, in price and quality of work. Estimates cheerfully made.

SEND for CATALOGUE and SAMPLES of WORK.

Paper Bags.

THE manufacture of Paper Bags is of recent origin. Only a few years ago they were unknown, and dealers seemed content to wrap their goods and wares in the old-fashioned paper bundles. But American genius, which contemplates convenience, as well as principles of science and mechanics, applied itself to the comfort of store-keepers and customers, with complete success. The Paper Bag now universally used, is an indispensable requisite to the business, and the economy of home. The most perfect Bag in use, is the invention of an American Lady. The machine which cuts, prepares, folds, and pastes the bag with the square ends is her invention; for which she should receive the daily thanks of sellers and buyers.

All articles designed for shipment or transportation, or home consumption, are packed neatly in appropriate bags; hence their manufacture has become a very extensive interest, and some of our largest Houses have made a specialty of them, with an invested capital of upwards of $250,000. The demand for them increases proportionately with growth of business, and during the past year we manufactured about one hundred millions, the sales of which amounted to $400,000, requiring about 800 tons of paper. A large portion of these were shipped to New York; and great quantities sold to the South and West, besides those used at home. On account of the great facilities which Baltimore possesses for the manufacture of Paper, and Paper-Bags, its Paper mills, which line the never failing streams of Maryland, its exhaustless stores of raw-material, and the cheapness of labor, render it the best market for the supply of this indispensable Paper Package.

Cotton.

THE Cotton Trade of Baltimore, is a growing interest. For many years, little was done in this great Staple, but the increased facilities for shipment to this Port, the enterprise and thrift of the men engaged in the trade, and the admirable system of warehouse storage recently introduced, have given an impetus to the Cotton business which promises to make it a very powerful auxiliary to the commercial prosperity of our city. A Cotton Exchange has lately been established, which publishes a daily Market Statement, and in many ways facilitates trade in this important branch of industry. Its officers are Messrs. George P. Tiffany, President; Geo. R. Gaither Jr., Vice-President; Jos. S. Whedbee, Treasurer; Fred'k. G. Whelan, Secretary; and its members are gentlemen of the highest standing and excellence in the community. The receipts of Cotton for the present year have greatly exceeded those of any similar period in the past; and the demand for exportation, and for home consumption, by the immense factories in and around our city for the manufacture of Cotton Duck and the lighter Cotton goods, leaves no doubt of the very rapid increase of the trade in the future. The system of warehouse storage established in 1867 under a charter from the State of Maryland by a number of our leading capitalists, is superior perhaps in perfection of detail and security, to that of any city in the country. Some of our leading merchants are engaged in the Cotton business, and they can now advance money on consignments with security to themselves, and their patrons. When the Cotton reaches this port, it can be stored at comparatively little expense in the vast reservoirs of the Company, where it may remain for a mere trifle, until a favorable opportunity offers for its disposal. In the meantime cotton-certificates are issued by the Baltimore Warehouse Company, incorporated 1867, which can be transferred as other negotiable securities. The capital of the company is $1,000,000, and the flattering auspices under which it was inaugurated leaves no doubt of its success in the future and its beneficial influence upon the Cotton trade of our city. In connection with the Cotton trade of Baltimore, a Cotton-Press has been established, with all the modern improvements in machinery, and with a capacity sufficient to accommodate the wants of the trade for many years to come. From data before us and for reasons which have been repeatedly urged, we think it safe to say, that Baltimore is destined in the future to become one of the great Cotton marts of the world.

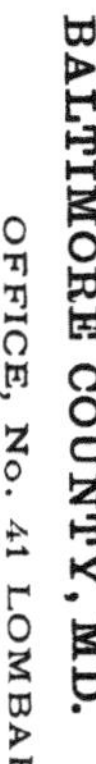

DRUID MILLS, BALTIMORE COUNTY, MD. GAMBRILL, SONS & CO.

OFFICE, No. 41 LOMBARD STREET.

Cotton Duck.

PRIOR to 1839 all or nearly all the Cotton Duck manufactured in this country was made by the Passaic and Phœnix Mills in Paterson, New Jersey, and the exorbitant prices demanded by these monopolists, did much to check the trade in this article. To-day, two-thirds of the Duck made in the United States is manufactured in the vicinity of Baltimore, and the above mentioned mills have discontinued its production. In the year 1839 the property known as the Old White Hall Flouring Mill, on Jones' Falls, was purchased by one of our distinguished citizens and converted into a Cotton Factory. The enterprize prospered, and in 1843 the Woodberry Factory was built, and its capacity doubled in 1845. The Mount Vernon Factory was constructed at the same time. The Old White Hall was burnt in 1852, and the Clipper Mill, a factory of great capacity, was erected on its site with such expedition, that it was in running order six months after the conflagration. This mill was destroyed by fire in 1866, but subsequently rebuilt, and its capacity doubled. The Druid Mill was commenced in 1865, and enlarged in 1872. The latter is at present the largest Cotton Duck Mill in the country. In addition, there are now at work in the vicinity of Woodberry, the Mount

Vernon Factory No. 2, the Park Mill, and the Washington Factory, all engaged in the manufacture of Cotton Duck.

Of course the war had a depressing effect upon the production of this commodity. Our domestic mills were cut off from their Southern supply of the raw material—Cotton advanced fabulously in price, and Russian and English looms for the time practically supplied the market. In 1866, the price of cotton fell rapidly—the new crop from the South was brought to the factories, and since that time foreign goods have almost been driven from the market.

The process through which the raw material passes before it is converted into Duck may be interesting to our readers. The cotton is first cleaned by machinery, and after seeds, lumps and dirt are removed, it is transferred to carding machines, which perform, on an immense scale, the operation which was formerly slowly effected by hand. It passes thence through several machines, by which the roll of fibres is gradually reduced in size, and becomes at last a firm, fine thread. A number of these are then twisted together, to make a cord of sufficient strength, and of these latter the "warp," or foundation of the fabric is formed; other cords, wound on bobbins, supply the "woof" or filling. These woven together by the looms make the cloth complete, and it is then rolled into bolts, and packed in bales for shipment. All this necessarily requires an immense amount of intricate machinery, and it is estimated that a force of two thousand two hundred horse power is used in these Mills. In addition to the manufacture of Cotton-Duck, Fishing Nets are made here by machinery, the only place in the United States where this is done to any great extent. Upwards of 25,000 bales or more than 12,000,000 pounds of cotton are consumed annually by these Mills. They employ fully 1,800 hands, and minister to the support of at least 5,000 persons. The Cotton-Duck is used extensively in the manufacture of sails, awnings, bags, and for a number of other purposes. It is unnecessary to add that the South and West can be supplied in this market on the most reasonable terms.

Cotton Bags.

AS an appendage to the manufacture of Cotton goods in the city of Baltimore, and especially to the manufacture of Cotton-Duck, the preparation of grain Bags and Sacks demands particular notice. Baltimore is favorably located for their manufacture. The many mill streams in the neighborhood of the city, the numerous cotton mills in and immediately around it, and the superiority of the heavier class of domestics especially suitable as material for their construction, enable the manufacturers to compete successfully with any of the Eastern cities; while the moderate cost of living, and low rents, give the trade an advantage over New York and Boston. The immense amount of wheat and corn which passes through, or is manipulated in our market, creates a demand for the manufacture of grain Bags and Sacks, which would at all times cause a degree of activity with the merchant engaged in that trade; but a system prevails at this Port which renders the market very particularly active. A very extensive business is done in hiring Sacks for shipment to Europe, the owner of the Sacks shipping under his own Bill of Lading, in the same manner as the dealer ships his grain. The capital invested in the trade is very large, all Jute Goods are landed by our European Steamers at lower freights than elsewhere. The facilities for the manufacture of the Bags are first-class, and the character of the men engaged in this branch of industry is a complete guarantee that persons dealing with them are sure to get what they buy. In this particular branch of manufacture, the Baltimore article can readily compete with that of New York or any other.

Curled Hair.

ABOUT the year 1836, a young German came to this country and shortly afterwards established a small factory for the manufacture of Hair, Bristles, &c., on Colston's Hill, near the Hookstown Road. The life of the factory was healthy from the first, and its business gradually enlarged, until in 1847 the location was insufficient for its pressing requirements. A lot of ground was purchased on the Frederick Road, and a new factory erected. From that time to the present the increase of the trade has been very rapid. The various uses to which Hair and Bristles are put, the rapid development of the country, and the incessant demand for goods of this sort for upholstering purposes and brush materials, and the toilet generally, caused an expansion of the trade, which rendered it difficult at times, to supply the orders that came to the factory. Its capacity was enlarged, agencies were created in the leading cities of the west for the procurement of raw materials; tenant houses were erected for the employees, warehouses for the storage of both crude and manufactured goods; and now a thriving village crowns the location which but a few years ago was a barren plat of ground. Others encouraged by the success of the young German, have invested money in the business, and a number of smaller factories have sprung into existance, whose business is only circumscribed by their capacity.

The factory on the Frederick road, known as Wilkens' Factory, turns out 40,000 pounds of manufactured goods per week; and it is estimated that at least seven hundred operatives are employed, and several million of dollars are invested in the business. The manufactured goods are consigned to Retail Merchants and Upholsterers throughout the United States; and large quantities are exported for consumption abroad.

The curled and manufactured Hair produced by the factories of Baltimore is unsurpassed for excellence, and the market price is lower than in any other city in the United States, because of the vast capital invested, the extensive experience, and thorough knowledge of the business, possessed by those engaged in its production.

Leaf Tobacco.

THE Tobacco market of this city has been of paramount importance at all times since the commencement of its history. In colonial times and indeed for a long period afterwards, it was the only crop raised in this State, by which she was known to outsiders, insomuch that the lands were impoverished, and farmers and planters driven to the cultivation of other products, to restore the soil to its original fertility. Early in the history of the State, inspection laws were adopted by the Legislature for the protection of planters and buyers. These laws were perhaps the most judicious of their kind ever devised, and have remained in force with but little alteration to the present moment. Under them, five large warehouses have been established in Baltimore, at points convenient to the shipping. The manner of inspection is so simple, and apparently equitable, that it may not be out of place to give a brief description of the process. One head of a hogshead of Tobacco having been removed and the hoops loosend, the hogshead is turned over, and the entire casing lifted off the Tobacco. The compact mass thus exposed, is broken into at five different points with an iron bar, and a sample taken from each opening.

An average of each of these samples is selected, and the whole tied together with a strong tape, sealed and labelled. The casing is replaced, and the hogshead coopered according to its necessities. The samples chosen and made official, are regarded as establishing the grade of the Tobacco, as well as the quality of the packing, and by these the sales are made. The fees, waste and cost of storage, &c., are so insignificant when compared with methods of inspection in other cities, that though the policy of the State of late years has been to discourage governmental inspections, the system with reference to *Tobacco* has not been disturbed. Four of the five Inspectors are taken from the rural districts, where the wiles of politics usually give place to integrity and fair dealing; and the consequence has been that with the rarest exceptions, the offices have been filled by high-toned, honorable gentlemen engaged in the cultivation of the plant themselves, and thoroughly competent to discharge the duties which pertain to the office.

The increase of the trade in this city, and the insufficient accommodations of the present warehouses, have led to the erection of another which will be completed in a few months. During the year 1872, there were inspected 51,209 hogsheads of Tobacco, in addition to 5,682 hogsheads remaining in the warehouses on the 1st of January of that year. The Foreign shipments during that period, and which were made to a large number of European ports were 49,983 hogsheads. The quality of the Tobacco grown in Maryland, and that brought to this market from Ohio, and Kentucky, is of coarse, heavy grade, and is consumed principally in portions of France, and Germany, where the people care more for quantity than quality. Shipments have been retarded to some extent by the scarcity of tonnage, but the increased facilities afforded by the improvements in the harbor to be completed by the first of May, and the very rapid augmentation of the shipping in the past few months, will lead in the near future, to a very large expansion of the trade.

Manufactured Tobacco.

OUR City has always been one of the leading markets for Manufactured Tobacco. It is contiguous to Virginia, North Carolina, and the great sections of America noted for the production of the best Tobacco on this continent, and also for the manufacture of the best Chewing and Smoking Tobacco in the world. Thus located, Baltimore commands a large portion of this trade, and is in reality the best distributing market in the country. The Commission and Jobbing Trade, with heavy capital is enabled to carry large stocks, and with the forwarding facilities of rail and water, gives us superior advantages over any other city. We have also several very large factories for the manufacture of Smoking Tobacco, Fine-cut, and Snuffs, with advantages unsurpassed by any others elsewhere. The Brands of these have attained a wide reputation in this country and Europe.

Cigars are extensively manufactured in this city, and their superior quality has gained for them, great popularity at home and abroad.

Responsible agencies of the Tobacco Manufacturers of any prominence in the trade of the country are established here, thus giving additional value and attraction to the Baltimore Market.

Lumber.

THE Lumber Trade of Baltimore city, is very great. We are so favorably located for the prosecution of the business, it would be really strange were this not the case. The Chesapeake Bay affords easy access to the vast Lumber regions of Virginia and North Carolina; the Susquehanna drains the extensive woodlands of Pennsylvania, while the railroad corporations which centre in Baltimore stretch out their arms into the almost limitless forests of West Virginia, Ohio and Indiana. In addition to the requirements for building purposes, this branch of industry has been greatly extended of late because of the vast increase in the number of Houses engaged in the Furniture Trade, the enlargement of the business of those already established, and the springing up in our midst of factories for the manufacture of Mouldings, Ovals, Mirror and Picture Frames, &c., &c.

The last few years have witnessed a decided change in popular taste with reference to the material out of which furniture is constructed. Fashion has greatly diminished the use of rose-wood and mahogany, and hence their importation is mainly for veneering purposes. With the increase in wealth and the development of taste, wants have become general which were formerly confined within a narrow circle, and the demand for highly wrought mouldings, handsome frames, passe-partouts, &c., has necessitated the establishment of extensive factories to meet it, where work of the most finished description is turned out.

Walnut, Ash, Poplar and White Pine are now used almost exclusively by furniture dealers, and immense quantities reach the market annually. The best Walnut is brought from the States of Ohio and Indiana; vast quantities of Poplar come from the forests of West Virginia, while the States of Virginia, North Carolina, Georgia and Florida furnish Yellow Pine, from the last two of which is obtained the finest material to be found in the world. Ash and White Pine reach this market in large quantities from Pennsylvania, Ohio and Indiana. About thirty large Houses are engaged in the Lumber business in this city with an immense aggregate capital. The gentlemen who compose the above firms are among our most reliable and honored citizens.

One hundred million feet of White Pine, one hundred million feet of Yellow Pine, and fifty million feet of other Woods, including Walnut,

Poplar, Ash, &c., are received in Baltimore annually. Much of the Wood is dressed in Baltimore and shipped from here to other places. The machinery used in the trade is of the most highly improved character, and the number of employees very large. The workmanship is superior, and the trade offer inducements to purchasers equal to those extended in any other market in the country.

It is a fact worthy of mention, as showing not only the facilities of the trade, but the reciprocity of the different sections of our country, that large quantities of the Lumber product of the South, Yellow Pine and Cypress, are sent to the distant cities of the West and North-West, where it is used almost exclusively in car building, and for other manufacturing purposes, in which cheapness, durability and strength, are essential qualifications. This Lumber is manufactured to order at the Southern mills, shipped direct to the consumer, and is ready for use upon receipt. The orders are received in Baltimore by those dealers who have large interests in the South, and of course minister to the importance of our City. The trade is growing rapidly and will ere long demonstrate the fact that the Western Lumber dealer appreciates the Lumber product of the South as thoroughly as we value the White Pine forests of the North and West. In addition to the Lumber Trade carried on with the South and West, large quantities of White and Yellow Pine are shipped to the West Indies and South America.

Agricultural Implements.

THE honorable position which the Science of Agriculture has occupied in Maryland in conjunction with the other Southern States, has made Baltimore at all times during her history an extensive market for Agricultural Implements. The present is unquestionably the era of improvement in labor-saving machinery. The farmers of Maryland, generally educated and cultivated, have not been slow to avail themselves of the advantages which have been thereby presented.

They early found that their lands, along with the saving of labor by the use of implements, exhibited also an increase of productiveness which amply compensated them for an appreciation of the prices of machinery. This exercised a fostering influence over the establishments engaged in their manufacture, and gave to the trade an impetus, which by judicious foresight and energy the manufacturers have been able to enlarge, until to-day our City ranks far ahead of most of the large cities in America; and surpassed by few if any, in the production of these essentials to farming. In fact, East of the Ohio no city can compete with Baltimore in this regard.

Ten large Houses are at present doing a thriving business in this branch of industry with a very handsome working capital, and a number of hands averaging four hundred. Formerly each House embraced in its operations all the various implements used in Agriculture, as also Seed and other goods belonging to that pursuit. The introduction of steam and the vast improvements in machinery made it cheaper for Houses to select a specialty and follow it. In this way certain labor-saving machines are manufactured at cheaper rates than formerly, and in a style excelled nowhere on this continent. Of course the number of machines or implements manufactured here has been reduced; but the usefulness of those produced has been proportionately increased, and the general dimensions of the trade greatly enlarged, while factories for all the very best labor-saving machines manufactured in the United States have here established agencies, where they can be purchased at the factory rates.

All the Agricultural establishments of Baltimore offer the strongest inducements to purchasers from abroad in the way of choice and carefully selected seed, large quantities of which, when not produced under favorable auspices in this country, are imported expressly for the Baltimore market. The annual sales in this branch of industry are very heavy and rapidly increasing, annually amounting at present to fully $3,000,000. Large invoices of Agricultural Implements, Seeds, &c., are shipped to the Southern States, and along the line of the Atlantic coast, in fact through all the country east of the Ohio. In this department of trade, Baltimore affords to dealers, a market equal in quality and prices, to any other in the United States.

Sash Factories.

SINCE the introduction of steam-power into the ordinary pursuits of life, vast improvements have been made in carpentry. Especially has this been the case with reference to the manufacture of Sash, Window Frames, Doors, Blinds &c. So great have been the advances in this department of industry, that the humblest and cheapest dwelling erected in the larger cities at this present writing, will compare favorably in interior finish with the most gorgeous edifices of former times. Baltimore has kept pace with other cities in this regard.

Thirteen Sash Factories, employing upwards of seven hundred hands, and manipulating $1,000,000 of capital, are at present in operation in this city. For fifty years the business of wood-working has been one of our most active industries, but in the last five years the trade has trebled. The quality of the work done by our factories is fully up to the standard established in other cities. Offices, churches, and public buildings are fitted by the trade, in a style of taste and elegance unsurpassed elsewhere, and which has commanded the admiration of parties from abroad. Baltimore has great facilities in the way of securing lumber of the most available description, and upon the most advantageous terms. The factories engaged in the business, turn out all kinds of work, and offer as great inducements to purchasers as can be obtained in any other city in America. As large as the demand is for home consumption it by no means disposes of the material turned out by these establishments; and large quantities of Sash, Window Blinds, and general Finishings for buildings, are shipped to the Southern States, South America and the West Indies.

Furniture.

THE manufacture of Furniture is usually a prominent feature in the business of large cities. Our own is not behind her sisters in this regard. The manufacture and sale of all kinds of Furniture have been for years a leading and rapidly increasing interest in Baltimore. Our facilities are superior to those of most American cities. For the lighter kinds of Cabinet Furniture the very best article of yellow-pine can be obtained via the Chesapeake Bay, from the forests of lower Maryland, Virginia, and North Carolina. For other classes of Furniture the forests of West Virginia furnish an inexhaustible supply of soft poplar, which by easy and cheap transportation over the Baltimore and Ohio Railroad, can be obtained on the most reasonable terms, while the competition between the western sections of this Road and the Pennsylvania Central, enables our manufacturers to obtain their supplies of black-walnut from the forests of Indiana, at less cost than those of the North and East, whose distance is more remote. This, in addition to the fact that the cost of living and labor is cheaper in Baltimore, has led to a very rapid development of the business; and in the last five years the manufacture and sale of Furniture have been more than doubled; while many new firms have been added to those already in existence.

As an indication of the enlargement of the trade and the low prices in this city, it may be stated that during the past year extensive orders for Sewing Machine Frames have been received by our manufacturers from the large towns of the North, and have been filled so satisfactorily as to lead to a repetition of the orders. Every style of Furniture, from the richest and most chaste designs for parlors, drawing-rooms, chambers, and offices, to the less pretentious cabinet setts, is manufactured with equal care and skill. Those engaged in the business have displayed great enterprise; and have not contented themselves with their own resources in the selection of patterns, but have made it a point to visit localities where Furniture is largely manufactured, and study the ingenuity and tastes of other sections. Thus the most fastidious and refined taste can be gratified in our city.

A certain amount of European Furniture is imported here, to supply the demand of those who can afford the luxury of foreign styles, but the skill of our handicraftmen has so thoroughly kept pace with the spirit of modern improvement that this is generally conceded to be totally unnecessary. From accurate information, we are able to state that fully $1,500,000 are invested in the business, 2,000 hands are employed, and the annual sales amount in the aggregate to $3,000,000. Besides the local trade, vast quantities of Furniture are shipped from this city to the South and West. During the year 1872, shipments were made to the West Indies and South America, giving promise of a valuable trade to that direction.

Pianos.

THE wonderful advances made during the present century in all departments of industry have been no-where more marked than in the development and improvement of Pianos—and it is a matter of just pride to Americans, that the world is indebted to this country, for many of the advantages which modern instruments possess. The largest Piano factories on the globe are located in the United States, and owing to the thrift and independence of the laboring classes, and the facilities for advancement offered them through our institutions, and mode of government, and the elevation of taste thus acquired, the number of these instruments sold annually is immense. During the year 1865, one hundred and eighteen thousand, two hundred and eighty Pianos were made in this country, and the trade in these instruments amounted to $59,284,673. What the increase has been since that date is a matter of conjecture, but the fact that the Piano has become almost as necessary in the humblest households, as the most useful article of furniture, forbids the idea that there has been any diminution in the statistics of the trade.

Baltimore has obtained her full share of this great and increasing business. There are a number of factories in this city, among which is the establishment of Wm. Knabe & Co., one of the largest in the United States. William Knabe, the founder of the firm, (since deceased), came to this country and commenced the manufacture of Pianos on Liberty street, in 1837. Their beginings were humble—large investments in an untried branch of trade were then unheard of, and a wide-spread and deeply rooted prejudice existed in favor of articles from abroad. The superior delicacy of tone, which still so distinguishes the instruments of the Firm, gradually attracted the attention of competent judges and the germ of a factory rapidly developed into mammoth proportions. The great increase in the business of the Firm, necessitated the abandonment of their original location, and the selection of another site; and since 1855, their factory has been in operation on Eutaw street. Wm. Knabe & Co. manufacture annually from 1,500 to 2,000 Grand and Square Pianos which are shipped to all portions of the United States, but principally to the South and West, with which sections their business relations are of an extensive character.

The prices of these instruments vary from $500 to $1,500. The difference in price, is occasioned chiefly by the outside ornamentation, carving, tracing &c.; the cheaper instruments being as melodious and powerful as the most costly. The advantages claimed for them by Knabe & Co., are that their method of constructing the "action" is peculiar, which imparts to the instrument an unsurpassed delicacy and fullness of tone; that the woods used in their construction are selected with the utmost care, and with all the known tests, and are thoroughly seasoned before being worked up; and that before a Piano is taken from the factory, the proprietors always assure themselves of its excellence and durability. That this is no idle boast is attested by the reception of more than eighty medals and premiums at various exhibitions and by the approval of such artists as Thalberg, Gottschalk, Heller, Strakosch, Marmontel, Vieuxtemps and others, and also, by the reception of a number of orders for work from distinguished artists in Europe. The firm has a branch establishment in New York, and an agency in Boston.

Musical Instruments.

MOST of the different varieties of Musical Instruments are manufactured in Baltimore, and in many instances rare skill is displayed in their production. For twenty years the manufacture of Organs has formed an important feature among the industries of the city and of late the orders from neighboring states have attested the estimation in which they are held for finish and excellence of tone. Church Organs, ranging in price from $1,000 to $50,000 are constructed here and large numbers of them are shipped to the South and West, and some because of their tone and compass are sent to Eastern markets. In a number of our finest churches are to be seen specimens of the Organs manufactured in this city.

Jewelry.

AMONG the many branches of industry which minister to the importance and add to the wealth of our city may be mentioned the manufacture and sale of Jewelry. A number of large houses are established in Baltimore, with extensive capital, and employing many hands. All the different styles of Jewelry known to the trade are manufactured with skill and neatness, and our Jewelers have always endeavored successfully to meet the popular taste so excessively variable in this regard. The various precious stones of which large and costly stocks are always on hand, are set in Baltimore with an elegance and finish that cannot be surpassed. Silver ware is manufactured here to a very considerable extent, and as every place has its peculiar styles, supplies of Baltimore-made Ware are eagerly sought by Jewelers from the neighboring cities. Watches of all kinds, both of American and foreign manufacture, from the most expensive to the least costly, are sold by the trade as low as can be obtained from the manufacturer. In addition, the rarest of foreign Bijoutry is imported direct to this city, and the shelves of our best Jewelers are beautifully adorned with these articles. A prominent characteristic of this branch of industry in Baltimore is the thorough reliability of the gentlemen engaged in it. They are among our most highly esteemed citizens and purchasers coming to this city can be assured that they get what they bny.

Established 1800.

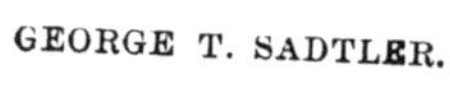

GEORGE T. SADTLER.

GEORGE W. SADTLER.

G. T. SADTLER & SONS,

OPTICIANS,

No. 212 West Baltimore Street, Baltimore,

Importers, Manufacturers and Dealers in

Spectacles, Watches, Jewelry, Silver Ware, &c.

Special attention paid to adaptation of Glasses to the Eye.

Prompt attention given to repairing Watches and Jewelry.

GEO. W. WEBB,

Goldsmith and Jeweller,

(Adjoining the Carrollton Hotel,)

DEALER IN

DIAMONDS, RICH JEWELRY, FINE WATCHES, CLOCKS & BRONZES, STERLING SILVER AND PLATED WARE.

Particular attention is paid to neatness and durability in the manufacture and repair of Jewelry. Watches repaired by experienced workmen.

CHARLES. W. BLAKE.

PRACTICAL.

Watchmaker & Jeweler,

AND DEALER IS

FINE WATCHES, JEWELRY, SILVER AND PLATED WARES,

No. 3 North Charles Street,

BALTIMORE.

Clocks, Watches and Jewelry Carefully Repaired.

Plated Ware.

THE manufacture of Plated Ware was begun in this City about twenty years ago on a small scale. The care and skill displayed in its production led to a gradual expansion of the business, and at present Baltimore can boast of an extensive establishment fitted with all the modern improvements in machinery, and with a capacity for all classes of work. Gold and Silver Plated Work and Britannia Wares are produced, which for excellence of workmanship and beauty of design will compare favorably with similar articles in any portion of the country.

The fact that the styles of the various factories in America are very different, and that dealers are compelled to have samples of each, has led to the introduction of Baltimore Plated Ware in all sections of the country, and it has been received with favor wherever sent. The business is largely on the increase and dealers can supply themselves in this market upon terms quite as reasonable as are offered elsewhere.

Tin.

THE Tin Trade of Baltimore, allusion to which has already been made in a previous article, has wonderfully developed in the last few years. The demand for Tin is always large in a great city, where it is so lavishly used for household purposes,and of late for coverings for the roofs of buildings; but this demand has been measurably increased of late by the rapid multiplication of oyster and fruit packing houses, and their immense consumption of the article in the course of their business. As no Tin mines exist in this country, the raw material is of course imported from abroad; but the favorable terms under which it can be brought to this market has led to its importation in large quantities. We give the statistics of importation from the books of the Custom House for the year 1871, and the first ten months of 1872:

For 1871.

	Boxes.	*Value.*
January........	150	$820.00
February.......	16,785	93,189.00
March...........	[illegible],900	170,648.00
April............	13,817	79,635.00
May..............	14,387	83,042.00
June.............	8,550	48,058.00
July	9,928	55,160.00
August.........	13,825	81,116.00
September.......	18,197	104,122.00
October.........	11,582	66,742.00
November......	10,289	58,224.00
December......	18,186	106,194.00
Total.........	165,596	$946,950.00

For the first ten months of 1872.

	Boxes.	*Value.*
January.........	16,261	$98,052.00
February.......	14,723	98,508.00
March...........	18,242	132,112.00
April............	15,898	119,933.00
May..............	25,452	205,489.00
June.............	8,186	73,860.00
July.............	11,095	101,880.00
August	20,668	188,246.00
September.......	29,562	272,921.00
October.........	18,569	164,518.00
Total.........	178,656	$1,455,519.00

It will be seen from the above that the importation of this article has increased in value in the first ten months of the year 1872, $508,569 over the entire importation of 1871. The demand for the raw material is increasing with each successive year. Oyster and fruit packing houses are springing up in the city, while the large wholesale houses which deal in the article are multiplying in number and extending their business. All materials requiring Tin for their manufacture are made in Baltimore in a style of finish and excellence comparable with any other sections of the country, and at rates which offer inducements to purchasers. Besides supplying the demand for the article in this city the wholesale trade is constantly in receipt of orders from Virginia, West Virginia, West Pennsylvania and all the Southern States.

Type Foundries.

AMONG the other industries in which Baltimore has made some progress, is Type manufacture. Two factories are in operation, employing a number of hands, and absorbing considerable capital. All the various styles of type are manufactured with skill and elegance, that rival the workmanship of any similar factories in the larger cities of this country, and orders are filled as cheaply here as elsewhere.

Brass and Bell Founding.

THE Brass and Bell Founding interest has been largely developed in Baltimore. The introduction of gas in our cities and towns, the extension of water facilities, and the almost universal application of gas and water to public and private buildings have created an enormous demand for the necessary fixtures, and have led to such expansion of the resources and capacity of the establishments in this city as enables them to compare very favorably with those in any other section of the country. All articles pertaining to this branch of industry, viz: Plumbers' Brass Work, Water, Gas and Steam Fixtures, and Apparatus and Bells of all descriptions, are manufactured by them in quantities to suit the increasing trade, and with a perfection and finish which are unsurpassed.

The metals of which the articles in this department are composed, such as tin, zinc, copper, &c., are usually obtained direct, and plumbers' earthenware is imported from Europe. So that Baltimore possesses every facility for supplying the trade at the lowest prices, and it gives us pleasure to state that the trade is rapidly increasing, especially with the South and West.

Henry McShane & Co.'s Brass Works were established in 1856. The firm has rapidly enlarged its sphere of operations, and is to-day one of the largest establishments of that character in the United States. The Works are located on North street, the building occupying a front two hundred and fifteen feet with a depth of one hundred and fifty feet. Two hundred and sixty hands are employed by the firm, of whom sixty are engaged in their Phœnix Iron Works, Holliday street, where six tons of iron are run down daily into light castings for plumbers' and machinists' use. Electro-plating in silver and gold forms a very important feature of the work of this firm.

The establishment of Regester & Sons, on Holliday street, is very extensive, and employs a large number of operatives, many of them skilled workmen. A special feature of this Foundry is its manufacture of Bells, the excellence of workmanship displayed therein recommending the firm throughout the country.

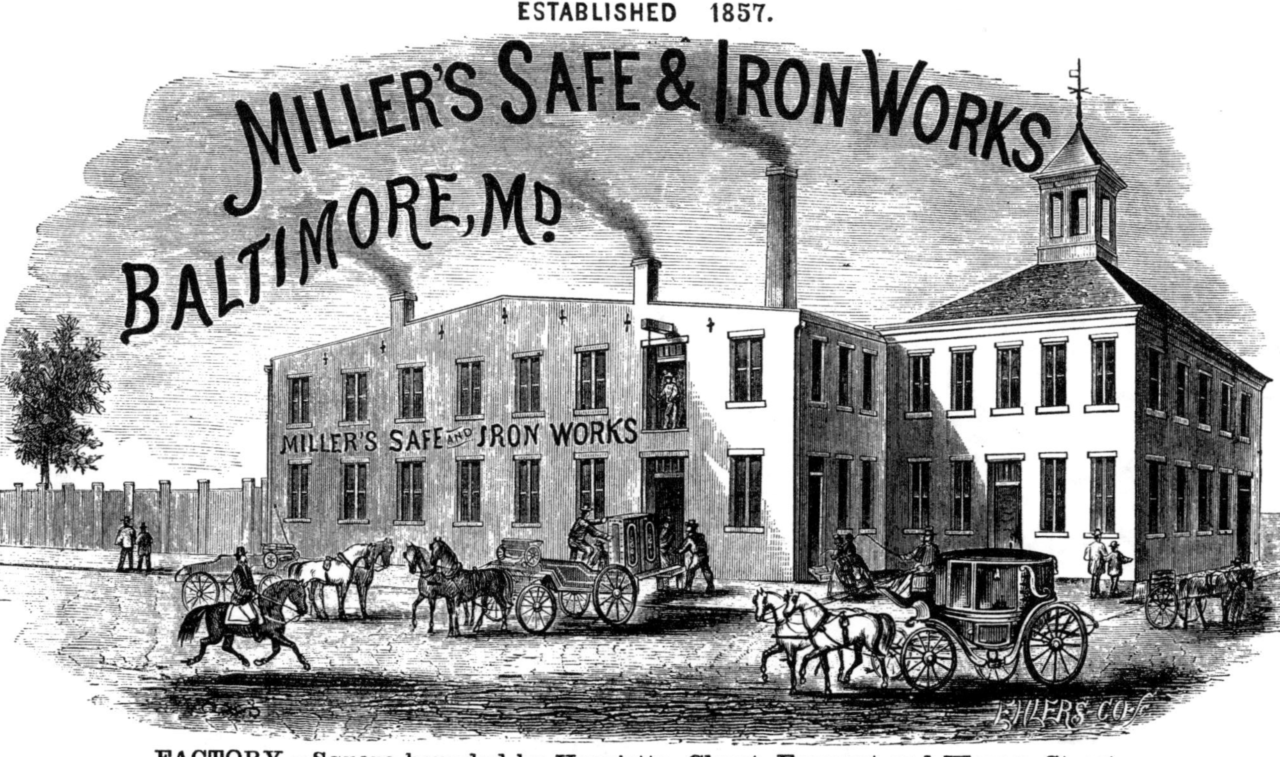

FACTORY.—Square bounded by Henrietta, Claret, Fremont and Warner Streets.

Iron.

THE Iron Trade of Baltimore is one of her most prominent interests. The very ground upon which the city is built is an ore-bank, and the neighboring hills teem with this valuable metal in the crude state, ready to be manipulated at the least possible expense, for the purposes of trade. The Iron made from this ore has the highest reputation for car-wheels and malleable purposes. It is known all over this country and is in great demand from the extreme East to the West, being considered by the trade superior to all other Iron for such uses. The numerous water courses in the vicinity of Baltimore immediately adjacent to the main lines of communication, offer admirable facilities for smelting ore, while the railroads running directly to the coal mines, or the localities where charcoal is prepared, reduce the cost and transportation of fuel to a minimum figure, which enables manufacturers to produce the metal with profit to themselves, and at reasonable rates to consumers. The furnaces which supply the trade of Baltimore are twenty-six in number, of which twenty-three are at present in blast, and doing a very active and increasing business. Of the above, fifteen are charcoal furnaces, four anthracite, and three are coke. The production of Iron in the aggregate, amounted in 1872, to 54,000 tons. In connection with these furnaces are a number of Bar and Plate Iron Works, which do a heavy business—one company alone running four Plate Mills, which yield an annual product of $1,000,000 in value. Aside from the Rolling Mills of the great railroad corporations, which have termini in this city, there are works for the manufacture of Railroad and Plated Iron, Car-Wheels, Rivets and Spikes, Boilers, Steam Engines, &c., &c., which in magnitude and excellence of workmanship will compare favorably with similar manufacturing establishments in any portion of the country.

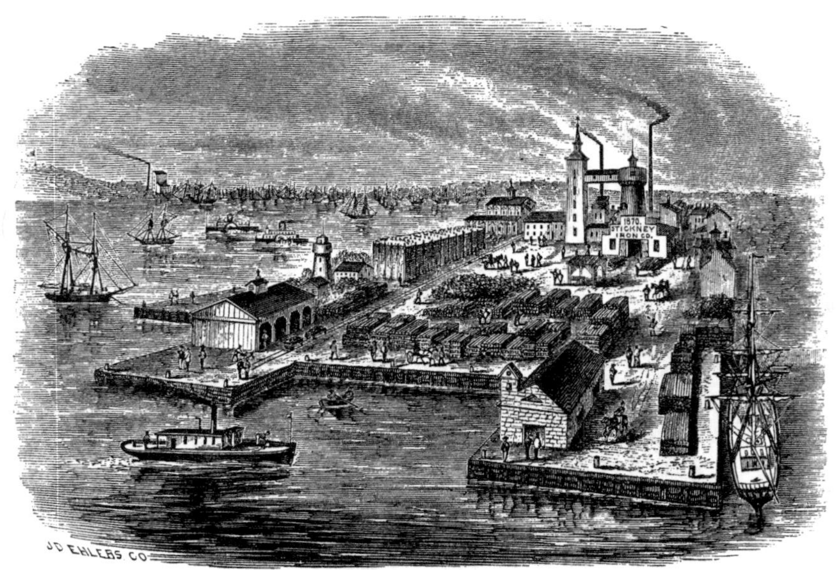

STICKNEY IRON COMPANY,

CLINTON STREET, CANTON.

CHARCOAL PIG IRON.

J. H. STICKNEY, PRESIDENT. WILLIAM OLIVER, JR., MANAGER.
WILLIAM HARVEY, SECRETARY. REED, STICKNEY & CO., SELLING AGENTS.

OFFICE,—No. 42 SECOND STREET,

BALTIMORE.

TROXELL, HANDY & GREER,

AGENTS FOR

ANTHRACITE, CHARCOAL AND COKE PIG IRON,

AND

CHARCOAL HAMMERED BLOOMS.

Dealers in Bar, Bundle and Sheet Iron; Cut Nails and Spikes; Horse and Mule Shoes, &c.

Corner Charles and German Sts. BALTIMORE.

THOMAS C. BASSHOR & CO.

28 Light Street, Baltimore,

Manufacturers and Dealers in

BOILERS, ENGINES, PUMPS,

Plain and Galvanized Iron Pipe,

Fittings, Brass Work, Heaters, &c.

Steam Heating in all its branches.

SOLE AGENTS FOR

Bacon's Hoisting Engines, Earle's Patent Steam Pump, Pickering's Governor and Valve, Champion's Patent Boiler Feeder, American Steam Guage Co.'s Steam Guages, Brown's Low Water Reporter, &c. &c.

☞ SEND FOR CATALOGUE.

C. REEDER & CO.

No. 51 Hughes Street, Baltimore,

MANUFACTURERS OF

MARINE

AND

STATIONARY STEAM ENGINES.

Machinery and Castings of all kinds.

FLYNN & EMRICH,

50, 52 and 54 North Holliday Street, Baltimore,

MANUFACTURERS OF

Steam Engines & Boilers, Iron & Wood Working Machinery, Presses, Punches, Dies and Tinners' Tools of every description, and all kinds of Machinery.

SOLE AGENTS FOR

Knowles' Patent Steam Pump, New York Safety Steam Power Company's Engines and Boilers, and Clogston's Patent Steam Heating Apparatus.

STEAM HEATING, WITH CLOGSTON'S HIGH OR LOW PRESSURE STEAM HEATING APPARATUS, for Warming and Ventilating Public and Private Buildings, Mills, Factories, Green Houses, Graperies, &c. The above apparatus may be seen in operation at our own establishment.

CUMBERLAND DUGAN & CO.

No. 26 SOUTH CHARLES ST., BALTIMORE,

KEEPS ALWAYS ON HAND A LARGE ASSORTMENT OF

ENGINES and BOILERS,

BOTH STATIONARY AND PORTABLE.

LATHES, PLANERS and DRILLS for working in Iron; LATHES, PLANERS and MOULDING MACHINES; MORTICING MACHINES and SAW TABLES for working in Wood; ANVILS, VISES, BELLOWS, NUTS and WASHERS; WROUGHT IRON and CAST IRON PIPE, for Gas and Water; PORTABLE FORGES and DRILL PRESSES for Blacksmiths; STEAM PUMPS, all sizes, &c. &c.

Rivets and Spikes.

IN 1865, a Factory was established in this city, under very modest auspices, for the manufacture of Rivets and Spikes. The concern prospered, and from time to time was enlarged. It passed subsequently into the hands of one of our most energetic citizens, and has become one of the largest establishments in America. That which was originally a mere machine shop possesses to-day a capacity almost unlimited for the manufacture of all the smaller articles known to the trade in connection with Railroads, Boilers, &c., such as Rivets and Spikes, Bolts of all kinds, Nuts, Washers, Wood Screws, &c. Already the trade in these articles from this Factory has assumed large proportions in our city and elsewhere. Large quantities of them are shipped through the country, North, South and West, and the trade is on the increase. Purchasers can be supplied in our city at the most reasonable rates, and the skill displayed in their production is a guarantee that buyers will be satisfied.

Removed to Corner President and Fawn Streets.

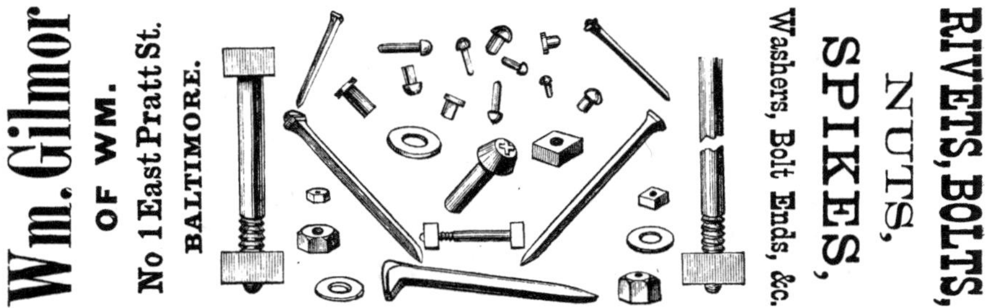

ENOCH PRATT. HENRY JANES.

E. PRATT & BROTHER,

27 and 29 South Charles Street, Baltimore.

IRON, CUT NAILS, SPIKES,

HORSE AND MULE SHOES.

Taunton Yellow Metal and Cumberland Coal.

Wm. Knabe & Co., Piano-Forte Manufacturers,

Ware-Rooms, No. 350 West Baltimore Street, Baltimore.

112 FIFTH AVENUE, NEW YORK CITY.

Architectural Iron Works.

OF the many uses to which Iron is put, none are more comprehensive than the modern application of it in the erection of warehouses. The advantages claimed for buildings constructed of this material are ease in embodying any architectural design, economy in cost, space, moving or rebuilding, security against atmospheric phenomena, such as lightning, moisture, &c.; ease of ventilation, durability of material and immunity from fire. We have in Baltimore one of the largest establishments in the country for the manufacture of Architectural Iron Works. Bartlett, Robbins & Co. began business in 1844 as stove founders. They soon added the manufacture of railing and ornamental work generally, and later on added the business of Architectural Iron Work proper. A large number of first-class iron buildings have been erected by them in this city; among which may be mentioned, as monuments of their skill, and admirable illustrations of the advantages of this new method of house-building, the following: the Tracy Building, Baltimore street; Numsen Building, Light street; Consolidated Building, corner German and South streets; Office Building of George R. Vickers, German near South street; McCreery Building, corner German and Sharp streets; Gary Building, on Hanover street; Noah Walker Building, on Baltimore street above Howard; and J. W. Bond & Co.'s Building, Nos. 90 and 92 West Baltimore Street, opposite Post Office Avenue.

The Works of this firm are very extensive, embracing every facility for the manufacture of material used in the construction or enjoyment of an iron building to the minutest detail; walls, floors, doors, windows, roof, porticoes, balconies, cornices, vaults, ventilators, fences, gates, fountains, vases, statuary, chairs, settees, gas and water fixtures, a heating apparatus, ranges or cooking stoves, parlor stoves, grates, brackets, stable fixtures, iron pavements, pots and kettles, culinary implements, bedsteads, in fact everything except beds and bedding, and science will doubtless ere long find some means of remedying this apparent difficulty. Independent of the work done in Baltimore by Bartlett, Robbins & Co., they are constantly in receipt of orders from other cities, and already have erected many iron buildings in New York, Richmond, Raleigh, New Orleans, Galveston, as far as Portland, Oregon, where they erected the "Corbett Hall," a building constructed at their works in Baltimore and carried around Cape Horn to its destination on the Pacific.

FOUNDRY, COR. SCOTT AND PRATT STS. OFFICE, 24 LIGHT STREET.

Iron Bridge Building.

IRON Bridge Building, since the advent of Railroads in this country has assumed mammoth proportions. The multiform character of the work, the exceeding nicety required in construction, and the eminent engineering skill necessary, have made it a very important branch of industry, and have led to the employment of some of the ablest minds in America. Baltimore in this regard occupies a prominent position, in fact she is not second to any of our large cities. Two extensive Firms, the Patapsco Bridge and Iron Works, and the Baltimore Bridge Company have been established in this city with branches in other places. The former especially has erected very extensive works in our midst necessitating a large outlay of capital and requiring for their operations a heavy laboring force. Collectively these Firms have manufactured twelve miles of Bridging and Trestle-work. To mention in this work the names of the various railroad corporations that have sought their skill would exceed the limits necessarily allotted to this department. Suffice it to say, their industry may be seen on nearly every railroad in this country, and on a number of railroads in South America. The Patapsco Bridge and Iron Company have built two and a half miles of Bridging and Trestle-work in North Carolina, crossing and connecting both branches of the Cape Fear River, and using Pneumatic Piles instead of masonry, and passing through three separate strata of rock in the bed of the river, encountering in the last two strata cypress trees from ten to thirty inches in diameter, and in a perfect state of preservation. They have also constructed Bridges in Cuba and Mexico; and the numerous Bridges built in this city and on the railroads and county roads leading out of it, bear ample testimony to the estimation in which they are held.

The Baltimore Bridge Company constructed the St. Charles Bridge across the Missouri River 6,675 feet in length and 90 feet above low water, the Rock Island Bridge across the Mississippi 1,840 feet in length, the great Varrugas Viaduct which spans one of the deep chasms in the heart of the Andes 12,000 feet above the level of the sea, on wrought iron pins at a maximum elevation of 252 feet, and a number of other works which attest their skill. The science of pneumatics has been specially availed of, and piles of the largest dimensions ever yet sunk have been successfully laid in the swamps of North Carolina. It must be borne in mind, in order to appreciate the extent of this business in Baltimore, that the Baltimore and Ohio Railroad builds its own Bridges. A better market than our city for those in need of this kind of work cannot be found in the world. There are very extensive iron and machine shops in Baltimore comprehensive in their scope, where every class of iron-work is done.

Coal.

AMONG the many branches of industry which have contributed to the development and financial advancement of Baltimore City, the Coal trade may be specially cited. The inexhaustible supplies of Bituminous Coal furnished from the Cumberland Coal regions, the superior quality of the article, the Gas Coal from West Virginia, and the Anthracite Coal brought to the City from the Coal regions of Pennsylvania, all point to Baltimore as a centre for that trade, and the lines of railroad now in process of construction, and the contemplated extension of others at no distant day, make it scarcely problematical that our City is to be in the future, the most extensive Coal market in America if not in the world. The Bituminous Coal regions, situated about two hundred miles from Baltimore and extending along the Georges Creek Valley from Piedmont to Frostburg, have never been fully explored. Hidden away there are endless mines of wealth which the labor of a thousand years will not appreciably diminish. It is only within the last few years that the real value of Bituminous Coal has been discovered. The strikes and difficulties encountered by operators at the Anthracite mines, and the sudden elevation of prices resulting therefrom, have led to its introduction where it was before unknown, and its use has been attended in every instance with a desire to repeat the experiment. The rapid substitution of steam in every branch of industry and trade for the ruder and slower appliances has already created an immense demand for its use, but what may be expected in the future can scarcely be hypothecated upon any data at present in hand. But a few years ago, 1,700 tons were considered a heavy shipment of Coal from the mines for one year—2,345,153 tons were shipped from the mines in 1871, and 2,355,471 tons in 1872, and this, though a very decided indication of the increase in the trade, gives but a feeble idea of what it will be in future years when competing routes are opened up and the supply is made commensurate with the demand for Bituminous Coal. There were shipped to Baltimore in 1872, 1,915,000 tons from the Cumberland Coal regions; of Gas Coal from Western Virginia, 250,000 tons; of Anthracite Coal from Pennsylvania about 350,000 tons. The completion of the Pittsburg and Connellsville Railroad has opened up to the market another region of Gas Coal from which doubtless in a short time large supplies will be obtained. The Coal at present received in Baltimore affords freight for 5,000 vessels, ranging in size from the largest class of ships to the smallest coasting schooners. It is shipped to all ports along the coast of the United States, and during the past eighteen months a foreign trade has sprung into existence which bids fair to rival that of any port in the world. Two years ago, Coal was seldom shipped from Baltimore to any foreign port except Aspinwall. Since that time, Cumberland Coal has grown rapidly into favor. A panic, caused by well-grounded fears of the exhaustion of the English Coal mines, has seized upon the operators in Great Britain and the prices have steadily advanced with no likelihood of any reduction. The result has been a demand upon the Baltimore market which it has been found at times difficult to meet, and to-day, Coal is shipped from this City to all quarters of the globe. The immense resources of the Baltimore and Ohio Railroad and the Chesapeake and Ohio Canal are taxed beyond their capacity to supply the market, and the extension of the Western Maryland Railroad to the Coal regions is merely a matter of time, while the Canton Company have it in contemplation to run a shorter and quicker route to the Bituminous Coal regions and to Pittsburg by means of which the trade [illegible] indefinitely extended.

Petroleum.

BALTIMORE offers great facilities for the refining and shipment of Petroleum or Coal Oil; and these are rapidly effecting an increase in the amount passing through this market. The double connection by rail with the oil region, the cheap rates of transportation, and the abundant means of storage, compare favorably with those offered by any other seaport. The completion of the Union Railroad, with its tunnel, will still farther promote this traffic; so will also the competition of the Baltimore and Ohio Railroad effecting a reduction in freights. As a market for southern purchasers, Baltimore is unequalled.

Paints and Chemicals.

MANY years ago the manufacture of Chemicals was an especial feature of the trade of this City in so much that cities of larger growth were dependent upon Baltimore for their supplies. For some unexplained reason the business dwindled down and the preparation of these articles fell away to almost nothing. The introduction of guano, however, as a fertilizer, and the discovery that its nutritive properties were vastly increased when in combination with other compounds dissolved by acid, led to a revival of the manufacture of Chemicals under circumstances which justify us in concluding if not at present, that it will ere long be one of the most important industries in our City.

The number of factories for the manufacture of Oil of Vitrol, Muriatic and Nitric Acids and Sulphate of Ammonia has doubled, and those already in existence have largely increased their capacity.

Immense quantities of Sulphuric Acid are required in the preparation of fertilizers, and as the manufacture of the latter article is largely on the increase in this City it is difficult to fix a limit to the expansion of trade in these articles.

Epsom Salts, (Sulphate of Magnesia) Glauber Salts (Sulphate of Soda) and (Sulphate of Iron) Copperas, are manufactured in great quantities for the use of the wholesale druggists. In these regards our City may be considered independent of any other community. Large quantities of indigenous roots possessing Chemical or remedial properties are also consumed in Baltimore by the wholesale dealers in medicines, and are sent to all portions of the country. The manufacture of medicines, with the exception of those already mentioned, has recently become an interest in the City, but the energy and enterprise displayed by those engaged in the business, lead to the conclusion that it is soon to become a very important branch of industry.

Large amounts of money are invested in the wholesale drug business, and the gentlemen engaged in it are among our substantial and leading citizens.

The only establishment in America for the manufacture of Bi-Chromate of Potash, is located here, and the largest factory in the world for the manufacture of Chrome Yellow is also located in this City. Paints of every description are manufactured at this factory, but Chrome Yellow has become a specialty and is exported in large quantities to all quarters of the globe. In South America, European manufactures have found it impossible to compete with Baltimore, and at this time trade with that country is practically monopolized by our dealers.

The reputation of Baltimore for the manufacture of Paints is equal to that of any city in the world. Large supplies of Soda, Roots, Dye Woods, Cochineal and Quick Silver, are imported from South America and West Indies, besides Nitrate of Potash from the East Indies, and Arsenic and Paris Green from other places. Salt-Petre, for packers in the West, is extensivly manufactured in Baltimore. It is estimated that fully $5,000,000 are invested in the manufacture of Paints and Chemicals in the city of Baltimore, and it is difficult to fix an estimate to the amount of sales made annually.

It may be added that the Maryland White Lead Company, who are very large corroders, have one of the most extensive establishments in the country. There are other houses largely engaged in the manufacture and grinding in oil of White Lead, White Zinc and Colors. Baltimore Lead is shipped to all parts of the United States, and has a reputation equalled by few articles of a similar character made elsewhere and excelled by none. Baltimore has also one of the oldest Varnish Factories in America for manufacturing fine Furniture and Coach Varnishes, Japan, Leather and Dormer Varnishes.—This house has been manufacturing these goods for forty years. Among the houses engaged in the manufacture of Linseed Oil is the firm of Thomas and John M. Smith, established nearly thirty years ago. The reputation of this house for the production of a pure article is national. Raw and Double Boiled Linseed Oils are manufactured by them and shipped to many points in the North, South, East and West.

Naval Stores.

THE steady improvement in the market for Naval Stores in our City is due to greater facilities as well as lower rates of freights arising from shorter lines of road, which enable Baltimore to compete favorably with Northern markets.

The establishment of additional lines of Steamers to Europe will soon restore the foreign freight room of which the introduction of steam lines temporarily deprived our city by monopolizing the more lucrative freights.

and thus dispensing with a large number of sailing vessels. The superiority of Baltimore over any one Southern market lies in the fact that, receiving from all points South, she can offer the produce of many markets, and forward in thorough order, merchandize which has been in transit from two to five days, the time requisite for reaching the City.

We append the receipts at this port for the last five years:

Years.	*Spirits.*	*Rosin.*	*Tar.*	*Pitch.*
1872,	21,407	77,990	10,207	3,168
1871,	22,852	79,352	11,302	1,941
1870,	15,523	66,003	8,088	781
1869,	14,434	51,520	5,686	870
1868,	11,646	53,904	6,629	649

Window Glass and Glass Ware.

FEW articles admit of more general consumption than Glass, and still fewer are liable to a more constant demand. Its varied uses and its brittle character make it the subject of constant solicitude alike to the housekeeper and the merchant, and its plentifulness and cheapness a matter of no little consideration. The attention of the trade of Baltimore was turned to the manufacture of Window Glass and Glass Ware in the very infancy of the City; and the matter of its production and sale was of great importance, when only the most sanguine of our citizens dared hope for the splendid future that has since dawned upon her. A Glass Factory known as the "Baltimore Glass Works," was established on Federal Hill, on the south side of the Basin, during the year 1790, and was among the first establishments of that description in America. For nearly eighty years it has been in continuous and successful operation, undergoing from time to time vast additions and extensive improvements. Sixteen years since, a new factory was started at the Spring Gardens for the manufacture of Bottles, Vials, Jars, &c. In 1858 this factory changed proprietors, and like its predecessor has undergone many improvements, its capacity having been enlarged at various times until at present there are in operation two furnaces for the manufacture of Bottles, Vials, Jars, Flasks, Demijohns and a great variety of other articles. One flint furnace from which are turned out Tumblers, Chimneys, Jars, Vials, Cologne and Extract Bottles and all the little Glass articles for the toilet, and the perfumers art. These works employ some two hundred hands and manufacture yearly $200,000 worth of Glass Ware. For the manufacture of this large amount of Glass it may be interesting to enumerate some few of the more important materials consumed. In the space of twelve months this factory uses 500 casks of soda ash, 2,000 tons of coal, 500 tons of packing hay and straw, 2,000 tons of sand, 50 tons of marl, 1,000 cords of wood, 500 tons of lime, 1,000,000 feet of lumber, 10 tons of iron, 50 tons of pot-clay, 300 kegs of nails, &c., &c.

The Baltimore Window Glass Works have two large furnaces in operation employing about one hundred hands and manufacturing 60,000 boxes of Window Glass and Coach Glass for cars and coaches, Picture Glass, &c., annually amounting to $160,000. In addition to the establishments mentioned above, there are also the Maryland Glass Works. This factory, erected some years ago on the Spring Gardens has rapidly developed into importance and is at present turning out at least 30,000 boxes of Window Glass annually, employing a large number of hands and consuming 250 tons of soda ash, 600 tons of sand, 1,600 tons of coal, 500 cords of wood, 40 tons of pot-clay and a large quantity of lumber. From the above it will be seen that the production of Window Glass alone, during the year, amounts to

90,000 boxes, being an increase since the year 1865 of 60,000 boxes. The increase in the manufacture of Glass Ware during that time has doubled, making the annual value of the manufacture of the two articles in this City at present, something under a million of dollars. The facilities for its manufacture are great. The reputation of Glass made in Baltimore has always been the highest; and the merchants engaged in the business are not only thoroughly acquainted with all its minutia, but are among our most influential and substantial business men, and they have made this City a market where all the articles of Glass manufacture can be purchased at the lowest prices, and on the most desirable terms.

BALTIMORE GLASS WORKS
WINDOW GLASS.
GLASS WARE.
BAKER BROS. & CO.
EHLERS CO.

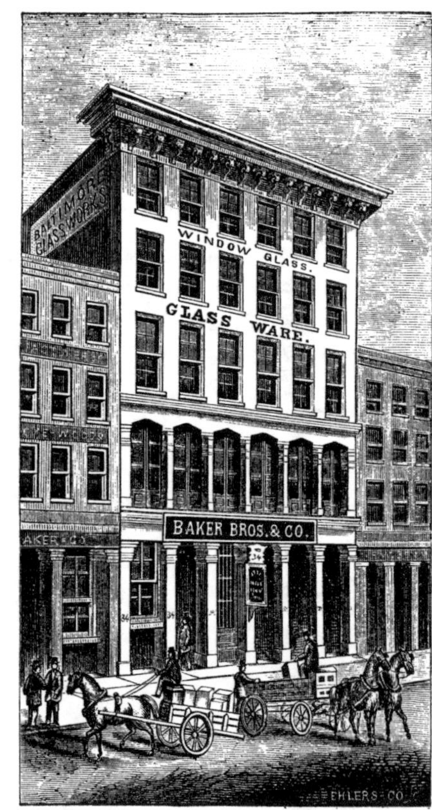

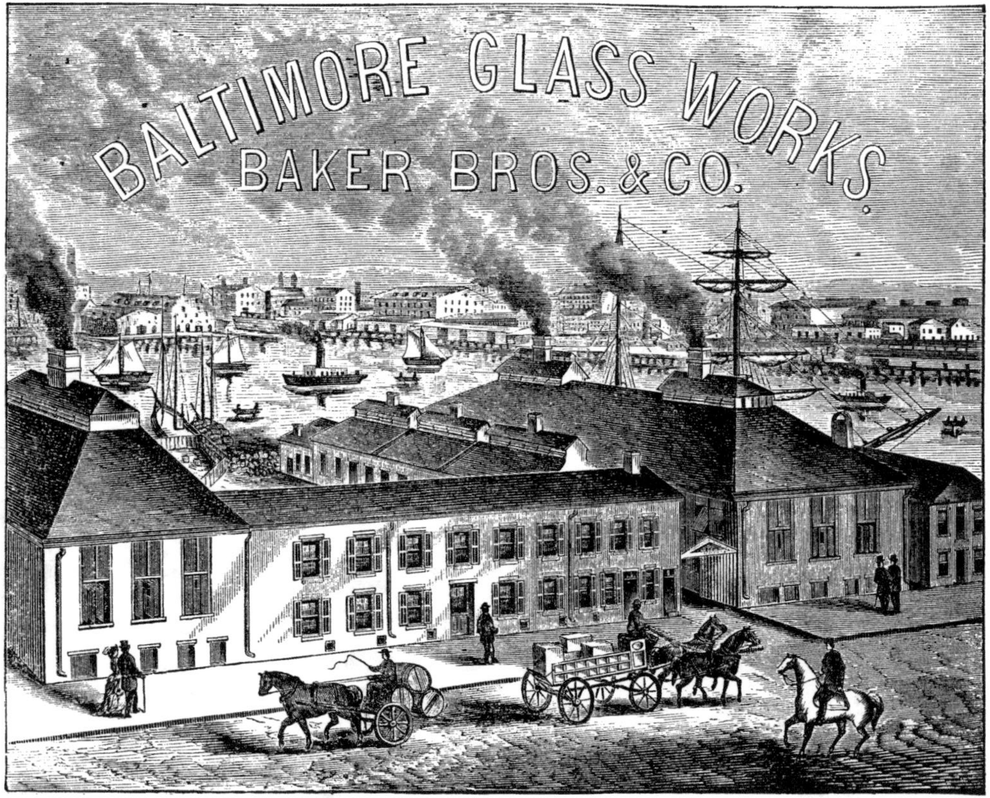

BALTIMORE GLASS WORKS.
BAKER BROS. & CO.

Guano and Fertilizers.

WHILE immense tracts of land are being cleared for cultivation in the West, and grain is becoming so plentiful as to be used in some instances for fuel, the soil nearer home in many cases is suffering a corresponding decrease in productiveness from the thriftless mode of tillage adopted by some, and the great tax of its powers by all farmers in their efforts to secure from it the very greatest possible yield. It is gratifying to know however, that this destructive policy has been in a measure checked during the last few years, and that more enlightened farmers and agriculturists have begun to learn the importance of recuperating worn-out lands by means of the various kinds of Fertilizers. Cotton planting, tobacco culture, and a number of the crops grown in the East and South, are more exhaustive in their effects upon the soil than grain, and hence the greater necessity for the use of Fertilizers in their cultivation. A growing conviction of the true value of these Fertilizers has caused their manufacture and distribution to become a most important branch of the trade of Baltimore. This City was the first and for many years the only port in the country for the importation and sale of Peruvian Guano—a business which was begun as early as the year 1832. For a long time the Guano was used in the crude state, just as it came from the Islands, but the advance made in the science of Agricultural Chemistry led to the discovery that the force of this Fertilizer might be greatly increased, and a large proportion of the amount imported is now used in the preparation of artificial Fertilizers. Into their manufacture also enter large quantities of bone, and the offal from the slaughter-houses, both of Baltimore and the West. The factories for the preparation of these articles are located chiefly in South and East Baltimore, and occupy a very considerable area of ground. In the same portion of the City are extensive Chemical Works for the manufacture of sulphuric acid, or oil of vitriol, of which agent an immense quantity is used in making Fertilizers. The analysis of new soils and numberless experiments largely increase the list of artificial manures from year to year, and so numerous are now the different compositions, from the same general basis, that almost all are designated by some proprietary name, to give a list of which would be outside of the purpose of this work.

The ease with which these Fertilizers can be adulterated makes the trade peculiarly liable to fraud. It is matter of congratulation that the gentlemen engaged in this business in our City are persons of such standing and tone in the community as to preclude the idea of deception in the manufacture or sale of these compounds.

Suffice it to say, that all the varieties of Fertilizers known to the trade and likely to be beneficial to any known soil, can be purchased in Baltimore on as reasonable terms as elsewhere, while the facilities for shipment to any part of the country are unrivalled.

Marble.

WITHIN a few miles of Baltimore on the line of the Northern Central Railway are located quarries of Marble practically inexhaustible, and of a quality which rivals that found in any other portion of the country. These quarries have been worked for many years. Their convenient location along one of the main lines of railroad leading out of our city, has enabled their owners to supply the material at prices remunerative to themselves, and favorable to purchasers. Immense quantities of the Marble have been shipped to Baltimore and other cities. The monolithic columns of the Capitol at Washington, and many of the public buildings in that city built of this material, are ample evidence of the quality of Baltimore County Marble, and the estimation in which it is held by those best qualified to judge, and the numerous buildings that have been erected in our own city are an indication of its appreciation by those who reside in Baltimore. The new City Hall, a magnificent edifice recently erected in our midst, has been constructed entirely of Marble from these quarries, as was also the Washington Monument.—Immense blocks of the crude stone can be taken out and shipped to market; blocks in fact, of any size likely to be required for practical purposes. It is susceptible of the very highest polish, and is largely used for ornamental purposes.

Large establishments exist in our city for cutting and dressing Marble, which employ a number of hands and are furnished with the most improved steam machinery.

BALTIMORE CAR WHEEL CO.

OFFICE, 15 SOUTH STREET,

CAPACITY 300 WHEELS PER DAY,

Manufacture Wheels of all Patterns, for City as well as Steam Railways, and with or without axles. Using strictly Baltimore Charcoal Iron, (which has no superior, and few equals, for making Car Wheels,) and annealing their Wheels by the Central Flue system, they warrant them free from strain, and equal in tenacity and uniformity of chill to any made.

Tensile Strength of Baltimore Iron IN PIG.	Tensile Strength of remelted bars made from Baltimore Charcoal Iron, same as used in Wheel Plates by this Company.	Tensile Strength, after two years service, of Wheel Plates made by this Company from Baltimore Charcoal Iron.
28560 lbs. per sq. inch.	42000 lbs. per sq. inch.	23800 lbs. per sq. inch.
33320 "	41600 "	33320 "
26180 "	40800 "	33900 "
23086 "		28560 "
27370 "		
33000 "		

WORKS, COR. ESSEX & BURKE STS., CANTON, BALTIMORE.

W. S. G. BAKER, President. J. M. LAWFORD, Secretary.

Fire Bricks and Potteries.

BALTIMORE possesses superior advantages for the manufacture of all kinds of Bricks. The surface of our soil is underlaid with clays which are manufactured into all varieties of ware constructed of clay—Stoneware, Pottery, Terra-Cotta, and Chemical Ware the most difficult and important of all. The largest kinds of Fire Blocks, and Retorts for the use of zinc works, sugar refineries and gas works, some of the latter weighing considerably over a ton, are manufactured in Baltimore. No place in the country affords such fine material for these varied industries. In Pottery Ware alone Baltimore should surpass Trenton, and command the trade of the West and South. With grounds for these establishments at a nominal price contiguous to rail and water transportation, and the clays often on their sites, it is a wonder that more capital and enterprise should not have sought investment in them with such assurance of success.

There is already one concern manufacturing refractory materials which is sending its Retorts, Fire Bricks, Sewer Pipes, Tiles, &c., &c., to the remotest sections of the country, from Maine to Louisiana and westward, even across the Mississippi, with a rapidly increasing business. The manufacture of artificial hydraulic cement, similar to the far-famed English Portland and Roman Cements, might be developed here to an almost unlimited extent with our variety of clays and limes in close proximity. These manufactures of raw material, direct from the soil where it is lying awaiting the skilled labor which capital can so easily provide, are the most solid source of permanent wealth to any community.

Bricks.

FEW persons who walk the streets or cast their eyes up to the substantial dwellings which line them, care to inquire how many distinct bricks were used in their construction, and yet perhaps could the number be ascertained, it would foot up an array of figures, by the side of which those that express the combined national debts of all the nations on the globe, would dwarf into insignificance. As new buildings are erected or old ones repaired, new streets paved or old ones mended, the number required is indefinitely increased; and the system adopted long since by the municipal authorities of this City to allow none but Brick, Stone or Iron dwellings to be built, save under peculiar circumstances, while a very great advantage to the City, has marvelously increased the demand for bricks. It will probably not astonish any of our readers then to be informed, that more than 100,000,000 Bricks are manufactured in and about the City of Baltimore annually. The clay in the vicinity of Baltimore, the finest in the world, is peculiarly adapted to the manufacture of Brick, and the materials used in burning them can be purchased at rates which render their production a means of profit to the manufacturer, while at the same time he can successfully compete in price with those of any other locality in the country. Extensive Brick yards are established west of Jones' Falls, on the Washington road, at Moale's Point, Locust Point, on the Frederick road, east of the Falls at Canton, Brooklyn and Belair Avenue. One million of dollars is invested in the business, 2,000 hands are employed, 25,000 tons of coal, and 2,000 cords of wood are consumed in their production. The quality of the Bricks made in this City is unsurpassed by that of any made in the United States, and Baltimore Pressed Brick are superior to any made in the world, as is evidenced by the fact that they are shipped to all seaport towns, and along all the different railroad lines leading out of Baltimore. The increased demand for Pressed Brick growing out of the fires in the East, has led to their use in that section to a greater extent than in our own City.

Horses and Mules.

A FEATURE of the trade of Baltimore is the traffic in Horses and Mules. With the exception of the Kentucky market, that of this City is the largest in the United States. The very best Mules raised in America are to be found in the sale stables of this City, and Horses of heavy draught, fed upon the blue-grass of the Western States, and notoriously free from the imperfections and disorders to which Horses are liable, are brought to this City for sale in larger numbers and in better condition than they can be found elsewhere, save where they are raised. In fancy Horses for road purposes the market does not pretend to compete with that of New York, where the best breeds of trotters are raised, and where the demand is always great, though of late years even in this respect, Baltimore has been by no means insignificant; but the market is always stocked with medium Horses at fair prices, and the character of those engaged in the business is a guarantee to buyers that their representations are correct. The finest Mules in the world are sold here in large numbers for home use, while many are shipped from this point to the South and the West Indies. The market is more active usually during the Fall and Spring months, but an adequate supply may be found in the City at all times. Baltimore possesses unusual facilities for the shipment of these valuable animals, and the Baltimore and Ohio Railroad is at present perfecting arrangements for the transportation of live stock, which will doubtless create a large addition to the trade. The Stable accommodations are admirable, and Western men have heretofore shown a very decided preference for our City.

It is estimated that from eighteen to twenty thousand Mules and Horses pass through this market annually, and with the increase of railroad facilities it is safe to predict a corresponding increase in the trade.

The Cattle Market.

THE Cattle Market of Baltimore has long been famous. The City occupying as she does a central position on the Atlantic Coast, in striking distance of the various grazing fields by her railroad connections and water communication, and contiguous to broad stretches of fertile country, where grass and forage of every description are plentiful, her market has always been supplied with superior beeves, hogs and sheep. The market is furnished from Virginia, West Virginia, Pennsylvania, Tennessee, Kentucky, Missouri, Illinois, Texas, North Carolina, Indiana and Ohio. The facilities offered to drovers in Baltimore are considered by stockmen from other cities the finest in the United States, both as regards stabling and the dues required of them. The trade is steadily on the increase, and the accommodations which competing lines of railroad now offer will give it an impetus in the future. We append the monthly receipts of live stock for the years 1871 and 1872, as reported at the State Scales:

	1871.			1872.		
	Beeves.	*Hogs.*	*Sheep.*	*Beeves.*	*Hogs.*	*Sheep.*
January,	5,974	18,172	11,175	6,632	29,306	6,941
February,	6,758	23,136	16,756	6,370	36,099	11,173
March,	3,115	17,552	5,351	4,202	27,471	6,170
April,	3,983	16,794	7,504	3,727	25,419	6,620
May,	3,684	22,811	12,598	3,703	27,101	13,537
June,	4,318	23,477	9,529	5,857	30,684	18,662
July,	5,959	20,181	20,313	4,457	24,879	11,995
August,	8,341	22,247	17,309	8,304	31,729	19,317
September,	12,939	27,233	16,370	12,313	36,271	16,161
October,	14,432	37,873	20,316	17,993	48,975	20,807
November,	14,658	45,811	15,631	9,394	37,579	11,628
December,	5,587	27,697	5,672	7,450	7,625	37,217
	89,748	303,284	158,624	90,402	363,138	180,228

Hotels.

PERHAPS no feature contributes more directly to the rapid development of a city than the number, convenience and comfort of its Hotels.—Without these indispensable adjuncts it is like a well selected library with no means of access to the shelves. The books may be very instructive and entertaining but the public will never discover the fact by personal inspection. For a long time Baltimore was behind the spirit of the age in this respect. Her public houses were few and far between, and partook more of the homeliness of the old road-side inns than of the elegance and luxury of modern caravanseries. Thanks to the spirit of enterprise which has manifested itself in the Monumental City during the past decade, old things have passed away, at least so far as they retard our progress, and Baltimore *to-day* is as well supplied with Hotels in proportion to the number of her inhabitants as any city in America—further, they are as splendidly fitted up and give as much

GUY'S HOTEL, ON THE EUROPEAN PLAN, BALTIMORE.

comfort to visitors. "The Carrollton," recently erected on Light Street, with a front on Baltimore Street, the main thoroughfare of the City, is admirably located. Situated in the very heart of Baltimore, it is convenient both for business and pleasure. Sumptuous in its appointments, it is furnished with every improvement that modern taste or ingenuity can suggest, and will compare favorably with any of the recently constructed Hotels in this country. We cite the Carrollton, not because it is superior to others, but as an illustration. "Barnums" is an old established house and has a cosmopolitan reputation. There is a number of other first-class Hotels in the City whose accommodations have proved ample for all the demands of the greatest exigencies that have occurred within the past few years. Baltimore is well supplied with a cheaper class of Hotels, whose outer finish, interior comforts and excellent tables, have earned for them an enviable reputation both at home, and with strangers.

The Houses kept on the European plan in this City are worthy of special mention. They are numerous and fitted up in a style of elegance combined with perfect taste which is really exceptional. Among these is "Guy's Monument House"—Established at an early period in the history of Baltimore, it has steadily preserved its reputation as a house where gentlemen are treated as though they were at their own homes. The Maryland Club, the oldest organization of that description in this country, was formed at "Guy's." This sufficiently expresses the character of the men who resorted thither years ago, and it is only necessary to say that there has been no alteration since then in the nature of the guests. The Guys were eminently a set of men who knew how to keep a hotel, and the mantle that fell from the shoulders of the last of the name has been very creditably worn by the present proprietor. The *cuisine* of this establishment has acquired fame in many portions of this country, and more than once has its excellence been attested by orders from Europe. A number of other houses conducted upon the same plan, offer to visitors during their sojourn in our City, both the comforts of home and all the luxuries that taste and money can supply, while their moderate charges especially recommend them to the travelling public.

G. R. VICKERS' OFFICE BUILDING.

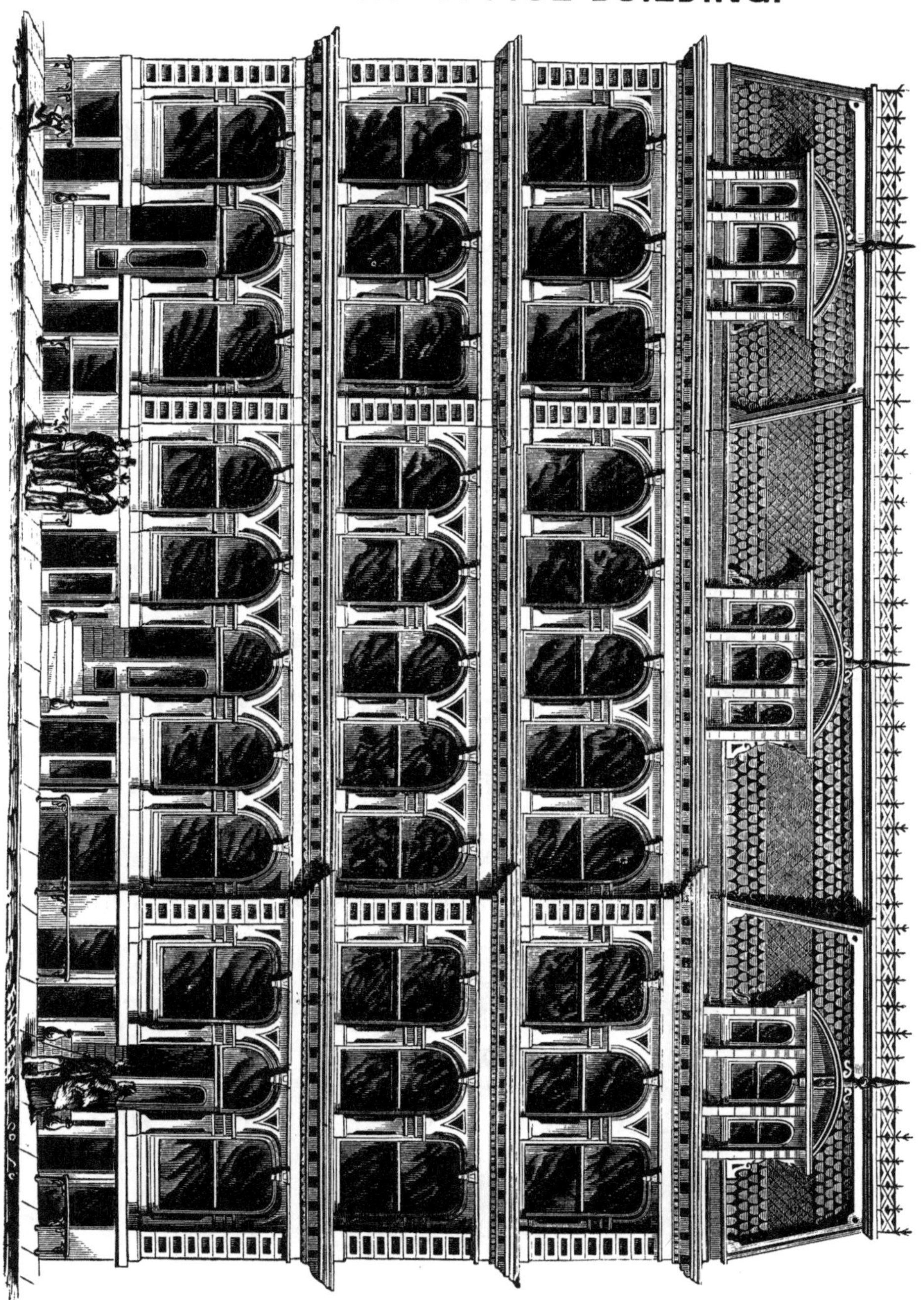

GERMAN STREET, NEAR SOUTH ST., BALTIMORE.

Banks and Bankers.

THE Banking Capital proper of Baltimore is about fifteen millions of dollars. Were this all, our City would offer but feeble inducements to enterprising men to make their homes with us. Such an amount seems totally inadequate to the necessities of a great commercial emporium, and a weak exhibit when placed in juxtaposition with the capital held by the Banks of other cities.

But this is supplemented in a variety of ways which, if not peculiar to Baltimore, at least find their fullest development here. The private Banking Houses are not only numerous, but solid and substantial. Those in charge of them are, with scarcely an exception, men of large capital and an extended experience, enabling them to rival the Banks in the magnitude of their operations, and at the same time affording the most ample security to those whose financial agents they become. There are no bogus Banks or Banking Houses in the City. While there are Exchanges for the convenience of business men, and the transactions of legitimate trade, speculation has not yet reared its front in our midst, and "puts" and "calls" are unknown terms save in the vocabulary of curb-stone brokers, or the under current of mercantile life, where obscurity begets immunity, and tends to the preservation of that high tone which should always characterize commercial communities.

In addition to that furnished by the Banking Houses, a large amount of floating capital in the hands of our wealthy citizens is constantly seeking investment, and the large towns of the State, such as Frederick and Annapolis, are supplied with Banks far beyond the requirements of the trade in those localities. The surplus capital of these Banks, and in fact that of the entire State, seeks Baltimore as its natural outlet, and in this manner an amount of money aggregating many millions of dollars and adequate to the wants of business is placed in this market.

The marked succcss of our Banks, their payment of large semi-annual dividends, and the fact that no failure has occurred among them for thirty years, are powerful inducements to capitalists from other sections to make similar investments in this City. The Banking Institutions and private Banking Houses of Baltimore have shown commendable enterprise, especially in the buildings they have erected, and some of our handsomest edifices, replete with architectural adornment and evincing decided taste, having been built to accommodate their increasing business.

There are in our City upwards of ten Savings Banks and Institutions embracing the "Savings" feature, with deposits aggregating nearly twenty-five millions of dollars. This is a creditable showing for Baltimore. These Banks are established principally for the benefit of the mechanics and laboring classes, and are dependent upon them for their success. Such an exhibit speaks volumes in behalf of the thrift and energy of the larger class of our population as well as of those to whom they have trusted their earnings.

The Savings Bank of Baltimore.

THE SAVINGS BANK OF BALTIMORE.

The Savings Bank of Baltimore was organized on the first day of January, 1818, and incorporated at December session, 1818, being the second of the kind formed in the United States.

The Bank is empowered to receive deposites of money and invest the same in public stocks, or other securities, and allow such interest as may be directed or provided by the By-Laws of the Corporation, the surplus profits to be divided every three years among the Depositors, as the Directors may think proper. The Depositors receive all the profits, there being no Stockholders.

Twenty-five Directors are chosen, annually, by the members of the Corporation, out of their own body.

The Directors have power to make such By-Laws, or other rules, as they may deem expedient. The Corporation is prohibited from issuing bills or notes in the nature of Bank Notes, and from lending any portion of the funds to a Director.

The object of this Institution was to encourage the laboring population, and all in moderate circumstances, to lay by something for the future, in the belief, that the habit of so doing would conduce, not merely to the better support of individuals, and families, but promote their moral, as well as physical well being. It is well known to those who have observed the operation and effect of the Institution on the welfare of the community, that it has been the instrument of enabling many to become owners of their own dwellings, and that without involving the necessity of paying forfeits, or running into debt.

For several years the Bank was opened only one day in the week, when its business was conducted by the Directors in person, these being divided into committees, and performing a large part of the clerical labor. The increase however in the number of Depositors, and consequent increase of general business, has made it necessary to employ permanently, officers and clerks, and at this time the daily services of a President, a Treasurer, an Assistant Treasurer, and several Clerks, are required.

The Depositors, on the first day of January, 1873, numbered 28,635, and the funds amounted to $10,735,394.

The rate of interest paid to the Depositors annually is 4 per cent, and the extra dividends of surplus profits have made the whole interest distributed more than 6 per cent, as much as 7½ per cent having been divided for the last six years to deposits of one year's standing.

The Bank is open daily, for the receipt and payment of deposits, and for the transaction of general business, from 10 to 1 o'clock.

OFFICERS.

ARCHIBALD STIRLING, President. **DAVID BALDWIN, Treasurer.**
SAM'L McDONALD RICHARDSON, Assistant Treasurer.

DIRECTORS.

ARCHIBALD STIRLING,
MICHAEL WARNER,
CHAUNCEY BROOKS,
DEETER BARGAR,
EDWARD KURTZ,
GALLOWAY CHESTON,
WILLIAM McKIM,
WILLIAM KENNEDY,
JAMES I. FISHER,
JOSEPH CUSHING, Jr.
THOMAS C. JENKINS,
NICHOLAS POPPLEIN,
SAMUEL KIRBY,
GEORGE S. BROWN,
GEORGE N. EATON,
THOMAS WHITRIDGE,
SOLOMON CORNER,
AUSTIN JENKINS,
THOMAS M. SMITH,
WILLIAM LAMPING,
LAURENCE THOMSEN,
CHRISTOPHER HINRICHS,
ENOCH PRATT,
HENRY W. DRAKELY,
HENRY JAMES.

THE FIRST NATIONAL BANK OF BALTIMORE,

No. 8 SOUTH GAY STREET.

Organized 1863. ***Capital, $1,110,000.***

DIRECTORS.

JOHNS HOPKINS,
WILLIAM J. ALBERT,
WILLIAM E. HOOPER,
THOMAS KELSO,
HORACE ABBOTT,
SAMUEL M. SHOEMAKER,
GEOGE SMALL,
J. SAURIN NORRIS,
THOMAS PEIRCE.

J. S. NORRIS, President. **THOMAS KELSO, Vice President.**
E. K. HOLTZMAN, Cashier.

The Eutaw Savings Bank of Baltimore

The Eutaw Savings Bank of Baltimore was formally organized by the corporators on the 16th April, 1847, by their acceptance of the Charter granted at the December session of the Maryland Legislature in 1846, and by the election of Directors and Officers.

At that time a number of public spirited and influential citizens interested in promoting the general welfare, considered that it was important to establish a Bank in the western part of the city for the purpose of benefitting widows and orphans, and that important portion of every large community, who desire the safe-keeping and profitable investment of their hard earned and careful savings.

The Bank was opened in a small room on Baltimore street, near Eutaw street, and for many years the services of its devoted President, the late Jesse Hunt, were given for an almost nominal salary, and the Institution was conducted upon the most economical system. At the end of 1848 its accumulated deposits and interest amounted to $52,895.21. In 1858, the business of the Bank had so much increased that it became necessary to erect a building suitable for its wants, and adapted for the proper care of the large amount of securities then in its keeping. The present building on the corner of Eutaw and Fayette streets was then occupied, and the popularity of the Bank continued yearly to increase.

The accumulated deposits and interest at the close of 1872 amounted to $4,197,901.96, and the number of depositors, having open accounts, to 11,585.

By its Charter, the Eutaw Savings Bank is prohibited from issuing any form of notes or bills for circulation, and its By-Laws provide that its investments shall be confined to the purchase of public securities, or to loans upon real estate, and such collaterals as the Board of Investment shall approve.

But in no instance has the discounting of commercial paper been authorized, the loans of the Bank being made only upon such securities as in fact represent the perpetuity and prosperity of the Nation and the State. Deposits are received in sums not less than one dollar, and interest is allowed thereon at the rate of 4 per cent. per annum. Every third year the surplus profits of the Bank are divided among the Depostiors, thus increasing the actual interest on balances remaining on deposit for three years, to an average of from 6½ per cent. to 7 per cent. per annum.

OFFICERS.

WM. F. BURNS, President. **ROBERT D. BROWN**, Treasurer.

DIRECTORS.

George Bartlett,
William H. Perkins,
J. Harman Brown,
Aaron Fenton,
Francis Burns,
Henry Snyder,
William J. Rieman,
Sam'l R. Smith,
William Devries,
James Harvey,
N. G. Penniman,
William Wilson, Jr.
Elisha H. Perkins,
Asa Needham,
William F. Burns,
Matthew B. Clark,
John L. Weeks.
Francis Dawes,
Hy. R. Louderman,
John Cushing,
Daniel M. Thomas,
George P. Thomas,
John Gregg,
Alfred Jenkins,
A. A. Hack,

FRANKLIN BANK,

CHARTERED 1810.

CAPITAL,

$626,750.00.

No. 15

South St.

OPPOSITE

German Street.

CHAS. J. BAKER,

President.

Chas. Goodwin,

Cashier.

DIRECTORS:

S. SPRIGG BELT,
ROBERT TURNER,
GEORGE SANDERS,
GERMAN H. HUNT,
WM. SEEMULLER,
CHARLES WEBB,
HUGH SISSON.

SAFE DEPOSIT VAULTS

Of STEEL and IRON,

For the Safe Keeping of Government and other Bonds, Securities or Valuables.

Western National Bank of Baltimore,

No. 14 Eutaw Street.

CHARTERED 1835.	CAPITAL - - -	$500,000
	SURPLUS - - -	170,000

CHAUNCEY BROOKS, President.

W. H. NORRIS, Cashier.

DIRECTORS:

CHAUNCEY BROOKS,
FRANCIS BURNS,
AARON FENTON,
WM. BRIDGES,
GEORGE BARTLETT,
JAMES HARVEY,
WM. G. POWER,
SAMUEL R. SMITH,
WM. F. BURNS,
MATTHEW B. CLARK,
WALTER B. BROOKS,
ROBERT GARRETT.

NATIONAL UNION BANK OF MARYLAND,

AT BALTIMORE.

CHARTERED 1804.

Reorganized as a National Bank 1865.

WM. W. TAYLOR, President.

R. MICKLE, Cashier.

Capital $1.258,725.

DIRECTORS:

WM. W. TAYLOR,
JOHN STELLMAN,
C. OLIVER O'DONNELL,
CHARLES W. LORD,
GERARD H. REESE,
WM. WOODWARD,
LEWIS N. HOPKINS,
WM. A. WILLIAR,
A. FULLER CRANE,
SAML. H. ADAMS,

STUDENTS CAN ENTER AT ANY TIME.

Night Session commences Oct. 1, 1873,

And continues in session until April 1, 1874.

The Business Department of this Institution is most thorough and practical. Consignments of Merchandise are daily received and Shipments made. Exchange Bought and Sold. Drafts and Collections upon all the principal cities of the United States and Canadas. The public are invited to call and examine the workings of the College, which will convince the most skeptical of the importance of young men attending our institution. For College Documents, address

W. H. SADLER, President,
Nos. 6 & 8 N. Charles Street,
BALTIMORE.

Baltimore Female College

This Seminary of learning, instituted for the liberal education of young ladies, was incorporated in 1849, with authority to confer degrees, and was liberally endowed by the State of Maryland in 1860.

There are two departments of instruction, the Preparatory Department, for young misses, and the Collegiate Department, for young ladies. In the latter are conferred the degrees of Baccalaurea Literarum, Baccalaurea Artium, and Magistra Artium.

Among its educational facilities the College has a well-selected library of 3,750 volumes, chemical and philosophical apparatus, including a good telescope, presented by Geo. W. Childs, Esq., of Philadelphia, a painting gallery, and cabinets of minerals, coins, medals and copies of antique gems.

In a few months the College will be removed to Park Place, at the intersection of Park and North avenues, where extensive buildings are being erected for its accommodation. These are beautifully situated in a grove on a lofty eminence that commands a view of the country around, of the city, and the river and bay for many miles. There are shady walks for exercise, and various arrangements will be made for recreation and amusement, which, with pure refreshing breezes from the adjacent country, will render it both healthy and attractive to the pupils. The buildings will embrace all the modern improvements for heating and ventilation, and will have study, recitation, and music rooms, separate, with every convenience for boarding and day pupils.

FACULTY OF INSTRUCTION.

Prof. N. C. Brooks, LL.D., *An. Languages.*
Prof. W. C. Robinson, A.M., *Mathem'cs, &c.*
Prof. Felix Aucaigne, *French.*
Prof. A. J. Volck, *Painting.*
Prof. C. Gola, *Piano and Singing.*
Miss Luella Kelly, *Belles-Lettres.*
Miss Fannie E. Jessie, *Mathematics.*
Miss L. A. Maddox, *Vocal Music.*
Mrs. E. A. Polster, *Piano and Guitar.*
Miss Emma Polster, *Piano.*

For catalogues containing full information as to regulations, tuition, boarding, &c.

Address

N. C. BROOKS, LL.D., President.

Cooperage Stores.

PREVIOUS to the war the business in Cooperage could not be called extensive, but since 1861 it has been constantly increasing in this City. A large proportion of the Oil, Pork, Syrup, Beef and Whiskey Barrels used in this and neighboring cities is made here of materials from West Virginia and Pennsylvania. Whiskey, Pork and Lard Tierces are shipped to Eastern cities in large quantities. Flour and Sugar Barrels, made of materials from Ohio and Michigan, are consumed principally by the mills and refineries in this vicinity. The demand for these articles keeps in constant operation four factories, besides a number of smaller establishments which employ from 800 to 1,000 operatives. One single House in our City aggregated more than $600,000 in its business during the past year. Barrels are sent in large quantities to Wilmington, N. C., and other Southern ports for the shipment of Turpentine. Cooperage for the West Indies is largely exported from Baltimore. During 1872, 300,000 Shooks, and upwards of 2,000,000 Hoops were shipped to those Islands and South American ports, and considerable demand has sprung up for Molasses Shooks and Hogsheads from the Eastern cities. They are made in the mountains of Pennsylvania and West Virginia for Houses in this City, and are brought here over the different railways. The Trade is rapidly increasing and the facilities possessed by Baltimore preclude a diminution in the future.

[From the *Baltimore Saturday Night* of May 3, 1873.]

SUBURBAN IMPROVEMENTS—HIGHLAND PARK.

It is questionable if there is any city within the United States surpassing Baltimore in her suburban advantages. This is not only the opinion of our own citizens, but it has been freely and frequently expressed by visitors (strangers) from almost every part of the world. Having been ourselves residents of Baltimore for many years, and noticed with especial interest her expansion into the surrounding country, particularly in northerly, northwesterly, westerly and easterly directions, we are not surprised, considering all these inducements, but gratified that such should have been the case.

There is, indeed, scarcely a limit to our growth as a centralizing and radiating commercial metropolis. It is only surprising these suburban attractions were not long ago more thoroughly appreciated and availed of. Fortunes were lying in them comparatively dormant equal to gold mines, waiting only development through energy and enterprise to insure actual realization. Fortunately, however, for a considerable number of our citizens, they had forecast sufficient to see what was in the future, and boldness enough to embrace opportunities thus offered. By so doing some have already become millionaires, and others are on the easy road to fortune. Scarcely an instance can be recalled within the past twenty-five, thirty or more years, where investments were made either in improved or unimproved property, bordering inside upon the city limits or outside her boundaries, extending far out into Baltimore County, that it did not rapidly—almost fabulously—advance substantially in value, making fortunate purchasers rich. The fact is—has been over and over again practically demonstrated—that fortunes, to a greater or less extent, have been more rapidly, surely, and more easily accumulated in this way than by any other means. It is free from all risk, and time, without labor, care or anxiety, adds value to such investments with each passing month and year. Numerous instances, surprising in themselves, could be adduced to prove what we assert. Many of our friends, we gladly know, have thus been successful. We could, if necessary, name them by scores, and trace their successes almost exclusiuely to speculations of the sort here mentioned.

It is evident that the increased and increasing population of Baltimore, the inevitable tendency of trade and business towards her existing limits, must in time disagreeably encroach upon present resident localities. This being the case, persons will gradually feel inclined to locate farther out, as many are now doing, choosing country villas as more agreeable. Within our own recollection this principle has realized most positive verification. Beautiful little towns and elegant villas—magnificent improvements indeed—have gone up where not long ago farms, barren fields, hunting grounds and unsightly prospects were only visible.

We might present numerous instances in proof of what is above asserted, but at present refer more especially to one as an example, challenging emulation. It is the enterprise of Messrs. Thomas R. Clendinen and Charles G. Wilson, representatives of the Chesapeake Land and Loan Company, the Franklin Land and Loan Company, and the Lexington Savings Bank and Loan Company, who. by their enterprise, their young active energy are accomplishing, and about to accomplish, improvements similar to those now existing within the vicinities of Boston, New York, Philadelphia, Chicago, and other large cities. It requires just such gentlemen, with quick forecast, expansive, liberal views, who have stepped far outside the confines of antiquarian notions, to see, appreciate, and outwork enterprises like those in which they have embarked. Baltimore needs more of them to insure her progress in every respect, and we hope the time is not distant when she can realize their presence, come from where they may.

The locality to which we here refer, and the scene of operations embarked in by these gentlemen, is only one mile from Baltimore, known as "Highland Park." It is a magnificent estate of 144 acres rolling land, superbly wooded and watered, rising to an elevation of about 500 feet above tide, on the Liberty or Windsor Mill road, reached by the Baltimore,

Calverton and Powhatan railroad, which leaves our city at the head of Baltimore street, and by the Baltimore and Randallstown railway, running from Pennsylvania avenue and Baker street. The first named road skirts along the western front of the property a dis, tance of more than 4,000 feet, and the last through the centre of the park 4,500 feet. The entire park has been laid out in lots twenty-five feet front, with a depth of 160 feet. Parties desiring to purchase, lease or improve, can procure one or more lots adjoining on advantageous terms. It is the object of the holders to offer such inducements as will meet a ready response.

This is the most extensive, complete, and inviting suburban improvement of its kind ever undertaken within Baltimore's vicinity, and promises great success. The first spade was struck 29th August, 1872, and now, less than nine months, some 12,000 feet of avenues sixty-six feet wide have been graded, planted with silver and sugar maples, white poplar and other trees. Gas works capable of supplying as large a quantity as is used in Hagerstown have been erected, and a dozen handsome villas, varying in value from $6,000 to $12,000, have been built, each of different design and style of architecture. All are furnished throughout with modern conveniences of gas, water, baths, ranges, furnaces, marble mantles, etc. They are substantial, airy, well ventilated, well lighted, commodious, elegantly ornamented, and finished in a superior style. Each one is advantageously located. The plan of the park, as also that of the building operations, is admirable.

CANTON.

THE Canton Company, by reason of its varied and extensive powers as a Corporation, its wonderful development and its future prospects, is entitled to special mention in any article professing to give a history of the resources of Baltimore City. The Company was organized in 1828, under a charter granted by the State of Maryland, giving the Corporation the right to hold land to the extent of ten thousand acres, and, to use the language of the fourth section of the Act itself, "to improve in such manner as may be conformable to the laws of the State, any lands which shall belong to said Company, by laying out streets, &c., in the vicinity of Baltimore on or near navigable water, and erecting and constructing wharves, slips, work-shops, factories, stores, dwellings and such other buildings and improvements as may be deemed necessary, ornamental and convenient."

Forty-five years ago this Company commenced operations. At the moment the community was not ripe for an enterprize which comprehended within its scope such vast improvements and that was likely in its developments to exceed any organization of a similar character in the country. Able and energetic men connected themselves with the Corporation; persons whose foreknowledge looked beyond the mere hour and its necessities and saw in the struggles of the youthful City the elements of a great emporium; men who discovered in Baltimore at that early period the materials for future growth, and a destiny not dreamed of in the most sanguine imaginings of her very worthy but somewhat sluggish citizens. Their enterprize and energy have already reaped for them golden rewards, scarcely comparable, however, with those which await them in the future.

Contrary to the general law which has obtained in the development of cities, (which usually leads them to spread in the direction of the West and Northwest,) Baltimore at an early period exhibited a capacity for, and a tendency to, expansion in the East certainly equal to that observable in either of the other sections. The spirit, too, which had originally created distinct towns on the opposite side of Jones' Falls was still at work, and the rivalry thus established was entirely favorable to the growth of the City as a whole.

The topographical features of the eastern section were similar to those in the west and northwest. A beautifully undulating country offered to builders and those in search of residences, eligible sites in either locality, and Canton in the east possessed the additional advantage of a magnificent expanse of water front, the natural haven of the shipping, and with accommodations ample for an almost indefinite increase of commerce. The Canton Company were not slow to avail themselves of these advantages. They bought lands and water-fronts and erected houses.

There came a period of stagnation. The enterprize languished, and the hopes of its well-wishers were dampened. Some imagined that the foreshadowings of Baltimore's future greatness were illusory, others that the opportunity had not yet presented itself, and that its founders had better await a more convenient season. The corporators were undismayed. New and vigorous elements were introduced into the management. Land in and about Canton was purchased whenever thrown upon the market—wharves were constructed—factories and warehouses built—streets were laid out, graded, and paved, until a vast extent of waste common was transformed into a busy and prosperous City. The community, slow to realize improvement in any shape, began to be attracted by this thriving seat of factories, dwellings and commercial enterprizes which appeared to have sprung from the very bowels of the earth.

They at length discovered that a great work had been quietly accomplished in their midst, but not before capitalists from a distance had been interested by the sturdy determination of the Canton Company, and after a careful examination of the progress and design of the work, these latter did not hesitate to embark in it their capital. The stock of the Company appreciated rapidly, and after a series of years the foresight of its projectors was abundantly rewarded and their judgment completely vindicated.

To-day the Canton Company owns 2,800 acres of land, comprising 18,000 building lots—laid out 20 by 100 feet—many of them binding on streets graded and paved, with water and gas convenient, part within the city limits and part without, in Baltimore County, on shelled roads or streets; also a wharf property and water front of 20,000 feet, with a depth of water from 16 to 26 feet.

The following is a list of factories and industrial enterprizes in active operation on the Company's grounds, together with the number of hands employed in each:

	No. Hands.		*No. Hands.*
12 Oyster and Fruit Packing Houses,	2,500	1 Sash Factory and Planing Mill......	25
1 Stone Cutting Yard..................	60	1 White Lead Work, (just started)....	
2 Stove and Hollow Ware Foundries..................................	200	3 Iron Smelting Furnaces................	150
1 Sugar Refinery..........................	40	1 Copper Smelting Furnace............	250
1 Fruit and Oyster Can Factory....	60	1 Bridge Builder and Machinist.......	160
1 Rolling Mill..............................	1,000	3 Distilleries.................................	
1 Axe Handle Factory.................	50	8 Coal Oil Refineries, (with capacity for refining 5,000 bbls. per week)	75
1 Dredging Company....................	100	6 Lager Beer Breweries..................	60
1 Transfer Company.....................		1 Packing Box Factory..................	10
2 Chemical Works........................		1 Ship Yard.................................	
1 Car Wheel Foundry...................	250	4 Fertilizing Manufactories.............	45
7 Brick Yards..............................	2,000	3 Lime Burners............................	30
2 Steam Saw Mills........................	40	1 Cotton Batting Factory...............	20
1 Agricultural Work.....................	30	1 Furniture and Wooden Ware Fac'y	300

NOTE.—In an article in another part of this volume the Canton Company was unintentionally mentioned, in enumerating the extent of the manufacture of Bricks in the city. This was an error. Without the mention of the Brick-Yards at Canton, the summing up on page 248 will be correct.

A number of enterprises have been established since the foregoing statistics were compiled, and the employees and residents have vastly increased during the last twelve months. The establishment of transatlantic steam-lines, the increasing trade of great rail road corporations with termini in this City, and the proposed construction of others have created a pressing demand for shipping facilities. Our rapidly increasing commercial marine needs much more extensive accommodation than the upper harbor of Baltimore, or even Locust Point, can furnish. In this emergency the attention of the public has naturally been directed to the Canton Company for relief. The Company have proved themselves equal to the exigency. An increased energy has been displayed in the construction of wharves, while immense numbers of piles have been driven for any necessity that may arise in the future. Preparations have been made for the accommodation of all the rail road corporations, which will afford ample facilities for an indefinite augmentation of the trade of Baltimore, and temporary measures have been adopted for immediate and pressing demands.

The Union Rail Road, recently completed, a work of great magnitude, was projected mainly under the auspices of the Canton Company. It consists for the most part of a Tunnel, constructed at heavy cost through a treacherous soil at a depth in some places of 65 feet below the surface, and finished in the most substantial manner. In addition to the long desired outlet it affords to tide-water, it constitutes a most important link in the great highway between the Metropolis and the Capitol of the nation.—This corporation was chartered to build a rail road around the City to connect roads centering here or passing through, and to obviate the delay and inconvenience of travel by horse-power through the streets of the City. The Canton Company subscribed for most of the Stock of the road, and endorsed the bonds of the Company to an extent sufficient to defray the expense of its construction.

CLAY CUTTING, UNION RAIL ROAD TUNNEL

Under a section of its charter, all the railroads passing through Baltimore are entitled to its use at a certain fixed valuation per mile. The Northern Central, the Baltimore and Potomac, the Western Maryland, and the Philadelphia, Wilmington and Baltimore will immediately avail themselves of this provision. The first named is now negotiating for 1,700 feet of water-front, sufficient to accommodate more than its present trade. The Baltimore and Ohio Rail Road Company has also obtained a crossing from their property on Locust Point, by which, the cost of transfer of Cumberland coal is reduced to 20 cents per ton, and thousands of tons are already passing over.

Negotiations are pending for the incorporation of a Company to build elevators of a capacity sufficient for any quantity of grain. Trestle works and transfers are already constructed by which grain, coal and produce generally, may be transferred from cars to shipboard, at the smallest possible expense. Arrangements are now being perfected for the extension of the Western Maryland Rail Road, by a route the shortest yet found to Pittsburg, the Lakes, the bituminous and gas-coal fields and coal oil regions.

The brick yards are to be removed to remote portions of the Company's land that the whole property adjacent to the four miles of water-front may be developed—in fact everything is being done that a careful foresight can suggest for the most liberal accommodation of trade that is already centering at Canton. Several enterprising New York Capitalists have been added recently to the Directors, and the Board is at present composed as follows:

Chas. J. Baker, George S. Brown, Charles Weber, Wm. G. Harrison, and S. Sprigg Belt, of Baltimore, and James H. Banker, Wm. Mertens, Wm. Butler Duncan and Samuel L. M. Barlow, of New York.

The influence exerted by the Canton Company is to be seen not only on their own grounds but through the entire Eastern section of the City, and the rate of improvement in the latter quarter is at present quite as great as in any other portion of Baltimore. The extension of Patterson Park, whence the finest views of the City and harbor, with their surroundings may be obtained, invites the erection of the handsomest residences, and enterprising builders are availing themselves of the opportunities thus presented. A feature of the Company's work and to which much of their success may be attributed is the fact that they are always ready to extend a helping hand to energetic mechanics or business men. Those desirous of prosecuting a certain business who do not possess the adequate capital nor machinery, have but to show their capacity and energy to be assisted.

The future of the Canton Company can be readily foretold, but how rapid will be its development, and how extensive its usefulness to the City of Baltimore, it is impossible to predicate from any data at present in our possession. The anthracite coal from Pennsylvania will seek here a depot, and an outlet by hundreds of thousands of tons,—the bituminous and gas-coals will pour into Canton in quantities of which the present receipts give but a feeble idea, while the facilities for shipment, indefinite in extent and of such easy accesibility throughout the entire year, leave no room for doubt that it will rival, if it does not supass all other marts for the exportation of coal in this country.

The rail roads centering here drain an immense extent of fertile country and will pour into Canton the great grain products of Maryland, Pennsylvania, Virginia, and a large share of the produce of the vast plains of the West, and the elevators to be erected will constitute it the most accessible spot for the shipment of grain on the Atlantic seaboard—but it is as a manufacturing center that Canton will be especially useful to Baltimore. The number of factories already established is but an earnest of its future development in this regard and the inducements held out by the Company, the moderate rents, the cheapness of living in Baltimore, and the character of the men who comprise the Board of Directors, substantial, high-toned and able to accomplish what they promise, all point to Canton as the future manufacturing center of the seaboard.

BALTIMORE AND OHIO RAIL ROAD.

CHARLES CARROLL of Carrollton, the last surviving signer of the Declaration of Independence, laid the corner-stone of the Baltimore and Ohio Rail Road on the 4th of July, 1828. The character of this illustrious man has shed its influence upon this great work from that hour. A long list of Presidents, whose judgments have been surpassed only by their integrity and successive Boards of Directors, with foresight and enterprise, tempered with prudence, have given tone to the Corporation in the past, and have brought the undertaking to a conclusion so eminently successful as to challenge the admiration of thinking men both at home and abroad.

When we consider that the Baltimore and Ohio Rail Road was the first *road* of that nature projected in this country, it is easy to imagine the difficulties attending its construction. From the very novelty of the undertaking, many untried problems had necessarily to be solved or their impracticability demonstrated. During the first few years of its existence these efforts to discover the best and most economical modes of construction, without precedents, and with the comparatively limited scientific acquirements of those days, presented obstacles by the side of which the trials of modern engineering shrink into insignificance and the solution of which has facilitated the construction of many similar works in America. But the perplexities encountered in building the road were slight in comparison with the financial difficulties which beset the Company until the road was completed to the Ohio river on the 1st of January, 1853. The opening to Wheeling, a distance of 379 miles, was attended with special ceremonies and really marked an era in the history of railway enterprise. Vast mountains had been tunneled, valleys filled up, and rivers spanned to admit the passage of the locomotive, and vexed questions in engineering set at rest forever. A country abounding in mineral wealth and fertile plains, which needed but the hand of the husbandman to "blossom as the rose," was opened up to civilization and made tributary to Baltimore; a traffic was begun in Coal which has since then developed into gigantic proportions—millions of tons passing over the road annually, and a line of intercourse established with the great West that gave an impetus to emigration, and has since added greatly to the trade and commerce of our City.

Mr. John W. Garrett, of the firm of Robert Garrett & Sons of this City, accepted the Presidency of this road in 1858. Financial difficulties had embarrassed its operations for some years prior to 1856. Mr. Garrett was first induced to interest himself in its affairs about 1857, and very soon thereafter the good influence of his wise counsels became apparent in its management, but an immediate and palpable change became manifest upon his accession to the Presidency. He surrendered to the Road his vigorous powers of mind, his vast financial experience and his great executive ability. His presence at its head acted like a spur upon the Corporation, and since that time the history of the road has been a series of uninterrupted successes.

The Baltimore and Ohio Rail Road Company have established permanent co-operative relations with the Marietta and Cincinnati and the Ohio and Mississippi Rail Roads, thus virtually extending the Baltimore and Ohio Rail Road to Cincinnati, and through that City to St. Louis, connecting by friendly Northern and Southern Roads with, and drawing business from the Southern half of the great States of Ohio, Indiana, and Illinois, also from Kentucky, having direct connection with Louisville, its chief city, and reaching Tennessee, Arkansas and other Southern States through other effective alliances.

Under the policy of President Garrett the Baltimore and Ohio has been extended to Columbus, Ohio, to Sandusky on Lake Erie and to Pittsburg by the extension of the Pittsburg and Connellsville Rail Road, now known as the Pittsburg, Washington and Baltimore Rail Road. The Winchester and Potomac Rail Road, the Winchester and Strasburg Rail Road, the Washington County Rail Road, and the Metropolitan or Point of Rocks Rail Road, have been established during this period. This Metropolitan Branch shortens the line between Washington and the great West 48 miles. By this route and the Connellsville Rail Road the distance from Pittsburg to Washington is but 300 miles; thence to Baltimore 38 miles; and only 10 miles further from Pittsburg to Baltimore *via* Washington than by the direct line; hence the name Pittsburg, Washington and Baltimore Rail Road. Under the auspices of the Baltimore and Ohio, a line of rail road is now being constructed through the Valley of Virginia, which will bring this wonderful agricultural region into direct communication with our City. By its connection with the Chesapeake and Ohio Rail Road at Staunton, the Coal, Iron and Salt territory of West Virginia is opened up to Baltimore, and by the extension of this Valley Rail Road to Salem, and connection with the Virginia and Tennessee Rail Road the salt and other minerals of Southwest

Virginia are reached, and also the products of East Tennessee, Georgia, Alabama and Mississippi. By the Orange, Alexandria and Manassas Rail Road, with its extensions under its new name, "Washington City, Virginia-Midland and Great Southern," the mineral regions of Virginia, the Carolinas and Georgia are reached, where gold, silver, lead, copper and iron are found, and where the climate and soil are favorable to agriculture, particularly so for fruits and vegetables.

This latter connection is formed by the Washington Branch of the Baltimore and Ohio, which leaves the Main Stem at the Relay House, about nine miles from Baltimore, and runs to the National Capital. Another short road is to be constructed from the Metropolitan Branch to a point in the neighborhood of the Annapolis Junction, by means of which passengers and freight from the West can be conveyed directly to our City by a much shorter route than that at present in use, while the line of rail road along the Patapsco and Monocacy, penetrating a region abounding in vegetable and mineral wealth, will still by its way-traffic add to the revenues of the Company.

At a point 90 miles above Newark, on the Lake Erie Division of the road, it is proposed to construct a line of Rail Road direct to Chicago, a distance of 260 miles. In addition to the trade directly from Chicago, and along the line of this road, it will have many important connections east of the Prairie City, which, in obedience to their interests, will be feeders to this Chicago extension. The Cincinnati, Sandusky and Cleveland Rail Road connects at Tiffin; the Dayton and Michigan Rail Road extending from Cincinnati through Toledo to Detroit, with connections penetrating the Michigan prairies, north and west of Saginaw, connects at Deshler, Henry County, Ohio, and the Toledo, Wabash and Western Railroad, connects at Defiance, Ohio. This road, with its branches, extends over Illinois and Missouri more than 1,200 miles. At Auburn, Indiana, it connects with the Fort Wayne, Jackson and Saginaw and the Eel River Roads, both extending south into Indiana, and north into Michigan. At Walkerton it crosses the Indianapolis, Peru and Chicago Rail Road, and by this route can reach Laporte and Michigan City, Indiana, the latter a port on Lake Michigan. Before entering Chicago a connection can be made with the Illinois Central Rail Road, which, with its branches, drain the greater portion of Illinois. This road can have no interest in opposition to the Baltimore and Ohio, but will seek over its line the port of Baltimore, as its best entrepot for the produce of the country, through which its main line of branches extend. Numerous branches are proposed to connect important towns in Ohio and Indiana, with this Chicago extension. The benefits that will accrue to our City from the completion of these great enterprises, are incalculable.

Already has the trade of Pittsburgh, the great manufacturing city west of the Alleghanies, begun to pour into Baltimore, and the time is not far distant when we shall compete successfully with the cities of Philadelphia and New York for the carrying trade of this great region of country. The Baltimore and Ohio, with its through connections South and West, has materially aided the development of those sections, by opening up territory, rich in mineral and agricultural resources, susceptible of great improvement and to which the rapidly increasing population of the Atlantic seaboard, and the tide of emigration pouring into our City may resort with confident hopes of at least realizing many of their anticipations by frugality and industry. Towns and villages have sprung up along the line of railroad, and even those sections but remotely connected with the road have felt its wonderful influence.

A spirit of enterprise has grown up in neighboring districts; roads and turn-pikes have been opened, and vast stretches of country that might have remained primeval forests but for this great work of internal improvement, have become productive and the inhabitants cultivated and refined. The extension of the road from Centreton on the Lake Erie Division to Chicago, gives the Baltimore and Ohio one continuous line of rail road from Baltimore to the Lake City of the West, the granary where is received the exhaustless products of the fertile plains which stretch out through the northwest. Thus Baltimore is enabled to compete with the great cities of the East for a share of this immense trade. The extension of the road from Pittsburg to Centreton, a mere question of time, will give another direct route from Chicago to Baltimore.

The scenery along the line of the Baltimore and Ohio Railway is picturesque and beautiful, but portions of the road merit special notice. "Harper's Ferry," the point at which the peaceful waters of the Shenandoah become lost in the more boisterous Potomac, has been described by Jefferson as "one of the most stupendous scenes in nature, and well worth a voyage across the Atlantic to witness." Jefferson's Rock, named after that illustrious statesman, a great overhanging cliff which looks frowningly down as though it would topple headlong upon the unwary traveler, offers an exhaustive view of the wonderful passage of these two rivers through the very heart of the mountains. The road from this point to the Ohio River gives to the sight-seer a succession of views embracing nature in almost every attitude. Long ranges of mountains, beautiful valleys, level plains, changed by the magic of the husbandman into boundless gardens, lofty precipices, mountain torrents, and the endless phases in which nature fantastically arrays herself, pass before the vision like the ever changing views in some gigantic kaleidescope. "Fort Frederick," whose hundred years have witnessed the downfall of one government and the uprearing of another, the vigorous growth of which has astonished the world, and with whose history the name of Washington will ever be connected, is located near the line of the road between Harper's Ferry and Cumberland. "The Glades" and "Cheat River Valley" are perhaps as rich in exquisite natural scenery as any portion of the world, and tourists at this early date have evinced their appreciation of what has been aptly styled "the American Switzerland."

Among those features on the line of the Baltimore and Ohio well worthy of inspection by sight-seers and travelers, are the immense rolling-mills or machine-shops of the Company, located at Cumberland, and the magnificent Hotel, recently erected by the corporation for the accommodation of travel over their roads.

The affairs of the Baltimore and Ohio Rail Road under the present administration have been conducted with prudence and economy, and yet, when the end appeared to justify the means, the Company has not hesitated to venture its capital in behalf of the boldest enterprises. Shortly after the war, a pioneer line of Steamers was established between this port and Liverpool under the auspices of this corporation, which, though not entirely successful, because of the very limited carrying capacity of the vessels employed, clearly demonstrated that as a port of entry, Baltimore was destined to become one of the leading Cities in America. This line was succeeded by what is known as the "North German Lloyd," or "Baltimore and Bremen" line of Steamships. Four first-class steam-ships have already been placed on this route (and two more are in process of construction) to ply between Baltimore, Southampton and Bremen.

The property of the Baltimore and Ohio Rail Road at Locust Point has been greatly improved to meet the requirements of these Steamers. The funds necessary for improving the harbor and channel having been provided by the Government of the United States and the City of Baltimore, this work, which has been in progress for some time, is rapidly approaching completion. When finished, the depth of water will be sufficient for the largest sea-going vessels,—all that is necessary to make Baltimore equal to any seaport in the country and without drawback from the advantages she possesses over all others in geographical position. Piers have been constructed at Locust Point, spacious and substantial warehouses built, and a grain elevator erected with a capacity for 600,000 bushels of grain. In addition, the Company proposes to erect immediately two more grain elevators with a capacity of 1,000,000 bushels each.

The success of the Bremen Steamships has led to the establishment of another Transatlantic Steamship Company, the Allan Line, which connects this port with Halifax and Liverpool. The cheapness of fuel in Baltimore gives these Steamers a great advantage over other cities. They are enabled to coal here at a reduction in cost of $2,000, for each voyage, and the port charges in comparison with other cities along the Atlantic Coast, are insignificant.

The great Workshops of the Company at Mount Clare, on the Western suburbs of our City, in which are employed more than sixteen hundred hands, form an especial feature of Baltimore. Here all varieties of work required by the necessities of a mammoth rail road are manufactured. Great Iron Bridges, Locomotives, Pullman Palace Cars and the most elegant Passenger Coaches, with all their polished veneering and rich upholstery, Stationary Engines, Boilers, Car Wheels, Axles, Bar Iron, Rail Fixtures, Springs, &c., are produced with a neatness of finish and skillfulness, and with strong and durable qualities not exceeded anywhere in the world. At various points along the line of road, similar workshops of very ample capacity for the repair and manufacture of machinery, are established.

The benefits which our City has reaped from this great road are simply inestimable. The impetus given to manufactures and the employment furnished to citizens would alone abundantly compensate the City for the assistance she gave the road in the early stages of its construction, but the vast amount of wealth, mineral and agricultural, poured into our City through this main artery can only be measured by her rapid increase in all the elements which make a great metropolis.

The financial condition of the City has been very strikingly affected by her relations to the Baltimore and Ohio Rail Road. Being a proprietor of $3,250,000 of the stock of the Company, she receives ten per cent. upon her investment, and, paying but six per cent. upon the debt created to aid this work, she realizes a profit of $130,000 annually for the benefit of the tax-payers.

It may be noted here as a remarkable fact that the assessed value of the real estate in Baltimore at the time the Baltimore and Ohio Rail Road was commenced, in 1827, was but $27,000,000, a sum less by $29,000,000 than the amount since absorbed in this great work.

The vast proportions to which this organization has grown, are shown by the fact that its control already extends over railway properties in many States, the cost of which exceeds $100,000,000. It possesses more than 500 locomotives, over 10,000 passenger and freight cars, and employs above 20,000 men in its working departments; its disbursements for labor, material and supplies exceeding $1,000,000 per month.

As the Baltimore and Ohio Rail Road, together with the vast net-work of railways co-operating with it, is used in making Baltimore a great manufacturing and commercial centre, and the most economical and desirable entrepot for the constantly expanding business of large portions of our extensive country, it requires but the concurrent energy and enterprise of our citizens to make the progress and greatness of the City unlimited in extent and thoroughly substantial in character.

The following is a list of the prominent officers of the Baltimore and Ohio Rail Road:

President—John W. Garrett; 1st Vice President—John King, Jr.; 2d Vice President—Wm. Keyser; Master of Transportation—Thomas R. Sharp; Master of Machinery—John C. Davis; Master of Road—John L. Wilson; General Freight Agent—N. Guilford; General Ticket Agent—L. M. Cole; General Passenger Agent—Sydney B. Jones, (Cincinnati); Auditor—Wm. T. Thelin; Assistant Auditor—A. D. Smith, (Columbus, Ohio); Treasurer—Wm. H. Ijams; Superintendent of Telegraph—A. G. Davis; General Superintendent Ohio Division, (Columbus, O.)—W. C. Quincy; Edward Potts, Secretary to the President.

NORTHERN CENTRAL RAILWAY.

IN that broad expanse of country with Niagara Falls, between Lakes Erie and Ontario, forming the apex and New York, Philadelphia and our own City marking the base of the triangle, may be found pretty fully illustrated the great wealth which Nature has given to man.

That its importance was thoroughly appreciated by all three of these large cities and that they desired to secure its advantages to themselves peculiarly, is evidenced by the fact that great lines of rail roads were very early in the history of our country projected through its entire length and breadth and now form a perfect net-work over the territory embraced in the triangle. The richest fruits of husbandry, the exhaustless mineral deposits which underlie the soil in that region, the great woods which furnish so luxuriously our best saloons and drawing-rooms, form together a combination of treasures which can be surpassed probably in no other section of the globe.

The range of territory embraced within the lines drawn from these cities to the point named above, has had expended upon it, perhaps, more of the muscular strength and exuberant energy of man than any other district of the same dimensions in this or the Old World, save the portions of Great Britain and the continent of Europe that have been for ten centuries inhabi-

LAKE ROLAND.

ted and cultivated by an enlightened race. Several causes have led to this wonderful development of a region not a whit better than many other parts of these United States. Proximity to our great cities and the vast capital which centres in those places, but especially the facilities for building rail roads, have brought about a result which must necessarily lead to the growth of the whole American Continent and the realization of the prophecies of our sanguine politicians with reference to its immense forces at the beginning of the next century.

Among those great Roads which have contributed to the progress of this vast section of our country may be mentioned with pride by Baltimoreans the present "Northern Central Railway," formerly known as the Baltimore and Susquehanna. Chartered by the State of Maryland on the 13th day of February, 1828, organized as a Company on the 5th of May following, with a Board of Directors whose names are historic, it commenced operations by the laying of the corner-stone on the 8th of August of the succeeding year. It was confidently expected that the Commonwealth of Pennsylvania would combine with our State in this great undertaking, and after long delay, in March, 1832, an act of incorporation was obtained from the Pennsylvania Legislature to extend the road from York to the Maryland line. The latter act was objectionable in its features, and it was not until November, 1835, that a satisfactory conclusion was reached between the Legislative body of that State and the Stockholders of the road. Our space requires that we should be brief in our notice of the early history of this Company.

Like all great works of internal improvements, planned almost in the dawn of our national life, it had its trials and struggles. The wisdom of our Legislators which had manifested itself so conspicuously with regard to other corporations was not slow to perceive the advantages that must accrue from this organization to the City of Baltimore and the State of Maryland. Timely aid was extended, and our own City contributed her quota towards its construction. It must be borne in mind however, that rail roads at that time were in their infancy—civil engineering was scarcely a distinct science outside of the army, and very able men with the best intentions in the world were liable to make mistakes in estimates, and did make egregious errors. The road was opened to the Relay House on July 4th 1831 and to Timonium and Owings' Mills in 1832. It was perhaps the first rail road corporation in this country to undertake gradients of any considerable magnitude. The Parr Spring Ridge was overcome by a grade of·84 feet to the mile, for two and seven-tenths miles.

An interesting feature in its early history was the importation of a locomotive from Liverpool, ordered in March 1831, and ready for delivery six months before a vessel could be obtained to bring it over—the third locomotive, by the by, in successful operation in America. The Baltimore and Susquehanna Rail Road was completed to York, in August 1838; the Wrightsville, York and Gettysburg Rail Road subsequently operated in connection with this road, was finished in 1840; to Columbia it was opened in the same year and communication secured with Pittsburg by means of a canal from that point.

The State of Maryland on the 10th of March, 1854, and the Commonwealth of Pennsylvania on the 3d of May following, passed an act with this title:

"An Act to authorize the consolidation of the Baltimore and Susquehanna Rail Road Company, with the York and Maryland Line Rail Road Company, the York and Cumberland Rail Road Company, and the Susquehanna Rail Road Company by the name of the Northern Central Railway Company."

THE ARTIST'S DREAM—WATKINS GLEN.

The connection of the Northern Central with the great Pennsylvania Road, its extension by means of its own branches or healthful connections to the Lakes, the West, the North-west, the South, and the Pacific Coast are so well known to the public at large, as to require no allusion in an article of this kind. That this road ramifying as it does, through its connections, the whole North American Continent as far as it has yet been settled, has accomplished incalculable good for our country, it is scarcely necessary to mention here, but there are features about it which belong to few rail roads, and which we feel bound to recount in an article setting forth its advantages in connection with the history of Baltimore. If we glance at any of the maps which exhibit its extensions, we shall find that along its line have sprung into existence towns and cities as though by magic. So thickly are they strewn from Baltimore to Canandaigua, that a map drawn with proper scales will hardly contain their names. The whole road appears to be a continuous city with here and there a more thickly settled portion to mark the greater enterprise of a particular class of the inhabitants.

The immense wealth underlying the surface of Baltimore County, iron, marble, granite and lime, is tapped and brought into our City. The road penetrates the wonderful anthracite region in Pennsylvania, and its exhaustless products are received in Baltimore by hundreds of thousands of tons. The Copper mines about Lake Superior contribute to its revenues,—the through travel from the great North-west, the products of that section and of the "Far West" and their vast resources, mineral, vegetable and cereal, are poured into our City through its means.

The gentlemen connected with the road have displayed an energy and have adopted a far-sighted policy that really rank them among those great practical men who have made the nineteenth century an extraordinary era in the annals of history. Whenever a connection could be profitably formed and was likely to lead to trade and travel to any of the larger cities where its termini are located the road was extended in that direction, and this has been done repeatedly when immediate profit could not have been a consideration, indicating clearly that it was the result of enlightened prudence, and that *future* prosperity was the object at which the Company was aiming. This policy undoubtedly in the early history of the road impaired its financial strength, but "it is an ill-wind that blows nobody good," and the terrific war between the North and the South which brought trouble to every community and almost every fire-side in the land, yielded a golden harvest to the rail roads located along or leading to the lines of the contending armies. This road was convenient to the capital of the country, and like similar corporations having depots in this City, its coffers were replenished by the revenue acquired from the Government for the transportation of troops and supplies and its embarrassments were consequently dissipated. A double track was completed over the greater portion of its length, and its monetary strength so considerably augmented that it was enabled to extend a helping hand to a new road projected through a very fertile section of our State but which had languished because of the impoverished condition of our people who resided in that region.

The latter, the Baltimore and Potomac, has since then been built through several of the lower Counties of Maryland to the Potomac river and also to the City of Washington, and forms close and continuous connections by locomotive power through the great tunnels under the Eastern and Northwestern sections of our City with all the leading Northern and Southern routes of travel.

THE EAGLE CLIFF AND FALLS—HAVANA GLEN.

The Northern Central Railway Company have not been content to rest on their oars; they seek now by means of the Union Rail Road an outlet to tide-water, which in view of the very great increase in the Coal trade of our City in the past 18 months, will be specially advantageous to our commercial interests. They have invested heavily in land at Canton and purpose the erection immediately of spacious piers, wharves and elevators for the reception of Western grain. But we shall devote the balance of our space to a summary of the more interesting and beautiful features along the line of this great road. A trip over it from Baltimore to Niagara cannot fail to interest, and its impressions will be stamped upon the mind forever. For simple beauty, splendor or sublimity the scenery along the route is perhaps not equalled by that of any road in the world. There may be lines of travel which, separately, illustrate more strongly any one of these features, but such a combination can scarcely be witnessed on any other road. The Rocky Mountain passes give us an idea of *grandeur*, some of the terrific declivities of the Andes, *sublimity*, and the beautiful little glades about Cheat River in the Alleghany range suggest simple loveliness, but along this line of road we have them *all*, and can enjoy them *seriatim*.

As the train passes out of the substantial depot on Calvert Street the traveller is confronted with the great machine shops which have given Baltimore such a reputation as a centre for manufactures. Through a line of villages, the natural off-shoots of a great city, teeming with busy life and echoing the sound of the manufacturer's hammer, the train glides until a beautiful little lake is reached which nestles peacefully in a smiling valley. So cosily is it located one finds it difficult to realize that the skill of man, not the hand of Nature, has created Lake Roland as a reservoir to supply the wants of a great city.

The road passes Timonium, at one time the great race-course of the State, where many of the contests that so delighted the distinguished heads of the old Maryland families, were wont to occur. Further on, beyond Cockeysville, are located the marble, granite and lime quarries and the iron works at Ashland, with great beds of ore that are likely to add for an indefinite period to the resources and prosperity of our City. The Gunpowder River, a small stream tributary to the Chesapeake Bay, intersects the road at numerous points until the Maryland line is reached. The river crosses beneath the railway in several places, and in some instances its windings and twistings among the overshadowing rocks give a decidedly picturesque appearance to the landscape. Long ranges of hills in the upper part of Baltimore County, discovering to the pleasure-seeker or traveller the various strata of rock so instructive to the geologist and attractive to all who take an interest in the workings of Nature, mark this portion of the Northern Central Railway.

There are so many features of general interest along the line of this road that it will be impossible for us to mention them all, and many omissions will necessarily occur of spots which travellers, once seeing, can never forget. The connections of the Northern Central with Gettysburg and its vicinity point it out as a delightful Road to excursionists. Here occurred what has been supposed by many to have been the crowning battle of the fratricidal strife which deluged some of the fairest portions of our country in blood. The Healing Springs of Gettysburg, a recent discovery, and the variegated scenery of the surrounding country, are strong inducements both to the sight-seer and the valetudinarian.

It is not, however, until after Harrisburg is reached that the more striking features of this great highway can be thoroughly appreciated. The Susquehanna comes in view, a stream, broad, majestic and prolific in points of interest, and, as the full moon at times casts its pale rays over the waters, suggestive of scenes far away, where the people traverse their city in boats, and shadowy forms glide from under the dark arches like phantoms from another world, with this difference, that the apparitions proceed from the numberless drifts which crowd the river, and the gondolas are lovely little islands studding its centre and sides.

SUSQUEHANNA, NEAR HARRISBURG.

But there is a region beyond Harrisburg on this road, a section of America which deserves special mention, where nature has invested the country with all the qualities alluded to above, and where the industry of man with his feeble auxiliaries, has utilized the boundless treasures she offers him. As we pass through the centre of Pennsylvania into the Western portion of New York, we encounter a succession of beautiful views,—lofty precipices, mountain torrents, rushing cascades, pastoral fields, awful chasms, headlong falls of streams and wonderful upheavals of the Earth's surface which cause us to gaze with admiration, and if reflection at such a time be possible, to think of the limitless phenomena produced for our pleasure and instruction by an all wise and all powerful Creator, in a space which occupies so small a portion of the planet on which we live. The exquisite beauty of the landscape along the canal near Millport; Watkins Glen, already world renowned, with its boundless variety of scenery, alternately awing us into soberness by its grandeur and calling forth exclamations of delight by its sweet peaceful beauty; the very names of the views suggestive and showing how man can only be an imitator of the manifold workings of nature, "the Cathedral," "the Artist's

THE BRIDAL VEIL—HAVANA GLEN.

Dream;" Havana Glen with its "Bridal Veil," its "Mystic Cascade," its "Eagle Cliff and Fall;" the little mountain torrents flowing through each of these vales displaying a multiplicity of motions, at one moment leaping with resistless fury from precipice to precipice as though they would rend the adamantine surfaces upon which they fell; at another gliding mildly along with graceful sinuosity as though they had never rushed and spouted and foamed; the mammoth walls of rock, with jagged sides which rear their lofty heads on either hand as these limpid fountains gush down their sides or seek the old and beaten pathway marked out for them at some preadamite period, when man was known only in the mind of the great Creator—all these varied and wonderful objects of interest widely known at present, are destined in the future to make this region the *mecca* of tourists, and the Northern Central Railway the route by which their pilgrimages are to be accomplished.

Genesee Falls are too well-known to need description here, and finally the great Falls of Niagara, the eighth wonder of the world, the apex of the triangle referred to in the beginning of this article are reached. Their grandeur and sublimity are known to the whole world, and the impossibility of doing justice to their magnificent features should be a sufficient apology for their mere mention.

In closing our remarks upon the Northern Central, it is due to this corporation that we should particularly specify the great benefits it has accomplished, not only for the sections of country through which it immediately passes, but for the whole of our vast territory as yet brought under cultivation and made tributary to the wants and luxuries of our people.

Beginning its efforts early in our history, it pushed steadily on with its work until that portion already alluded to had been penetrated, and its rich treasures,—mineral, agricultural and beautiful,—exposed to the gaze and collected for the use of mankind.

The development of one region leads to the advancement of all. How far the Company has been instrumental in assisting the progress of civilization to the far West, it is impossible to estimate; it is sufficient for our purposes to state,

UNDER THE FALL, LOOKING TOWARD THE CATHEDRAL—WATKINS GLEN.

that, as in the *past*, it has sought connections and extended its road wherever they were likely to prove mutually profitable to the corporation and the City of Baltimore, so for the *future*, the present energetic and prudent management of the Company is a satisfactory guarantee.

The following are the officers of the Northern Central Railway:

President—J. D. Cameron; Vice President—J. N. Du Barry; General Manager—A. J. Cassatt; Secretary—R. S. Hollins; Treasurer—J. S. Leib; Auditor—S. Little; General Passenger Agent—Edwin S. Young; General Eastern Freight Agent—J. M. Drill; General Western Freight Agent—Isaac M. Schermerhorn.

BALTIMORE AND POTOMAC RAIL ROAD.

THE five lower Counties on the Western Shore of Maryland contain a population, intelligent, educated and refined, and possessing characteristics very similar to those which distinguish the inhabitants of our own City; moreover, in each of those counties may be found broad tracts of country remarkably fertile and productive and most beautifully located, and yet until within the last year or so, but little has been known of these people or the section in which they live.

A number of reasons may be urged for this apparent obscurity. We shall, however, suggest but one, so self-evident, that its bare mention will cause its recognition. Until a very recent period there were practically no avenues of communication between Baltimore and large sections of these counties, not forty miles distant from the city limits. The fact is the "iron-horse" had penetrated the vast wildernesses of the West and scaled the lofty altitudes of the Rocky Mountains before he had entered the "forest of Prince George" or the great tobacco growing country of Charles and St. Mary's, while much the larger and richer portions of Anne Arundel and Calvert are still without rail

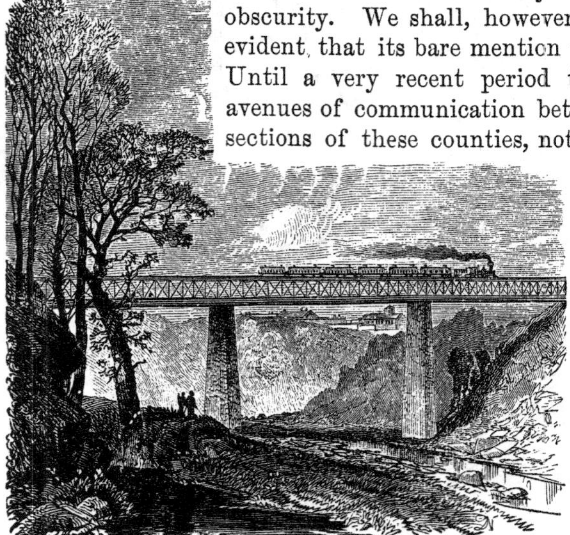

HIGH BRIDGE OVER GWYNN'S FALLS, B. & P. R. R.

road communication. The steamboats which ply between Baltimore and different points along the shores of these counties, though furnishing safe and commodious means of access, do not of themselves afford sufficient outlet for the trade of the Southern portions of the Western Shore, even when not obstructed by the inclemency of the weather during the winter season. Though they contribute their quota to the development of that portion of our State they are not able to bring about that rapid improvement which would seem to be necessary to enable these sections of Maryland to keep pace with the great march of progress and advancement taking place in many other parts of the country.

Before the war, the gentlemen from these counties lived like feudal barons. Surrounded by their slaves, nearly all were independent as far as this world's goods were concerned, and the spirit of money-making, at present the prevalent feature of all communities, had made but slight inroads among the wealthy neighborhoods which so thickly dotted this lower tier of counties.

Hospitality, the brightest gem in Maryland's crown, the jewel which has made her far better known in foreign lands than some of her wealthier and more enterprising sisters, seemed to be both the business and pastime of the inhabitants of this portion of our State, and as there was no urgent necessity for the exercise of energy, at that time but little of it was exhibited. There were bright exceptions even then to the rule. Some men were conspicuous in these localities for their clear appreciation of the real needs of lower Maryland and endeavored to arouse a spirit of enterprise. As early as 1853, a number of these gentlemen applied to the Legislature and obtained a charter for the Baltimore and Potomac Rail Road. The preliminary organization was not effected until 1859, and the following gentlemen were selected as Directors of the road: Hon. John Stephen Sellman, of Anne Arundel County; Hon. William D. Bowie and Col. W. W. W. Bowie, of Prince George's County; Hon. Walter Mitchell and John W. Jenkins, of Charles County; Edmund S. Plowden, of St. Mary's County, and Edwin Robinson, of Virginia.

Unavailing efforts were made to commence the construction of the road during the year. No State or City aid had been secured, and as was said above the large majority of land owners did not at that time realize the necessity for railroad communication with Baltimore. The Hon. ODEN BOWIE, since then Governor of our State, was made a Director of the road, and very soon thereafter its President, in 1860. He immediately suggested a more active policy, and two sections of the work, from Upper Marlboro to the Annapolis and Elk Ridge Rail Road, were put under contract. Had the contractors completed their work, Upper Marlboro, the county seat of Prince George's, would have been placed in communication with our City by means of the Annapolis and Elk Ridge Rail Road and its connection with the Washington Branch of the Baltimore and Ohio Rail Road. Unfortunately the civil war broke out and a long period of inactivity followed. Governor

Bowie never relaxed his efforts, but the political agitation which convulsed the country for the next four years rendered abortive every attempt to build a road that did not minister to its necessities in some form.

The war over, the people of Prince George's and Charles became alive to the almost absolute necessity of the road, but they were in no condition to respond financially to the demands of Governor Bowie. The system of labor in these counties had undergone a complete revolution. Millions of dollars worth of property had been swept away—hundreds of households were impoverished, and those who had escaped bankruptcy had not yet adjusted them-

EASTERN ENTRANCE OF BALTIMORE AND POTOMAC RAIL ROAD TUNNEL.

selves to the great change that had taken place in their mode of planting and farming. With what rapidity they assimilated themselves to the change in their condition and put their shoulders to the wheel, it is hardly necessary to state here, but at this juncture, no local capital could be raised and the prospects of the corporation were desperate. Governor Bowie was undismayed. He had seen all along the great advantages to be derived from its construction, not only to the portion of Maryland through which it would pass, but also to Baltimore, which it would place in such close connection with the great Southern and South-western lines of travel and which through its branch road to Washington gave another means of approach to the National Capital.

The capitalists of Maryland had very generallv invested in the great corporations which had served to extend the trade and commerce of Baltimore, and the financial pressure which had followed the close of the war, and which has not altogether abated at this writing, did not leave many of them in a condition to aid in the construction of another road. Struggles, too, ensued with rival corporations, and it was not until 1867 that legislative enactments were obtained that enabled the corporation to commence its work.

In the meantime, the President had not been idle. Finding it impossible to interest the capitalists of our own State because of the crippled condition in which they were placed, he went elsewhere. The Pennsylvania Rail Road Company appreciated directly the advantages likely to accrue to Baltimore and its own system of roads from its completion, and the requisite funds were secured for its construction. The road was put under contract immediately throughout its entire length.

It was to be built first from Baltimore through Anne Arundel, Prince George's and Charles Counties, to Pope's Creek, on the Potomac River, a distance of 73 miles, and its lateral branch to Washington, from Bowie Junction in Prince George's, was to be 17 miles long, making its entire length 90 miles. The Baltimore and Potomac was opened from Baltimore to Washington on the 2d day of July, 1872, and from Bowie to Pope's Creek on the 1st of January, 1873.

The most prominent features of the road are its great tunnels under the cities of Washington and Baltimore. The tunnel in our City passes directly under the streets and houses, is one and a half miles in length, and at some points 55 feet below the level of the streets. It is cut in many instances through solid rock. Water and other obstacles were encountered, but the most scientific principles of engineering were brought into play to surmount them, the magnitude of which will be better understood when it is known that its cost has been more than two millions of dollars. Indeed there is no such work under any other city in the Union. The road itself from Baltimore to Pope's Creek is a model of engineering skill. The Company have availed themselves of all the modern improvements in rail road construction known to Engineers. Its superstructure is substantially built and laid with durable rails weighing 64 pounds to the yard.

The immediate results to follow to the city of Baltimore are, an impetus to farming and planting through an extended and very fertile region of our own State, by which the productions of that section, such as corn, wheat and tobacco, are likely to be increased four-fold, and fruits and vegetables of every description brought into the city at prices which will place them within reach of the whole community; an enhancement of the value of property along its line, and an offer of sites for summer residences for our successful merchants, together with small farms, for their recreation and pleasure, at prices likely to render unnecessary the expensive exodus of our people during the hot months of summer to the various fashionable and uncomfortable resorts and watering places.

To the country through which it passes it will simply be an inestimable auxiliary. Its more remote benefits to our City will manifest themselves at an early day when the plans at present in contemplation have been carried out and the extension to Richmond completed. Already, through its Washington branch, intercourse with the Southern lines of rail road has been secured, and the completion of the Baltimore tunnel gives a perfectly agreeable and convenient route to through trade and travel. The road is abundantly provided with the finest equipment of engines, passenger coaches, palace and sleeping cars, and has already fulfilled the most sanguine hopes of its friends.

The following is a list of the present officers of the corporation:

Hon. Oden Bowie, President; J. N. Du Barry, Vice President and General Manager; E. L. Du Barry, Superintendent; S. Little, Secretary and Auditor; J. S. Leib, Treasurer; Edwin S. Young, General Passenger Agent; James M. Drill, General Freight Agent.

THE author begs to say, that in compiling this account of "The Monumental City, Its Past History and Present Resources," he has had to contend with peculiar difficulties. In the effort to represent all interests, it has been necessary to seek information from many sources, and to accept it in various shapes. The facts obtained were sometimes a little highly colored by the prejudices of those from whom they were derived.

Whatever may be the faults of the work, he feels that he has gathered a mass of information in regard to our prosperous and growing city, and that in acting the pioneer, he has materially lightened the labors of those who will come after him.

GEO. W. HOWARD.

J.W. BOND & CO.
90
BOOKSELLERS
J.W. BOND & CO.
90
J.W. BOND & CO.
EILERS

National Fire Insurancc Company

OF BALTIMORE.

Incorporated by the State of Maryland, Dec. Sess. 1849.

Chartered Capital,

$300,000.

Cash Capital,

$100,000.

Assets,

$207,000.

JOHN B. SEIDENSTRICKER, President.

DIRECTORS.

HENRY M. BASH,
GEORGE BARTLETT,
JOSEPH W. JENKINS,
WILLIAM WOODWARD,
EDWARD J. CHURCH,
GEORGE SMALL,
HUGH SISSON,
ROBERT LAWSON,
DECATUR H. MILLER,
OLIVER A. PARKER,
ROBERT LEHR,
GEORGE C. JENKINS.

H. C. LANDIS, Secretary.

THOMAS C. JENKINS, Jr., Clerk.
WILLIAM C JENNESS, Clerk.

Office at the North-West cor. of Holliday & Second Sts.

ILLUSTRATIONS.

GENERAL INDEX.

* NOTE.—Inadvertently, the name of DR. RICHARD S. STEWART was omitted in our mention of the Maryland Hospital, now Spring Grove Asylum. That he was the originator of this institution and has nurtured it to the present moment, when it has assumed such grand proportions, is a fact with which every intelligent Marylander is familiar.

The treatment of the Insane, in our State at least, has been advanced to a Science mainly through his efforts.

INDEX TO ADVERTISEMENTS.

ERRATA.

On page 39, line 29, read "passes" for "passed."

On page 73, line 20, substitute "of" between "earnest" and "what."

On page 76, in the note at the bottom, read "University" instead of "Unviersity."

On page 123, in the Article on Soap and Candles, at the 5th line, read "*the* Cape of Good Hope" instead of "Cape of Good Hope."

On page 133, in the Flour Article, at line 6, read "are" instead of "is."

On page 142, leave out "colon," at 12th line.

On page 183, at line 18, read "existence" instead of "existance."

Top of page 207, read "Established 1851" instead of "Established 1871."

On page 248, read "200,000,000 Bricks" instead of "100,000,000 Bricks." This includes the manufacture of Bricks at Canton.

NOTE.

The Firms of Woodward, Baldwin & Co. and Norris & Baldwin have dissolved since this work went to press, and a Co-Partnership has been formed under the name of

WOODWARD, BALDWIN & NORRIS,

Nos. 9 and 11 Hanover Street,

Dry Goods and Commission Merchants,

And Selling Agents for the Savage Manufacturing Company and Warren Cotton Mills. See Pages 177 and 180.

APPENDIX.

SINCE the Publication of this Work a new impetus has been given to the movements of the MONUMENTAL CITY, and many important enterprises have been either completed or inaugurated, which the Author deems necessary to include in his exhibit of the City; and therefore he has added as many pages to it as practicable, that he might set forth the additional attractions and new features of its enterprise and trade which are of the most recent date.

It will appear from these that BALTIMORE is progressing surely and grandly in the great march of the Nations. Even during a year of unparalleled financial troubles, when the wheels of trade have been clogged, and the great burden-trains of commerce have moved slowly, she has advanced steadily, adorning her streets and avenues with stately and magnificent edifices; inaugurating and prosecuting the grandest schemes of improvement which she has ever undertaken; stretching out new lines of communication to the South, West and North-West; enlarging and deepening her harbor, and advancing her moral, educational and benevolent interests.

To keep pace with her progress and herald anew her advantages and claims, the Author sends out his Book thus Appended, with the earnest hope that it will contribute an essential part to the increased trade and reputation of our magnificent Metropolis.

THE CITY HALL.

AMONG the many objects of which Baltimoreans may be justly proud is the new City Hall.

It is one of the most elegant structures in the United States. Occupying the entire square on which it is erected, it stands out in bold relief, impressing the observer at every point of view with its gracefulness and grandeur.

The purity of the marble of which it is constructed, the consistency of its details, and the harmony of its proportions, all combine to produce the most pleasing effect.

The Architect has eminently succeeded in doing what is exceedingly rare in the design and construction of large buildings; he has given it that completeness, which merits and receives the enconium of the educated and ignorant, the connoisseur and boor alike; having produced an entire effect, without protruding any prominent feature at the expense of the rest. This completeness, this absence of an undue prominence of one idea, is indicative of the highest order of architectural skill—and it is with pride we claim the Architect, Mr. George A. Frederick, as a native Baltimorean, whose education was received in our own city—and we take this occasion of commending our City Authorities for giving one exception to the proverb, "a prophet is not without honor, save his own country," in employing in every department our own artisans.

In May, 1854, Mayor Hollins approved the ordinance authorizing the purchase of the entire square bounded by Fayette, North, Lexington and Holliday Streets.

In January, 1866, an act was passed authorizing the Mayor and City Council to build on this site a New City Hall, and on the 18th of October, 1867, the corner-stone was laid with appropriate rites and ceremonies, by the Grand Lodge of the F. A. A. M. of the State of Maryland, and an eloquent oration was delivered by our highly esteemed and justly distinguished fellow-citizen, Hon. John H. B. Latrobe, who still continues among us ever ready to give us the benefit of his talent and wisdom in all great enterprises, as well as in works of benevolence and art.

The Building Committee then in charge of the work were His Hon. the Mayor John Lee Chapman, President, Thomas B. Burch, John W. Kirkley, James Smith and Thomas C. Basshor, Esqrs.

In 1868 a new Committee was appointed consequent upon a change of municipal administration, consisting of His Hon. the Mayor Robert T. Banks, President, George A. Coleman, John Ellicott, Thomas J. Griffiss, George W. Stinchcomb, Ogden A. Kirkland and George A. Davis, Esqrs; and in October, 1869, the present Committee were appointed, viz: His Hon. now the Mayor, Joshua Vansant, President, J. Hall Pleasants, Samuel H. Adams, Ichabod Jean and John W. Colley, Esqrs.

A brief description will show it to have no superior in style and appointments.

The front length of the Building is 239 feet, the width 149 feet.

Its size may be inferred from the area which it covers, 29,000 square feet. The area of the square including the pavements being 50,500 feet.

Its general style is the Rennaissance, preserving the simplicity and dignity of the ancient, and adding sufficient of the modern to adorn without encumbering it. This is accomplished by dividing and relieving the extensive fronts and faces with projecting pilasters, columns and arches over the openings of each story, and graceful cornices, balustrades, parapets; all of which together enhance the grandeur that naturally belongs to great structures like this.

The general plan consists of a centre structure four stories high, and two connected lateral wings three stories high, with Mansard roofs. The centre preserves more distinctly the ancient order, terminating on the east and west fronts with pediments adorned by sculpture in high relief representing Trade, Commerce and the Arts. From the central roof rises the rotunda surmounted by a grand dome and lantern, composed of iron, in the construction of which six hundred and fifty tons were used. The dome at the base has a circumference of one hundred and seventy feet, divided into twelve parts by rich Corinthian columns, between which are arched windows. At the base of the lantern is a projecting balcony two hundred feet from the pavement, from which the most magnificent views may be obtained of the City and surrounding country and Chesapeake Bay, amply repaying the toiling ascent of the steps constructed within the wall. The entire height from the base to the finial is two hundred and fifty feet.

Above the windows and columns referred to, and at the base of the dome is the town clock; its four illuminated dial plates facing the cardinal points of the compass, and each plate five feet six inches in diameter; and each apartment is furnished with a clock-dial regulated by electricity from the dome clock.

In the lantern, "Big Sam," the City Bell, is placed, weighing 6,500 pounds, manufactured by Joshua Regester & Sons, of Baltimore—which strikes the hours, sounds the fire alarms, and is managed by electricity.

The heights of the stories are respectively, the cellar ten feet six inches; basement fifteen feet; first and second principal stories twenty feet six inches; the Council chambers and large Hall thirty-five feet.

Four large and commodious stairways are on each floor on spacious marble-tiled corridors. The rooms are well lighted, and heated by hot water on the indirect radiating principle, and ventilated by special ducts leading to four shafts eight feet square and one hundred feet high.

Each department is furnished with dressing rooms and all necessary conveniences, both public and private.

Although the building is strictly fire-proof, every department has secure vaults, very large, lined with iron and steel; the doors, which are of iron, were made by the American Steam Safe Company, of this City.

All the municipal offices are contained within the building. In the basement are the departments of the Water Board, Board of Health, City Commissioners, Inspector of Building, City Fire and Alarm Telegraph, Port Wardens, Inspector of Illuminating Gas, Board of Police and Detectives.

On the first principal story are the Governor's Room, the Mayor's Department, City Register's Office, Board of Finance, City Comptroller, Tax Department, City Counsellor, Board of School Commissioners, Park Commissioners and Harbor Commissioners.

On the second principal story are the First and Second Branch Council Chambers, each forty-two feet square and thirty-five feet high, and the large hall forty-two by one hundred and forty feet, thirty-five feet high; all finished in the most elaborate manner, in hard wood, with Corinthian pilasters in Scagliola of various colored marble highly polished, crowned by rich gilt caps cast of pure brass, and surmounted by an elegant entablature. The ceilings are covered and richly decorated. On this floor also are the Council Committee Rooms and City Library.

In the Mansard story the rooms are used for storage and safe-keeping of the Municipal Records, beginning with those of 1797.

There is an entrance to the building on each street; the principal one on Holliday Street is by a marble portico, with six fluted columns and capitals of the Composite order. The door is in bronze of heavy dimensions, and beautiful in construction and design.

The whole building is furnished in the most approved manner; the furniture is of handsome style and finish; each apartment is supplied with that which is admirably adapted to it; the desks, tables, cases, &c., are arranged in the most convenient order, and there is no more complete Municipal Hall in the United States.

From this description, together with the engraving on page 33, our readers at a distance may form a correct impression of our great City Hall. We may be allowed to indulge a seemly pride in this edifice, since it is pre-eminently the result of the genius and skill of our own workmen, built of stone hewn from our quarries and material wrought in our founderies and factories.

As it rears its lofty sides, white with the purest marble, and lifts its grand dome above the City which it represents, we feel that we have erected a monument which will stand for ages, commemorative of the dignity and strength, the culture and enterprise of the people of the Monumental City.

BALTIMORE AND OHIO RAIL ROAD.

OUR readers will find an accurate sketch of the rise and progress of the Baltimore and Ohio Rail Road on pages 285–290, which was prepared from the most authentic sources and with great care.

The magnitude of this Corporation and the importance of its relations to Baltimore justify us in devoting additional space to it as the great institution of the Monumental City.

The citizens of Baltimore should thoroughly acquaint themselves with its history, and appreciate its significance to their City, for no other City in the world has such a Road sustaining to it the same or similar relations, those relations being of such a nature and so intimate, that the two are really identical. The Road may truly be regarded as a part of the corporate existence of the City. Thus the interests of the two can never be antagonistic; they are mutually dependent on each other. We hold it, however, to be especially incumbent upon the citizens of Baltimore to foster and encourage this Road, and to manifest an enlightened appreciation of its splendid achievements in the behalf of our City.

Whatever of commercial greatness Baltimore to-day possesses, must in the largest measure be accredited to the Baltimore and Ohio Rail Road. The genius of its entire conduct from its origin has been to enhance the growth and importance of Baltimore. This was the inspiration of the movement that resulted in its organization, which appears in the language of the invitation of Mr. Geo. Brown and Mr. Philip E. Thomas to certain citizens to meet in consultation at Mr. B.'s residence on Feb'y 12th, 1827, "*to take into consideration the best means of restoring to the City of Baltimore that portion of the Western trade which has lately been diverted from it by the introduction of steam and other causes.*"

At every step in its progress this has been the ruling purpose of its Officers and Directors, to make it subserve the interests of Baltimore, and to be the great tributary to her wealth and commercial grandeur; and at the cost of personal ease, against the opposition of inveterate enemies, under the most perplexing discouragements, and with the pledge of their private fortunes, they have executed that purpose to a degree far beyond their most sanguine hope.

The original purpose of the founders of the Road was to connect Baltimore directly with the great West in order to make her the entrepot of its vast and growing trade; and this has been steadily prosecuted by every administration; they have never lost sight of this, as the chief point of attainment. The earlier administrations, guided by the consummate wisdom and commercial sagacity, and sustained by the financial strength of

CENTRAL OFFICE BALTIMORE AND OHIO RAIL ROAD COMPANY.

N. W. CORNER BALTIMORE AND CALVERT STREETS.

E. F. Baldwin, Architect.

such men as the Brown's, Thomas', Carroll's, Oliver's, Patterson's, McKim's, Hoffman's, &c., surmounting obstacles that would have defeated ordinary men, completed the Road to Cumberland; at that time considered a marvellous achievement of financial and engineering skill. From this point it was vigorously pushed on by those who are still among us, the true representatives of the wisdom and commercial activity of Baltimore, under the most trying circumstances and in seasons of great financial depression, until it reached the Ohio River at Wheeling on January 1st, 1854.

The present administration, with a zeal not surpassed by their illustrious predecessors, and with a generous yet judicious spirit of enterprise, have adhered to the text of the original founders and enlarged upon it, carrying it out into relations which even their penetrating and expansive vision had not caught. The Baltimore and Ohio Rail Road has not only *reached* the Ohio River, as meditated in 1827, but it is advancing Westward with its mighty tread, touching lakes, crossing rivers, penetrating forests, enchaining Cities, and if we mistake not the profound intent of its present powers, destined to plant its stations on the Pacific Coast and bring the wealth of the Indies, the trade of China and the Isles of the Sea, into our waiting arms.

We have alluded in our former article to the extensions and connections of the Road in the West and South. These have been effected by uniting with and leasing other roads, and constructing new lines running through the richest sections of Virginia and the Western States; thus opening up and bringing into direct communication with Baltimore the whole West, with its illimitable resources.

The latest triumph of the enterprise of this Company is the CHICAGO EXTENSION. This extension begins at Lake Erie junction, 89 miles North of Newark, Ohio, and runs midway between the Lake Shore and Michigan Road on the North, and the Pittsburgh, Fort Wayne and Chicago on the South, passing through a series of flourishing towns; the entire distance from Lake Erie junction to Chicago being 268 miles—the road deviating as little as possible from an air line, having low gradients and favorable curvature.

The utmost caution was exercised in its construction, and it is unsurpassed by any other Road in the country. An important feature of this Road is the numerous connections which it makes with other Roads converging towards Lake Erie and Buffalo, thus draining all portions of the Northwest and shortening the distance between Chicago, Toledo and other important points. At the Junction with these Roads elevators are to be erected for the rapid and economical transfer of grain. Ten or more are now in the course of erection along the line, which, by the increased facilities they provide for the farmer and grain operator, will secure an immense trade to the Road. The Company has secured one of the most desirable and convenient locations in the City of Chicago for its passenger and freight stations, and has formed close and amicable relations with other lines terminating on the Lake Front, and has made arrangements for securing access to the immense stock and lumber yards, elevators and packing establishments of that enormous City. At South Chicago the Company has purchased 40 acres, upon which will be erected its water stations, machine and construction shops, &c. It has also secured ample Dock facilities, and is in every way thoroughly equipped to compete for and do the carrying trade of Chicago and the Northwest, and bring it to our doors.

By this extension Chicago is 152 miles nearer to Baltimore than to New York, over a road of the lowest grades, with a minimum tariff on freight and passenger travel.

The Map which accompanies this article gives a better and more complete view of this great Road, with all its extensions, than can a verbal description. From that appear not only the magnitude and extent of the relations of that Road, but the eminent wisdom with which the extensions have been laid out; penetrating in each direction the richest sections of the country, and binding to Baltimore by the shortest routes, the great cities of each section. In order to impress this fact upon the country we herewith give a table of comparative distances, which speaks more powerfully for Baltimore than the most eloquent appeal.

BALTIMORE AND OHIO RAIL ROAD TIDE TER TERMINUS, ELEVATORS ETC., LOCUST POINT, BALTIMORE.

DEER PARK HOTEL, SITUATED ON THE SUMMIT OF THE ALLEGHANIES.

THE QUEEN CITY HOTEL, CUMBERLAND.

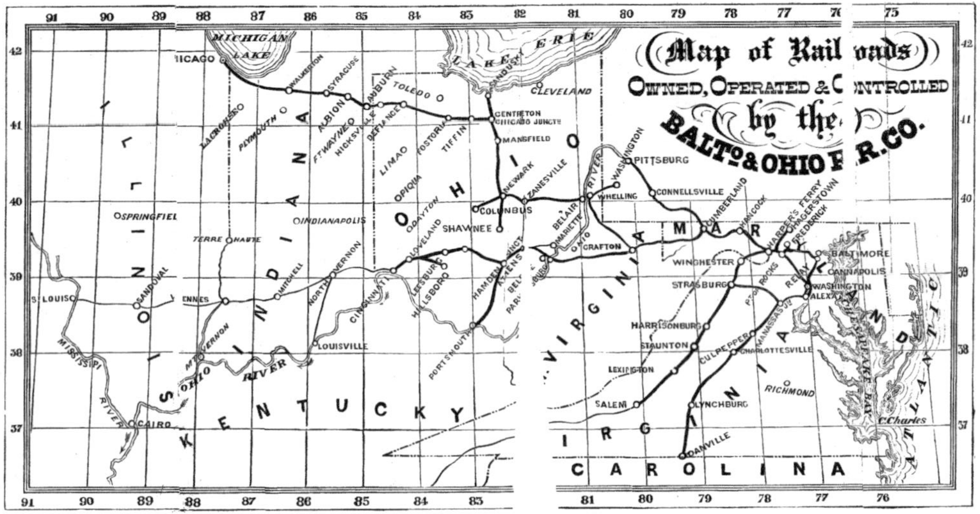

Map of Railroads
Owned, Operated & Controlled by the Balt^o & Ohio R.R.Co.

MICHIGAN LAKE
LAKE ERIE
ILLINOIS
INDIANA
OHIO
KENTUCKY
VIRGINIA
MARYLAND
CAROLINA
ATLANTIC
MISSISSIPPI RIVER
OHIO RIVER
RIVER
CHESAPEAKE BAY
C.Charles
CHICAGO
WALKERTON
SYRACUSE
AUBURN
TOLEDO
SANDUSKY
CLEVELAND
LACROSSE
PLYMOUTH
ALBION
FT.WAYNE
HICKSVILLE
DEFIANCE
FOSTORIA
TIFFIN
CENTRETON
CHICAGO JUNCT'N
MANSFIELD
LIMA
PIQUA
DAYTON
NEWARK
ZANESVILLE
COLUMBUS
SHAWNEE
SPRINGFIELD
INDIANAPOLIS
TERRE HAUTE
ST. LOUIS
SANDOVAL
ENNES
MITCHELL
NORTH VERNON
CINCINNATI
LOVELAND
LEESBURG
HILLSBORO
HAMDEN JUNCT.
ATHENS
BELPRE
PARKERSBURG
MARIETTA
BELAIR
CAIRO
CRAFTON
WHEELING
WASHINGTON
PITTSBURG
CONNELLSVILLE
CUMBERLAND
HANCOCK
HARPER'S FERRY
HAGERSTOWN
FREDERICK
BALTIMORE
ANNAPOLIS
WASHINGTON
ALEXANDRIA
RELAY
POINT OF ROCKS
WINCHESTER
STRASBURG
HARRISONBURG
STAUNTON
CULPEPPER
MANASSAS
CHARLOTTESVILLE
LEXINGTON
RICHMOND
SALEM
LYNCHBURG
DANVILLE
MT. VERNON
LOUISVILLE
PORTSMOUTH
CAIRO

VIADUCT HOTEL, RELAY STATION.

DISTANCES FROM BALTIMORE AND NEW YORK.

FROM CHICAGO.

To Baltimore via Baltimore and Ohio Rail Road............ 815 miles.
To New York via New York Central Rail Road............ 980 "
" via Erie Rail Road........................ 961 "
" via Pennsylvania Rail Road................ 899 "
Less to Baltimore than the average distance to New York, 132 miles.

FROM ST. LOUIS.

To Baltimore via Baltimore and Ohio Rail Road............ 929 miles.
To New York via New York Central Rail Road............1167 "
" via Erie Rail Road........................1201 "
" via Pennsylvania Rail Road................1050 "
Less to Baltimore than the average distance to New York, 210 miles.

FROM LOUISVILLE.

To Baltimore via Baltimore and Ohio Rail Road.. .... 696 miles.
To New York via New York Central Rail Road............ 989 "
" via Erie Rail Road........... .... 987 "
" via Pennsylvania Rail Road................ 851 "
Less to Baltimore than the average distance to New York, 246 miles.

FROM CINCINNATI.

To Baltimore via Baltimore and Ohio Rail Road............ 589 miles.
To New York via New York Central Rail Road............ 882 "
" via Erie Rail Road........................ 861 "
" via Pennsylvania Rail Road................ 744 "
Less to Baltimore than the average distance to New York, 240 miles.
Less from Pittsburgh to Baltimore than to New York.....104 "

From all points South of Baltimore the distance in her favor is 200 miles. Thus the Baltimore and Ohio Rail Road has not only put in the power of Baltimore to compete with the other cities of the Atlantic Coast for the Western trade, but has made her to surpass them all in her facilities and advantages.

But the vision of this Company has not been confined to the West. Looking at the signally advantageous position of Baltimore at the head of our magnificent Bay—so far inland and yet with an admirable harbor—its attention was directed across the ocean to the ports of Europe, and it was determined to make it the entrepot of European trade. Mr. Garrett, as the present honored and efficient President of the Company, appreciating the advantages of our situation, inaugurated the enterprise of establishing a line of steamers between this Port and Europe, declaring that this would place Baltimore in the front rank of the commercial cities of the world, a prophecy rapidly approaching fulfillment.

Thus having provided every facility for bringing both the inland and oceanic trade to Baltimore, the Company has, at an enormous expense, made every accommodation for it in the City itself.

The terminal facilities which have become indispensable to the increasing trade of the country are vastly superior to those of any other City in the East. These consist of the TIDE WATER FREIGHT AND SHIPPING DEPOT AT LOCUST POINT.

LOCAL FREIGHT AND RECEIVING STATIONS ALONG THE CITY WATER FRONT.

CAMDEN STATION.

MOUNT CLARE STATION.

LOCUST POINT is the marine terminus of the Road. The Company owns about 80 acres, with a water front of 3600 feet. The Point derived its sole importance from the coal trade, until the establishment of the line of steamers, when the present extensive improvements were begun which appear in the engraving; these consist of large piers for the ocean steamers, which are covered by iron sheds, into which the cars are run on double tracks.

The Docks alongside and between these piers are 100 feet wide and sufficient to accommodate 4 or 5 steamers at once. Freight can be transferred directly from the hold of the vessel to the cars, thus economizing in time and expense in the handling of cargoes.

The accommodations for emigrants are also very complete. There is an office of a German Banking House on the pier, next to which is a ticket office, and the emigrants can exchange their foreign notes for current money and purchase a ticket to any part of the country; and without any delay and extra expense can enter the cars of the Baltimore and Ohio Rail Road and proceed to their destination.

On Locust Point also the Company has erected two immense Grain Elevator Buildings, which occupy a conspicuous position in the engraving. Their capacity is over 2,000,000 bushels of grain. They contain 331 storage bins, 21 receiving and 11 shipping elevators, which are furnished with every facility for the rapid transfer of grain.

Between the Elevators is the Rail Road Ferry, for the transfer of freight to the Canton side, where connection is made with the Philadelphia, Wilmington and Baltimore Rail Road, which forms a continuous through freight line from New York and the East, to the South and West.

Between the Rail Road Ferry and the large Elevator, a Coffee Warehouse is building of immense dimensions, and a Sugar Warehouse is projected on a similar site. The effect of these extensive improvements, as it is the design of the Company, will be not only to increase importations at this port, but to enlarge the commerce of Baltimore by drawing hither additional steamers and sailing craft; attracting them by offering tonnage at the lowest rates, and making this the most profitable and convenient port of entry for the whole country, South, West and Northwest.

Our space does not permit us to particularize concerning the facilities provided along the water-front, at Mount Clare and Camden Station. It is only sufficient to note, that in the way of handling cars, transferring freight, and storage, the arrangements are most ample and complete, so that no City or Rail Road in the country can present better inducements or offer greater facilities to trade and commerce.

In its great desire to increase the commerce of the city, and the transportation of freights, the Company has not been unmindful of the comfort and convenience of the travelling public. Elegant and luxurious coaches are manufactured at the Company shops, provided with all possible conveniences for passengers. But a special feature of this Company, which indicates its superior wisdom and consideration, is the system of Rail Road Hotels which it has adopted. At Benwood, Parkersburg, Grafton, Cumberland, Martinsburg and Washington Junction, hotels have been established, where passengers are served with first class meals and accommodations. All of them are kept in the very best manner, and have already proved the practical wisdom of the Company in the great influence which they have exerted in determining passengers to this route.

A slight review of the history of the trade of Baltimore will show the effect of the Baltimore and Ohio Rail Road upon it, and reveals the fact that the large increase of both inland and oceanic trade is immeasurably due to the facilities which it has regardless of expense provided. We select but two departments as illustrative of this, the Coal and Grain trade.

In 1843, when the Road was finished to Cumberland, the tonnage for the year was 4,964; in 1845, when the terminus was made at Locust Point, it suddenly increased to 108,000 tons; and since the additional facilities were provided there, it has multiplied steadily, and in 1873 amounted to 2,019,718 tons.

The benefit of the terminal facilities offered by the Road is even more apparent in its grain traffic. The opening of its first Elevator, Feb'y 23d, 1872, increased the receipts of that year to 6,049,430 bushels, and necessitated the erection of the new and larger Elevator of double its capacity. In 1873 the amount received was 7,510,657.

The effect of these accommodations is seen in the exportation from this port. In 1870 the amount was not worth recording. In 1871, 3,004,868 bushels. In 1872, 5,232,163. In 1873, 7,251,717. At this rate of increase alone we will soon compete with New York, as we are now second only to that city in grain exportation.

Having presented in a general way such facts as we deemed important in showing the magnitude of this Road, and its incalculable importance to our city, it will afford an additional element to our pride and satisfaction in it, to know its financial standing. It is established upon the soundest financial basis, having no *watered* stock, no large *nominal* capital upon which it must earn dividends—but with an actual capital sufficient for all practical purposes, with economy of distances, at reasonably low rates to attract and retain the growing business of the West, the Road has steadily prospered until it enjoys the confidence of the world, as evinced by a loan of $15,000,000 at the lowest rate of interest, negotiated by Mr. Garrett during his recent visit to Europe, at the time our country was passing through a fearful financial crisis; and when the New York Central and Erie Companies found it hard to meet their current obligations, the Baltimore and Ohio Rail Road paid two dividends of 5 per cent. each and increased its surplus fund $2,880,861 82.

The Company has uniformly pursued the policy of making moderate dividends and applying the surplus earnings in the construction of new works and securing valuable connections, until with a nominal capital of $16,711,100 has, by investing its undivided earnings, a surplus fund of nearly $30,000,000. By this policy it has been enabled, by cash contracts, to have many of its most important enterprises affected at the lowest cost, as, for instance, its Chicago Extension, which was built at the extremely low rate of $23,000 per mile. When the history of the Baltimore and Ohio Rail Road shall be written, as it ought to be by a competent hand, it will present one of the most interesting volumes of American enterprise and skill, and will signalize the men by whom it was originated, and those through whose genius and resolute will it has been carried on to its present colossal proportions.

The Presidents of the Company, with order of their succession:

Philip E. Thomas, Esq., Hon. Louis McLain, Hon. Thomas Swann, W. G. Harrison, Esq., Chauncey Brooks, Esq., John W. Garrett, Esq.

The Hon. J. H. B. Latrobe, now the Company's senior counsel, has been in the service of the Company uninterruptedly from the commencement of the earliest surveys.

The first Board of Directors was composed as follows:

Charles Carroll of Carrollton, Wm. Patterson, Robert Oliver, Alexander Brown, Isaac McKim, William Lorman, George Hoffman, Philip E. Thomas, Thomas Ellicott, Talbot Jones, William Stewart, Solomon Etting, Patrick McCaulay and John B. Morris, the only surviving member.

CENTRAL OFFICE OF THE BALTIMORE AND OHIO RAIL ROAD CO.

THE vast expansion of the Freight and Passenger Traffic of the Road demanded greater accommodations, and a centrally located Office, both for the convenience of the Road and the travelling public. In consideration of this the Company purchased the most eligible site in the City, on the north-west corner of Calvert and Baltimore Streets, upon which the old Baltimore Museum stood, and are now erecting one of the finest structures for this purpose in the United States. One which will be an ornament to the City, and worthy of the Road.

As seen in the Engraving, it will be five stories high with an attic, in the style of the Rennaissance. The walls to be of fine cut granite, with red Scotch granite columns to the porticos and windows, surmounted with elegant carved capitals.

The main entrance is to be on Calvert Street, and consits of a handsome portico thirty-six feet high, with red Scotch granite columns. Over the doorway the spandrel panels are to be enriched with carved cornucopias of grain and fruit.

The whole building will be surmounted with a heavy balustrade, and over the pediment on Calvert Street will be a pannel fifteen feet high, with the name "Baltimore and Ohio," in raised letters.

The interior will be arranged in the most convenient manner, and elegantly furnished.

The Building is the design of Mr. E. F. Baldwin, in charge of the Architectural Department of the Road, upon whose skill it reflects great credit, and our citizens will not only take a pride in it as a splendid contribution to the beauty of Baltimore, but find it a great convenience.

UNION ELEVATOR.

IN our article upon CANTON, to which we call special attention as a complete description of that valuable and enterprising adjunct to our City, we indicated on pages 283 and 284 certain enterprises which had been recently undertaken, and were then proposed; among which were the construction of Elevators for the handling of grain. We are enabled to record the completion of at least one of these, which together with those already and about to be erected will constitute Baltimore the best grain entrepot on the Atlantic coast.

Mr. John Gardner, of great enterprise and large experience in the construction and use of Elevators, having thoroughly identified himself with the interests of our City, and in spite of herculean difficulties has triumphantly suceeeded in the erection of one of the best appointed Elevators in the country, which will be seen in the Engraving is ornamental as well as an immense advantage to Baltimore.

In April, 1873, he obtained permission of the Canton Company to erect an Elevator and Warehouse at the foot of Fifth Avenue, and the Company, with its usual promptitude in advancing all true interests and encouraging enterprise, placed at his disposal nine hundred feet of tide-water front, including Fifth to Sixth Avenues. It further advanced him a most liberal sum to enable him to prosecute the work. He immediately improved the opportunity thus generously offered, and was ready at the beginning of 1874 to transfer grain.

The building consists of an Elevator of large capacity, and storage floors. The important feature of this Elevator is its great capacity for the transfer of grain, &c., and in this respect exceeds that of other Elevators.

The arrangements for passing grain from cars to vessel lying along side of the piers are most complete. The piers are so arranged that vessels can discharge cargoes on one floor and receive from the other at the same time, thus economizing both time and labor.

Steam power is used, and so employed that freights can be moved from one floor to the other and hoisted from vessels simultaneously, and thus with a depth of water to accommodate vessels drawing twenty-two and twenty-four feet, Baltimore possesses the perfection of terminal facilities. There is in addition an outside berth where bulk grain can be transferred from barges or vessels to ships in waiting by means of a ship-leg. The grain can also be thoroughly cleaned by means of a powerful improved cleaner. Every precaution against fire has been taken. A tank containing 2,500 gallons of water is placed at either end, with connecting and distributing hose at proper points.

An Artesian well, in connection with the Elevator, has been bored, whose flow of water is very strong and abundant. It is sixteen inches in diameter, and furnishes not only the

GARDNER'S
UNION RAILROAD DEPOT
ELEVATOR & STORAGE.

boilers but the vessels with the purest water without changing their berths. There is another convenient arrangement by which steamers can "coal" direct from the Elevator while receiving their cargoes; and facilities are now being provided for the deposit of coal from the Northern Central Railway and Western Maryland Rail Road, by which Canton and the Union Elevator can accommodate all that can be shipped hither.

These complete arrangements in connection with the concentration of Rail Road lines from the North, South and West, and the completion of the two magnificent tunnels, the "Union" and the "Baltimore and Potomac," give to this locality an advantage which should command the attention of producers and shippers.

Our citizens have not yet begun to appreciate the bearing of these improvements at Canton upon the wealth and growth of the City, but the few sagacious minds who have begun and prosecuted them, understood their relative importance to us, and with consummate foresight and princely expenditure they have aided in doing that which will yet make Baltimore illustrious among the great seaports of the world, and second to none of the cities of the United States in trade and manufactures.

RECEIPTS OF GRAIN AT THIS PORT DURING THE PAST TEN MONTHS TO NOVEMBER 1ST, 1874—(see page 129.)

Wheat	5,668,532	bushels.
Corn	7,928,896	"
Oats	1,013,932	"
Rye	113,004	"
Total	14,724,364	"

NUMBER OF CATTLE, HOGS AND SHEEP RECEIVED IN BALTIMORE FOR THE TEN MONTHS ENDING NOV. 1ST, 1874—(see page 250.)

	Cattle.	Hogs.	Sheep.		Cattle.	Hogs.	Sheep.
January	8,207	32,377	10,454	July	10,043	29,670	25,907
February	5,988	34,130	6,950	August	11,087	28,490	24,437
March	4,438	26,010	7,497	September	15,545	23,386	23,425
April	6,313	39,802	10,958	October	30,828	36,381	21,687
May	4,902	31,972	13,906				
June	5,623	27,448	18,177		102,974	309,766	163,398

BALTIMORE CAR WHEEL COMPANY.

FEW, if any, of our manufacturing enterprises are of more importance to us than our iron manufacture. Made out of the very ground under our feet, the full price of every pound of Baltimore iron that is sold is an actual addition of that amount to the material wealth of Baltimore. About 20,000 tons of the best "wheel iron" in the world are made here annually. For many years nearly the whole of this yield was shipped *in the pig* to distant points. The Baltimore Car Wheel Company's Foundry, recently erected at Canton, now converts a large quantity of this iron into car wheels of the very best quality, and promises ere long to consume all that is produced here.

At the great Industrial Exposition held at Cincinnati from the 1st to the 30th of September, 1874, general attention was drawn to this Company's wheels, which were subjected to a series of very severe tests by a committee appointed for that purpose by the officers of the Exposition. The committee consisted of Mr. H. M. Britton, Chief Engineer and General Superintendent of the White Water Valley Railroad and President of the American Railway Master Mechanics' Association; Mr. Samuel M. Cummings, Master of Machinery of the Pittsburgh, Fort Wayne and Chicago Railway, and Mr. Alexander Gordon, of the Niles Tool Works.

A very interesting account of these tests appeared in the Railway Gazette of October 10th, 1874. We have only space for a short extract. An engine truck-wheel of the neat hollow-spoke pattern was placed in one of the powerful wheel presses exhibited by the Niles Tool Works. With a bearing of four inches on the outer rim at top and bottom, the maximum power of the press (400,000 lbs.), brought to bear directly upon the centre of the opposite side, had no effect upon it. Nor could a fracture be made with a taper steel pin ⅛ inch larger at its thickest end than the "bore" of the wheel, into which it was driven up to the maximum pressure of 400,000 lbs., without the wheel showing a sign of giving way. When afterward broken under a drop, it showed a uniform chill of ⅝ inch and soft gray metal of uniform thickness of a little less than ¾ inch in the arms and ribs. Below we give the report of the committee:

CINCINNATI INDUSTRIAL EXPOSITION.
CINCINNATI, O., September 25, 1874.

At the request of Mr. W. S. G. Baker, President of the Baltimore Car Wheel Company, we, the undersigned, acted as a committee to test the strength of his wheels by different processes, as follows:

Wheel No. 1 was a 30-inch double-plate car-wheel, weight 460 lbs., having 12 11-16 in. holes drilled through and across the diameter. Six taper steel pins, 7 inches long, ½ in. at one end and 1 in. at the other, were alternately driven by a sledge-hammer weighing 26¾ lbs.; 148 blows were struck, when it showed a crack to the rim. It then required 36 more blows to make the fracture complete. The wheel showed a uniform chill of 5-16 in.

Wheel No. 2 was a horse-car wheel, single-plate, and required 23 blows of the same sledge to break the web, which was about ⅝ in. thick, and 43 more blows to break a piece out of the rim. It showed a uniform chill of ⅝ in.

Wheel No. 3, a 31-inch double-plate car-wheel, was placed in a hydrostatic press, so that it had 5½ inches bearing on the upper and lower rim. It required 250,000 lbs. to break it in two. The pressure was brought to bear directly on the hub. Uniform chill of ½ in.

Wheel No. 4 was a single plate 30-inch car-wheel, weight 460 lbs. This wheel was broken by same press, but the maximum hand of guage having caught, we could not determine the pressure. Uniform chill of ⅝ inch.

Wheel No. 5 was a 26-inch engine truck-wheel. This was a cored arm and rim pattern, weight 445 lbs., and was forced on an axle 1-16 in. larger in diameter than the bore of the wheel, at a pressure of 300,000 lbs. It was then removed from the axle, and underwent the same test as No. 3, with a pressure of 400,000 lbs. without a fracture; this being the full capacity of the press.

Wheel No. 6 was a single-plate 30-inch car-wheel, weight 460 lbs., and underwent the same test as employed in No. 1, requiring 133 blows on pins before a fracture could be seen, and then 92 more blows were required to break a section from rim, when an even chill of ⅝ inch was shown, and a soft fibrous plate.

Wheel No. 7 was a double-plate 33-inch car-wheel, weight 510 lbs., pressed on an axle, having a taper of 3 16 inch in 7 inches, and having bearings on outer rim same as in No 3. This required a pressure of 100,000 lbs. on the centre of hub to crack the plates, and the wheel was not broken open.

(Signed) H. M. BRITTON,
S. M. CUMMINGS,
ALEX. GORDON,
Committee.

THE HARBOR.

ON page 82 reference is made to the harbor of Baltimore and to certain improvements in the channel. Since the publication of this book these improvements have been completed, which are of such importance as to demand further notice.

Two main channels have been widened and deepened, called the Brewerton and Craighill channels. The Brewerton extends from Fort McHenry by a direct line to a point one and a half miles below Fort Carroll, and thence in another straight line 9 miles, to the ship channel entrance buoy, 4½ miles below North Point. It is 150 feet wide, with a depth of 22 feet at mean low water; $304,317 were expended in its construction.

The Craighill channel was commenced in 1866 and completed in April, 1874, under the direction of Col. W. P. Craighill, of the U. S. service, at an expense of about $400,000. The channel is 250 feet wide, with a depth of 24 feet at mean low water.

There were added to the width of Brewerton channel 100 feet, which give to the harbor continuous channel to the deep waters of the Bay.

By the ingenious management of Col. Craighill, in making the narrowest parts of the channel where the sides are of soft mud, so that if struck by a vessel no injury ensues, and where the material is hard increasing the width to 400 feet, he has supplied the great need of our port, viz: a channel wide and deep enough for the largest vessels engaged in ocean commerce to pass easily and safely.

The value of this to Baltimore cannot be overestimated, and taken in connection with the geographical position, at the head of the Chesapeake Bay, from 100 to 200 miles nearer to the great cities of the West than any other Atlantic city, enables her to offer the greatest advantages to the trade in exporting and importing.

BALTIMORE PRODUCE EXCHANGE.

THE rapid growth of the population of the United States and its accumulation in large cities have greatly increased the consumption of all kinds of provisions, and this has necessitated a special as well as general classification of the trade of these articles. Thus the Dairy and other product have become a separate department of trade, and constitute a very large proportion of the business of the country. The traffic in Butter, Cheese and Eggs is especially very heavy. The amount of capital invested in it is enormous, and will surprise not only the public but those engaged in the trade.

The statistics show that the Butter product of the United States is $436,000,000; Cheese product, $60,000,000; Egg product enormous, figures not known.

The trade having grown to such proportions in our city, the gentlemen engaged in it determined to organize an Exchange, and on August 1, 1874, the Baltimore Produce Exchange was established, with the following officers: Edward L. Kemp, President; Daniel F. Pope, Vice-President; Ed. B. Owens, Treasurer; Mark J. Cornell, Secretary, and eight Directors.

With this Exchange every facility is offered to the trade in this city, and producers may be assured that they have advantages for the disposal of their articles not surpassed in any other city.

PEABODY INSTITUTE.

(See page 38.)

THE Peabody Institute has four separate departments—a free reference Library, a Lecture Department, a Conservatory of Music, and a Gallery of Art. The Library now contains 56,000 volumes of books in a thousand different languages and dialets; and it has a fair representation of the most valuable literature of the world. As a consulting library it contains few modern novels and no juveniles whatever, but it possesses a large collection of books representing the light literature of the past, and of books in belles lettres, history, biography, geography, travels, antiquities, philosophy, philology and science in all its branches; and it receives 278 serial publications, representing the best periodical literature of the day and the most advanced science of America, England, France and Germany. All of these are offered to the public without money and without price. The library is absolutely free, strangers having the same rights and privileges as citizens. It is open every week day from 9 o'clock, A. M., till 10, P. M. The reading room is a large, comfortable apartment, well warmed, well lighted, and free from noise.

The Institute gives from 30 to 120 lectures every winter, at merely nominal prices for admission. In its General Course about 30 lectures are delivered by the most distinguished scholars, literary and scientific, that can be procured, and all lectures requiring it are fully illustrated. The charge for admission to these 30 lectures is $1.50, an average of five cents for each lecture. The experiments at the lecture often cost more than the amount of admission fees.

Several courses of Class Lectures, each course running through the entire lecture season, are also given. The lectures are intended to give more extended instruction in language, literature, and science, than can be given in the more popular lectures of the general course. Usually during each season one of the class courses on literature is given in the French language and one in German. To these will be added Italian lectures so soon as required.

The Conservatory is designed to give a thorough education in vocal and instrumental music. Besides cultivating the voice, and giving lessons on the various musical instruments, it gives instruction in harmony, thorough bass, counterpoint, form, figure, composition, instrumentation, reading, and orchestral playing.

During each season a course of lectures is delivered by the Director on the history of music and on the great composers and their works. A series of Symphony Concerts, at which the best works of the great masters are performed by a trained orchestra, led by the Director of the Conservatory, and numerous concerts by the students are given at regular intervals during the winter. Professors of the highest grade of excellence, most of whom have been trained in the great schools of Europe, are employed as teachers. The students are instructed in classes at less than one-fourth the prices at which instruction of the same grade can be procured from private teachers, and they have free admission to all the concerts of the Institute besides.

The Gallery of Art must await the completion of the new building before it can properly be said to have an existence. It has, however, three beautiful pieces of sculpture on exhibition at the Institute—* the Clytie, by Rinehart, a bust of Pocahontas, by Powers, and a copy of an antique marble, the crouching Aphrodite. It also possesses a full copy in plaster of the frieze of the Parthenon, and about fifty of the most celebrated antique and other marbles, but it has no proper place for exhibiting them.

An extension of the Institute building, which will more than double its capacity, and will furnish ample accommodations for all its departments, has been begun on Mount

* See page 73.

Vernon Place. The new part, like the present building, will be built of white marble and in the Grecian style of architecture. The entire structure will have a front on Mount Vernon Place of 170 feet, and on Charles street of 150 feet.

The annual amount derived from the funds and available for the support of the Institute is $50,000.

Having given a complete description of the Peabody Institute in the body of this book on pages 38, 39 and 40, and a full account of its various departments above, it is eminently proper and desirable that our citizens should hear from Mr. Peabody himself in reference to his munificent gift to our city.

On the occasion of the dedication of the Institute, October 25th, 1866, at which he was present, and formally received by the Trustees and our citizens, Hon. Thomas Swann, then Governor of the State, addressed him, on behalf of the city, in an appropriate and eloquent speech, saying:

* * * * * * * *

"We receive you, sir, not as a stranger. Your early life was commenced here in this city, partly in our State. The sympathies and associations contracted here have followed you throughout life. In the financial crisis of 1837, which spread over this whole Union, affecting more or less almost every State within our limits, when we required countenance and support abroad, you, sir, stood the fast friend of the State of Maryland [applause], and by your efforts, by the weight of your great name, pointed us to that career of prosperity and success in the management of our financial affairs, which has placed us to-day, I will not say in advance, but by the side of the most prosperous of our sister States.

"And we are here to announce to you that this great Institution is now ready to enter upon the work of practical development in the great cause of human advancement, which it was your purpose to accomplish in the letter of instructions which you placed in the hands of the Trustees entrusted with this charge.

"And no man, Mr. Peabody, whether living or dead--in this country or any country—has attracted a larger share of the public attention by works of disinterested charity and benevolence. [Applause] You have not lived for yourself alone. Two hemispheres attest your princely liberality. Retiring to your native country, after so many years' absence, crowned with all the honors that human applause can bestow upon a private citizen, not excepting the applause of royalty itself, I feel proud, standing within the walls of this noble Institution, the work of your own hands, for which we are indebted to your unaided liberality, to say, sir, that I speak here to-day, not only the sentiments of the vast crowd before me, but of the whole State of Maryland, when I assure you, that in honoring George Peabody we honor ourselves." [Applause.]

To which Mr. Peabody replied:

* * * * * * *

"But I am sure you will pardon me, my fellow-citizens, if on one point to which Governor Swann has eloquently alluded—the spirit of harmony in which all should be carried out—I speak a few words, coming as they do from the very depths of my heart, and appealing to you, *you* the people of Baltimore, with whom rests the success or failure of this Institute. For, as years advance, and what were forebodings for the future have become merged in the past, the earnest desire for unity and brotherly feelings which I cherished and expressed ten years ago, in the terms referred to by the Governor of Maryland, has become deeper and more intense. It is my hope and prayer that this Institute may not only have and fulfil a mission in the fields of science, of art and of knowledge, but also one to the hearts of men, teaching always lessons of peace and good-will, and especially that now it may in some humble degree be instrumental in healing the wounds of our beloved and common country, and establishing again a happy and harmonious Union—the only Union that can be preserved for coming ages, and the only one that is *worth* preserving.

"To you, therefore, citizens of Baltimore and of Maryland, I make my appeal, probably the last I shall ever make to you. May not this Institute be a common ground, where all may meet, burying former differences and animosities; forgeting past separations and estrangements, weaving the bands of new attachments to the City, to the State and to the Nation. May not Baltimore, her name already honored in history as the birth-place of religious toleration in America, now crown her past fame by becoming the day-star of political tolerance and charity; and will not Maryland, in place of a battle-ground for opposing parties, become the field where milder counsels and calm deliberations may prevail; where good men of all sections may meet to devise and execute the wisest plans for repairing the ravages of war, and for making the future of our country alike common, prosperous and glorious, from the Atlantic to the Pacific, and from our Northern to our Southern boundary."

And in an address to the children of the Public Schools, who surrounded him as he spoke, he said:

* * * * * * *

"With such an assemblage as this, therefore, I am glad to have my name associated, as I see that it is, by the badges worn by many of you, and I shall feel it to be a very great honor if the medals thus bearing my name shall continue, as I am informed they have heretofore done, to prove incentives to application, diligence and good conduct, and I shall ever take a sincere interest in those to whom they are awarded.

"There is another relation in which I look upon you, and that is the future guardians of the Institute from which I speak to you. For in a few short years you will have left the places you now occupy, and taking the positions of those at present in active life, will have the care and enjoy the privileges of this Institution. And I hope most earnestly that it may be the means of all the good to you that was contemplated in its foundation, and that you, on your part, may see that it is carried on always with kind feelings and harmony. And so I trust, my dear young friends, that in passing by this edifice—young as you are now—you will feel in looking upon it, not that it is one for grown-up men and women, and with which you have no concern, but that it is yours also; that you will at no distant day have a right in it as your heritage, and so will even now in your tender years take an interest in it and all things connected with it.

"I have now but little advice to give you, for I am sure that your parents and teachers have bestowed, and will always bestow upon you, the kindest and most earnest counsel; but I would say, attend closely your studies, and remember that your close attention to them is a thousand times more important to you than to your teachers. Bear in mind that the time of your studies, though it may now appear long to you, is in reality very brief, and at a future day, when it is perhaps too late, you yourselves will feel that it is so. Do not be ashamed to ask advice and take counsel from those older than yourselves; the time will come when you, in your turn, may advise those younger than you, and who will follow in your footsteps. Strive always to imitate the good example of others. I am glad that your assemblage is in this most interesting place, for I hope that your future recollections of this occasion may be connected with the thought of him whose statue crowns yonder beautiful monument, the illustrious Father of his Country, and that you may be induced to take him more and more for your model; for he, pre-eminently great among men, was also great and good in his boyhood and youth.

"Finally, strive always to act as if the eye of your Heavenly Father were upon you, and if you do this, His countenance will always smile upon you."

May the people and youth of the Monumental City honor the memory of this great and good man, by employing this Institute as he intended, and by enacting in their lives the pure and noble sentiments with which he accompanied his princely gift at its dedication.

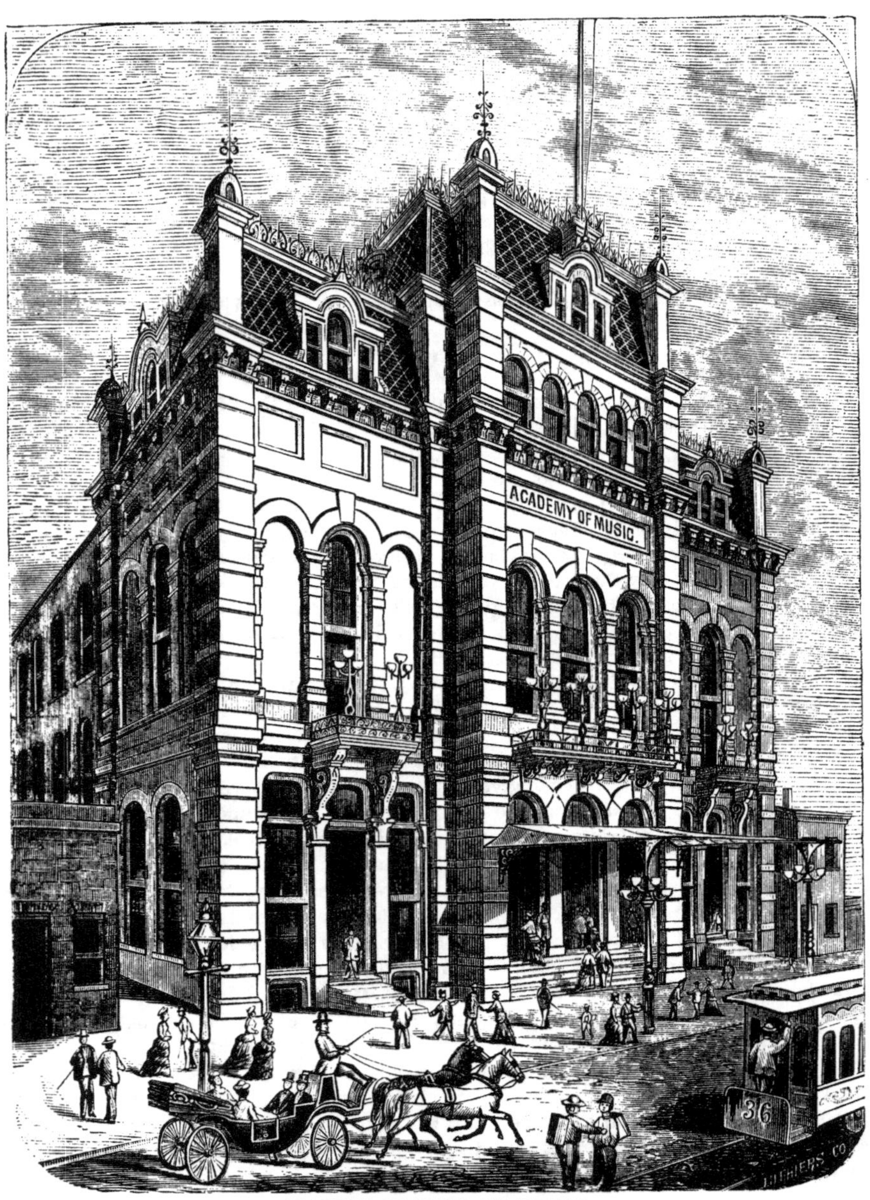

ACADEMY OF MUSIC, BALTIMORE.

(NORTH HOWARD STREET.)

*The Author acknowledges the courtesy of the proprietors of the Baltimore Gazette for the use of this Cut.

THE ACADEMY OF MUSIC.

BALTIMORE, not to be behind her sister cities in the department of Music and the Drama, has erected an Academy of Music, which is unsurpassed in the United States. About two years ago a number of our most highly cultivated and enterprising citizens projected and liberally subscribed towards it, and though we had a number of fine edifices for the purposes of the drama and music, such as *Ford's Opera House, Concordia Building, Masonic Temple, Raine's Hall, &c., there was no building, which, in all respects just suited the wants of our community, and that could compare with the grand halls of other cities. But, on the completion of this building, we have one that will compare favorably with any similar structure in the world, which includes spaces and features not found in any other. Its magnitude may be inferred from the size of the lot which it covers, 120 feet by 250. Its facade is in the Romanesque style, and rises to the height of 100 feet, presenting an imposing view. The grand entrance on Howard street is through arched doorways into an elegant hall with the purest marble floors and richly decorated walls and ceiling. The hall passes between two splendid and brilliantly lighted cafés, exquisitely frescoed. Over the hall and cafés, on the second floor, is a Concert and Lecture room, with dancing floor, and sitting capacity for 1200 persons. Its rich ceiling, whose span is 100 feet, is divided into three long compartments by arcades forming the front of spacious galleries, under which are dressing rooms and pantries with dumb-waiters, and every appliance for large entertainments. The approach to the hall is by two grand stairways, 14 feet wide, whose walls are beautifully painted in decorated panels.

Occupying the centre and rear of the edifice is the Grand Opera House, to which the main hall on the first floor leads; this is surrounded by a wide lobby, from which there are numerous openings into the auditorium, which is beautiful beyond description. This is arranged according to the most approved plan, so that the entire stage is visible from every seat in the house, on the floor and in the dress circle and galleries. The stage is perfect in its appointments, and the machinery so complete as to produce every possible variety of scenic effect. It is 80 by 75 feet, with a height of 80 feet above and a depth of 36 feet below it.

The arrangement of boxes is peculiar to it; the box-circle having two rows of boxes with four seats and rows of single seats for those desiring but one.

The Green and Dressing rooms are commodious, and finished in the most approved manner, with every possible convenience.

From the centre of the Crystal Dome, hangs the great Chandelier of the most magnificent style, unsurpassed in any other city in the United States, it is 27 feet from the dome to the foot-knob, and has a major circumference of 52 feet. It is constructed of gilded metal and glass with 240 candle-shaped burners and 994 strands or chains of crystal, festooned from the bands with tassels of prismatic drops. The electric battery produces a spark seven inches in length. When lighted it is brilliant beyond description and forms a perfect completion of this grand Auditorium; a similar Chandelier, with 120 burners is in the Concert or Ball Room described above.

Standing upon the stage, and getting a full view of the house, the effect is gorgeous. From the magnificent ceiling, with its exquisite frescoes and transparent crystal centre, to the floor, there is perfect elegance. The walls are traced in gilt and colors. The fronts of the galleries are beautifully decorated; the columns are graceful, and the "tout ensemble" is the expression of highest art and the most cultivated taste.

The builder, Mr. B. F. Bennett, and the architect, Mr. J. Crawford Neilson, deserve special commendation in their respective parts in the construction of this grand building.

* Pages 60, 61, 72, 78, 79.

MARYLAND ACADEMY OF SCIENCES.

THE Maryland Academy of Sciences, encouraged by the public spirit of some of our generous citizens, has laid the foundation of an enterprise which ought to appeal to the sympathies of this entire community. It has erected a Hall for the use of its members and for the delivery of public lectures, and has placed therein large glass cases, which are being rapidly filled with choice specimens of Mineralogy, Geology and Natural History, illustrative of the resources of our own State and of the region adjacent to it.

Alive to the deficiencies which exist in our systems of higher culture, it aims to supply a want that is felt by many who desire to gain an intimate knowledge of natural objects and of their relations to each other, and to the region to which they belong. Aware that our mineral resources are still almost untouched, that our birds and fishes need protection and development, and that our wealth of shell-fish is capable of being enlarged indefinitely, it desires to increase and diffuse the knowledge which is necessary to promote their successful and intelligent cultivation.

Hitherto our city has not been very quick to apprehend and to appropriate her natural advantages for improvement; for, with all the possibilities of superior position, climate, and beautifully varied surface, it has taken a long time to secure many of the improvements of which we are now so justly proud. But now a new era seems to be opening, fresh energies have been stirred, and some progress has been made towards a more advanced, while more active, civilization.

Still, many issues have to be met; a more ample and permanent supply of pure water has to be provided, (both for the domestic uses of our steadily increasing population and for our rapidly extending manufactures); a system of perfect drainage has to be established; and departments for the teaching of the sciences and their applications have to be added to our higher schools.

As a contribution towards these objects, the Academy has made a beginning. Explanations and lectures, descriptive of our region, and of its natural phenomena and resources, have been projected and will soon begin, and to this feast, as well as to the treasures in its Museum, all will be admitted gratuitously. Our citizens cannot afford to let such an enterprise remain in embryo. A large building is requisite to contain and display only those natural objects which belong to our territory or which characterise some of its past or present areas.

Our hydrographic basins and the ocean need to be carefully studied, both to afford the ready intercourse of an unobstructed navigation and to aid in perpetuating their bountiful supplies of food.

None of our natural features remain stationary—the frosts of winter, the heats of summer, and the sharp teeth of chemical agents, unite in levelling the summits of our granite mountains and primeval hills, while the currents of the sea and of our rivers, and the impetus of winds and rains, scoop out vast reaches of our Eastern peninsula and deposit their fragments in the path of an increasing commerce. To us, far more than to our Northern neighbors, these forces echo, that eternal progress is peculiarly our destiny—we can stand still only at our future peril.

To such interests the Academy is devoted; to represent them and make them widely known, a large Museum and its facilities are needed. To the enlightened spirit which has prompted such benefactors as George Peabody, Johns Hopkins and others to establish here perpetual monuments of wisdom and sagacity, we look for the means to accomplish a part of our manifest duty in advancing the prosperity of this community.

PUBLIC SCHOOLS.

THE *Public School system of Baltimore is the growth of nearly half a century, and during that period it has accomplished such grand results, and promises so much more in the future, that it has become an important element in the prosperity of our community.

BALTIMORE CITY COLLEGE, NORTH HOWARD STREET.

An act was passed by the General Assembly of Maryland, on the 28th of February, 1826, which authorized the Mayor and City Council of Baltimore to establish Public Schools and to levy and collect such taxes as were necessary for their support; and on the 17th of January, 1827, the City Council adopted an Ordinance accepting the Act of Assembly.

* Pages 36, 37, 38.

Three Public Schools were established in the City in 1829, under the control of three teachers with two hundred and sixty-nine pupils. They soon secured public confidence and increased in number; and as they became more thorough and efficient their beneficial influence was felt and appreciated by the community. The growth of these schools has been regular and rapid, and in view of the fact that the attendance of pupils is voluntary and not enforced by any compulsory laws, they have increased in number and influence as rapidly as those in any other city.

During the year 1873 there were one hundred and twenty-three schools, with six hundred and twenty-four teachers, containing over forty thousand pupils in attendance, about one-half of the number being girls.

The system embraces Primary, Grammar and Collegiate Institutions, adapted to every class and sufficient to furnish the most liberal education.

Baltimore City College was established in 1839, and the Female High Schools in 1844, and many of our most valuable and honored citizens are graduates of the former, whilst a large number of our most accomplished women have received their education in the latter schools. In addition to the regular schools for instruction in English there have also been established English-German Schools, for the purpose of enabling the children of German parents to receive the full benefit of Public School education. These have been deemed necessary in view of the large number of Germans in our city, who contribute much by their labor and industry to its material prosperity. These schools will enable their children to acquire a thorough English education, whilst at the same time other pupils can obtain such instruction in the German language as may aid them in future business relations. This extension of our Public School system has met with general approval, and will popularize our schools.

There are thirteen schools exclusively for colored children, containing over three thousand pupils. They are under the charge of white teachers, who are as well qualified as those of the schools for white children, and who furnish every grade of instruction which may be needed. The colored people of our city fully appreciate these educational advantages, since they have never demanded mixed schools, which would necessarily be injurious to the educational interests of both races.

In view of a recent Act of Congress, it is contemplated to establish here a Nautical School, under the auspices of the School Commissioners and the Board of Trade. The object of this school is to impart instruction in navigation, seamanship, and all matters which pertain to the proper equipment and sailing of vessels. A suitable United States vessel will be furnished at this port, and nautical instruction will be given by competent officers of the Navy and assistants. This school will be of great benefit to the merchant service of our city, by the promotion of nautical education, which has heretofore been so much neglected.

The new building for the Baltimore City College is one of the most commodious and elegant public structures in our city. The lot is one hundred and twenty feet front, with a depth of two hundred feet, and cost $60,000. The building is designed in the College Gothic style, and cost about $120,000.

The maximum dimensions of the place are ninety-nine feet four inches in width by one hundred and sixty-nine feet in depth, and the building is three stories high, and contains all the necessary class-rooms for six hundred pupils. It is thorough in all its appointments, and will furnish accommodations equal to any school building in the country.

MARYLAND STATE NORMAL SCHOOL.

THE State Normal School was established by Act of the General Assembly, in 1865, and was organized in January, 1866.

It is intended for the education and training of Teachers for the Public Schools of the State, and is supported by an annual appropriation of $10,500. The school was first opened in the Red Men's Hall, in Paca Street, and was very slimly attended, the first session averaging not more than thirty students, but it grew rapidly in numbers and popularity; and in 1872, having entirely outgrown the limited accommodations of the Red Men's Hall, it was removed to the spacious building, corner of Charles and Franklin Streets, formerly occupied by the Union Club, where it is held at present.

The Legislature made an appropriation of $100,000 for the purpose of erecting a new building for the use of the school. The Board of Public Works have selected a site on the corner of Republican and Townsend Streets, opposite Lafayette Square, and will build a handsome and commodious house. The plans having been already prepared by Mr Frank E. Davis, Architect, and approved by the Board.

The number of students at present in attendance in the Normal School proper is one hundred and fifty-eight, and in the Model School connected therewith fifty-three.

FRONT STREET THEATRE.

ON Thursday evening, September 10th, 1829, the "New Theatre and Circus" (now * Front Street Theatre) was first opened with an audience of about 3000 persons. Many prominent actors and actresses made their appearance in this theatre, and it at once became a favorite resort for the pleasure seeking society of the city.

* Page 79.

On February 3d, 1838, a disastrous fire destroyed the building. It was occupied by Mr. Cooke with his celebrated equestrian troupe and a stud of 50 splendid horses. His entire stock, fixtures, machinery, wardrobe decorations, including the horses, twelve of which were extremely small, were destroyed.

The theatre was rebuilt by Mr. Wm. Minifie (architect) the same year, 1838, and on May 22d a furious tornado swept over the city and blew down a large portion of the old wall; the theatre was opened again on December 3d, 1838.

It has been under various management, not always satisfactory to its best patrons, but six years ago Col. Wm. E. Sinn assumed the exclusive control, and appreciating the difficulties of such a large enterprise, as well as the wants of the community, he has sought to introduce and carry out a regime which is more satisfactory and gratifying to the immense audiences which nightly fill the spacious building. In his conduct of the entire establishment he has displayed signal ability and knowledge of his profession.

EVENTS CONNECTED WITH THIS THEATRE.

It has been identified with many important and exciting public events, having been a favorite place for holding great meetings and conventions. On February 22d, 1832, the centennial anniversary of the birth of George Washington was observed with extraordinary demonstration by the citizens of Baltimore. An immense concourse of people assembled in it, and W. H. Collins, Esq., read Washington's Farewell Address, and Hon. J. H. B. Latrobe delivered an eloquent oration.

In December, 1850, Jenny Lind, the "Swedish Nightingale," gave four concerts here to delighted audiences, the receipts of which amounted to $60,000.

On June 18, 1860, the National Democratic Convention, according to the order of its adjournment at Charleston, reassembled in this city and chose Front Street Theatre for its sessions. Hon. Caleb Cushing presided. The session was a stormy one; on the fourth day (21st of June) the reports were submitted, which occasioned a bitter wrangling of the two parties in the Convention; upon the adoption of the majority report, filling the vacant seats of the Gulf States with Douglass men, several States, with Virginia, California and Oregon in the lead, withdrew. Mr. Smith, of California, remarked, "this Convention has properly been held in a theatre, and upon that stage a play has been enacted this evening that will prove a tragedy, of which the Democratic party will be the victim." After the withdrawal of delegates, the Convention remaining nominated Stephen A Douglass for the Presidency. On the morning of the 21st, at the moment of the most intense excitement, while the Committee on Credentials were reporting, a loud crash came from the centre of the floor and over 100 delegates were seen going down through the stage; for a moment the wildest confusion prevailed, but order being restored, it appeared that the front of the stage and covering of the orchestra had given way and sunk about three feet, throwing those seated there into a confused mass, from which they were with difficulty extricated.

On the 7th of June, 1864, the Union National Convention assembled in Baltimore and held its sessions in this theatre, and nominated Abraham Lincoln for the Presidency and Andrew Johnson for the Vice-Presidency.

On November 20th, 1866, Baltimore was the scene of one of the finest civic displays ever witnessed. The occasion was the laying of the corner-stone of the new Masonic Temple. Members of the Fraternity came from all parts of the country. Upon the conclusion of the ceremonies the Knights Templar of Baltimore entertained the visiting Commanderies with an elegant collation in the Front Street Theatre, which was described as a most brilliant affair.

YOUNG MEN'S CHRISTIAN ASSOCIATION BUILDING.

THE movement inaugurated in December, 1870, by the public meeting held at Masonic Temple, has culminated in the splendid edifice now nearly completed—(*see page* 43.) This meeting embodied a singular representation of the wealth, public spirit, social and religious influence of the city. It signalized the interest of the gentlemen present in the great idea of utilizing in the interests of religion, good morals and liberal charity, the organized efforts of the young men of the city, who, being members of the various churches in the community, were believed to offer a most valuable agency for the accomplishment of these great results.

The result of the meeting was to devolve the execution of the project upon a Board of Trustees, who were to hold the funds subscribed for the purpose of erecting a suitable building, and on whom the trust imposed the responsibility of carrying the project into effect upon a large and liberal scale, which would gratify the intentions of the generous donors of the fund, both as to the religious influences of the enterprise and its value generally as an auxiliary to the social and intellectual advancement of the community.

The building is situated on the corner of Charles and Saratoga streets, in a very central position, and occupies a point well calculated for perfect lighting and ventilation of the apartments.

The first or ground floor, with the exception of the stairways, is entirely occupied by first class store-rooms, the revenue from which will form a very important item in the finances of the Association. The second floor is reached by a wide, easy flight of stairs, from a conspicuous entrance on Charles street. On the right of a spacious and handsome vestibule is a large conversation room, having at one side the beautiful bay window afforded by the corner tower. On the left is the reading room, 36x40 feet beyond the grand stairway; the business office and the Secretary's room are both large and convenient.

In front of the stairway, and in the vestibule before mentioned, are the entrances to the grand hall and lecture room, capable of containing 1200 persons, triangular in shape, and presents a large area in the floor and in the two galleries, while yet no seat is over 45 feet from the speaker, and the lights are most conveniently arranged.

This room extends through three stories of the building to the floor of the Mansard roof.

On the third story are large Class Rooms, Editor's Rooms, Board Room, and a splendid Library, about 45 feet square.

The Cloak Rooms, Wash Rooms and Closets are distributed about the building so as to be quite private, while easy of access.

The fourth floor contains also several Class Rooms and two Gymnasiums.

The large space of the French roof is not appropriated as yet to any purpose.

This building is peculiarly well lighted and ventilated, especially in the Lecture Room. It is heated by steam, and the chimney shaft has been largely used for the purpose of extracting air, other shafts being used to supply it.

The exterior of the building is rich in trimmings of Cleveland stone in our best pressed brick walls—the angle tower and all the first story being entirely stone.

It is an imposing building, having something of a collegiate character, and is most advantageously situated to show the fine effect of its roofing and towers.

This enterprise was carried out by the liberality of a large number of citizens, whose donations supplied the means, judiciously expended. It was constructed by Mr. William Ortwine from the designs of Niernsee & Neilson, architects.

MARYLAND INEBRIATE ASYLUM.

HARLEM LODGE.

THE Maryland Inebriate Asylum, known as Harlem Lodge, is an incorporated Institution, for the care and treatment of Inebriates.*

It is controlled by a Board of Trustees; its chief executive officer is Joseph Parrish, Physician, with the title of Superintendent, who resides upon the premises, and is also Secretary of the Board.

There is a certain number of free beds, which are occupied by beneficiaries of the State and City of Baltimore. There is provision also for those in moderate circumstances, who pay but a small sum per month, and there are private apartments for men of means who are willing to pay for extra space and accommodation.

The location is a beautifully retired spot on the old Frederick road, about five miles from the city. Thirty-five acres of land are laid out in groves, orchards and gardens, in which are included a green-house, ten-pin alley and billiard-room, which furnish ample opportunity for entertainment and for useful occupation.

The discipline is mild and skillful, the officers having always in view the cultivation of the self-respect of the inmates. A good library is supplied, and a literary society or guild for mutual aid and improvement is maintained.

Cards containing on one side a diagram of the different routes to the Institution and on the other the names of the Trustees, have been placed in the hands of physicians, clergymen, policemen and hackmen of Baltimore, that strangers arriving in the city, as well as residents, may learn from these several sources of information the locality of the Institution and the address of the Trustees.

MARYLAND LYING-IN HOSPITAL.

THE College of Physicians and Surgeons of Baltimore was chartered in 1872, and its powers enlarged and extended by the Legislature in 1874, with Drs. Harvey L. Byrd Thomas Opie, William W. Murray and others, as coporators. At the same session the Legislature by special act appropriated twenty thousand dollars, and empowered the College of Physicians and Surgeons to use the same in establishing a Lying-in Hospital in connection with and under the control of the Faculty of the College. A suitable building was soon secured, and the Asylum opened on Lombard Street, between Hanover and Sharp Streets. The Asylum has been arranged and furnished with special reference to the comfort and health of its inmates, and will compare favorably in all respects with any similar institution in this country; offering the advantages of a *home* to the poor and destitute during the most trying and important period of female life.

Hitherto this class, always considerable in every large community, and found in greater or less numbers in rural districts also, are invited to come when in need of the skill and nursing which they require during parturition, without money and without price, until they and their offspring can return to their homes.

Provision is made also for such women as have not the means of procuring suitable nurses during confinement at their own homes, at moderate charges. Private rooms are likewise arranged for those who might prefer the privacy and attention the Asylum offers, to the boarding-houses and hotels in which they reside.

The State has probably never made an appropriation which is likely to prove of such great advantage to the deserving poor as that for the establishment of this noble institution.

* See page 50.

"HOMEWOOD PARK."

THIS beautiful Park has recently been added to the attractions of the "Monumental City."

It was generously *presented* by its owners to the Mayor and City Council, on conditions that will ensure its improvement and use as a public pleasure-ground for all coming time. It embraces about sixteen acres, bounded by Charles Street and Waverley Avenues, Holmes and Oak Streets. The most noble oaks, tulip-trees and other magnificent monarchs of the forest already adorn it.

The Engineer of Druid Hill Park, A. Faul, Esq., says, "that without altering the natural surface, it is susceptible of great beauty in laying it out in winding walks, dells, miniature water-falls and lakes."

It is immediately opposite the elevated grounds of the "Peabody Heights," which are to be occupied only by elegant, first-class residences; and the grand projected avenue, which is to connect "Clifton" and "Druid Hill," will pass in its vicinity; in short, it is destined to become, both in its own natural beauty and its delightful surroundings, one of the most charming and attractive spots in Baltimore or its suburbs.

MILITARY.

THE close of the war between the sections of our country found the State of Maryland utterly without a militia force.

In the year 1867, however, the General Assembly, acting on the Declaration of Rights, Article 28, "That a well regulated Militia is the proper and natural defense of a free Government," passed a law which, while very imperfect, still caused a revival of the military spirit in a State always renowned for the bravery and discipline of her troops. Under the stimulus of a newly-awakened spirit and the liberality of the General Assembly, nine Regiments of Infantry, two Batallions of Artillery, and three Companies of Cavalry were raised in the City of Baltimore alone, while in the counties several other Regiments of Infantry and Cavalry were formed. The principle on which this force was created was wrong, and soon worked its destruction, so that, in 1870–1, the Fifth Regiment of Infantry alone remained of that arm, and the three small Companies of Cavalry. The Fifth Regiment not being dependent on the State for its support, and imbued with a spirit not to be quenched, continued to prosper, until at this time it has a national reputation and fame.

Commencing with the year 1869, the Fifth has gone into Camp of Instruction for a week to ten days, annually, and has improved itself in discipline and knowledge of camp duties, while affording to the officers and men a cheap and pleasant mode of summer recreation. Twice, viz: in 1870 and 1873, it encamped for ten days at Cape May, and while there was reviewed severally by Gen. Meade and Gov. Randolph, of New Jersey, and Gov. Hartranft, of Pennsylvania, and was the recipient of the most distinguished courtesies from the press and people congregated from all parts of the United States. In 1874 its encampment was at Long Branch, where the President of the United States reviewed and complimented it for discipline and appearance, as he had previously done in Washington. From Long Branch the Regiment visited New York, and under the escort of the celebrated New York Seventh were received with an enthusiasm hardly ever equalled in New York; and by the critic of the "Army and Naval Journal," the Fifth was awarded the front rank of the Militia of the United States. This result, so gratifying to the members of the Fifth, has been attained only by good conduct, strict discipline, gentlemanly intelligence and honorable conduct of officers and men alike. Socially equal and personally intimate out of the ranks; when on duty no familiarity or favoritism is desired by the men or permitted by the officers.

The Fifth Regiment is now regarded as one of the institutions of our City, of which the citizens are justly proud. In recognition of the good-will of the city authorities, the Mayor and City Council of Baltimore, in 1871-2, built for the Regiment an Armory--for purposes to which it is devoted—unsurpassed in the United States. The main drill-room, without a pillar, is one hundred by one hundred and forty feet, with a large gallery, accommodating about twelve hundred people to view the drills; beside the main hall, there are some sixteen large rooms used for Companies head-quarters, band, &c.

The Regiment has about five hundred men, fully armed with Springfield breech-loading muskets, and equipped thoroughly for immediate service; the repressive influence of such an organization upon the rowdy and turbulent elements of our city is worth many thousands of dollars to the people.

Within the last two years another Infantry Regiment has been raised, viz: the Sixth, It has a large Armory on the corner of Calvert and Saratoga Streets, where it is undergoing that discipline and training which will make it a credit to our City, and a pride to the members themselves. Under the fostering care of the State it has continued in successful organization, with a full list of officers and members, and upon occasions of public drill is very much admired and praised by our citizens.

The Cavalry still consists of three Companies, in a prosperous condition, all under the command of Major Harry Gilmor.

The Colonel of the Fifth is J. Stricker Jenkins, and of the Sixth, Clarence Peters.

THE SALVAGE CORPS.

IT has always been evident that there is an enormous destruction of property at fires from reckless handling and by damage from water. Various attempts have been made to adopt a system to prevent this, with only partial success.

The Salvage Corps of this City seems to be the most efficient means yet devised for this purpose. It was organized through the efforts of Messrs. Andrew Reese, President of the Howard Fire Insurance Company, the Fire Inspector Mr. Charles T. Holloway, and other gentlemen connected with the Insurance interests, who have brought it to its present state of efficiency. It is as yet a voluntary Association, supported by various Fire Insurance Companies, to whom its operations have been of most material advantage.

Its equipment is two elegant silver mounted wagons, with six of Holloway's Chemical Extinguishers, buckets, axes, and water-proof covers.

The specific duties of the Corps are:

1—To extinguish incipient fires; 2—Prompt use of water-proof covers on perishable goods; 3—Removal of goods to a place of safety; 4—Taking charge of damaged goods; 5—Notifying Companies of the perilous condition of premises. These and such other duties as the case may demand are performed without conflict with the Fire Department. Such an organization, which has abundantly demonstrated its necessity and value, should be liberally supported, and the gentlemen who through much difficulty and opposition organized it, deserve the thanks of the whole community.

STATE HOUSE OF CORRECTION.

BY an Act passed at the Session, January, 1874, of the Legislature of the State, an appropriation of $250,000 was made for the purpose of purchasing a site and erecting thereon a State House of Correction.

The Board of Public Works and Attorney-General of the State were constituted a Board for the purpose of carrying out the provisions of this act. The object and want of such an institution must commend it to the people of the State. In this, as in every community, there exists quite a large number of degraded and evil disposed persons of all ages and both sexes, who, from confirmed habits of idleness and dissipation, become habitual violators of the law, and entail a heavy expense upon the taxpayers, through repeated trials in the courts and incarceration in our jails, without returning any compulsory labor, or having the benefit of reformatory instrumentalities by which their characters and habits may be amended. This Institution is designed to supply the want which this state of things creates. Under the intelligent and efficient management to which, by the law, this Institution is entrusted, we believe that it will not only be self-sustaining but one of the most valuable and salutary in the State, especially so to the City of Baltimore, to which it will be conveniently located, 15 miles on the Washington Branch of the B. & O. R. R., near Jessup's Cut.

SUNDAY SCHOOLS.

WE would be false to the spirit of this Work if we failed to give more than a passing notice of an institution in our midst, which perhaps is doing more than any other agency to mould the character and determine the status of Baltimore. The Sabbath School has become a recognized power in the world. It is not only a school in which specific instruction is given upon Bible truths, but an institute where are training the men and women who are to be the guides of the Nation in its various departments of civil and social life. The Sabbath School exerts the preponderating influence upon the community. Gathering within its sacred folds every week the children of all classes and from all quarters, under the instruction of earnest and devoted teachers, and there invested with the most impressive influence, and receiving the most useful of all knowledge, they are being prepared after the highest model for their future relationships and positions in the world. As an educational institution the Sabbath School is of immense value to the nation. In it are thousands of children who have no other opportunity of learning the language and acquiring the principles of knowledge. Beginning with their A B C's—they are carried along until they are able to read and understand the WORD OF LIFE, and through its divine tuition are fitted for manly occupations and noble stations.

No city in the world owes more to the Sabbath School than Baltimore. In every department, civil and professional, commercial and literary, many of the leading, controlling men, were Sabbath School boys, and they will willingly attribute to its influence much of their success. In our domestic life, in the sanctity of our homes, in the good order of our community, its effect is visible.

No city is more thoroughly furnished with Sabbath Schools than ours. Upon our avenues, amid the palaces of wealth, on almost every street, in the lanes and alleys, out upon the hills and fields as pioneers of an advancing population, the Sabbath School is planted, to do its benign work alike among the rich and poor, the high and low, teaching all the same lessons of truth and purity.

We have compiled from the most authentic sources the number of teachers and scholars of all the schools in our city—which are as follows:

Methodist Episcopal—Teachers 1,018, Scholars 9,874; (colored,) T. 385, S. 3,179. Meth. Epis. (South)—T. 136, S. 1,241. Meth. Epis. (German)—T. 101, S. 578. Indep't. Meth.—T. 75, S. 631. Meth. Prot.—T. 186, S. 1,556; colored, T. 15, S. 118. Presbyterian—T. 477, S. 4,231; Baptist—T. 331, S. 2,503; (German)—T. 8, S. 45; (colored)—T. 49, S. 448. Prot. Epis.—T. 785, S. 6,485; (colored,) T. 13, S. 70. Lutheran—T. 248, S. 2,070; (German,) T. 107, S. 979. Reformed, T. 161, S. 1,432. United Brethren—T. 117, S. 949. Evangelical—T. 8, S. 78; (German,) T. 68, S. 765. Friends—T. 33, S. 474. Associate Reformed—T. 60, S. 475. Christian—T. 34, S. 361. New Jerusalem—T. 24, S. 79; (German,) T. 20, S. 62. Congregrational—T. 15, S. 172; (colored,) T. 9, S. 77. Young Men's Christian Association—T. 11, S. 200. Maryland Penitentiary—T. 47, S. 536. Oheb. Shalom. (Hebrew)—T. 4, S. 196; three other Hebrew Schools to be formed. Universalist—T. 30, S. 150. First Independent—T. 10, S. 65. Roman Catholic—S. 12,000. Total, Teachers—4,585; Scholars—51,964.

THE WESTERN MARYLAND RAIL ROAD.

In July 1857 a work was undertaken, whose relative importance to the City of Baltimore has never been properly appreciated. The originators themselves, perhaps did not at the time, fully prospect the results which must yet flow from its completion.

The Western Maryland Rail Road chartered January 1852, begun July 1857 and extended in 1873 to Williamsport, may clearly be demonstrated to be one of the most valuable enterprises ever projected by our citizens. The public mind absorbed in the truly grand and stupendous operations of the Baltimore and Ohio Rail Road, has been to a great extent oblivious to the important bearings of this Road upon our material advancement. We hail the interest, which under the present efficient administration is being awakened, as indicative of a growing appreciation of it.

In whatever aspect it may be viewed, its relative importance to the trade and the citizens of Maryland is conspicuous. The entire country through which it passes is uninterruptedly beautiful, and is filled with scenes and incidents of interest to the tourist and resident. Starting out from the lovliest suburban country of Baltimore, crossing one of its most exquisite valleys, with Druid Hill Park and its grand old forests to the east and Highland Park to the west; surrounded by beautiful hills, many of which are crowned with graceful villas, it enters Carroll County, renowned for its mills and dairy farms; passing through Westminster its delightful county seat, thence along the Pipe Creek valleys abounding in rich meadows and sparkling streams, crossing the Monocacy it opens up Frederick County, whose rich ores will greatly contribute to Baltimore's prominence among the great manufacturing cities; thence it enters Washington County; ascending the Blue Ridge, it presents mountain views unsurpassed, and displays on every side "little hills that drop their fatness," teeming meadows and vales of abundance; passing through the flourishing City of Hagerstown, it terminates at Williamsport on the Potomac River and the Chesapeake and Ohio Canal, whence it may assist in bringing the Coal of Cumberland hither, to brighten our firesides and drive the pondrous wheels of our industries.

For Summer recreation this Road offers unequaled facilities; within three hours ride of Baltimore, the summit of South Mountain is reached, where our citizens, worn and wearied with the anxieties and toils of the year, may luxuriate in the mountain air surrounded by scenes of beauty and sublimity unexcelled.

For suburban residences, this Road offers unsurpassed opportunities. From Baltimore to Westminster, thirty miles, the country is high, healthy and charming, and those who desire to escape the turmoil of city life, can find no more attractive and convenient locations.

Its material importance to Baltimore, appears from the varied interests which it is developing and will indefinitely multiply. For the Produce trade which has become one of the heaviest in the country, this Road presents unlimited opportunities, in a country unsurpassed in dairy facilities; the Counties of Carroll, Frederick and Washington being among the richest in agricultural and dairy resources. It will also largely increase trade in limestone, marble, copper, iron and other ores in which these counties abound, the iron being the best quality for rail-heads, and the marble equal to the celebrated Texas quarries. Thus in agriculture, mineral and manufacturing interests, this Road developes inexhaustible resources and possibilities.

With proper terminal facilities in Baltimore and at tide-water, even with its present length and Western terminus, it must contribute largely to the trade and industries of our city. But the proposed extension to Johnstown on the Pennsylvania Central Rail Road via Bedford, adhering as closely as possible to the air-line between Baltimore and Pittsburgh, when perfected will be of prime importance to Baltimore and the great Cities and States of the West. This line runs through and taps the three great Coal deposits of Pennsylvania and Maryland; the Broad-Top, Alleghany and Cumberland Beds, and opens a new direct route to the Pennsylvania Oil Regions, and would thus constitute another great medium of supply to this market of these two articles of Commerce. In addition a very large proportion of the Pennsylvania iron trade, and the grain and produce of its central and border Counties would be diverted hither.

The present necessity of this Road is a depot conveniently situated and a tide-water terminus. The President and Managers have largely overcome the inconvenience of Fulton Station by an arrangement with the Citizens Passenger Railway to have cars starting from Eutaw and Fayette Streets where the offices of the Company are situated, so that passengers virtually have a depot at one of the most accessible points in the city. Strenuous efforts however are making to effect a better entrance, with a depot sufficient for all purposes.

The President of the Road J. M. Hood, Esq., who has attained a high reputation in the management and construction of rail road enterprises, with the encouragement of the Directors, is rapidly improving its condition and overcoming to a commendable degree the difficulties which attach to all new Rail Roads.

The City of Baltimore is the largest Stockholder, its entire interest at the close of the last fiscal year being $3,279,500. The manifest improvement in the condition and prospects of the Road affords general satisfaction, and the President's annual report for 1874, shows a great increase of its revenue over the year 1873 and demonstrates its ability ere long, to appropriate a large amount of its earnings annually, to paying the interest on the bonded debt; in the language of the report "economy with due regard to efficiency is being practiced in every department of the Road." The present officers are: J. M. Hood, President and Manager; Alexander Rieman, Vice President; J. S. Harden, Secretary and Treasurer; B. H. Griswold, Auditor and General Agent; Charles Webb, Assistant Manager; William Lannan, Master Machinery, and twelve Directors.

WM. H. RINEHART.

Since the publication of this book and our reference to the exquisite works of this eminent Artist on pages 72 and 73, he has passed away. He died in Rome, October 28th, 1874, where for nineteen years he pursued the study of his favorite art, and attained a reputation among the first Sculptors of the age. Having made liberal bequests to his surviving brothers, he left the residue of his estate including his private Collection of works, for the promotion and cultivation of Art in his State and City, appointing his personal friends Wm. T. Walters and B. F. Newcomer, Esqrs., his sole Executors, without restrictions, to fulfil the purposes of the noble and public-spirited disposition of his estate.

* RAINE'S HALL.

Among the Public Halls of Baltimore this deserves special mention. It constitutes the third story of the German Correspondent Building. It is a spacious and beautiful Room, admirably proportioned and complete in its acoustics. The walls are handsomely decorated, the end wall in rear of stage having a fine fresco of the Druid Hill Park Mansion, upon the ceiling are figures representing Art, Industry and Science, the centre piece a large oval with the figure of Apollo. A balcony in the forward end of the room provides for the musicians at balls and on festive occasions. The convenient location and fine construction of the Hall make it a very desirable one for public assemblies and musical entertainments. The whole building is an ornament to the city, and testifies to the success of the Correspondent.

THE HOUSE OF REFORMATION AND INSTRUCTION FOR COLORED CHILDREN.

One of the most recently instituted enterprises of philanthropy in our midst, is the House of Reformation and Instruction for Colored Children.

The only places of commitment and detention for this class were our common Jails and Penetentiaries, in which they could not receive that care and attention which would result in their reformation. The scheme of a House of Reformation similar to the House of Refuge for white children, excepting that there is no rigid system of incarceration, was undertaken by a few philanthropic gentlemen, among whom we especially mention the late Mr. Benjamin Deford, who was one of the first to inspire the movement, and contributed by his means and counsel to its success, and whose public spirit, geniality and practical wisdom, made him most highly esteemed by the citizens of Baltimore.

An act of incorporation having been obtained from the Legislature in 1870, with a donation of $10,000 on condition of $30,000 being secured by private subscription, one of our most useful and public spirited citizens, Enoch Pratt, Esq., donated the handsome farm "Cheltenham," 752 acres, in Prince George's County, valued at $22,600. The Board were thus enabled to secure the appropriation of $10,000; subsequently in 1872 and 1873, the State and City together gave $40,000, and the State recently $15,000 additional for a building, and this with other private donations of money and material amounted to about $90,000, and the institution was put at once into successful operation in February, 1873.

There are now about 100 inmates on the Farm, who have been committed by the courts for various offences, and thus delivered from the debasing and hardening effects of prison life, and are under that moral and intellectual discipline which is most conducive to their improvement and reformation.

Since the organization of the Board one of its most efficient and liberal members has died, a gentleman whose enterprise, christian nobility and benevolence, have made his death a public calamity; whose heart and hand were ever open to respond to the pressing wants of a sinful and suffering humanity. We refer to the late Henry W. Drakeley, Esq.

The present officers are, President, John R. Cox; Vice President, G. S. Griffith; Secretary, Wm. M. Boone; Treasurer, William E. Woodyear; with a Board of sixteen Managers on the part of the City, State and Subscribers.

* See Pages 60 and 61.

STATE NORMAL SCHOOL, (LAFAYETTE SQUARE.)*

FRANK E. DAVIS, ARCHITECT.

THE building is 120 by 105 feet, of the best pressed brick, with Berea stone trimmings. The tower is 175 feet high. The basement contains the gymnasium, dressing rooms, and three large class rooms, &c. In the principal story are the parlor, library, offices, reception rooms and six large class rooms. In the second is the assembly room, seating 600 persons; also, a students' library and other rooms. On the third floor is the lecture room, laboratory, apparatus, and cabinet of natural history. The roof is covered with slate in ornamental shapes. The gables, dormers and ridges are finished in great taste with richly wrought finials and castings.

The whole building is perfectly lighted and ventilated. It constitutes another handsome addition to our city, and reflects great credit upon the Architect.

* See page 337.

FRANKLIN STREET PRESBYTERIAN CHURCH, (FRANKLIN AND CATHEDRAL STREETS.)

THE I. O. O. F. OF BALTIMORE.

ON the 2d of September, 1817, arrived in this city, a plain, earnest, noble-hearted young man from England. Locating at Fell's Point, he soon found himself amid the ravages of the Yellow Fever. Though a stranger, he fearlessly applied himself to the work of humanity. Deeply inspired with sympathy for the suffering, at the risk of his own life, he took his post by the sick and dying, facing perils before which many citizens fled in terror. This was a grand and fitting introduction to his life here, which was to become monumental by his organization and development of that society, which has so nobly amplified throughout the world the spirit with which he begun his career amid the distress of his adopted city.

This young man, Thomas Wildey,* together with John Welch, John Duncan, John Cheatam and Richard Rushworth, on the 26th of April, 1819, organized the Washington Lodge, No. 1. This was the origin of the I. O. O. F. on this continent. From this unpretentious origin, through many trials and struggles which have made it all the sturdier and nobler, it has grown and diffused itself through all climes. Prior to 1830, four feeble Lodges existed, but upon the erection of their Hall they began to strengthen. Its dedication on the 26th of April, 1831, was the signal of new life; and henceforward the Order everywhere advanced, receiving most valuable accessions. The membership rapidly multiplied, and Lodges were introduced into the States and Territories, until in 1860 representatives from all of them assembled in this city in convention; and now from Baltimore as the centre it radiates to every city, town and village of the United States, and has become established in Canada, British Columbia, Sandwich Islands, Germany, Switzerland and South America, and negotiations are pending with the government for its introduction into Austria, whose polity has hitherto forbade the existence of such societies. In Great Britain the Order is independent of this country.

Its usefulness is coextensive with its prevalence; under the administration of its national Grand Lodge, it has performed a mission, which not only endears it to the members but commends it to all men, and makes it illustrious in the realm of benevolent achievement. The following statistics are a grand exhibit, and must produce a profound impression of its magnitude and importance. From 1830 to 1873, the initiations amounted to 869,181; members relieved, 647,603; widowed families relieved, 85,118; members deceased, 56,887. Total receipts, $50,811,704.93; total paid to relieve the sick, bury the dead, educate the orphan, $19,720,950.97. Number of Grand Lodges in America, 46; Grand Encampments, 36; Subordinate Lodges, 5,494; Subordinate Encampments, 1,533; Lodge members, 414,825; Encampment members, 80,131.

Lodges in Maryland, 101; State members, 13,386; city, about 10,000.

Grand Lodges in other countries, 6; Subordinate Lodges, 74; Subordinate Lodge members, 13,529.

The total revenue of the Order for 1873 was $4,434,001.08, and the aggregate relief bestowed, $1,490,274.72.

Its ability and benevolence were displayed in its munificent contributions to the relief of Chicago, Peshito and Memphis and other places stricken by fire and disease. To Chicago it gave $131,120.62; to Peshito and other towns of the Northwest, $25,272.25; to Memphis, about $40,000. For an organization which thus responds to the call of distress, whose treasury is ever open, and under whose sheltering ægis the widow and orphan find protection from man's inhumanity, and refuge from the blows of misfortune, there are only words of praise.

The educational aspect of this Order is quite as important as its benevolent. Through the education of its youth, the medium of its press, and literature, and the general influence it has acquired a moral and intellectual position, from which it commands mighty social forces all over the world. Its appliances for this result are well ordered. The State

*See page 70.

Library in the Hall on Gay street contains 40,000 volumes of the best selected literature, ancient and modern, one portion of which is in the German language. Thirty journals, weekly and monthly, are published, and frequent lectures delivered upon literary, historical and scientific subjects.

Among the membership are many of our most useful and respected citizens. James L. Ridgely, Esq., has been the Grand Secretary for thirty-five years, who has devoted to its advancement his eminent abilities and culture, and through whose counsel and administration it has largely attained its present efficiency and reputation. The Grand Treasurer is our present worthy mayor, Hon. Joshua Vansant, who has earnestly labored in its behalf, and by his zeal and influence has greatly promoted its welfare.

We cheerfully record this Order as one of the grand forces of Baltimore; that here is the centre of so vast an organization, exerting such wide and benign influences. Through its channel of communication we are sending out to the world the pulsations of our life, and awakening in thousands sentiments of good will for our city, as the Birthplace and Home of American Odd-Fellowship.

THE MASONIC ORDER.

THIS Order was introduced into Maryland by the Provincial Grand Lodge of Massachusetts, which issued the charter for the establishment of the Grand Lodge at Annapolis in 1750. Five other Lodges were subsequently chartered by the Provincial Grand Lodge of Pennsylvania, and one in 1765 at Joppa by the Grand Lodge of England. On July 31, 1783, five Lodges convened at Talbot C. H. and *informally* organized the Grand Lodge. On April 17, 1787, the Grand Lodge was *duly* organized, and the Grand Chapter in 1812. There are now in this city 32 Lodges with 3,800 members; in the State 92 Lodges with 5,800 members.

The corner-stone of the original Hall was laid in 1814. This was occupied for a half-century, when the present mammoth Temple* was built, the corner-stone of which was laid November 20, 1866. This Temple, built of pure white marble, cost $450,000, and is very spacious and imposing. The third story is devoted exclusively to the purposes of the Fraternity; the second floor contains the large Hall, with a sitting capacity for 2,500 persons. On the first floor, besides stores, is a smaller Hall, or Lecture Room, seating about 600 persons.

This Order has always held a high position in Baltimore, many of its members being among our most highly respected and influential citizens. In the various departments of life, professional, commercial and mechanical, it has exerted a large influence, and has been closely identified with most of the great interests and movements of the city. Like all other great associated institutions it has had its trials and vicissitudes, but through the zeal and fidelity of the members it is successfully outriding them all. To its M. W. Grand Master, one of our most honored citizens, Hon. J. H. B. Latrobe, is due the greatest mead of praise, since through his judicious counsel, and administration, it is overcoming its financial difficulties, and has attained a position in which to fulfill its noble and benevolent mission.

BALTIMORE PROVISION EXCHANGE.

Officers: T. Robert Jenkins, President; W. L. Hill, Secretary; John Black, Treasurer; Directors: R. D. Armstrong, J. C. Nicodemus, W. P. Harvey, H. G. Vickery, J. D. Oakford.

On pages 106 and 109 the Provision trade of Baltimore is presented, whence it will appear that no city occupies a better position as a provision market.

The aggregate amount of sales of Bacon, Lard and Pork at this Port, for the last year was 200,000,000 pounds; the Bacon was principally distributed South, and Lard largely to Europe; 400,000 hogs were slaughtered for City use and cured on ice, and the business is steadily increasing.

*See Page 72.

FINANCIAL STATEMENT OF BALTIMORE,

For the year ending October 31, 1874.

The Funded Debt		$30,103,725 77
Guaranteed Debt		1,992,000 00
Total		$32,095,725 77
Deducting from which, Water Loan interest paid by revenue from water rent	$5,000,000 00	
Druid Hill and Patterson Park loans, interest paid by City Passenger Railway Companies	755,066 25	
		5,755,566 25
Leaving a debt of		$26,340,159 52
Against this the city has available assets to the amount of	$26,155,296 15	
and an annual revenue from market houses, improved wharves, and real estate rented, of 110,077 34, which, capitalized at six per cent., amounts to	$1,834,622 34	
giving a total of		$27,989,918 49
Thus the excess of the city's assets over its present liabilities is		$1,649,758 97

This statement does not include the city properties, such as the City Hall, Court Houses, Record Office, Jail, Police Stations, Fire Engine Houses and Apparatus, School Houses, Almshouses, Steam Tugs, Public Parks, City Yard, &c., &c., which must be estimated by millions of dollars.

We question whether any other city can make a more favorable exhibit. It cannot fail to impress the commercial and industrial mind of the country, and if spread abroad will induce capital to invest here in trade and property, as the most favorable city where taxes are necessarily light, and the expenses of living consequently moderate. As "figures speak louder than words," the city of Baltimore has *the* most powerful argument in her favor, which needs only publication to be convincing.

STATE FINANCES.

As the financial and commercial character of a city is largely affected by the condition and credit of its State, we publish with pride the following statement of the financial standing of Maryland, which adds force to the above.

The Funded Debt of Maryland to Oct. 1, 1873, is $10,741,215.60, the interest on which ranges from three to six per cent. Against this the State holds Bonds and Stocks paying interest, aggregating $4,522,043.46, to which are added the amounts reduced by redemption, and exchange, and due from incorporated institutions, taxes, collections, fees, &c., &c., viz: $2,608,053.72, thus diminishing the debt to $3,611,118.42.

The unproductive assets of the State in Stocks and Bonds amount to $21,608,694.51.

The rate of taxation is 17 cents on a hundred dollars of property, only two other States being taxed as low.

The six per cent. non-taxable stock is selling to-day readily at 108.

The revenue for the present year has been largely in excess of previous years, and the next financial exhibit will show an improved condition, which will place her most favorably in comparison with any of her sister States.

THE GERMAN ORPHAN ASYLUM, (AISQUITH AND ORLEANS STREETS.)

INDEX TO APPENDIX.

THE

MONUMENTAL CITY,

ITS

Past History and Present Resources,

WITH A DESCRIPTIVE ACCOUNT OF
THE CITIES OF

WASHINGTON AND ANNAPOLIS

AND THE

U. S. NAVAL SCHOOL,

BY

GEORGE W. HOWARD.

BALTIMORE:
J. D. EHLERS & CO., ENGRAVERS & STEAM BOOK PRINTERS,
87 Second Street,
1876.

DESCRIPTIVE ACCOUNT OF

WASHINGTON CITY.

THE view we have taken in this volume of Baltimore's national centralism on the Atlantic seaboard is quite demonstrated by the close connection between that city and the Capital of our country.

Baltimore is but forty miles from Washington by rail. The Baltimore and Ohio R. R. Company has a double-track road and the *Baltimore and Potomac R.R. a single-track road between the cities. At present, no less than 66 trains run daily, back and forth, between them—41 over Washington Branch, B. and O. R. R., and 25 over Baltimore and Potomac Road. Practically, we may say without exaggeration, that these metropolitan cities are suburbs of each other. A striking illustration of this was given on July 25th, 1873, when the great fire happened in Baltimore, threatening to be almost as destructive as the conflagration of Chicago, in the fall of 1871. It was thought, at one time, that the fire department of our city, numerous as was its apparatus, and thoroughly organized as it is, would not be able to stop the devastation. It was resolved to ask aid from Washington. The telegraph was quickly used, and the Baltimore and Ohio Railroad Company notified of the demand. Its officers instantly ordered a train to be put at our city's service in Washington, and in sixty minutes from the time that the first message was sent from our city to the authorities in Washington, the fire apparatus of that city had been ordered out, loaded on cars, expressed over the Washington Branch, and was playing on the flames in Baltimore. In fact, the train passed from Washington to our city in the unexampled time of forty-three minutes. This seems to demonstrate the near annihilation of space between the cities, and proves that they are practically one in everything but government. By means of the telegraph, they have been really identical, since electro-magnetic telegraphy was *first* tested in America on their wires. All the business relations of the two capitals have long shown this fact, and made Baltimore the favorite residence of numbers whose official duty or business require their daily presence in either of the cities.

*Double track now being laid.

It is natural to suppose that there is hardly an American, and surely not a foreigner, coming to the Atlantic seaboard who is not anxious to see the National Capital, even when not in its winter ferment. Of late it has become attractive not only on account of its political relations to all parts of our country and its well known historical collections, but from the remarkable changes in its civic improvements and adornments; its superb, new buildings; its vast libraries and museums; its national edifices of charity and munificence; its rapidly increasing crowds of wealthy citizens and the spendid residences they have built for permanent homes; its closeness to Mount Vernon; and its gathering of intellectual people for a large part of every year. Indeed, it is quite surprising to notice the numbers of opulent men and women of leisure, who have adopted Washington as a residence, independently of business, politics, or statesmanship. In its mild climate, varied society, and numerous institutions of art, science and government, they find delightful, varied resources, while, by the proximity of Baltimore, they obtain in our city, whatever may be lacking in Washington All these attractions are independent of the fact that Washington is the annual residence, for many months, of the National Legislature, and at all seasons is the official post of the President, the Cabinet, and the administrative officers of the Government.

Thus Baltimore, without its political turmoil, may be considered a part of the National Capital, and as few will come to our city without going to the other, we believe it would not be unacceptable to our readers to possess, in short compass, a condensed view of Washington and the Federal District.

It is unnecessary, in such a sketch, to "begin at the beginning" and recount the old story how it came to pass that the political Capital of the States was placed on the Potomac; how the site was quarrelled over in committees and in Congress, in the Confederacy and under the Constitution; how New York, Philadelphia, Princeton, Baltimore, Wright's Ferry on the Susquehanna, and other places, were pressed for the prize; how men talked of centres of territory, and centres of population, and of centres of wealth, in turn as the proper umpires of selection; and yet came to the conclusion that all such centres were constantly changing in *all* countries, and that there was no true national centre but patriotism. And so, at last, it was, in all likelihood, the known opinion, and probably the known wish of Washington, that turned the scales in fixing the "Federal Capital" on the banks of his favorite river. But even after the removal of the seat of government to Washington, the city may be fairly said to have had a rickety existence—a sort of semi-uncertainty as to whether it would live or die—whether it would travel bodily northwardly or probably westwardly—until long after the war of 1812 with Great Britain. In that war, Washington got a bad reputation as a city of refuge. The enemy captured it easily, drove out the functionaries, and destroyed the public buildings. Indeed, it was not until the "Capitol extension" was determined on, dome built, and the great building finished during the civil war, that men felt certain that Washington was no longer adrift on the sea of sectional politics. The war did much in realizing this solid and wise conclusion, for Washington became the centre of all action not only as the seat of executive power, but from central convenience; and thus the crowds who saw the Capitol either from business or curiosity for the first time in their lives, cheered on the workmen to complete the dome as the perpetual home of confirmed national unity.

Though much attention had been paid before this to public buildings, and even to some municipal improvements in Washington; and though the Patent Office and Post Office were built, as well as partly the Treasury and the President's House, yet the great civic start dates from the modern Capitol and the war. Before that time the "Federal City" was always a straggling, ugly village; "a city of magnificent distances," as it was called; distances to be traversed in clouds of dust in summer, and waded through in mud in winter; a city cut in two by that sluggish worm of a rivulet which, as Moore sang, "was

Goose Creek once but Tyber now;" a town of some 15,000 inhabitants in 1830, a sort of national boarding house, or badly kept hotel, for politicians and contractors, with a quiet, reserved, aristocratic, old fashioned Maryland and Virginia society, in the background, which kept aloof from the political turmoil, whose refined life and courteous hospitality and whose dinners and suppers of canvasbacks and oysters, with "old Madeira imported by Gen'l. Smith, of Alexandria, in 1800," were the most desirable things to the stranger in Washington.

It was one of the desires, if not one of the designs of those who resolved on this city's site, that it should not become a *Commercial* Metropolis, but remain confined to its official character—legislative, executive and judicial. Washington probably thought, as others certainly did, that Alexandria's commerce and activity would not corrupt the political virtue of our legislators. But it was to be kept as pastoral and patriarchal as possible. *Anno Domini* 1800, however, was anterior to *Anno Domini* 1875, by three quarters of a century, and *very* long before rail and electricity had unified not only neighboring cities, but the world. Thus, before the war, it was the habit to undervalue Washington. As it had few attractions or comforts, folks got away from it as soon as possible if not compelled by law to abide there. But the war convinced men that Washington was a sort of neutral ground on which all sections could come without the rivalries of trade, and in free society become better acquainted with each other, and learn that they did not differ much in the essentials of character or opinion, and thus lay the basis of nationality. So, thousands, (may we not say hundreds of thousands ?) became national by coming for the first time in their lives to Washington city, and realizing that *there was* such a thing as a national focus of people as well as of government. In this manner the Federal City obtained a hold on hearts in all quarters of our country. The State system of local government, and the National system of State defences and supply of arms, had localized the ideas of men, by familiarizing them only with local capitals and local defences in arsenals, forts and navy yards. All felt, it is true, a pride in these things as possessed by their own States, partly from the power they manifested and partly from the profit they brought to the neighborhood. But, it was only when they came to Washington and comprehended the vast machinery by which the power of a *Nation of States is concentrated and wielded*, and saw the easy operation of that mighty engine, like a central heart throwing fresh blood to every quarter of the land, and sending its mandates in a minute throughout the world, that they got confirmed in their Nationality. *They understood that Nationality was a necessity.*

There are few fairer prospects in a lowland country than the one beheld either from the western collonade on which the Capitol-library opens, or from the upper galleries of the Capitol-dome, at a height of about three hundred feet above the Potomac. It is a view of great beauty as far as nature is concerned, and of increasing grandeur every year in its civic and architectural aspect. Bursting forth suddenly from the thick verdue of trees that clothes the steep western terraces of the Capitol-hill, the whole western part of Washington city starts out in strong relief; its broad avenues radiating star-like from the base. Directly in front, wide and thronged for about a mile, stretches the well known "Pennsylvania avenue," striking off near the Presidental grounds and Treasury towards Georgetown and its "Heights." On the right is New Jersey avenue, and on the left are Maryland and Delaware avenues; while from the top of the Capitol's dome the prolongation of these avenues may be descried, intersected by other avenues and streets, northwardly and southwardly, bearing the names of other States, until the city's limits are reached, on the one hand, at the shore of the Potomac, and, on the other, at the wood-crowned hills of

Maryland. This civic design or plan of radiating or concentrating streets bearing the names of the various States, is a practical sentiment of National unity in a common Capital.

The observer on Capitol Hill stands on a wide plateau overlooking a great, green basin formed by the slopes of that undulating tract which lies on the left bank of the Potomac, between Rock Creek and the Anacostia. From the lower Falls of the Potomac, where the broken spurs of the Blue Ridge make nature somewhat rugged, a low chain of elevations ranges along the north, and continuing on the opposite shore of the river and of the Anacostia, merges in the circling sweep of the Virginian hills. These form a superb amphi-theatre, belted with the silver river, in which the city stands. Seen from the great elevation of the dome on a bright, clear day of June, and across the groves of the Capitol, and the flowers and verdure of the Botanic Gardens and the Mall, it is a picturesque marvel. It is as grand and beautiful, and somewhat resembles, the view of the Connecticut winding in silvery coils through its charming meadows and hills, as beheld in summer from the top of Mount Holyoak. In the upper stillness and distance of the dome, sight and sound are mellowed and harmonized, so that the rougher features and discords of a big city are lost to eye and ear, and the prospect is rather a picture than nature. Away off to the west, flow southwardly the bright waters of the Potomac, spanned by its famous "Bridge," across which, on the Virginian side, are seen the steep, bare hills of "Arlington," formerly the home of Custis, now the National Cemetery of 15,000 citizens who fell in the civil war. These heights, crowned with original forest as far as the eye could reach up and down the river, were stripped of trees during the conflict, and are now only beginning to resume their former aspect. Directly at the observer's feet, at the base of the western terrace, betwixt Pennsylvania and Maryland avenues, are the superb National Conservatories and Botanical Gardens, rich in choicest native and exotic plants and trees. Beyond these, in the same plats, is the Mall, in whose midst, among gardens and groves, rise the quaint towers and crenelated walls of the Smithsonian Institution, an edifice built in the nineteenth century to revive, if possible, the mixed architecture of the twelfth, and to make a picturesque exterior of stone, mask an inconvenient interior. It is odd indeed, that a building designed for scientific purposes, should have been built on the plan of edifices that were erected in tasteless times, and if we may judge from their irregularity, were but patchworks of various dates, pinned together as the wants or vagaries of their builders required. This building has always reminded us of an old fashioned table-castor with unequal cruets. Beyond its unequal towers and roofs, loom up the rectangular lines of the "Department of Agriculture;" while further off at the end of the Mall, near the Potomac, stands that unfinished, *appealing* Obelisk, a nation's broken promise to Washington's memory.

Still further onward, northwestwardly of the Obelisk, are the twin domes of the "National Observatory." Southwardly, at Greenleaf's Point, where the waters of the East and West Branches unite, is the "Washington Arsenal;" while southeastwardly, on the Anacostia, or the East Branch, may be seen the "Washington Navy Yard" with its warlike shipping. North, among the more distant hills, stands the single tower of the "Soldier's Home;" and, closer to us still, the "Howard University." Directly in front, at the opposite end of Pennsylvania avenue, is the "White House," the goal of so many Presidental aspirations and sorrows. This plain mansion, like most of those we have already noticed, is embowered in grounds laid out with charming taste, while around it, according to the advice of President John Adams, are grouped the new "Treasury" and the old "War and Navy Departments." The more recent "Post Office" and "Patent Office Departments" are half a mile nearer to us on the right. President Adams was of the opinion that Secretaries, as his Cabinet counsellors, were necessarily in closer communication with the Executive throughout the year than with Congress in its winter sessions; and, doubtless, he believed they would be freer at a mile's distance from the interruptions of members whose legislative functions ought to keep them busy at the Capitol. In the primitive days of 1800, a mile was not as easily or quickly travelled in Washington's snow, sleet and mud, as it is now on the city's asphalt. All these public edifices, amid their groves, gardens and embellished grounds, are surrounded by elegant private dwellings lately built, by superb churches, tall spires, society halls, and the comely houses of charitable or humane corporations.

But turning around entirely from these western views of Washington, and looking eastwardly from the dome-top over the less densely occupied parts of the town, we see the streets and avenues, which a few years ago were but paths and lanes amid a straggling suburb beyond the "Old Capitol Building," now crowding with houses which stretch off from the planted grounds of the Eastern Capitol plateau embellished with statuary, and across the Congressional Cemetery with its embowered monuments, towards the gently waving levels of Maryland, dotted with villas, farms, cottages and forest. Then, letting the eye drop southwardly towards the Potomac—that river so anxious a boundary to millions during four years of war—its silvery water is seen winding away in graceful lines, until Alexandria is descried; and, in clear weather, the sites of Forts Foote and Washington, and even of historic Mount Vernon, are seen like blue dots on the horizon. This is an impressive panorama, an impressive massing of the Union's physical and intellectual forces. All the Nation's apparatus of war and peace is within our view. It is the focus of the country's strength and wisdom ; of its strength, because of its guarded seaboard centralism; of its wisdom, because here the most enlightened citizens, as well as the Representatives of popular power and leglislation, have not only the charms of nature, but all the appliances of culture to delight and instruct them.

But the reader may be anxious to quit this high perch on the Capitol, and to descend, too, from the lofty strain our admiration has drawn from us. It would be hardly proper to describe the city minutely in a book like this. That is the duty of "Guides" with which travellers arm themselves when they attack a new place. Yet it will be well to note a few, at least, of the Capital's principal attractions rather in the form of a catalogue, with a running commentary, than a complete narrative.

With the bird's-eye plat of town and country we have given, it is likely there will be no difficulty in finding places. Beyond the departments, gardens, public institutions, and neighboring drives and some fine houses, there is yet not much to absorb our time. These, to be seen and enjoyed as they ought to be, will require "a season." Private collections in art, literature, virtu and science, which are increasing in number and value as wealth and taste establish themselves permanently, are to be reached through personal introductions and hospitality.

The traveller who comes to Washington after ten or even five years absence, is instantly struck by the radical change and improvement of the streets, their drainage grading and paving, particularly in the western part of the city, where the Board of Public Works dealt remorselessly with old thoroughfares, widening, reducing th m to a pleasant level, and compelling some degree of elegant uniformity. This has played havoc with many a house-front and entrance, perching some on banks, and hillocks, and reducing others below their ancient level. It has given all, however, an opportunity, and especially those that have money, to terrace and adorn their fronts, and to gird themselves with marble and brick, or flowers and vases, as threshold welcomes to their visitors. Nevertheless one may say confidently, that, after a few years, all must confess the work has wrought a magical and proper change in the symmetrical elegance of Washington, as well as in comfortable access to all parts of it. Yet civic taxation will always blur a city's beauty to eyes that see it through "Collectors" bills! But happily the "deed is done," and all those parts of Washington, west and north of the President's House and the Departments, are now easily traversed, afoot and in vehicles, by night as well as by day. The Nation, during the war, became ashamed of a Capital which could scarcely be used by pedestrians (unaccompanied by a boot-black) in bad weather. The mode in which the improvements were done is unimportant to the visitor who does not come hither as a detective; nor shall we digest the *three thousand six hundred pages* of the "Senatorial Investigation" which Congress has printed as a warning or a guide-book for future Boards.

As originally laid out, the "Federal District" was a square of ten miles, comprising one hundred miles in its quadrilateral. Maryland and Virginia were both eager to cede land and bestow money for public buildings; Maryland gave $72,000, and Virginia $120,000, and when the Government came to want, as a builder, gave or at least guaranteed, more. So, the "District" continued to be the "Ten Miles Square" of early times, until 1846, when all that portion of it on the western shore of the Potomac, about 36 square miles, which had belonged originally to Virginia, was retroceded to that State, reducing the area of the remainder to 64 square miles, obtained originally from *our* State, and which the Nation still holds. The modern District, so diminshed, is divided into the City of Georgetown, the City of Washington and the County of Washington. In 1871, Congress made this into a Territory with a kind of Territorial Government, vesting the executive power in a Governor to hold office for four years, who was nominated by the President of United States, and confirmed by the Senate, with a Legislative Assembly or Council, appointed by the President and confirmed by the Senate, consisting of eleven members, and a House of twenty-two members, elected by the people. These, with a Board of Public Works, a Board of Health, and a delegate in Congress, made the Executive and Legislative apparatus of the dwarfed District or Territory of Columbia, yet raised and entitled it to something like National wardship. But, as early as a year after this bantling's birth, doubts arose as to the wisdom of the new device. Complaints and investigations were made, and after a bitter conflict, the territorial form of government was abolished in 1874,—the Board of Health alone being retained, with a provisional government of three Commissioners, until Congress shall enact a permanent system. The financial condition of this inchoate Government is not flourishing or flattering. Its Board of Public Works, mostly wealthy men, went to their duties with a bold hand, and the cost of completing them was heavy. With a population of about 132,000 of whom some 90,000 are *whites* and 40,000 *colored*, the District is estimated to possess a real estate of $200,000,000, and a revenue from taxation and other resources of about $2,100,000. Its bonded debt is $9,902,251, or within one hundred thousand dollars of the ten millions to which Congress has limited its power to contract debt. The rate of taxation is two dollars on the hundred dollars in Washington and in Georgetown, and one dollar and fifty-eight cents in Washington county. It is reported that the population of the District, as now founded, increased over seventy thousand in the fifteen years, between 1860 and 1875. With their increasing numbers, the prosperity of this region, (of which Washington City is the Capital and Georgetown the port and the main support of the District, together with the favorable climate in which the percentage of deaths is 1–53,) seems extremely probable.

All the crops of the temperate zone grow finely, while the products of large portions of Western Maryland and Virginia—coal, iron, wheat, corn and provisions—are poured into Washington and Georgetown, which are now practically one, by the Chesapeake and Ohio Canal, that ends at the latter city. Fruits and vegetables of the greatest variety and best flavor and species, together with the "mountain mutton of Virginia;" the choicest beef from the upland meadows of the Potomac, the Glades and Ohio; the excellent fish and oysters of the Chesapeake, the deer of Alleghany and the "canvasbacks" of Maryland, supply the markets abundantly.. The great Potomac Aqueduct now pours sweet water into all parts of the city. Hotels, which in former years were not renowned for good accommodations of bed and board, have been improved, while new ones, of late years, were added, which are unsurpassed in comfort and luxury, by the best of our northern cities. In fact Washington and the District are no more what they were in the days of our fathers, nor what they were supposed likely to continue forever. Those were the days of the "Stage Coach," with its "six or nine inside," for which we were "booked" the day before our journey, at the "Stage office in Baltimore, kept by Stockton & Stokes," and had to be punctual to the hour to secure good places in the interior. Five or six hours were spent upon the dusty or muddy "pike" betwixt the cities, until at last we entered them in the dusk of the evening, the driver blowing his horn, and the bar-keeper rushing to the coach-door with his movable step-ladder to aid the descending guests, and welcome them to "Gadsby's," in Washington, or to the "Indian Queen," or the "Fountain Inn," in Baltimore. The steam engine, capable of driving from thirty to sixty miles an hour, and the electric telegraph, were not even imagined; so that with these vastly altered laws of intercourse, supply, and distribution, changing almost all the bases of business and society, we should not be surprised, as years go by, to find Washington become a city of commercial importance.

Alexandria was such a city in the times of the "Old Dominion's" mercantile and agricultural pride, when the tobacco planters and farmers in semi-feudal days, maintained hospitable homes on their lordly estates, and imported, through Alexandria, many a thousand cask of "Madeira," a few hereditary, cob-webbed bottles of which still linger in the cellars of Baltimore *bon vivants*. It was, indeed, to Baltimore and Washington—and it is proper it should be remembered in the story of those cities—that we owe the first experimental trial and success of the electro-magnetic telegraph of Morse; for it was between them that the test-wires were laid in 1843, and the writer recollects with pleasure that his name was one of the first "ticked" by the instrument from Baltimore to Washington, and instantly returned from Washington to Baltimore.

The stranger who has but a short time to survey the National Capital, should begin his round of visits by the Capitol and its surroundings. He will find minute descriptions of this great edifice for sale in the building, as well as in the book stores. The Capitol is, indeed, almost a museum itself. Without entering into details which would be cumbersome, we would particularly direct the visitor's attention to the central rotunda and dome, for their wonderful architectural impressiveness. The embelishments of the rotunda in painting and sculpture are chiefly historical, and therefore of national interest, though some of them do not rank in the highest grades of art, especially the paintings of Trumbull. These, however, have inestimable value as portrait-pictures, while the paintings by most of the other artists are rather allegorical or imaginative than historical. Vanderlyn's "Landing of Columbus" is perhaps the best of that school owned by the Nation, while Powell's "Discovery of the Mississippi" is as fanciful in figures as those figures are fantastical in costume. Vastly different in appearance and clothing from this glaring group of Spaniards on parade, was the torn and way-worn band that reached the great river after its long and dangerous wanderings through the tangled forests and swamps of Florida. The sculpture by Caucici and Greenough, on the east-front of the Capitol, and on the sides of the great entrance,—particularly "Columbus Discovering America," as it has been facetiously called,—is not in our opinion worthy of so distinguished a place in a National Capitol. The first works of art that greet the visitor in such a place should be supreme in excellence.

Greenough's "Washington," and his colossal group of the "Pioneer protecting his Family from Indian attacks," though wrought with skill, are simply bits of good workmanship in statuary rather than works of high ideal art, illustrative of our forest-founders, and of the Father of his Country. The "Old Hall of Representatives," since the new one was occupied by Congress, has been devoted to the reception of sculpture and paintings, and we hope it will become, in time, an American Pantheon, where memorials of all who are worthiest in the land, in all classes of human endeavor, will be properly selected and kept, instead of continuing, as it was for a while, a show room of adventurers for Congressional patronage. In that way it will become worthy of the country, and a niche under its roof an object of ambition; but to insure so good a result it ought to be put in charge of an *independent* committee, whose taste and firmness could not be demoralized by the promise of a picture or a bust. The wretched "jobs" that have so often been won from Congress by these adventurers, should be replaced by works of unquestionable merit in design and execution, by artists who do not beg patronage or work "on commission."

THE CORCORAN ART GALLERY.

The foundation of Mr. CORCORAN's superb gallery, given by him to the United States—and, with the Smithsonian Institution, the noblest intellectual gift to our country—will produce a good influence on those who hold the purse-strings of national patronage. They must go to these collections, if only for pastime, and the eye, habituated even casually to art, must soon become interested as it observes, and so taught to be tasteful, even without study. The Nation can hardly be too grateful to Mr. Corcoran for his costly present. It was a wise, benificent display of the true uses of wealth. The collection of statuary, paintings, bronzes, casts and objects of *virtu*, and the splendid building that contains it, have probably cost the generous and tasteful bestower over a million of dollars. The stranger will surely visit this museum at the corner of Pennsylvania avenue and Seventeenth street, and we doubt not he will agree with us as to the intellectual effect it must have on the country, and especially on the legislators whose duties compel them to live so long in Washington, many of whom enjoy, in those halls, the first glimpse they ever had of true art. Elsewhere, throughout Washington, the stranger will find embellishments in the nature of works of art of various merit. The "bronze doors" in the Capitol, following and emulating the style of the great Pisan doors of Italy, are, we think, the best works of the kind we have seen dating since mediæval art. They are of exquisite design and execution, and though their embellishments may be catalogued, and will be found at length in the descriptive catalogues of Washington, it is difficult to *describe* them with any likelihood of conveying a correct idea of their character. They must be seen, as they doubtless will by all visitors, and then *studied.* The main bronze door of the Capitol, the portal of the east front to the rotunda, was designed and modeled by Randolph Rogers, the American sculptor, in Rome in 1858; the other bronze doors designed by the American, Crawford, and, after his death, modeled from his drawings, in Rome also, by the Maryland sculptor, Rinehart, lately deceased, are also suitable companions to the superb works of Rogers. These vast metallic valves, laced all over with historical and allegorical relievos, delicate yet bold in execution, framed in tracery and foliage worthy of Raphael, are sombre in their color, and not so well calculated perhaps to please as groups and figures of white marble, but they are not the less worthy of admiration and pride. Statues, single figures, and equestrian, of noted men, distinguished for civil and military deeds, will be found distributed over the city. Admiral Farragut's is to be set up in Farragut Square. In a square still unnamed, north of the President's House, stands the colossal equestrian statue of Winfield Scott, the work of Brown, ordered by Congress. In the square opposite the "White House," Jackson in bronze, rears a bronze horse perpetually on his hind-legs, and shows how Mills solved the sculptor's problem of sustaining so massive a statue without attaching the animal's tail to the pedestal by the bronze ligature of a serpent, as Peter the Great's horse is sustained in St. Petersburg. In other places there are statues of Washington, Lincoln, Hamilton, Gen'l Rawlings, Franklin, Hancock, Benton, General Greene, Roger Williams, Trumbull, Roger Sherman, G. Clinton, Livingston, R. Stockton, Kosciusko, Gen'l Kearney and Jefferson, the last in bronze, and certainly one of the best executed of our American portrait-statues.

These slight notices of National Art in Washington are made, because in all countries we find memorial art the *first* out-cropping of taste that distinguishes nations as they grow and naturally desire to surround themselves with objects, which are not only "things of beauty," but incentives to honor and tokens of popular gratitude. Painting and sculpture in bronze and marble, therefore, demand our earliest and most careful scrutiny, for they are the lasting records not only of our time but also of our national taste and intelligence.

There is much *fresco* adornment all over the Capitol, mostly ornamental arabesques and floral fancies. These were chiefly done by foreigners, and are mechanical rather than artistic. Over the first landing of one of the staircases of the "House" extension of the Capitol is a *fresco*, called a silica chromo, by Leutze, for which the Government gave him $20,000. It is best seen from a balustrade opposite, at the head of the stairs. It represents an emigrant train apparently descending the last slopes of the Sierra Nevada, and first beholding the Pacific at the Golden Gate. "Westward the course of Empire takes it way" is the motto affixed to his work by the great artist, who, in his picture, has given a grand composition of American energy, hardihood and enterprise, while the colors, we fear, are beginning to suffer change from the materials with which they were imparted, on the wall and plaster on which they were painted.

Do not quit the Capitol without going to the Library Halls, occupying the principal floor on the western projection of the building. Here are stored 260,000 volumes, and

50,000 pamphlets, 30,000 *volumes* alone, belonging to the *Law* Library. Piled on the collections originally bought by the Government from Mr. Jefferson and others, are the Smithsonian Library, deposited after the fire in that Institution in 1866, and the really great collection of the late PETER FORCE, who devoted his life to historical studies and to the gathering of his library. The Government, after some years of improper delay, paid him $100,000 for 23,000 volumes, exclusive of the immense collection of *pamphlets* which passed with the books. The early printed books *in* and *on* America; the early American newspapers from 1735 to 1800; the 300 early atlases and maps, many still unpublished, covering our whole territory; some fifty volumes, in folio, of historical autographs, embracing a collection of military and political letters of the Revolutionary times from 1765 to 1787; an "Eliot's Indian Bible" and 41 different works by Increase and Cotton Mather; are cited as *specimens* of the rarities and the excellence of this addition to the National Library. Dying very soon after the sale and transfer, Mr. Force did not long enjoy the money for which he had exchanged the greater treasure, his books. But it was a satisfaction to him to know at least, that they were not scattered by auction, but secured *by the Nation and made forever accessible to students.*

This spirit of intellectual refinement naturally leads us in our quest through the Capitol to the Government "Botanic Gardens and Conservatories," where the authorities have gathered all the beautiful flowers, plants and trees of the world. It is a self-paid compliment to the Nation that had the taste to collect this grand assemblage of the perennial charms of nature, its flowers and herbage, from all climates of the globe, and to bring them within the observation of every citizen. Into these luxurious grounds we enter, when we descend the western terrace of the Capitol; and through groves of flowers and verdure we may drive thence to the President's grounds, and even far beyond them. A lover of botany, and even a mere lover of pretty flowers, or even of a "belle's bouquet," will have his senses of sight and scent gratified for hours daily. A true botanist might spend weeks in study. From this establishment every citizen can be supplied with choicest seeds, and reproduce, in his distant home, the handsome flowers, or the more useful grains he has found in Washington. Beyond, but in the same westward line, we come to the "Smithsonian Institution," the legacy of a learned Englishman to our country. The quaint building we have already described is occupied by its scientific corps, museum of natural history and ethnological collections, and here every man of culture should pause, not only to visit the halls, but, if possible, to be presented to the acknowledged head of American Science, JOSEPH HENRY, who has been the virtual creator of the Smithsonian; the wise director of its energies, in collecting, investigating and publishing for the purpose of "diffusing knowledge among men," according to the will of the British founder.

The Department of Agriculture, with its collections, comes next, and will attract farmers and planters especially. A glance at the unfinished and, we think, ugly monument to Washington, may suffice as we go onward, resolving perhaps to give our mite towards its completion, though we disapprove the design.

In the "National Observatory," next reached, and in the "Signal Office," we shall find the superb apparatus collected by the Government, and get a glimpse of the busy scientific men, whose observations and calculations guide our ships over the sea, and give us daily bulletins, with our breakfasts, of the weather all over our coasts and country. The "President's House" is more remarkable for its beautiful groves, gardens, drives, walks and conservatories, than for its architecture, or the elegance or comfort with which it lodges the Chief of such a country as ours. For many years it has evidently not been suitable, in size or style, as the social focus of foreign and American statesman, and citizens who throng the Capital for half the year and congregate at the "White House." It was designed, we believe, to display "American simplicity," and to suit as well as prove the unostentatiousness of democracy. But, democracy requires accommodation, and is not indifferent to comfort or entertainment. The President has become a sort of national host. Unlike the heads of the Old World's governments, the Executive of the United States must not only be accessible if he wants to be popular, but he must be accessible if he wants to be useful. President Lincoln opened his office-doors daily during specified hours; and letting in the waiting crowd, received each person in turn, sitting at his writing table; and inviting the visitor to be seated, listened to his wants, complaints, projects and suggestions, his nonsense or his wisdom. These he called his "public opinion baths." Presidents, husbanding their valuable time, must organize their system of popular communication independently of *levees* or *receptions*, so as not to clash with executive business, which is increasing so rapidly, and exacts so much personal supervision from any conscientious man who does not allow himself on public affairs to be compromised by Ministerial Government alone. The *personal government* of the President is extensive, and it is the source of his *personal responsibility* as distinguished from the British Government, which throws responsibility on Ministers and saves the King or Queen, but converts that functionary into a figure-head instead of a power. Besides this, the relations of our country with all nations require the presence of a large Diplomatic society in Washington, and many Governments are beginning to build homes for their representatives in that city, and to fit them up in a manner commensurate with the dignity of the countries represented.

This adds much to the style of Washington life, and doubtless to its luxury and expense. The President's House, without being a palace in extent or surroundings, should be suitable at least in elegant and ample accommodations, and we regret to say we have not seen much improvement, save in the addition of conservatories, which are but ornamental, in the thirty years we have known it. Most of our late Presidents seem anxious to get away from it as soon and as often as they properly can, except at the end of their four years term.

Of the new buildings commenced by the Government, the Treasury, we believe, is the only one nearly completed. The new War, Navy and State Departments will be edifices of which the country will be justly proud when they are finished. The plans are certainly excellent. The Post Office and the Patent Office were built many years ago. Both are handsome and convenient, but of different styles. In the Treasury, official life deals for six hours every day with the machinery of revenue and expenditures, and so carries on Government which could not exist without money. To men of our day it has an especial interest. It is a manufactory of money. It makes the money or "currency" of the country, by coining its credit *in paper*. It not only makes the money by issuing it, but makes the plates to print it; it makes the ink that prints it; it makes the engravings that embellish and identify it; *fac-similes* the names that legalize it; it prints the notes; and makes or made the very paper on which the notes are printed. As much of this mintage of currency as is allowed to be visible should be seen by strangers. It is very pleasant to remember that this delicate fabrication, counting, classifying and packing, have been the means of giving employment to thousands of American women who "get their rights" in this gentler task, but would not be equal to the labor of impressing the Nation's credit on *metal*, if we dealt in solid coin instead of "Greenbacks."

In the marble halls of the Post Office Department, the vast machinery of our foreign and domestic correspondence by letter, postal cards, newspapers, hand-bills, pamphlets, books and packages should be observed with a competent and *willing guide*. One may rather wonder that a Post Master General does not go mad after a few weeks dealing with the myriad mails that are the life-blood of the world. When the superb system and remorseless discipline of this Department are understood, surprise gives place to admiration. Obedience and order are more implicit then in the army. It is difficult to lose a letter, and equally difficult not to get one after it reaches its destined office. A bank-note *will* slip out occasionally; but the *slipper* is generally soon detected. In this Department the *Dead Letter Bureau* and its collections should be asked for.

It is in the "Patent Office" that American ingenuity and mechanical science are strikingly displayed. Its model museum is a wilderness of conceptions that have come to no good, and of inventions that have been of more or less utility. Some (the sewing-machines for instance) have been of immense value, especially to woman. Since the ruinous fire of 1836, *one hundred and fifty-six thousand* models of inventions have accumulated in the Museum! What monuments these are, in forty years, of seething brains, disappointed hopes, extravagant speculations, of lucky hits, of genius, of enterprise! What would they have been, in point of curiosity, had not that fire burnt up *four thousand* models gathered since 1790, when the first patent was issued to one Sam. Hopkins for making potash! So great is the facility of our inventive power, that patents are issued at the rate of about 13,000 yearly.

In this building are also, at present, the offices of the Secretary of the Interior, and of the Indian, Pension, Census and Land Bureaus. An inquisitive man will feel inclined to call on the Minister of the Interior and ask his opinion of the "Indian problem!"

But, independently of the inventive talent displayed in the dusty samples of the Museum, the Patent Office has for many years interested us, as antiquarians and historians, in its collection of Revolutionary relics;—*personal* things, which bring the original possessors palpably before us. It is there we find Franklin's Printing Press, at which he wrought, as workman, in London in 1728; Washington's china, given to him by the Cincinnati; Washington's uniform, worn when he resigned his commission in our Maryland Senate Chamber at Annapolis in 1783; his tea table, writing case, compass, cane, *sword* and *tent*, and tent poles; his camp chest and furniture, andirons, two chairs, curtains worked by Mrs. Washington, and his *commission* as *Commander-in-Chief of our Revolutionary Army.*

Near these objects of personal but national interest is hung the ORIGINAL DECLARATION OF INDEPENDENCE, somewhat marred by the moisture applied, many years ago, in the State Department, when a fac simile of the document was made for an engraver. The signatures should be carefully retouched with India-ink by an experienced penman before they fade entirely under the oxidizing process to which they have been subjected. The Government Printing Office is an object of interest to citizens from its fine organization and the quantity of business systematically transacted in it. The "Museum of the Ordnance Department," (under the War Department, but not in that building,) should be visited, as it contains many curiosities in arms and military relics of great historical interest. The "Arsenal, and Navy Yard, and Marine Barracks," are also vast storehouses of military strength, and museums of articles of warfare, the relics of well-fought fields of land and sea.

We have alluded to the Smithsonian Institution already, but we neglected to mention that its halls have been made a NATIONAL MUSEUM of the collections of the United States Exploring Expedition under Admiral Wilkes, U. S. N., which were originally placed in the Patent Office, but transferred to the Smithsonian in 1858. Since then, this neucleus of a National Museum has been augmented by specimens from more than fifty expeditions of the United States Government, and by investigations of the Institution, and contributions from individuals, representing all quarters of the globe and all branches of national and human history. It is very complete in European and North American mammals—their skeletons as well as skins,—while the *ethnological* specimens of our continent, relating to native tribes, surpass, it is said, those of all other collections. The mineralogical, lithological, ore, mettalurgical, meteoritic and geyserite collections are rich and large. Not the least interesting memorials of Naval explorations are the "Polaris"-Arctic collections, saved from the wreck, with relics of the ill-fated Hall, of Parry, Franklin, Frobisher and Kane. Here, too, is the alleged "Sarcophagus of Alexander Severus," which Commodore Elliott, U. S. N., brought from Beyrut, in Syria, and presented to

Andrew Jackson for his sepulture. It was an odd gift, which the republican President declined, being unwilling to be coffined as an Emperor, and especially in a second-hand shell!

This interesting Museum, which is daily thronged by wondering crowds, gazing particularly at the quaint relics of our Indians, and the sculptures and monuments from Central America, is scientifically arrayed, and is not the mere "curiosity shop" that some have imagined. It will be added to every year, and before many pass, will require additional halls for the scientific display of the gathered objects and their study.

We have already alluded to the improvements, in the open air aspect, of the Capital, made in the last five or six years, under the Board of Public Works. They are most striking in the grand streets and avenues. In making these improvements, the main purpose has been to give the avenues—as the characteristic feature of the city—easy and uniform grades. The green-bordered footways along wide streets became instantly popular, so that Washington grew into a vast garden, in which the boundary betwixt town and county is almost lost. Public and private gardening closely followed the street-builders, and the new highways were planted with trees as soon as the seasons permitted. Large spaces of ground between curb and dwelling, allowed in some avenues the monotony of system to be broken and relieved by *double rows* of trees; so that this plan of *parking* the Capital has, to some extent, indemnified property holders by adding a parterre of turf to their lots, parting them from the dust of the street by a fringe of verdure and flowers. Many drinking fountains were also set up for man and beast, and provided with service pipes. The extent of this embellishment may be judged from the fact that, even at the beginning of last year, the parking then completed amounted to nearly six hundred thousand yards; while the finished sidewalks counted 208 miles; the improved roadway 118 miles in the city, and 39 miles in the county of Washington. The grading done between the middle of 1871 and the beginning of 1874, reached the enormous sum of three millions three hundred and forty thousand cubic yards. And so the success with which the streets of Washington and Georgetown were thoroughly *regenerated* in a short time and on novel principles, may justly be said to be unparalleled in the history of cities. These avenues and streets now afford drives for many miles, and display the increasing luxury of life and equipage, in the Capital, among our statesmen, resident citizens and the Diplomatic Corps. The elegant entertainments of the latter class, as well as of the Executive officers and wealthy residents, have, since the war, given the character of an European capital-city to Washington. We advise the stranger not to leave it, (especially if his visit is in the spring or summer, or in autumn—when the rich foliage of that season glows with red and purple and golden light—) without taking one of these pleasant drives through Washington's improved thoroughfares, and to end the excursion by a halt either at the superb Aqueduct over the Potomac; or in the groves of "Oak Hill," that beautiful but solemn cemetery-gift, too, of the princely philanthropist Corcoran; or among the embowered monuments of the Congressional Cemetery; or, again, at the *Soldiers' Home*, which a grateful people dedicated to the repose of veterans who have served their country faithfully in war. The Colleges at Georgetown, the Columbian University, and the Churches in the city should be inspected by him. The Theatre, which was the scene of President Lincoln's assassination—but was bought by the Government to be, monumentally, converted into a Medical Museum of the Army—contains surgical and anatomical collections, (the result of the civil war,) which are unequalled as scientific specimens for students, and are interesting even to the unskilled in surgery. Here are found the 16,000 volumes of hospital records of the war, forming the basis on which *pensions* are granted by the Governernment, *while the alphabetical registers contain nearly* 300,000 *names of the dead who fell in the fight.* It is a striking summary of that dreadful conflict! This Army Museum was not founded to gratify curiosity, but for the scientific use of the most benificent of all professions. It is considered the finest of its kind in the world, and is visited by numbers from abroad to study the results of our experience, not only in surgery and treatment, but in the construction of barracks, hospitals, ambulances, surgical instruments, artificial limbs, and all that terrible apparatus which attends the battle field, and by which man instantly tries to save life after attempting to destroy it!

Turning from the Museum, which grew up on the ruins of a Theatre, we must not forget that our fellow-citizen, Ford, its former owner, has re-established himself in Washington, and, with the facilities of travel between the cities, (in both of which he maintains Theatres,) could doubtless play a second piece in Washington with the actors who performed the first piece in his house in Baltimore. His Theatre, with other halls, and several edifices devoted to music and concerts of the higher class, afford ample entertainment to residents and strangers in Washington during autumn, winter and spring.

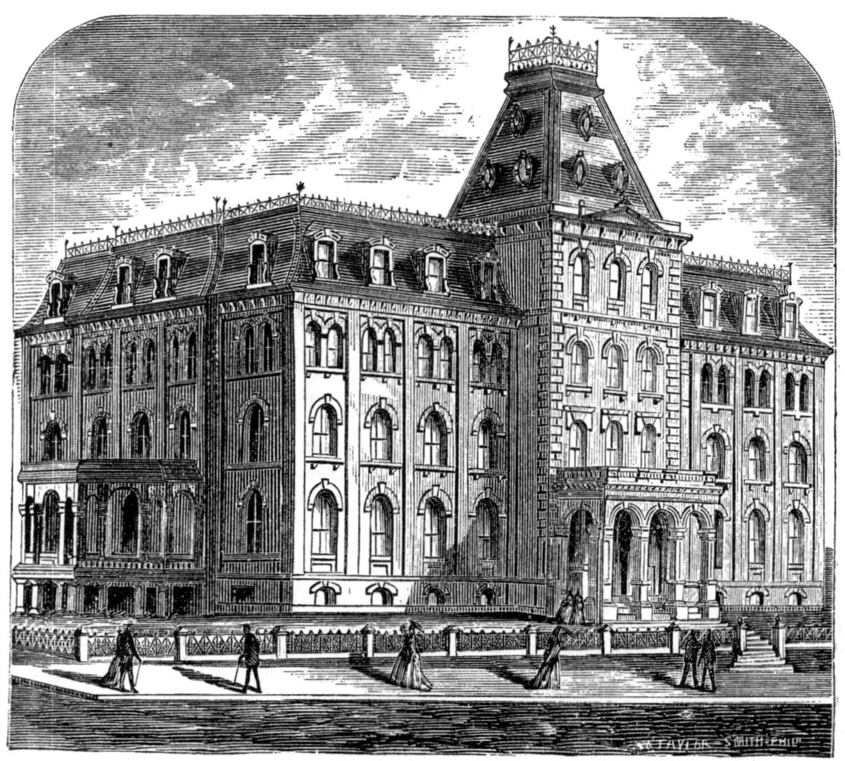

LOUISA HOME.

Among the many hospitals and asylums of Washington and the District, we should specially mention the LOUISA HOME, another of the benefactions of Mr. Corcoran. His "Art Gallery," to teach taste to the living, and his "Oak Hill Cemetery," for the repose of the dead—both gifts to the people—were aptly supplemented by this noble Asylum for gentlewomen of refinement and education who have been impoverished. It is a substantial edifice, built with care under his personal supervision, at an outlay of near a quarter of a million, while an equal sum has been set aside by him for its maintainance. Its name is monumental to the memory of the benefactor's wife and daughter.

This sketch of Washington is but a jotting down of hints, showing the attractive objects of the Capital, independently of "midnight sessions of Congress," the quest of "Government contracts," or attendance on "the Lobby."

The great questions of national interest which agitated the Union between 1800 and 1865 are settled—many by public opinion, or law, and many by the war. Thus there is no longer need, and hardly a chance, for our statesmen to deal with those broad, general principles which lie at the foundation of free, constitutional governments. We are out of the formative state,—the gristle of nationality,—and are quickly hardening into the bone of solid power and union. Hence there is rarely an occasion for our legislators to display that kind of oratory which made the first four decades of this century remarkable, and produced famous speeches, from the days of Samuel and John Adams, to those of Clay, Calhoun, Webster and others. Our best oratory of the classic class ended with those statesmen. Since then a larger country, and numerous interests or affairs to be dealt with, exact the closeness of quick, business debate, allowing little time for oratorical expansion. We legislate more perhaps on head than heart. Party, too, has drilled men to vote rather than reason. Accordingly, while a visit "during the session" will always be agreeable; for men of leisure, it will be mainly so from the society congregated in Washington during winter.

In old times, besides being only a politico-official place, Washington was not considered healthy. As in most new settlements of lowlands, there were marshes, the nests of *malaria*. These were drained long ago, and, as far back as 1848, the health reports showed the average of deaths was not more than two per day in a population of not over 25,000. Since the war the health of the city has been still more improved by proper sewerage and grading and sanitary police. It is recorded that of all those whose names are cut on the monuments of the Congressional Cemetery, the greater number died of diseases contracted before they came to Washington, or from the natural results of irregular habits. There could hardly have been anything more trying than the official, and often the private life, of an M. C. cooped up in the foul air of the halls and committee rooms, four, six and sometimes even twelve hours daily, often with evening sessions, late dinners and late suppers at the haunts of fashionable vice, which were unfortunately too much frequented by members and visitors in the high old days of cards, dice and the *duello*. Those were days of "Gadsby's," "boarding houses," "lodgings" and "Congressional *messes*," when it was the fashion to come hither *en garcon*, and play the gay bachelor, while the country family hibernated at home. Disease prevailed at times to such an extent, that we have heard a famous senatorial doctor relate how he was often consulted as to when he would "have his patients in condition to adjourn and go home." But in later times, Washington has lost its bivouac character. It is no longer an encampment of political gypsies, but an abode. Numbers of Representatives and Senators live there permanently in elegant houses, entertaining in style suitable to that of the Executive officers, the Supreme Judiciary, the Diplomatic Corps and the citizen-residents, who have built that sort of large and showy house which is commonly called "palatial." Many of these Senators and Representatives live there continuously, going to the watering-places in summer, and returning to their constituents only in time for fresh elections. Sessions are generally longer. Pay is higher. Money is buoyant. Presidents no longer ride on horseback to their inauguration, Harrison being the last we saw perform that exploit. Almost every married member brings his wife and family, educating his children in the schools of the District, or in neighboring Baltimore. The rickety Virginian hack, tattered driver, and the anatomical horses with ragged harness, have disappeared. Superb coaches, phætons, drags and roadsters are in vogue. Rivalry in splendor and costliness makes each yearly entertainment an upward step on the stair of extravagance. The architecture and furnishing of modern mansions surpass in luxury and cost nearly every thing below the grade of "Ogontz;"* but the rich man's luxury is the poor man's wealth, and so extravagance benefits society while it weakens the squanderer. In fact, Washington is a capital place, not only to visit, but to dwell in—provided you are an independent citizen and not an office-holder.

It is certain that the aspect of Washington—civic and social—underwent a marvellous change since 1860. There were two phases of this change—one during the war, another at its end. The war made that city an outpost of the battle-fields, though it remained the actual Capital of the Nation. Washington instantly became what it had never been before, a scene of enterprise in business on a vast scale. But this activity was, of course, limited to people from the North, East and West. For a time it was even the resort of hundreds of thousands connected with the conflict—as statesmen, soldiers, contractors, political adventurers, mere observers, or humane citizens, bent on mitigating war by succoring the sick and wounded. Woman was not missing at such a time of anxiety and need. After a while, the war's aspect changed, and society's face changed with it as one of Southern society's institutions vanished with Slavery. It would be absurd to deny that this had been a power in Washington life, but, at the war's end, that power was gone. Indeed, the dominion of *any* section's influence that interfered with free speech and action, was broken forever; and, with this wholesome establishment of perfect equality, feelings changed, imperious manners became ineffectual, duelling ceased, and the Nation no longer doubted that Washington would remain our Political Capital. Its foundations, in fact, were relaid in Universal Liberty, without which a Republic is a deceit. Then came necessarily the second change—the immigration of active, opulent people, with the sanitary improvement and becoming embellishment of what was to be forever the seat and centre of AMERICAN POWER. Hence the grand public works which have made Washington so beautiful and habitable; the increasing attractions of art, literature and science; and the rapid growth of a fresh, permanent society of wealth, culture and refinement. Few, we believe, will go there without visiting Arlington and the first battle fields of 1861; Bladensburgh, six miles east, the battle field of 1814; and the home and tomb of Washington at Mount Vernon. Little is to be seen now at Manassas. The interesting points where battle was fiercest will be shown, and balls picked up or bought; but nature has a kinder heart than man in rubbing out the stains of war. Wheat and verdure have obliterated them, and wild vines embroider the scarred fields that were wet with brother's blood.

At Bladensburgh there is hardly a trace of the battle of 1814; yet, with Lossing's Field Book at hand, one may study the ground, and fight it over on the spot. But the "duelling ground," where so many public and private citizens fell, when the pistol was still umpire of personal honor, will surely be pointed out by some of the old gossips of the village.

Washington's Mount Vernon has become *almost* national property, and, we believe, will shortly become so in reality, and so fall properly under the protecting guardianship of the Government. That is a Mecca towards which every American's foot turns, at least once in his life; and, as a day can seldom be spent more pleasantly, we advise the traveller to go down by water on the daily steamer, and so not only see Mount Vernon, the tomb and sarcophaguses of Washington and Martha his wife, and the personal and historical collections gathered in the halls and rooms of the house, but get, also, a passing glance at picturesque old Alexandria; of Fort Foote on its steep, towering cliff above the Potomac; and of Fort Washington, on the Maryland shore, in sight of Washington's estate, rising on its hill-top like some of the old castles that crown the heights of the Rhine.

---

*Jay Cooke's villa, near Philadelphia.

THE EBBITT, WASHINGTON, U. S.

C. C. WILLARD, Proprietor. ARMY AND NAVY HEADQUARTERS.

DESCRIPTIVE ACCOUNT OF

ANNAPOLIS CITY and U. S. NAVAL SCHOOL.

As Sir George Calvert, who was afterwards made by the King, Baron of Baltimore, in Ireland, had visited America, and personally inspected the country which in after years was to become Terra Maria, or Mary's Land, under his auspices, it is likely that when the first colony was sent thither by his son and successor Cecilous, under the care of his other son Leonard, it had already been determined in England that the emigrants were to be planted on the Potomac. The Potomac was the dividing line from Virginia, and its shores not remote from the elements of an already seated though very imperfect civilization. Accordingly, when the colonists landed from the vessel, a town was at once laid out, temporary lodgings built, and the place destined to be the first, and for a long time the seat of Provincial Government, was distinguished by the name of "Saint Marie's Town." Emigration continued. The Baltimore family was eager to improve its fortunes under the royal grant of American lands and the almost royal powers conceded in the charter. Bounties for settlement and liberal terms of transportation were offered. Pamphlets, descriptive of the Province and its resources, together with maps showing the "lay of the land and rivers," were liberally disseminated; and so the country filled up gradually under the Proprietary's care, and in the midst of an aboriginal population which seems to have been either gentler than the savages of the plains, or better managed by the settlers of that age than of ours. Thus the Calverts were active colonial planters, and all classes came hither under their inducements. The charter was peculiar; it created a Count-Palatine government—the first Province of the British Empire—and was not only attractive to folks who wanted to mend their fortunes by hard work in field and forest, but to well-born classes—younger sons of moderate means—who hoped to find in large manors and manorial rights the means of founding "families" for themselves by the law of entail. His Lordship had even the power to confer titles. There was a large influx of this better class of people who always kept up their tie with the mother country by frequent correspondence and visits, as well as by sending their children to England and the Continent for education. The numerous Episcopal Church parishes which in time grew up in Maryland, afforded a patronage to the Lords which was liberally bestowed on Oxford and Cambridge men of culture. Indeed, it was England that was looked on by perhaps the majority as "*home*," and Maryland only a tarrying place; so that, even within the last quarter of a century, we have heard a lineal descendant of one of the early settlers—brought up at Annapolis under the old *regime*—speak of going to England in the next year as of "*going home*."

These adventurers and landed men, fully comprehending at that early day the value of the province for the *trade and agriculture* to which the law then limited them, had already, towards the close of the seventeenth century, caused "the Assembly" to create no less than thirty-three towns, three of which were in the limits of what was then Baltimore County. But, of all these towns, which in truth were only "ports or places of landing" for the convenience of farming or planting neighborhoods, Saint Marie's and Annapolis maintained supremacy. Saint Mary's, the original capital of the Province, had been settled under Roman Catholic auspices. Annapolis was colonized by Puritan refugees from Virginia, who planted themselves at a place called by some "Providence," by others, "the town-land of Proctor's, where the town formerly was;" by others, "Anne Arundel Town;" "the Port of Annapolis;" and finally, by charter in 1708, "the City of Annapolis." The history of early Maryland's civil warfares cannot be properly recounted here. Emigration seems to have gone on without reference to creed, and it is likely that the Reformed Churches soon numbered more inhabitants in the province than the Roman. Be that, however, as it may, Saint Mary's was abandoned as the seat of Provincial Government. It was thought to be inconveniently placed at the southern part of the province, and too remote from all other important members of the commonwealth, especially as trade in large vessels grew up with the mother country. Accordingly Annapolis, centrally situated, became the politcal and social capital; and maintained at least its *political* character during the latter days of colonial power in the Revolution and under the Republic. But, even when tonnage was not of modern character or size, and great depth of water was not required for our ancestor's keels, Annapolis, with all its other advantages, was found inadequate as a harbor. In the latter days of the Province, that city had already waned as a commercial centre and "port of entry." In the interior, "Frederick" had grown up a nucleus of agricultural enterprise, though the savages were still disagreeable neighbors. In the first quarter of the eighteenth century, "the Monocacy and some three miles west of 'Frederick' were the extreme boundaries of American civilization," for the fringe of English people on the Atlantic. But those rich interior border lands had become attractive to emigrants from the Palatinate and other Germanic States, who laid the foundations of Western Maryland. Their early steadfast habits of labor, industry and thrift subdued that part of our wilderness, and their success brought numerous followers from the old world; so that Frederick already exceeded Annapolis in size and inhabitants at the outbreak of the Revolution. But, even in those times when legislation was thought conclusive in mastering men, the authorities were taught there were some things that nature and not arbitrary power controlled. The headwaters of the deepest navigable streams were sought, and the site of the predominant rival of all other towns in Maryland was finally found by Dr. John Stevenson, at the place which is now Baltimore. Circumstances led him to settle there as a physician. Finding the land good and well planted, and communication easy with the interior—east, west and seaward—he bought grain, freighted vessels. sent cargoes to England where they brought good prices, and brought back lucrative returns. People of enterprise saw the value of his settlement and flocked there; so that marshes were drained, the town grew, and within forty years from its beginning, "Baltimore Town," according to Eddis, was not only the most populous in the Province, but inferior to few on our Continent. The same writer rather pompously tells us that when the Governor, Sir Robert Eden, presented Dr. Stevenson to the renowned "Sir William Draper, then on his tour through the British possessions, that distinguished man was so charmed with the Doctor's town and success, that he hailed him as 'the American Romulus.'"

So, while Baltimore rose, Annapolis sank; but it never lost its "Court character," as the home and centre of a great part of the best society in America. Where the Governor dwelt, laws were made and public affairs carried on, was the rallying point of the cleverness and culture of such small populations as then existed in separate colonies or provinces. Opulent men built costly, elegant houses as their city dwellings, if, as was commonly the case, they had large plantations or manors, where they dwelt at other seasons, superintending Maryland's grand staple at that time—Tobacco. Tobacco from America became smoke in the old world, but brought back very solid revenue, together with all the luxuries of life. Troops of slaves, docile as in the Orient, supplied service. Lumbering equipages, or very rickety stage coaches, but generally *superb horses*, bore the colonists about the country. In town they visited in sedan chairs, borne by laqueys in livery. They sat on carved chairs, at quaint tables, amid piles of ancestral silver-ware, and drank punch out of vast, costly vases from Japan, or sipped Madeira half a century old. At Annapolis they laid out the best race course in the Colonies, and built certainly the first theatre. Here the best law-learning of America was gathered—the Jenningses, Chalmerses, Rogers, Stones, Pacas, Johnsons, Dulanys. Dulany's "opinions" were sent for even from London. Perhaps there were not enough educational establishments; but as the fathers preferred sending their children "home" to England for college, they thought the plain schools good enough for those who were not classed with the "gentry." Social ranks were then very marked and kept up. They built a superb ball room, which a British traveller calls "elegant," and says was "illuminated to great advantage," while at each extremity were apartments for cards, "where select companies enjoy the circulation of the party-colored gentry, without having their attention diverted by the sound of fiddles and the evolutions of youthful performers." There were no less than forty-four parishes of Episcopal Churches, many very extensive and populous. The clergy were, commonly, men of culture, sent from England, and portioned on the province by the proprietary. Generally they were men of excellent education and manners. Seldom would one of different character be tolerated by the high-toned men who composed the vestries. These clergymen did not abandon their classic pursuits when they crossed the sea, and familiarly wrote Latin notes to their boon companions of Annapolis, whose culture, in those days, enabled them to answer in the same language. Two of these notes now lie before us. They were free, hearty livers, importing and relishing their old Madeira; and it was in Annapolis that soft crabs, terrapins and canvas-back ducks first obtained their renown as the greatest delicacies of the world. The style of the time was, in winter, to enjoy the Capital, but, in milder seasons, to travel a social round among the great estates and manors—until the principal families of Calvert, Saint Mary's, Charles, Prince George's and Anne Arundel counties, and across the Bay on the Eastern Shore, were visited. They were bold riders, expert in hounds and horse flesh; and the daily fox chase, in season, was as much a duty to our systematic ancestors as it was to go to the parish church with proper equipage and style on Sunday. They had their "*Tuesday Club*," celebrated then, and even down to our times, for its conversational cleverness and *bon hommie*. If we may judge from the proceedings, which were minutely recorded by its secretary in volumes still preserved in the Maryland Historical Society's MSS. and in private hands, this club of wits and scholars must have been a match for those of London in the times of Addison or Johnson. With races each fall and spring; theatres in winter; assemblies every fortnight; dinners three or four times a week; a card party whenever possible; athletic fox-hunting; private balls on every festival; wit, learning and stately manners, softened by love of good fellowship, we are not surprised to find this character recorded of Annapolis in 1775: "I am persuaded," says a British traveller, "there is not a town in England of the same size as Annapolis which can boast a greater number of fashionable and handsome women; and, were I not satisfied to the contrary, I should suppose that the majority of the belles possessed every advantage of a long and familiar intercourse with the manners and habits of your great metropolis."

Indeed, of the old Colonial and Provincial capitals which did not become important as great municipalities after the Revolutionary war, there are none of such sweet savor in American memories as Annapolis and Williamsburg; of sweet savor not only for social and intellectual refinement, but for brave patriotism. Both were seats of culture and manly elegance, centres of the best company of colony and province; but they believed loyally in the "old country which they called *home*." They imported bricks from England to build their houses, many still standing to-day and one in Baltimore,* in the midst

* Mount Clare (Carroll's.)

of soil known to make the best bricks in the world. They called the streets of their Capital Hanover, Duke of Gloucester, Duke of York and Prince George; and they continue to call them so to this day, and at least four of their belles became Duchesses and Marchionesses in England.

But, as we remarked, from the date of its decline as a commercial place, Annapolis continued what it then became—a political Capital—a focus of legislative, judicial and executive power. Baltimore captured and kept the commerce. It became for many years a city of repose; cynical progressives called it "the finished city." It was and is a place without bustle, rush or noise, where one has the "unbounded satisfaction to find himself where no restless wheels beat time to, and no panting chimneys breathe forth the smoke of a vast multiform industry of the nineteenth century; where the sacred stillness of quiet conversation is yet undisturbed." A sort of Indian-summer of life and society prevails, where the heat is not parching or the cold pinching; the colors not too florid or gaudy, though perhaps a little frostbitten; while over all, a mellowing haze hangs like a veil, as dotted gauze which enhances well preserved beauty in its "fortys."

A society composed of the gentry, the Executive, the clergy, physicians and especially of the aristocratic lawyers, in such a province, where slavery prevailed and labor was cheap, was, with all its high-toned elegance, manliness and culture, very likely *conservative*. There were large classes of working people and emigrants of all grades, voluntary and involuntary. All were not exceptionally well-to-do and refined. But there was always a decided independence of character, a love of liberty and free expression, an understanding of inborn rights, which acted and re-acted on the upper and lower ranks of society. Some were so conservative that they remained loyal to the King and quitted America when the Revolution broke out. Indeed, at the time of the Stamp Act and non-importation discussions, and at the Declaration of Independence, the virile character of our best Marylanders displayed itself. They were not rash, they deliberated. The great body of the gentry was perhaps not ready for separation from Great Britain. We have had within the year a centennial festival in honor of those who destroyed a tea ship, the "Peggy Stewart," which was burnt a hundred years ago at Annapolis, by command of public opinion and evidently against the will of the conservatives.. From the best contemporary accounts it seems that most of the gentry would have been satisfied if Mr. Stewart had returned his ship and tea to England, and were willing to accept an apology from him instead of a holocaust. But the burghers willed otherwise, and the gentry had to see Mr. Stewart himself kindle the burnt offering. So it was at the Declaration of Independence. The Maryland conventionalists, the best minds of the Province, deliberated long and calmly at Annapolis. They weighed the consequences of severance from Great Britain and of Independence.

They were not the first to come into the field, but once there, they became staunch adherents during the war, never bating a jot or tittle of heart and hope until the final success which insured a peace that was as delightful to them as victory. At the burning of the Peggy Stewart, Marylanders in the main were still loyal to the throne, believing and really hoping that resolute conduct would secure their *rights* as freemen from the authorities in Great Britain, who saw they had to deal with determined men, acting from principle and not from passion. Though liberty was "always their right," independence was still unclaimed. But as in all revolutions, the greater heat was at the bottom, for while the surface was yet cool, the elements were boiling below. Opulent *conservatives*, intelligent and calm, with much at stake besides life, were not reluctant to negotiate, but those whose thoughts went swiftest on the impulse of natural reason, felt that *acts* were the impressive things, and that lessons taught by firebrands burned deepest in men's coffers, and thereby deepest into the judgments of Parliaments and Kings. And so the Peggy Stewart was burnt at the landing, and her owner forced to kindle the fire. Such was the society and public opinion of Annapolis in the olden time.

In our day, we know few pleasanter excursions from Baltimore or Washington than to our political Capital. We may be prejudiced, but we think it is a gem—in its way. From Washington it is easily reached by rail, and from Baltimore by rail and steamer. Both routes are quickly passed over; but we prefer to visit Annapolis by water when the excursion is purely one of pleasure, and to be made, as it should be, with a party. One travels so much by rail in our country, that a water-trip is becoming rare; and in the one to Annapolis a stranger has an opportunity of observing the fine harbor of Baltimore; the grand quays and conveniences, for European steamers, of the Baltimore and Ohio Railroad; a suberb view of the city rising on its amphitheatre of hills; the extensive town growing up in the suburbs of Canton and on the eastern highlands; the charming villas and residences on the borders of the Patapsco; the numerous bay craft and steamers for which our city is famed; the grand expanse of the Chesapeake Bay; and, just before reaching Annapolis, the blue outlines of the vast "Isle of Kent," which, in Provincial times, was once near becoming a principality.

After two and a-half or three hours of delightful steaming through this scenery, your attention is caught by the tall, shapely dome of the "State House" looming over the shore line on the west. The steamer soon quits its channel in the bay and heads directly for this object. The approach on a fine, mellow autumn day—when the trees are yet in leaf, but every leaf is rich with the royal colors of the season; when the air is full of misty gray sown with sunlight and sparkling like an opal—is a delightful compensation for whatever trouble one may have had in reaching the spot. The ancient city, apparently bowered in a green island, seems floating on the water. To your left, as you approach, the massive pile of the Catholic Church, founded on the old home of the Carrolls, stands out in bold relief from the green oaks, the golden hickories and the flaming maples. Thence the town begins to slope gently upward, with its quaint old houses, to the central Capitol and its dominating dome and spire, forming an absolute point in the perspective; and thence, towards the north and the water again, the houses slope downward in an easy bow, until they end in the gardens, groves, lawns and parades of the Naval Academy, terminated at "old Fort Severn" with a war-vessel or two at anchor; and the whole picture—town, trees and vessels—doubled by reflection in the waters of the Severn. You land at an old time wharf, and find a crowd of old time colored folks hanging around the piers, precisely as in the old times; but no where is there a distracting clamor for your baggage or your boots as you find, to your sorrow, when stepping ashore in wide-awake cities. You seem to arrive, as a matter of course, and no one is eager to ask your patronage for a hack or a hotel. No whip is poked in your eyes. You can walk; for the distances are not so great that three-fourths of a mile will fail to put you across the city in every direction. It is compact yet roomy. It has green lanes every where. You enter it. "Prince George's" street lets you know, by its aristocratic name, that you are in the domain of "quality," and not entirely out of the eighteenth century. It displays its dark brick, time-stained houses, hip roofed and broad-porched, drilling along the highways with that delightful irregularity which one likes so much in rural towns, whose streets are green lanes rather than dusty roads. There is none of that "paralellogramatic infringement of individual eccentricity," which so provoked Hamilton, the English traveler, in Philadelphia, half a century ago. These bricks are British bricks—bits of British soil solidified by fire for our ancestors, more than a hundred and twenty-five years ago; still preserved here as in a sort of museum of American antiquities. You go forthwith by a gently upward sloping street to the State House, and, being a wise traveller, go directly to the upper external gallery of the dome, surveying the scenery from a point nearly two hundred feet above the bay. The ground-plan of the city, spread map-like below, reminds you of that of Washington City from the capitol dome. You wonder whether Major L'Enfant, designer of the federal city, stole his plan of radiating streets from the earlier design of Annapolis; they make the Capitol on which you stand the hub of a big wheel, with streets for spokes. And how quiet is the rural-civic scene beneath you softened by distance, and richly tinged in its embowering foliage of autumn colors. The city covers not over one hundred and fifty acres, fifty less than were built over in Baltimore City during the last five years! It stands, as you behold it from this elevation, on a well marked peninsula, made by Acton's Creek on the south and Covey's Creek on the north, the head-waters of each approaching within half a mile. Thus it is nearly belted with a girdle of water; silver relieved on a garment of green. In front, eastward and southwardly, you have a wide view of the Chesapeake, forty or fifty miles; on your left is the broad entrance to the Severn with its war ships; and north, west and south a remarkable diversity of water, woodland and meadow, rolling away in easy undulations, extremely picturesque in a region so devoid of hills, and which may be called almost a lowland country. Across the river, one sees the National Hospital, and the new establishment and grounds added by the United States Government to the Naval Academy. But the beauty of the scene is mainly in its sylvan features, which make one feel he is in the country, though he knows he is in a city. On those fields Rochambeau and other French Allies were encamped, and in those fine houses the French gallants trod the stately minuet with the republican belles. Many, nay most of the buildings are, as we have said, of antique cut, and rarely touched by the destroying hand of the "modern improver." They are not desecrated with fresh red on bricks, or fresh white on boards; but even amongst the humbler substantial classes of the past, you are shown quite a number of manorial times and construction, while few are without gardens and even abundant groves. When Eddis came here in 1755, Annapolis appeared to him "an elegant village rather than the metropolis of an opulent province." The failure of its trade stunted the vigorous village of a century ago, but has left it the dower of beauty with which it was born.

The vitality of Annapolis was maintained, and always will be by its State-official character; yet it was a good idea, both for the old city and the United States Navy, that induced the federal government to establish the NAVAL SCHOOL on the banks of the Severn, with the old fort as a nucleus. It was precisely a safe and central spot for young men of America to learn seamanship and study marine warfare. They have all the advantages of a refined neighborhood of the best quality in America, without being endangered by the dissipations of a large city. They are at once near enough and far enough from the National Capital, to be aloof from personal influence, yet ready for personal protection; while their parents and guardians can visit them in a healthy city, and by easy access from every part of the Union. In fact, the Naval School and Annapolis assimulate as if they had been designedly constructed for each other, and so act and re-act to each other's mutual advantage. As an old-time beautiful town, of great historic interest by its connection with the Revolution, the early Congresses and Washington's last personal act in command of the army, Annapolis would always have been interesting to Americans; but the Naval Academy has made it a National as well as a State City. Every naval pupil who dwells within its bounds for four years has a sympathetic chord running to this old capital, from the Pacific, the Gulf, the Lakes, the Atlantic and every nook and corner of the interior; and after graduation, there is not a day that does not recall Annapolis affectionately to his memory.

The planting of this Naval School in our Capital has been of use to the city; yet without destroying its rural features or imparting a metropolital air. As you look down from the dome you observe, that, from Fort Severn Point, at the northeast part of the town, the Federal Government has acquired and included in the Academy's grounds the ancient "Governor's House," which was used by our Executives since 1775; and now the whole margin of the Severn as it stretches westward, and the beautiful woodlands across the creek, and the woods and fields again on the northern side of the Severn, have become the property of the Nation. The controlling influence of so orderly and systematic an Institution, where taste and means of accomplishment abound, have been of vast service to the old city, in matters of modern elegance. When the Legislature is not in session every second year, the large body of Cadets, Naval Officers and Professors at the Academy is said to be "the life of the town," so that when *tattoo* beats, at nine o'clock, a citizen declared that "Annapolis went to bed."

As you veer around the dome gallery on your survey, the large buildings below, on the west and on the north, are, first, the renowned and rebuilt "St. Anne's" Church and the modern Government House which was erected by the State within the last ten years. In another direction, nearly to the right, are the great tasteful gardens and beautiful dwellings of the hospitable Randalls and Hagners. Yonder are the ancient Chase mansion, Brice mansion, Scott mansion, Steele mansion and Harwood mansion—spacious, solid, gray, time-stained, antique houses of Provincial times—containing the great apartments, comfortable offices, deep windows, polished, narrow-planked parquettes; their easy stairways and carved balustrades; tall ornamented mantels and elaborate wainscoating. One still stands, built after the style of English manor-houses, enclosed by a large brick wall, embracing three acres. "St. Anne's" is a historical church. The modern phœnix that has arisen from the ruins of the old church is by no means venerable; and as we look on it, *at noon*, the clock-hands point to six, for just so much is this substantial ancient town of brick and mortar, which will last forever, behind the brisk cities of boards and plaster meant to last a decade. We find it really difficult to quit this steeple-perch on so balmy an autumn day, looking in any direction—landward, downward, or over the bay to the misty outlines of Kent, flocked by fleets of bay craft bound up or down, and memorable to most of us, as catchers of the Chesapeake oysters, that *bonnebouche* of Americans in San Francisco as well as Boston.

But, we must descend, and as we go down the inner stairway, observe the massive timber our ancestors used when they set up this State House, for the skeleton of part of it is, as usual in such buildings, still bare in the audit to the dome. They had to build strongly when they built honestly, and as they thought forever; erecting then dome and spire, two hundred feet high, on the apex of the central hill. The main entrance to the grand hall under the dome is from the east. In front of the door, on a pedestal, is the sitting statue of Chief Justice Taney, in bronze, by our Maryland sculptor Rhinehart—a good work and good likeness, but badly placed for *observation*—though suitably for *sentiment*—at the portal of a Capitol. The ground *descends* in front of it and the vista is short, so that no proper point of view for full effect can be got in the grounds. Still it is a worthy memorial of a distinguished Marylander, and honorable to him, the State and the young artist who executed it.

Let us enter the grand hall under the noble dome, which is surely very impressive. There is nothing modern about its architecture, which is of the English style of Sir Christopher Wren and his followers. The stucco ornamentation of the dome is remarkably good. A massive balustrade stairway rises at the western end, by easy tread; leading from its first platform to the Library, and then by branches, left and right, to the Court Rooms, the Governor's apartment, the Armory and the Adjutant General's office.

Standing on the floor of the Hall, on your left as you enter, is the Chamber of the House of Delegates; on your right, the Senate Chamber. These are spacious, in their original solid forms and size, and were very little meddled with by modern architects or upholsterers. They retain therefore the effect their designers intended.

The Chamber of the House of Delegates is adorned with Charles Wilson Peale's original full-length portrait of General Washington, accompanied by General Lafayette and Colonel Tilghman—a picture ordered by the State, and of artistic as well as historical merit. It is one of the few *votive* things ordered by States in early times, when fuller of gratitude than money, that were accomplished. The hall itself is spacious and well adapted for a popular assembly. Lafayette was "naturalized" there by Legislative act. On the opposite side of the Hall is the Senate Chamber—the true, historic Chamber of Maryland—in which the Congress of 1783 met; the Treaty of Peace with Great Britain, recognizing our Independence, was ratified; and where Washington resigned his commission as Commander-in-Chief of the Army. Here it was that the war really ended, and so consecrated a Chamber which, to the honor of our State, has never been *modernized.* It stands, architecturally, as it did in '83. Chairs and desks, carpets and fittings wore out and were replaced, but the grand whole has been untouched in style, so that it requires little imagination to conjure up the scene of the 23d of December, 1783, when, "according to order, his Excellency the Commander in Chief was admitted to a public audience;" and, being seated, the president (General Mifflin), after a pause, informed him "*that the United States, in Congress assembled,* were prepared to receive his communications;" whereupon he arose, addressed Congress, and, as he concluded, advanced and *delivered his commission* to the president. "Having finished," said he, "the work assigned to me, I retire from the theatre of action, and bidding an affectionate farewell to this august body, under whose orders I have so long acted, I *here offer my commission, and take my leave of all the employments of public life.*" The "Maryland Gazette" of the time, printed at Annapolis, remarks that "few tragedies ever drew more tears from so many beautiful eyes as were affected by the moving manner in which his Excellency took his final leave of Congress." Yet it is evident that the General's farewell, as a military man, to Annapolis was not, on that occasion, altogether doleful; for when he reached the city with his suite on Friday, the 17th of December, he was met, in great ceremony, a few miles from the city by Generals Gates and Smallwood, together with the principal inhabitants, who escorted him, amid salvos of artillery, to Mr. Mann's tavern, where apartments were prepared for him. Next day he waited on the President of Congress, with whom he dined, in company with the members of that body and the chief civil and military men of the State. On Sunday he returned the visits made to him. On Monday Congress gave him a dinner and ball at the Assembly rooms, entertaining upwards of two hundred distinguished guests, drinking toasts at night, accompanied by discharges of cannon, and illuminating the State House when the ball was given; at which, it is recorded, "General Washington opened the dancing with Mistress James Maccubbin of Annapolis, one of the most beautiful women of her day!"

The Senate Chamber of our Capital has always been an object of Maryland's pride in all the shifting scenes of politics. It has been a purpose of our statesmen to adorn it with historical portraits and pictures. Not many years ago a picture by Edward White was set up in it of "Washington's Resignation," which is meritorious, and contains, it is said, good portraits of as many congressmen as could be fairly placed and delineated on a canvas of such size. Of Provincial times there is only one portrait—that of Frederick Calvert, the last of the Barons; perhaps the most worthless, though a man of much college culture. There are excellent full lengths of Charles Carroll of Carrollton, by the late Thomas Sully, painted from life; and of Paca, Stone and Chase (from portraits), by the late John Beale Bordley. These where ordered by the State in commemoration of our four signers of the Declaration of Independence. In an adjoining committee room is a full length, fanciful in Roman costume, of Lord Chatham, the friend of America, executed in London by our American artist Peale, while in England.

In the old Annapolis ball room, many years ago, we remember seeing hung on the wall a begrimmed, full-length picture, black with age and smoke, which the person who guided us declared to be a portrait of Cecilous Calvert, son of Sir George, and second of the Lords Baltimore, consequently the receiver of the Charter and planter of the Province. This canvas, we were told, had lately been in worse plight, until a peripatetic "picture cleaner took it from the frame, spread it on the floor and *scoured* it with soap and brush!" A human form in antique dress, and a glimmer of tanned features could be descried through the load of varnish with which the traveling tinker had glossed the canvas. Where that picture is now, we do not know. The excellent full length of Charles, fifth Lord Baltimore, painted we are persuaded by Sir Godfrey Kneller, a gift from the Lord to his province, and which fell to the State by regular descent, was bartered many years ago by the authorities for portraits of certain Governors, painted by Charles Wilson Peale. The artist who made this improper bargain with the State authorities is long since dead; yet the picture we understand still continues in the possession of one of his descendants who is anxious to sell it. In 1853, the late Thomas Sully, (the Sir Thomas Lawrence of our country,)—copied this large portrait on a canvas of full size, and presented his masterly work to the Maryland Historical Society, on whose walls it is carefully kept in the Athenæum at Baltimore. The *original* should be recovered by a Government which was at least heedless in parting with such a pictorial prize, independently of its personal interest in our history. The State has not done much to patronize art. The few things we named comprise all worth noting. On the front of the Capitol, near the eastern gateway, is a long thin iron gun, whose surface is vermiculated by rust, and is said to have been found in the water near St. Mary's, and presented by the Rev. Mr. Carberry, as a relic of the founders of the colony and province. It may have fired a salute at Leonard Calvert's landing. The apartments reached by the hall-staircase we have described, viz: the Court-room, the Armory, the Adjutant-General's office and Governor's Chamber, are worthy of the antique building. They are spacious. The Armory as we saw it lately was in disorder, cumbered with boxes and old-fashioned arms in disarray. Standards of State Regiments of the late war, and of other wars, which we believe were once there are not apparent; while some banners lean against the walls in tatters. The relics of civil war should be either preserved *or* destroyed, but not left to perish from neglect. That species of ruin indicates indecision or timidity. Of all the upper apartments, the most important is the vast room known as the Governor's or Council-chamber. In days that preceded the era of furnaces and steam heaters, we remember the lofty mantel and grand baronical fire-place, which gaped on the west side of the chamber like a cavern, and was said to consume near a cord of hickory daily, to warm an apartment of forty feet frontage by thirty-four in width. This grand saloon basks in the southeastern sun; and from its deeply embayed windows in the thick walls, you have a broad view of the Severn, the town, Chesapeake Bay and the Naval Academy. It is a very quiet chamber in "off" times, when there is no legislation or governing astir. Its high walls, near the cornice, hold portraits of Thomas Johnson, the first Republican Governor; of Plater, Paca, Sprigg, Howard, Smallwood, who in turn have presided over Maryland; and an excellent full length of T. Holliday Hicks, who was Governor at the outbreak of the civil war. Nearer the observer are hung several interesting printed and autographic memorials of the Revolution, as, a letter of Washington; the first official printed copy of the Declaration of Independence, *signed* by John Hancock; the remarkable Proclamation of rights and principles of liberty, by Maryland notables before the Revolution, signed by most of the leading men of the Province, who afterwards became republicans; an original official copy of the Proclamation of Peace, &c. In the Library, in the Adjutant-General's office, in the Land Office building, there are original State papers of Proprietary and Revolutionary times; but we are sorry they are in such disarray as to be useless to the Government or to historical students. Attention to the duty of assorting and indexing these State papers, chronologically, in proper classes, and of binding them in volumes, before they suffer more from time and neglect, was warmly invoked by a Maryland student during the government of the Hon. A. W. Bradford, who approved his conservative effort. We hope the task will now be undertaken and thoroughly accomplished.

This sketch of Annapolis may suffice. We must, however, note the fine fountain, throwing up its water on the southwestern front of the Capitol, which is now hemmed in by a high iron fence on granite base, and by planted grounds which we would be pleased to see better kept from the inroads of *poultry*. Some of the old buildings which we remember in this *enceinte* are gone, especially one near the north wall of the Capitol. Within the circle enclosing the State House, still stands the old Treasury building, on the easterly margin of the hill. This building is very old, and was used as the Legislative "Hall of the *Provincial* Government"—the "Upper House" sitting in the smaller, and the "Lower House" in its larger apartment. Northeastwardly from the Treasury building is the modern Comptroller's and Record office. It is said to be a fire-proof building, and is certainly a comfortable one, heated, like the State House, by steam. Here the archives of the State are said to be deposited, (at least the greater part of them,) with the records of the Chancery Court and its office, long since abolished. In this building, too, is the Land office and its immensely valuable records—of which some of the earlier books or "Libers" are extremely entertaining in their details of Court cases, trials and events. The new Government House, first occupied, we believe, by Gov. Oden Bowie in 1869, stands about two hundred yards west of the Capitol. It is a stately pile, costing probably a quarter of a million for grounds, building and equipment, and is quite worthy of the State. It lacks, however, the nice grounds and water view of the old mansion of the previous hundred years. From the Government House, the State House and St. Anne's Church circles, respectively, most of the important streets radiate, as we have seen, while others intersect them at convenient points. St. John's College still stands on its eminence at the end of Prince George street. There, too, is still its "College Green"—the camp ground of the French warriors as they returned from Virginia—of Rochambeau, Lafayette and others—the camp, also, of American troops in the war of 1812. An industrious and perhaps somewhat credulous "Monkbarns" might detect some traces of these encampments. Certain it is that the grave-mounds of many who died in the service are still pointed out to curious travellers. One antiquity unquestionably remained on the grounds east of the College, and probably may be there still—the "American Tulip Tree"—a huge but ragged poplar of vast unknown age, which the gossips say "was growing here when Annapolis was settled by the Puritans, Anno Domini 1649;" was "commemorated in verse by a distinguished graduate of St. John's, the late lamented Dr. Shaw, a native of our city;" and is still held in veneration by Annapolitans. They have a sort of superstitious feeling about this poplar; for it is said that when it was accidentally set on fire in 1839, the excitement was as great, and the efforts for its salvation as prodigious, as if the Capitol had been in flames. A bit of antique sentiment like this is creditable to the people. The fire was quenched, the tree saved, and, though it was sadly scarred, Annapolis rejoiced!

The Churches—Methodist, Episcopal, Presbyterian, Naval and Roman Catholic—are not remarkably fine, architecturally. The old St. Anne's, as we said, was burned down; the present is a reconstruction. The big silvery bell—gift of Queen Anne to the parish—was destroyed. The silver communion service, enriched with arms and monogram of William the Third, was saved. Within the enclosure are some ancient tombs of the Carrolls, and some with elaborate sculptures of the Taskirs, one of whom was President of the Province. St. Mary's Roman Catholic Church stands on Duke of Gloucester street, on land given by Charles Carroll of Carrollton. This was the site of the *family mansion* in Annapolis, and we believe we are not wrong in saying that the original dwelling was included in the monastery or college of St. Mary's, a foundation of the order of the Redeemer, which is one of three in the United States through which candidates for the order's missions have to pass. Of all the ecclesiastical edifices, we think the Chapel of the Naval Academy the handsomest, though not largest. The old "City Hotel" and the "old ball room" are things of the past—the ball room being destroyed, but replaced by a fine modern Assembly Room, built since the civil war on the site of the ball room on Duke of Gloucester street. The main apartment, a-blaze with gas, is said to be superb when filled with beauty and belles. The "Maryland Hotel," at the head of Main street—a fresh institution—we hope will win the renown of the old "City Hotel" in the days of the bar-dinners, when Mr. Chief-Justice Buchanan used to sit at the head of the table, surrounded by such men as Wirt, Taney, Pinkney, Johnson, Nelson, Mayer, Meredith and McMahon in the palmiest days of the Court of Appeals.

But Annapolis has its national attraction, independently of its historical and antiquarian, in the hundreds of youths sent here by the United States, from all quarters of the country, and admitted even from foreign countries, to study Naval Science. These are our future Admirals. He who strolls northward, down Maryland Avenue, finds himself, after a short walk, face to face with a wall, a gate, a sentry-box and a sentinel. A step takes him out of the eighteenth century into the nineteenth, from the repose of quiet old Annapolis to the life and activity of the NAVAL ACADEMY.

We believe the country owes mainly to George Bancroft, the historian, while he was Secretary of the Navy, the permanent establishment of this National Institution. On the 10th of October, 1845, it was formally opened by Commander Franklin Buchanan, U. S. N., of our State, with an Academic Board of able men. When the civil war broke out in 1861, Maryland was thought too close to the fields on which the contest was to be fought. Accordingly, the Academy was removed to Newport, Rhode Island, Fort Adams being assigned for the School, and used until it was found unsuitable. The pupils were then quartered on the frigate Constitution in the harbor, during summer; and in winter, in the Atlantic Hotel, which was occupied until the Academy reopened for service at Annapolis some time after the war ended. During the war they had been used for military purposes, while Annapolis was a sort of hospital camp, or depot for sick soldiers, paroled men and recruits.

After the return of the Cadets to Annapolis at the end of the war, there was a stringent effort to withdraw the Academy from that city. Various northern interests contended for it. The temporary removal of the pupils to Newport, Rhode Island, and the limited area of ground belonging to the Government at Annapolis, then only twenty-one acres, together with the inadequate accommodations in the structures already built, were thought or urged as sufficient grounds for agitating the abandonment of the site and the purchase of a larger tract elsewhere for the erection of proper permanent buildings. In his report of December, 1865, the Secretary of the Navy called attention to the *insufficiency of the accommodations*, as well as to what he was pleased to style "the temptations" to which youths were exposed from being "in the heart of a city," as "serious and insurmountable difficulties" for continuing Annapolis as the site of the School, and making the idea of further expenditures for its improvement inadmissable. The report said that inquiries had already been made to ascertain more desirable locations; and the Secretary recommended that "the Department should be authorized to secure the refusal of one or more eligible sites for a Naval Academy." In the mind of that functionary, "removal" seemed to be a foregone conclusion; and surely, "removal" was furthered in this way by official suggestion. Of course, this was a popular hint to all sections in which there was the possibility of a competing location.

But we had an active, influential representative from Baltimore in the thirty-ninth Congress, in General Charles E. Phelps, who soon descried the dangerous character of the movement against Annapolis. General Phelps was a member of the Committee on Naval Affairs of the House, and the *only* member of it representing constituencies south of Pennsylvania. To check the eagerness of rival aspirants, soon after the meeting of Congress, he offered a resolution directing the Secretary of the Treasury to report the amount of money already invested by the United States Government in the Naval Academy at

Annapolis. The response that nearly a million of dollars had been spent there in land and improvements, furnished a conclusive reason for throwing the burden of abandonment or removal on those who proposed that the United States should incur so serious a loss of property, especially on emerging from war.

Admiral Porter was at that time the superintendent of the Academy at Annapolis, to which the Cadets had been returned. He, like most naval men of judgment and distinction, was decidedly in favor of keeping the School at the Maryland Capital, and was prompt and warm in urging its unrivalled advantages. It was suggested that the Naval Committees of the United States Senate and of the House of Representatives, should together visit the ancient city, and judge personally of its claims for the permanent Academy; and accordingly invitations were issued, not only to these Legislative Committees, but to "many prominent members, Senators and their families." The day fixed for the visit was unfavorable in weather, yet large numbers responded personally when the special train left Washington for Annapolis. Our Senator at that time, the Honorable Reverdy Johnson, accompanied the party, and the late Wm. Prescott Smith, then master of transportation of the Baltimore and Ohio Railroad, contributed greatly by his lively tact and address to the pleasure and success of the excursion. The Committees visited the grounds and the Academy buildings, inspected the Cadets, partook of the hospitality of the Admiral, at his quarters, and of Governor Swann, at the Goverment House, while many ladies and the younger folks were entertained by a ball and the excellent music of the Academy's band.

It might be difficult to say whether legislative judgment was not, on that occasion, helped to vigorous exercise by the old-fashioned hospitality of Annapolis; but, it is avered that when the toasts were given at these entertainments and short impromtu responses made, the result was a downright committal of Members and Senators in favor of Maryland's capital. The chairman of the Senate's Committee, Mr. Grymes of Iowa, was entirely satisfied with the place, and his opinion virtually secured the Senate.

But this did not end the contest. All the opposing combinations threw their united strength on the House of Representatives, using the rivalry of competing interests to prevent, if possible, an appropriation for the purchase of additional grounds and erection of suitable buildings. The House and the Senate disagreed on the Naval appropriation bill—the Senate having added an appropriation of $25,000 for the purchase of the Executive Mansion and grounds at Annapolis, $25,000 for more land in that city, and $120,000 for the erection of additional buildings. A "committee of conference" was demanded; General Phelps became a member of it on the part of the House of Representatives; and the result was a report *in favor* of the Senate's amendments. These were finally adopted by the House, and, the appropriations being thus granted, the sum of $170,000 was added to the Nation's stock in Annapolis.

These things happened in the spring of 1866. The fall elections in Maryland of that year were exceedingly unsatisfactory to the congressional majority. We have not space, nor would it be proper in a descriptive work of this kind, to set forth the political variances then existing. It is enough to say that in consequence of them—and perhaps with a hope that a charge of *disloyalty* would insure the Academy's removal—a resolution was passed by a party vote in the Congress of 1866–67, instructing the Naval Committee "to inquire into the propriety of an immediate removal of the United States Naval Academy from its present location in the State of Maryland to some point in a *loyal* State, where the pupils in that institution will be secure against the surrounding political influences, hostile to the National Government, which now prevail at Annapolis."

This menacing movement in Congress aroused prominent citizens of Annapolis to action. Such persons as Alexander Randall, Hagner and Mason, backed by numerous others without regard to party lines, expostulated wisely and vigorously in a memorial to Congress, which produced a greater impression than such things commonly do on Representatives. But the action of the Committee and of the House still continued adverse. It is impossible to state here in full the tactics of the combatants on either side. In the final debate in the House of Representatives, Gov. Francis Thomas and Gen. Charles E. Phelps distinguished themselves by defending not only the loyalty of their State to the country, but by demonstrating the suitableness of Annapolis as the site of the Academy. The last serious effort to withdraw it from its present excellent location was therefore defeated signally by a vote of 108 to 37 at that session; and should the controversy ever be re-opened, the argument for Annapolis will be found triply fortified by the obvious central and natural advantages of that city; by the decisive action in the face of party, just stated; and by the magnitude of the General Government's investments at the Academy's grounds since the year 1866, which we shall hereafter describe.

Fort Severn, an old-fashioned round-tower battery, at the northeast corner of Annapolis on the water, was a nucleus of the Government's possessions. This and its small territory were enlarged by several purchases, the first of which, we believe, was made in 1847 and followed by others, until in 1869 the Government acquired the old "Governor's House" and grounds, which had been built and laid out in early times by the celebrated provincial lawyer, Edmund Jennings, and sold by him for an Executive's residence to the last British Proprietary Governor, Sir Robert Eden, who added to the tall turreted centre two wings and the long room, so well known to all who enjoyed the winter hospitalities of Annapolis during the last hundred years. The United States bought this provincial relic for $25,000, and in that way laid the foundation of our modern Government mansion near the Capitol. In 1867 nine and a half acres had been purchased from St. John's College. In 1868, 1869, the "Strawberry Hill" farm, together with the land betwixt it and the Severn river and Graveyard creek—nearly one hundred and fifteen acres—were bought and joined to the original properties by a drawbridge over the creek. Thus a large domain has been gradually acquired, giving the United States control over a great space of land and water on the northern and western sides of the city, so that it enjoys not only ample room for academic quarters, but insures ventilation, drainage, room for exercise and amusement, and all those sanitary securities so important in public institutions. In fact, its spacious territory and numerous, separated buildings make it quite a town, independent and aloof from Annapolis.

On an elevation in the last bought tract beyond the creek, a cemetery for naval people has been laid out; while beyond its groves is a charming park, diversified in surface, covered with trees, herbage and meadows, made accessible by five miles of woodland paths. This has become the favorite afternoon resort of the seven thousand Annapolitans, as well as of the Academy's pupils and professors. The remainder of Strawberry Hill has been planted with gardens and orchards, to supply the school with vegetables and fruit, which grow so well in this prolific soil. It is pleasant to those who saw the "Naval Academy" grounds during the civil war, and observed their decadence with sorrow, to notice the improvements of the last ten years, not only in the rural portions outside of the walls, but within the academic enclosures, where fountains have been built, low grounds filled, shrubs, flowers and trees planted, roads and pathways laid out; so that what was once a waste, especially in rear of the quarters, is now one of the most attractive parts of the Academy. These charming grounds are made interesting by monuments set up along the walks, especially those to Clemson and Hynson, lost in the U. S. brig Somers off Vera Cruz in 1846; to Pillsbury and Shubrick, wounded and killed in the naval battles at Vera Cruz in the same year; to Commander Herndon, the brave sailor who lost his life on the mail steamer "Central America" in 1857, while gallantly trying to save his ship and passengers; and the well known "Naval Monument" which stood so long in Washington city, first, from 1808 in the Navy Yard, where the British mutilated it in 1814; next on the Capitol grounds, at the base of the grand steps on the west front—*in the midst of a fish pond*—where it remained until, in 1860, Congress placed it in the Academy's grounds. Erected to the memory of Captain Somers, Lieutenants Caldwell, Decatur, Wadsworth, Israel and Dorsey, who fell in attacks on Tripoli in 1804—early in our national life—this monument and the others are now properly planted in these grounds, where they constantly meet the eyes of naval aspirants, demonstrating that courage and fidelity to country are never forgotten. In the chapel of the Academy—a beautiful edifice—memorial tablets are set up to other naval officers and men; and we were particularly glad to see commemorated the brave Lieut. Talbott, Quartermaster Francis, Coxwain Andrews, and Muir, the Captain of the Hold, who were drowned in December, 1870, while trying to land on the Island of Kanai, in the North Pacific, after *a boat voyage of* 1500 *miles, which they had voluntarily undertaken in search of aid for their wrecked shipmates on Ocean Island.*

A catalogue of the Academy's buildings would be no more than an inventory of every possible appliance for comfort, health, discipline and instruction. The old Governor's House has been fitted up in good style as a Library, well stocked with scientific and literary works and periodicals—over 15,000 in number—which the pupils can use freely. Coins and curiosities; a valuable collection of American minerals, the gift of the late Hon. Joseph Wilson, of the Land office; an ornithological collection; several copies, in plaster, of celebrated statutes, and busts of military and naval men and artists, together with a number of paintings of naval engagements and portraits of renowned naval officers given by the Navy Department, adorn the library and halls. The old round Fort, stripped of its war paint and artillery, has been converted into a "Gymnasium," where fencing and other athletic or military exercises are taught to the Cadets who, moreover, from time to time trim, dress and decorate the vast apartment as a ball-room, when those celebrated midshipmen's parties are given once or twice a year, to which the belles flock from all quarters of our country. "Jenkins" has cautiously announced that these "hops are *believed* to have a very refining influence upon the young gentlemen, and are certainly very attractive to officers and to guests present." The Cadets are encouraged to sustain base ball and boat clubs, while their evening parades are as attractive as the celebrated sun-set drills at West Point. The "middies" are instructed thoroughly in *infantry tactics.* It has been said, that in a competitive exercise, they excelled the military Cadets at West Point in the *manual of arms,* though the West Pointers surpassed them in *marching.* For music, our "paternal government," supplies its naval *eleves* with a band of twenty-eight performers, who are obliged to play for an hour, each morning and evening, as well as for drills and parades. Of course they are always utilized at the "hops." Each young gentleman is obliged to bathe regularly at a bath provided by the Academy, and to be shaved, if he has a beard, as well as to have his hair trimmed, by a regulation barber, at a regulation price. His laundry-bill is limited to three dollars a month. His mess-bill to the commissary averages somewhat over twenty dollars for the same time. He goes to meals on a march, listens erect behind his chair to "Grace" from a Cadet Lieutenant-Commander, is seated by order, rises by order, and quits his mess-room by a march again. The Government spares no expense in the equipment of the Academy for pupils or professors with excellent lodgings, as well as with pure water and gaslight. All the apparatus of modern science is supplied. Among the branches taught at the Academy, it was due to good naval service that a *Department of Steam Enginery* should be added. This was done some years ago, and a large building erected, in which *the practical and experimental duties of a steam engineer are taught.* Old fashioned "navigation" is of course not neglected, but wind and sails are rapidly yelding to valves and vapor. Steam and iron for vehicle as well as motor, are to be controllers of the seas in commerce as well as warfare; and naval men, no matter how reluctant they may be to mix up a mechanical with a military life, must learn, if they wish meritorious distinctions, to make as well as manage an engine, and not to study it simply as a toy. We hope this will be impressed on the mind of every Superintendent of the Naval Academy, and that the Secretary of the Navy will see to its enforcement. "Engineers in the Navy," until recently, were rather overshadowed in official rank, by men who had neither their scientific learning or skill, yet depended on them for the management of their vessels, in calm or storm, in chase or battle.

This summary of the Naval Academy is all we think necessary to set down in a book like ours, which is rather directory than descriptive. Annapolis will be visited by all classes of travellers, and especially by those connected with the pupils or administration of the Naval Academy. It will be chiefly attractive to Marylanders as the seat of Government, Legislation and of our Appellate Court. A few will come as Antiquarians to see the old town, the old archives, the historical places. Many more, whose motives we particularly approve, will visit Annapolis to enjoy its delicious repose, charming scenery, and the still more charming society with which its ancient dwellings is filled.

DECLARATION OF INDEPENDENCE.*

The National Intelligencer, of Monday, contains the following article in relation to CHARLES CARROLL of Carrollton, the last survivor in 1826 of all those who signed the Declaration of American Independence.

In the year 1826, after all save one of the band of patriots whose signatures are borne on the Declaration of Independence had descended to the tomb, and the venerable Carroll alone remained among the living, the government of the city of New York deputed a committee to wait on the illustrious survivor and obtain from him, for deposit in the public hall of the city, a copy of the Declaration of 1776, graced and authenticated anew with his sign manual. The aged patriot yielded to the request and affixed, with his own hand, to a copy of that instrument the grateful, solemn and pious supplemental Declaration which follows:

"GRATEFUL TO ALMIGHTY GOD for the blessings which, through Jesus Christ our Lord, he has conferred on my beloved country in her emancipation, and on myself, in permitting me, under circumstances of mercy, to live to the age of 89 years, and to survive the fiftieth year of American Independence, and certify by my present signature my approbation of the Declaration of Independence adopted by Congress on the 4th of July, 1776, which I originally subscribed on the 2d day of August of the same year, and of which I am now the last surviving signer, I do hereby recommend to the present and future generations the principles of that important document as the best earthly inheritance their ancestors could bequeath to them, and pray that the civil and religious liberties they have secured to my country may be perpetuated to remotest posterity and extended to the whole family of man.

"CHARLES CARROLL of Carrollton.

"August 2nd, 1826."

* For this valuable historical relic we are indebted to our esteemed citizen, Alexander M. Carter, Esq.

ESTABLISHED 1832.

J. NEEDLES & SON,

No. 44

N. Charles St.,

BALTIMORE.

RETAILERS

OF

FANCY

DRY GOODS

Laces, Ribbons,

TIES,

EMBROIDERIES.

Best Quality Kid Gloves, &c.

R. C. Shipley & Co.

DRESS

SHIRTS

AND

Fine Furnishing

GOODS,

301 West Baltimore St.,

BALTIMORE.

HUTZLER BROTHERS,

WHITE GOODS, EMBROIDERIES,

LACES, MOURNINGS,

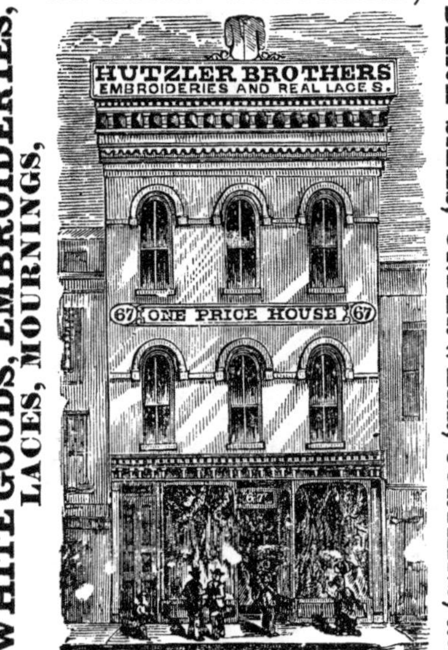

BLACK SILKS, UNDERWEAR, CURTAINS, &c.

67 NORTH HOWARD STREET.

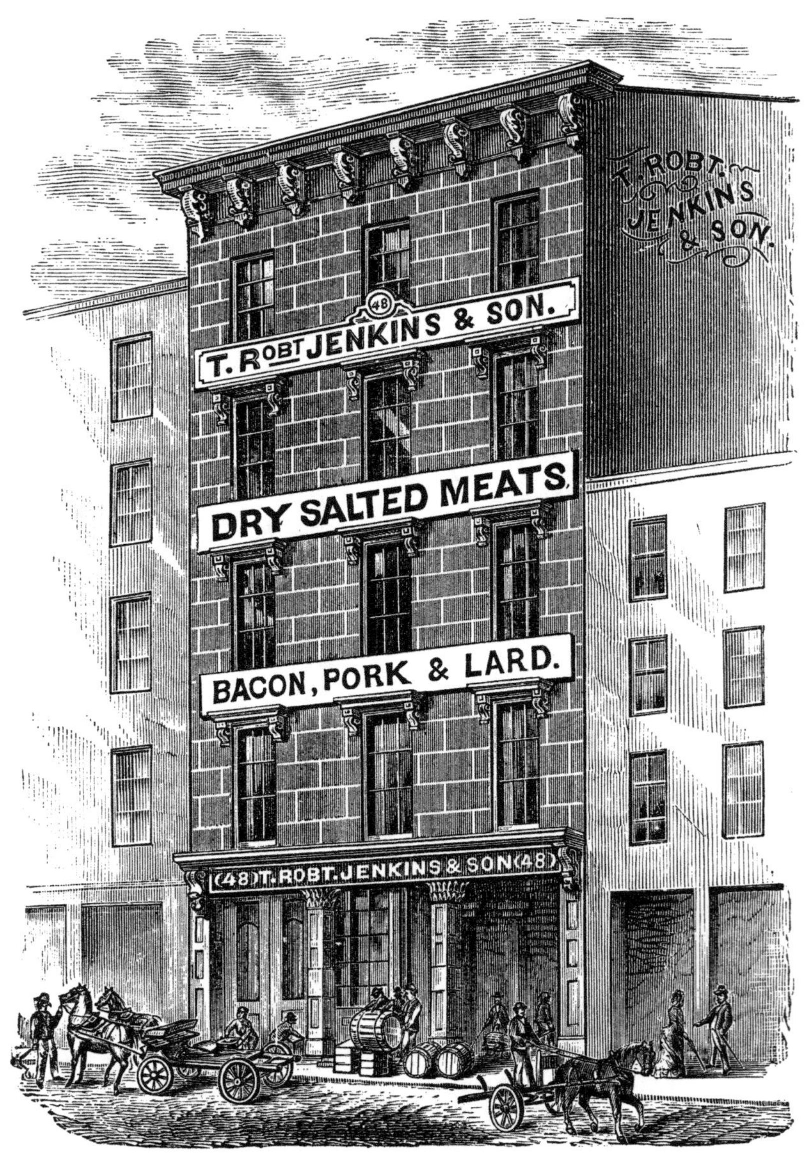

T. ROBERT JENKINS & SON,

Wholesale Provision Dealers,

And Curers of the "MARYLAND HAM,"

[See page107 .] BALTIMORE.

4

[See page 224.]

[See page 212.]

See Page 242.

See page 211.

See pp. 33, 316-17-18.]

OFFICERS OF THE

Corn and Flour Exchange,

FOR 1876.

PRESIDENT, - - - - - - *Chas. D. Fisher.*
FIRST VICE-PRESIDENT, - - - - *W. B McAtee.*
SECOND VICE-PRESIDENT, - - - *Geo. H. Baer.*
TREASURER, - - - - - - - *R. M. Wylie.*
SECRETARY, - - - - - - *Wm. F. Wheatley.*

EXECUTIVE COMMITTEE.

J. B. Hall, *Jas. Knox,* *W. D. Fullerton.*

BOARD OF DIRECTORS.

Chas. D. Fisher,
W. B. McAtee,
Geo. H Baer,
R. M. Wylie,
J. B. Hall,
Jas. Knox,
W. D. Fullerton,
Wm. R. Howard,
E. D. Bigelow,
Jacob D. Michael,
J. I. Middleton,
James Lake,
Geo. T. Kenly,
W. B. Graves,
J. A. Merritt.

Qualification for membership requires the applicant to be a citizen of the State engaged in business in Baltimore, and election by the Board of Directors. The present charge for membership is one hundred dollars initiation fee. Premiums for the choice of tables, ranging from five to ninety-five dollars. The roll of membership for the year 1875 contained four hundred and seventy-seven names. ☞ *See page* 135.

BOARD OF TRADE.

OFFICERS FOR 1875-76.

PRESIDENT,
J. HALL PLEASANTS.

VICE-PRESIDENTS,
ISRAEL M. PARR, HIRAM WOODS, D. H. MILLER, HENRY C. SMITH.

TREASURER,
J. STRICKER JENKINS.

SECRETARY,
GEORGE U. PORTER.

DIRECTORS—1875-76.

ROBERT A. FISHER,
P. H. MACGILL,
JAS. CAREY COALE,
JOSEPH H. RIEMAN,
HAMILTON EASTER,
W. W. SPENCE,
EUGENE LEVERING,
PHILIP T. GEORGE,
S. P. THOMPSON,
A. FULLER CRANE,
ANDREW REID,
DAVID L. BARTLETT,
GEORGE P. FRICK,
W. H. PEROT,
W. S. YOUNG,
GEO. H. BAER,
J. R. SEEMULLER,
J. B. BRINKLEY,
HOLLINS MCKIM,
STEPHEN BONSAL,
C. MORTON STEWART,
CHRISTIAN AX,
W. H. COLE,
W. B. MCATEE.

[See page 61.]

[See page 110.]

(See p. 200,)

Baltimore Retort and Fire Brick Works

Office, No. 3 South Holliday Street.

Manufactory, Locust Point.

GEO. C. HICKS & CO.

[See page 247.]

BALTIMORE.

J. FRANKLIN DIX. WILLARD C. WILKINS.

DIX & WILKINS,

Importers and Dealers in FOREIGN FRUITS,

No. 123 W. LOMBARD STREET, BALTIMORE.

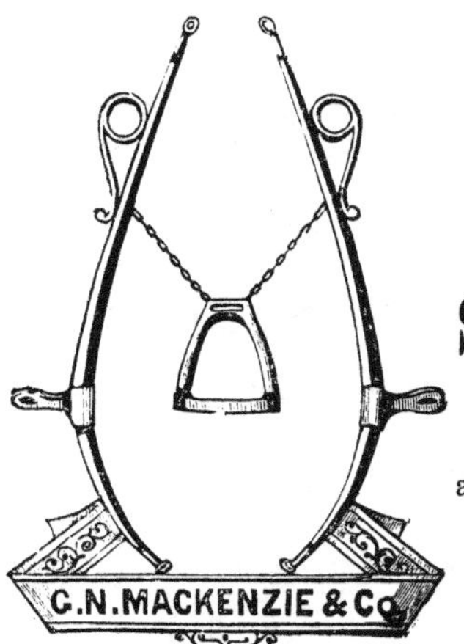

ESTABLISHED IN 1820.

GEO. N. MACKENZIE & CO.

SOLE SUCCESSORS OF

Thos. Mackenzie & Sons and Mackenzie Bros.

Importers and Wholesale Dealers in

SADDLERY HARDWARE,

Comprising everything in the line.

No House in the United States can offer a better assorted Stock on better terms.

Orders by Mail receive Prompt Personal Attention.

NO. 18 SOUTH CHARLES STREET,

BALTIMORE.

E. AUSTIN JENKINS, ALFRED JENKINS, JR. ROBERT H. JENKINS.

EDW. JENKINS & SONS,

IMPORTERS AND DEALERS IN

Carriage and Saddlery Hardware,

No. 180 W. Baltimore Street,

BALTIMORE.

HENRY R. CHAMPAYNE,

Carriage and Express Wagon

MANUFACTURER,

No. 84 German Street,

Betw. Eutaw and Paca Sts. **BALTIMORE.**

☞SECOND-HAND CARRIAGES FOR SALE OR EXCHANGE.

SEE PAGE 193.

5

ALEX. BROWN & SONS,

(Organized 1811.)

153 W. Baltimore Street.

[See page 267.]

BROWN BROTHERS & CO.

59 Wall Street, New York.

Bills of Exchange on

Great Britain and Ireland.

COMMERCIAL AND TRAVELLING CREDITS ISSUED,

Available in any Part of the World.

Telegraphic Transfers of Money

MADE TO AND FROM

LONDON AND LIVERPOOL.

☞ Advances Made on Cotton and other Produce.

[See page 270.]

[See page 263.]

[See page 272.]

REVERDY JOHNSON.

THE distinguished life and public services of Mr. REVERDY JOHNSON induced us to make special notice of him in our comments upon the Bar of the City and State in the first edition of our work, (see page 74.) Although, then, almost an octogenarian, he was apparently as vigorous as he ever was, both in mind and body. The labors and the excitements incident to the high and responsible offices he has filled had never, in the slightest degree, abated his ardent love of the profession he had made his own, and the power and dignity of which he had done so much to illustrate.

Returning from his mission as Minister to England in 1869, he had quietly resumed the practice of Law, and his services were eagerly sought for the trial of important causes, as they had been years before, in Maryland and in other parts of the country. Few persons, indeed, who did not know Mr. Johnson personally, would credit the fact of his very advanced age, and wherever he went, or wherever he was heard, he commanded the most marked attention. Almost the last of the living contemporaries of Pinkney, Wirt and Taney, of our own ever-memorable Bar, and of Clay, Webster and Calhoun in the Senate of the United States, he was looked upon, both by lawyers and politicians, with a reverence seldom now accorded to any man. He had outlived all partisan bitterness and jealousy, and was so far removed from current political influences, that his views and opinions upon the leading questions of the day were taken, not merely as the quick perceptions of his wonderful intellect, but as the calm results of the study and experience of half a century. The life of one so gifted and so useful to his fellow-citizens was, as we thought, very properly referred to, among the objects of our State and city pride. His recent and lamentable death certainly claims at our hands some tribute to his memory. A biography, and the relation of the important and interesting events in the history of the State and the country with which his name is associated, will doubtless be written. But we feel that we should not do justice to our own book, if we omitted to record in its pages the prominent physical and intellectual features of this very remarkable man.

Mr. Johnson was born at Annapolis, Maryland, on the 21st of May, 1796, and consequently, at the time of his death, on the 10th of February last, was within four months of the completion of his eightieth year. His family were among the very early settlers in Maryland, and some of its members had held prominent positions under the Colonial Government. His father, John Johnson, was an eminent lawyer, who, after serving in both Houses of the General Assembly, was successively Attorney General, Judge of the Court of Appeals, and Chancellor of the State. His mother was the daughter of Reverdy Ghiselin, long and well known as the Commissioner of the Land Office, at Annapolis. Educated at St. John's College, in his native town, Reverdy Johnson entered the Grammar School at six and left the institution at sixteen years of age. He immediately commenced reading law under the direction of his father, and was afterwards, for a while, a student in the office of the late Judge Stephen. He was admitted to the Bar and began practice in Prince George's county, in the village of Upper Marlborough, in 1816, when only in his twentieth year. Although thus under age, he was appointed by the then Attorney General his Deputy for the Judicial District, and performed the duties of that responsible office in the most creditable manner until November, 1817, when he removed to Baltimore and started in his career as a lawyer, which for brilliancy and success has seldom been equalled. Developing thus early that vigor of intellect and force of character which so distinguished him, he took at once an excellent position; and notwithstanding his youth, was recognized by lawyers and laymen as a man of unusual ability. He became, very soon, the professional associate and intimate companion of Robt. Goodloe Harper, Luther Martin, William Pinkney, Roger B. Taney, William H. Winder and others, who had already made the Bar of Maryland famous. Laboring with untiring energy and earnestness of purpose, Mr. Johnson obtained a large and lucrative practice, which, to the day of his death, was only interrupted by the discharge of his various public duties. In 1821 he was elected to the State Senate for a term of five years, and was re-elected for another term, but, after serving two years of the second term, he resigned, that he might give more exclusive attention to his practice Although frequently urged to do so, he always refused to be a candidate for the House of Representatives, and never held a seat in that body. In 1845, however, he was elected to the Senate of the United States, and soon took a conspicuous place among its leading members. In 1849 President Taylor offered him the position of Attorney General, which he accepted and filled with distinction until the accession of Mr. Fillmore, when he resigned and resumed his practice. From that time his fame as a lawyer became national, and he was retained on one side or the other of almost every important cause in the Courts of Maryland and in the Supreme Court at Washington. His advice and services were sought from distant States, and his appearance in Court in Connecticut and New York, in Missouri, Louisiana, California and elsewhere, in cases involving large interests and the most intricate questions of law, is a part of the history of the profession in America. In 1854 he was employed by an English House to argue a case before the joint English and American Claims Commission, then sitting in London under the provisions of an international treaty. Mr. Johnson there had as his associate the late Lord Chancellor Cairns, who was then in the House of Commons, and a leading member of the English Chancery Bar. Mr. Johnson had visited England and travelled in Europe, some years before, when comparatively unknown, but on this occasion he received very great attention from public men and members of the English Bar. Returning home, he was unceasingly engaged with his immense practice, and took no active part in public matters until in the winter of 1860-61, when he was forced to do so by the exigencies of that memorable period. He was chosen one of the Delegates from Maryland to the Peace Convention which assembled in Washington. Although avowing himself a Union man, and utterly repudiating the doctrine of secession as a constitutional right, Mr. Johnson was conspicuous in that Convention for his earnest and eloquent efforts to avert the threatening calamities of civil war by measures of compromise and conciliation; and it was only when all hope of a peaceful adjustment of the sectional difficulties had vanished, that he advocated the preservation of the Federal Government by its military power. When the supremacy of that power was re-established, Mr. Johnson was among the first and most determined defenders of the rights of the Southern States to be restored to their former places and privileges. In the winter of 1862-63, when the war fever was at its height, the Legislature of Maryland elected Mr. Johnson to the Senate, and he resumed his seat in that body after an absence of fourteen years. He participated in all the great debates, and though by no means a party man, and not always acting with the Democrats, he was invariably found in the front rank of those who resisted extreme and cruel measures of oppression and retaliation towards the Southern people. In 1868 President Johnson appointed him Minister to England, and during his official residence in that country he was the recipient of attentions never before paid to an American Ambassador. The settlement of the "Alabama Claims," which then excited the temper and severely taxed the self-control of both nations, was a very difficult task for Diplomacy, and, although the treaty negotiated between Mr. Johnson and Lord Clarendon was not ratified by the American Senate, it is universally conceded that the agreements it involved accomplished the great object—that of preventing war—while the subsequent arrangement of the mode in which those agreements were to be enforced, gave no additional security for peace, and established no new principle whatever.

With the advent of President Grant's administration, Mr. Johnson's recall from London became a matter of course, and in the fall of 1869 he was again in Baltimore, engaged as formerly, in the daily occupation of his profession. Although past the period of life when most men of competent fortune seek the retirement and ease of their homes, and abandon the cares and anxieties of business, Mr. Johnson manifested, even then, no such disposition. He was as ready as ever to undertake the trial of any case of sufficient importance to justify his employment by a litigant, or in which he was asked to defend the cause of public or of private justice.

One of the many unhappy results of the civil war, and of the attempted reconstruction of the States, in their relation to the General Government, was the frequent exercise of powers never before recognized, and the discussion of Constitutional questions never previously raised. In many of these cases Mr. Johnson appeared, and his arguments will ever be held as among the ablest modern expositions of the intent and meaning of the framers of our fundamental law. Retaining to the very last his robust health and cheerful temperament, he seemed likely to live on for some years yet, and this fact made his sudden death all the more shocking. He had only returned, a few weeks before, from London, where he had spent a month or two in the transaction of some business, and the two voyages across the Atlantic Ocean had been made by him without the slightest apparent discomfort. He had been welcomed back to Baltimore and Washington by his family and numerous friends, and in his unpretending manner had gone right to work again to try cases, the arguments of which his temporary absence had delayed. At the time of his death he was in Annapolis awaiting the call of one of these cases in the Court of Appeals of the State. It was one in which his interest and kindness of heart were warmly enlisted in behalf of the son of a friend of his early life, and had he been spared twenty-four hours longer, he would doubtless have closed his professional career by the exhibition of all his usual vigor of intellect and power and ingenuity of reasoning. He was taken off, however, "in a moment, in the twinkling of an eye," and, as if Providence had so ordained it, in the very place where his remarkable life began. To the very last his faculties of mind seemed perfectly unimpaired, for, but one hour before the announcement of his death, his delightful humor and fund of anecdotes had made him the charm of a dinner party at the Governor's House, where some of his intimate friends had been assembled. The only reasonable mode of accounting for the sad occurrence is upon the theory of an attack of apoplexy. The startling information of his death caused profound sorrow, not only in Maryland, but throughout this country and in England; for wherever American Independence or American Statesmanship were understood or recognized, Mr. Johnson was both known and respected. His loss to the community in which he lived will be long deplored. Simple in all his tastes, and absolutely free from all affectation of manner, he was the friend of all who knew him. Frank and manly himself, he rarely thought ill of any one, and was ever ready to encourage or assist those who approached him. He always manifested the deepest interest in the public welfare, and his presence and his earnest eloquence not unfrequently promoted the great efforts in our midst for moral as well as political reform. The life and character of such a man are a precious legacy to his countrymen, and an example which should not be lost sight of or suffered to be forgotten.

RESOLUTIONS ADOPTED BY THE GENERAL ASSEMBLY OF MARYLAND.

Hon. F. P. Stevens (by unanimous consent,) from a Joint Select Committee, appointed to prepare a suitable testimonial to the memory of the late Honorable Reverdy Johnson, presented the following

JOINT RESOLUTIONS.

Resolved by the General Assembly of Maryland, That the General Assembly of Maryland, have heard with profound grief and sincere regret, the annunciation by his Excellency, the Governor, of the sudden decease of the Honorable Reverdy Johnson, in the full vigor of life, and in the crowning years of a long period of usefulness to his state and country.

That by the death of this distinguished Jurist, Statesman and Diplomatist, the people of the State of Maryland have lost one in whose unquestioned fame, at home and abroad, they have ever felt a just pride, and whom they have delighted to honor, as one of her pre-eminently worthy and most illustrious sons: and the nation and the world have been called to mourn the deprivation of a wise counsellor and a devoted patriot.

That the State of Maryland will ever cherish and hold in grateful remembrance, the invaluable public services he has rendered, and would hereby express a tribute of honor and respect, to the consummate ability, and commanding intellect, which exalted him as the foremost Jurist of America.

To the patriotic impulses which animated him in the discharge of grave and responsible duties to his state and country.

To his unsullied private character, and ennobling virtues, which are inscribed upon, and enshrined in the hearts of his countrymen.

That as a further testimonial of respect to the memory of the deceased, an engrossed copy of these resolutions, signed by the President and Secretary of the Senate, the Speaker and Chief Clerk of the House of Delegates, be transmitted to the family of the deceased, and that a similar copy suitably framed be placed in the Library of the State.

FRANCIS PUTNAM STEVENS.
LEWIS H. STEINER.
Committee on the part of the Senate.

EDWARD J. CHAISTY,
BENJAMIN LANKFORD,
HENRY R. ATKINSON.
Committee on the part of the House of Delegates.

PEABODY HEIGHTS.

The suburban country of Baltimore is extremely beautiful, and no portion surpasses that lying to the north of the city. That section extending from Druid Hill Park to Clifton, the seat of Johns Hopkins University, and Lake Montebello, is one of the most picturesque in America. It is a panorama of uninterruped beauty, diversified with almost every variety of scenery, to which man has contributed the works of art and industry.

Graceful villas crown its heights, luxuriant gardens repose on its valleys and hill sides, lakes and streams sparkle amid its emerald fields. In the midst of this scene and on one on its crowning heights, the property of the *Peabody Heights Company* is situated. It is only three quarters of a mile north of Washington Monument, and nearly on a level with its top, bounded by Charles Street and Maryland Avenue on the west and North Street on the east. It is an elevated plateau containing about fifty acres, which have been laid off into broad streets and avenues to conform with the city, which ere long will incorporate it with itself.

ITS SITUATION IS BEAUTIFUL AND ADVANTAGEOUS. Overlooking the city, it affords comprehensive views of it and the surrounding country. From its elevation, the view embracing Druid Hill Park with its primeval forests and its lakes, Mount Royal with its Reservoir and Fountain, the City with its numerous spires and monuments, the Bay with its wide expanse whitened with the sails of our commerce, is beyond description. Opposite to it is Homewood Park, the generous donation of Mr. Wm. Wyman and others to Baltimore, whose shady groves will be a favorite refuge from the heat and dust of the city.

Upon the grounds are the handsome residences of Messrs. Holmes and Ulman, and in the near vicinity are the country-seats of many of our most prominent and cultivated citizens, as "Guilford," the property of A. S. Abell, Esq., and the elegant homes of Messrs. Perine, Wyman, Wilsons, Reese, Whiteley, Whitridge, Brady and others. Thus by its situation and surroundings it is truly beautiful.

ITS ADVANTAGES are evident from its relative position to the city and county, and the means of communication with both. The Baltimore, Peabody Heights and Waverly Railroad runs through its entire length connecting it with the York Road and Towsontown, the county-seat; also by the Park Avenue and Calvert Street Lines with all parts of the city. The Hampden and Woodberry Cars pass near, giving close communication with Druid Hill Park. It is within walking distance of Union Depot on Charles Street, where trains arrive and depart to all parts of the country. It is convenient to schools and churches of all denominations in the county and city. In fact it contains all the advantages of a country and city residence, having the charm and healthfulness of the one, and the social privileges and conveniences of the other. The Boulevard or Grand Avenue, which is to connect Clifton Park and Lake Montebello with Druid Hill Park, will pass near the property. It is impossible to conceive of a situation more beautiful and desirable.

The Company have laid it off into building lots, which they are leasing or selling at rates that make them desirable either for a home or investment, as the city is rapidly growing towards it with first-class improvements, its advance being largely along the line of which it is the very centre.

The Company is composed of some of our most prominent citizens and capitalists, whose names are a sufficient guarantee to any who may desire to purchase or locate here. By the express stipulations of the terms of purchase, there is perfect immunity from everything which may be objectionable to the purchasers.

The officers are—President, FRANKLIN WILSON; Vice-President, WILLIAM DEVRIES; Treasurer, CHARLES W. LORD; Secretary, J. APPLETON WILSON; Directors, GEORGE W. ROBINSON, WM. HOLMES, A. J. ULMAN, CHARLES WEBB, SAMUEL H. ADAMS.

231 BALTIMORE ST. BALTIMORE, MD.

N. H. BUSEY'S

PHOTGRAPHIC AND ART

GALLERIES,

N.W. Cor. Charles and Fayette Sts.,

BALTIMORE.

THE LARGEST AND MOST COMPLETE IN THE CITY.

Occupying the four-story building on the corner of Charles and Fayette Streets, and employing none but FIRST-CLASS ARTISTS.

The work produced at this establishment cannot be excelled in this country or in Europe.

Every kind of picture, from CARTE-DE-VISITE to LIFE SIZE PORTRAITS in Oil or Pastel, finished in the highest style of the art.

Particular attention given to copying and enlarging from old Daguerrotypes, &c.

Any orders by mail promptly attended to. Also a fine collection of

STEEL ENGRAVINGS,

ENGLISH, GERMAN AND FRENCH

CHROMOS, PHOTOGRAPHS

From Paintings, &c., &c.

ALL KINDS OF FRAMES ON HAND,

AND MADE TO ORDER,

AT VERY MODERATE PRICES.

SATISFACTION GUARANTEED.

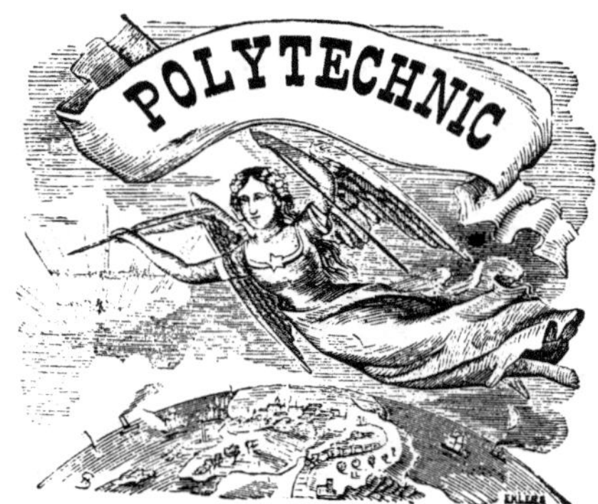

INSTRUCTION CO. OF MARYLAND,

CORNER OF

Baltimore and Charles Streets,

BALTIMORE, MD.

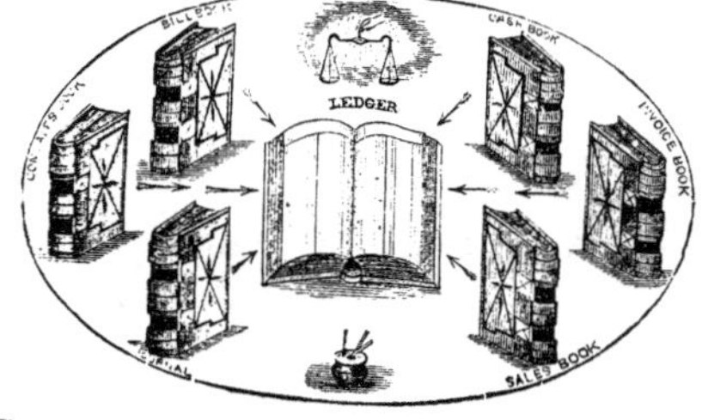

Diagram indicating the practical method of Posting directly from the Books of Original Entry to the Ledger.

PRACTICAL BOOK-KEEPING!

PRACTICAL INSTRUCTION!

Based entirely on the various operations of Finance and Trade.

No Copying from Printed or Manuscript Forms in Learning Book-Keeping at this Institution.

☞ Thirty Phonographic, Telegraphic, Banking, Writing, Shipping and Business Instruction Papers sent free to any address enclosing return postage.

JOHN H. ALLEN,
Superintendent.

C. T. LAWSON,
President.

OLDEST AND BEST
Actual Business College
IN THE COUNTRY.

Established in 1852.

Incorporated in 1854.

The only Incorporated Institution in the State practically instructing, viz:

Commercial Book-Keepers, Mathematicians, Commercial Correspondents in our own and Foreign Languages, Business and Ornamental Penmen, Stenographers, Mechanical and Architectural Draughtsmen, Telegraph Operators, Commercial Shipping, Express and Railroad Accountants, and Landscape Gardeners.

PHONOGRAPHIC DEPARTMENT.

Receiving Office of Telegraphic Department.

Emmart & Quartley,

FRESCO, SIGN AND HOUSE

PAINTERS & DECORATORS,

Execute every branch of FINE PAINTING, and make Special Drawings in Color for Wall and Ceiling Decoration, for Halls, Churches, Theatres, Public Buildings and Private Mansions.

Fine Imitations of Wood and Marble executed to invite the closest examination. Parti-Colors and Ivory Finish, and every description of HOUSE PAINTING.

SIGNS of every kind; ENAMELED GILDING on Glass; BANNERS and FLAGS for Societies and Lodges; Monograms, Figures, Tablets, Devices, &c.

TINTING for Walls and Ceilings, in Fresco, Oil or Encaustic finish.

The Latest and Best European Works on Decorative Art received soon as published, and are at all times open to the inspection of our Patrons.

The superior excellence of our work is attested by the numerous Private Dwellings done by us in this City, the address of which we will be pleased to furnish on application, and also by reference to the following Public Buildings, &c.

New City Hall, Baltimore.
" " Frederick, Md.
" " Cumberland, Md.
Academy of Music, " "
Second National Bank, " "
Fifth Reg't Armory, M. N. G., Baltimore.
Traders' National Bank, "
National Bank of Baltimore.
Alexander Brown & Sons' Bank, "
Drovers and Mechanics' " "
Wheeler & Wilson Manufacturing Co.
St. Joseph's Academy, Emmittsburg, Md.
The Sisters' Exhibition Hall, " "
St. Joseph's Chapel, " "
St. Patrick's R. C. Church, . Baltimore.
St. Ann's R. C. " "
St. Francis Xavier's R. C. Church, "
Ascension P. E. " "
Johns' Memorial P. E. " "
Ascension P. E. Church, Washington. .

St. Luke's P. E. Church, . Baltimore.
New American Building, "
Eastern Female High School, "
Deaf and Dumb Asylum, Frederick, Md.
Lodge and Chapter Rooms, New Masonic Temple, Baltimore.
Knights Templar Asylum, New Masonic Temple, Baltimore.
Carrollton Hotel, Baltimore.
St. Clair " "
Eutaw House, "
Rennert House, "
Mount Vernon M. E. Church, Baltimore.
Charles Street " " "
Grace " " "
Fayette Street " " and Chapel, Balto.
New M. E. Church, Chestertown, Md.
St. Paul's Lutheran Church, Baltimore.
First Lutheran Church, "
Safe Deposit Co. New Building, "

And other work in different parts of the Country.

We Refer by Permission to the Following Gentlemen:

P. Hanson Hiss & Co.
Hamilton Easter & Sons,
Geo. A. Frederick, Architect,
Dixon & Carson, "
W. S. G. Baker, "
Frank E. Davis, "
E. G. Lind, "
Markland & Bro., Builders,
S. H. & J. F. Adams, "

Jackson Holland, Builder,
J. Hall Pleasants, Esq.
James Hodges, Esq.
James A. Gary, Esq.
Joseph A. Sprigg, Esq.
Woodward Abrahams, Esq.
S. Eccles, Jr.
Thomas Shields, Esq.
Hugh Sisson, Esq.

Walter S. Wilkinson, Esq.
C. C. Fulton & Son, Balto. American,
Henry A. Thompson, Pres. National Bank of Baltimore,
Wm. M. Laffan & Co., Baltimore Bulletin,
Hon. Henry W. Hoffman, Cumberland, Md.
Col. Chas. E. Trail, Frederick, Md.

Respectfully, **EMMART & QUARTLEY,**

Designers, Decorators and Painters,

Late of 276 Baltimore St. **No. 32 PARK STREET,**

Third door above Lexington—Rooms on First Floor.

GUNTHER
1874
BUILDINGS
L. W. GUNTHER
LEAF TOBACCO.
A. SCHUMACHER & CO.
Gambrill Sons & Co
9 L.W. GUNTHER 9
J.D. EHLERS-CO

[See page 254.]

[See article on Western Maryland Railroad.]

UNIVERSITY OF MARYLAND.

Hon. SEVERN TEACKLE WALLIS, LL. D., Provost.

FACULTY OF PHYSIC—1875-76.

NATHAN R. SMITH, M. D.,
President of the Faculty and Emeritus Professor of Surgery.

WM. E. A. AIKIN, M. D., LL. D.,
Professor of Chemistry and Pharmacy,
178 *W. Baltimore Street.*

GEORGE W. MILTENBERGER, M. D.,
Professor of Obstetrics,
S. E. cor. Eutaw and Monument Sts.

RICHARD MCSHERRY, M. D.,
Professor of Principles and Practice of Medicine,
189 *N. Howard Street.*

CHRISTOPHER JOHNSTON, M. D.,
Professor of Surgery,
82 *Franklin Street, cor. Park.*

SAMUEL C. CHEW, M. D.,
Professor of Materia Medica and Therapeutics, and Clinical Medicine,
141 *Lanvale Street.*

FRANK DONALDSON, M. D.,
Professor of Physiology and Hygiene, and Clinical Professor of Diseases of the Throat, Lungs and Heart,
112 *Park Avenue.*

WILLIAM T. HOWARD, M. D.,
Professor of Diseases of Women and Children, and Clinical Medicine,
181 *Madison Avenue.*

JULIAN J. CHISOLM, M. D.,
Professor of Ophthalmic and Aural Surgery,
55 *Franklin Street.*

FRANCIS T. MILES, M. D.,
Professor of Anatomy and Clinical Professor of Diseases of the Nervous System,
14 *Cathedral Street.*

L. MCLANE TIFFANY, M. D.,
Professor of Operative Surgery,
31 *Cathedral Street.*

J. E. MICHAEL, M. D.,
Demonstrator of Anatomy.

[See page 95.] **S. C. CHEW, M. D., Dean of the Faculty.**

WASHINGTON UNIVERSITY

FACULTY—1875-76.

CHARLES W. CHANCELLOR, M. D.,
Emeritus Professor of Surgery and President of the Faculty.

JOSEPH E. CLAGETT, M. D.,
Professor of Obstetrics.

MARTIN P. SCOTT, M D.,
Professor of the Diseases of Women and Children.

JOHN F. MONMONIER, M. D.,
Professor of Physiology.

JAMES E. LINDSAY, M. D.,
Professor of Chemistry.

ABRAM B. ARNOLD, M. D.,
Professor of the Principles and Practice of Medicine.

H. B. TRIST, M. D.,
Professor of Anatomy.

JOSEPH A. WHITE, M. D.,
Professor of Eye and Ear Diseases.

WILLIAM GREEN, M. D.,
Professor of Materia Medica and Therapeutics.

JOHN N. MONMONIER, M. D.,
Professor of Operative and Clinical Surgery.

ISHAM R. PAGE, M. D.,
Professor of Principles and Practice of Surgery.

GEORGE E. NELSON, A. M.,
Lecturer on Medical Jurisprudence.

J. H. HARTMAN, M. D.,
Lecturer on Diseases of the Throat and Chest.

JOHN P. VAN BIBBER, M. D.,
Clinical Lecturer on Neurology.

GEORGE B. REYNOLDS, M. D.,
Demonstrator of Anatomy.

[See page 96.] J. E. LINDSAY, M. D., Dean of the Faculty

The COLLEGE OF PHYSICIANS and SURGEONS

OF BALTIMORE, MD.

Hon. ROBERT GILMOR, President.

FACULTY OF PHYSIC.

EDWARD WARREN, M. D.,
Emeritus Professor of Surgery.

THOMAS OPIE, M. D.,
Professor of Obstetrics.

PETER GOOLRICK, M. D.,
Prof'r of Medical Jurisprudence and Toxicology.

JOHN S. LYNCH, M. D.,
Professor of Principles and Practice of Medicine.

E. LLOYD HOWARD, M. D.,
Professor of Chemistry.

THOMAS S. LATIMER, M. D.,
Professor of Physiology and Hygiene, and Clinical Professor of Diseases of Children.

AUGUSTUS F. ERICH, M. D.,
Professor of the Diseases of Women.

THOMAS R. BROWN, M. D.,
Professor of Clinical and Operative Surgery, and Diseases of the Genito-Urinary Organs.

AARON FRIEDENWALD, M. D.,
Professor of Diseases of the Eye and Ear.

CHARLES F. BEVAN, M. D.,
Professor of Anatomy.

ARCHIBALD ATKINSON, M. D.,
Professor of Materia Medica and Therapeutics.

OSCAR J. COSKERY, M. D.,
Professor of Principles and Practice of Surgery.

JAMES G. WILTSHIRE, M. D.,
Demonstrator of Anatomy.

SILAS W. HUNTER, M. D.,
Prosector, &c.

The regular Winter Session begins October 1st, and terminates the last of February. The MARYLAND LYING-IN ASYLUM (see page 432) affords Students of this College special advantages for the practical study of Obstetrics and Gynecology.

MEDICAL AND SURGICAL CLINICS are held daily at 12 M. at "The Clinic Hall."

For further information write for a Catalogue, or address

THOMAS OPIE, M. D., Dean.

ELISHA RIGGS.
[Moved to New York from Baltimore in 1824, and was a prominent Merchant in New York until his death in 1853.]

GEORGE PEABODY.
[See pages 38, 329, 330 and 331.]

RIGGS AND PEABODY,

Congress Hall, Market St., near Liberty,

.ave received by the Dumfries from Liverpool, and New York Packets, an additional supply of seasonable Dry Goods, viz:

6 Cases assorted Bed Tickings,
10 Trunks Calicoes,
2 Cases Furniture Prints,
2 " Imitation Shawls,
1 " Scarlet Cassimere Shawls,
6 " Assorted Patent Threads, from No. 12 to 100,
2 Trunks Dog Skins and Bêaver Gloves,
1 Case assorted Pearl and Glass Buttons,
3 " Cords and Velveteens,
2 " Levantines and Florantines—Black and other colors,
1 " Levantine Shawls,
3 " Linen Cambricks,
1 " Ostrich and Down Feathers,

Which, with a general assortment of British, French and Indian Goods, will be sold on moderate terms.

—*Taken from the Federal Republican and Baltimore Telegraph, Monday, Oct.* 27, 1817.

GEORGE PEABODY

Died in London, England, November 4th, 1869, (aged 74 years, 9 months, 17 days,) was honored by a burial service in Westminster Abby, where a slab, commemorative of him, rests amidst those of the princes, heroes, statesmen and poets of the past. His remains were brought to Portland, Maine, in the "Monarch," turreted iron-clad, the finest vessel in the British Navy, by command of the Queen, and convoyed by an American and a French frigate.

"They brought no crowned king;
Theirs was a holier trust:
They bore a treasure from afar,
A good man's sacred dust."

"Mourned by the rich he taught,
Mourned by the poor he fed,
Mourned by a race with whom he broke
A nobler food than bread."

Prince Arthur attended the remains from the harbor of Liverpool to that of Portland; and although an officer in the British Navy, he was present at the funeral in Danvers, dressed in a full suit of black.

England and America buried this citizen of two-fold nationality, and France looked on with sympathy at the funeral.

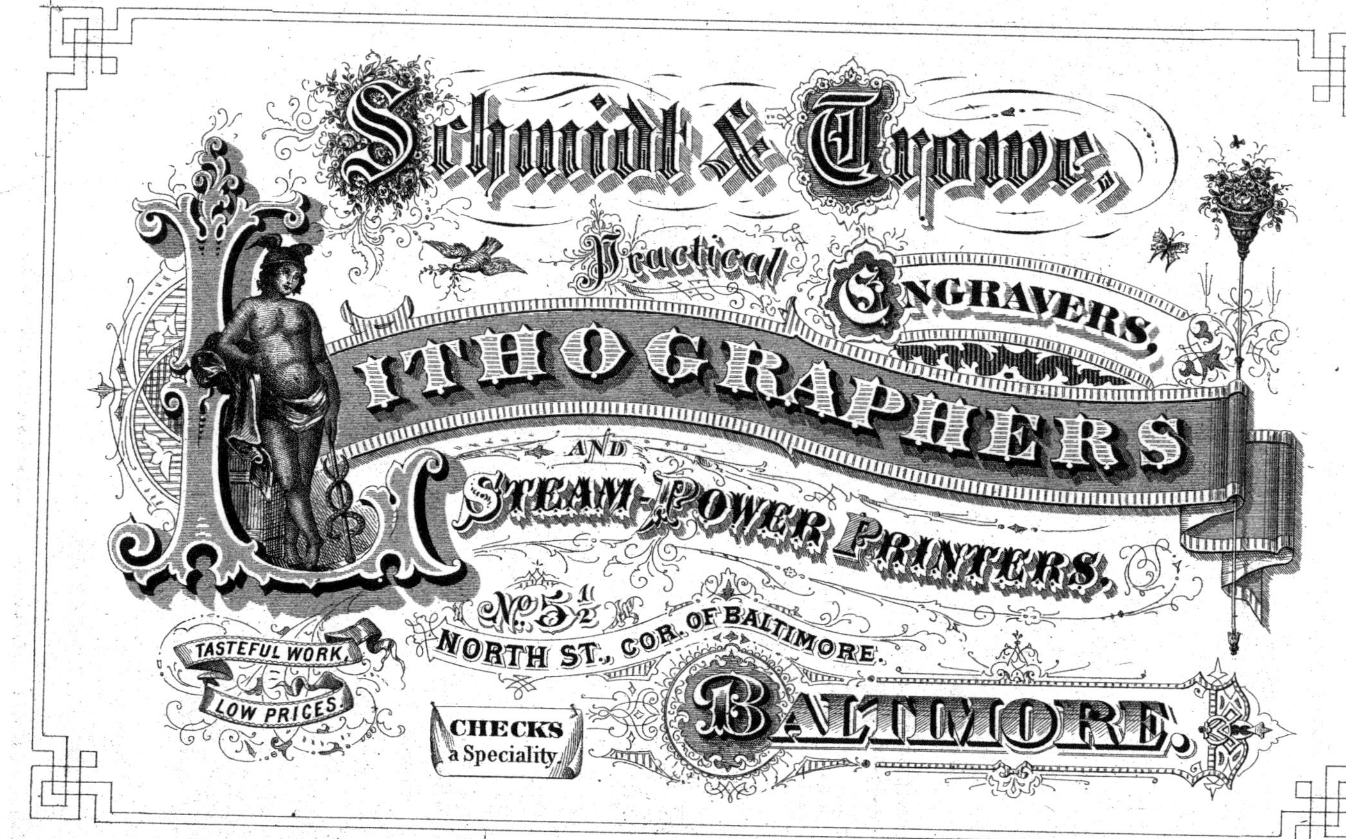
Schmidt & Trowe,
Practical Engravers,
Lithographers
and
Steam-Power Printers,
No. 5 1/2
North St., Cor. of Baltimore.
Baltimore.
Tasteful Work,
Low Prices.
Checks
a Speciality.

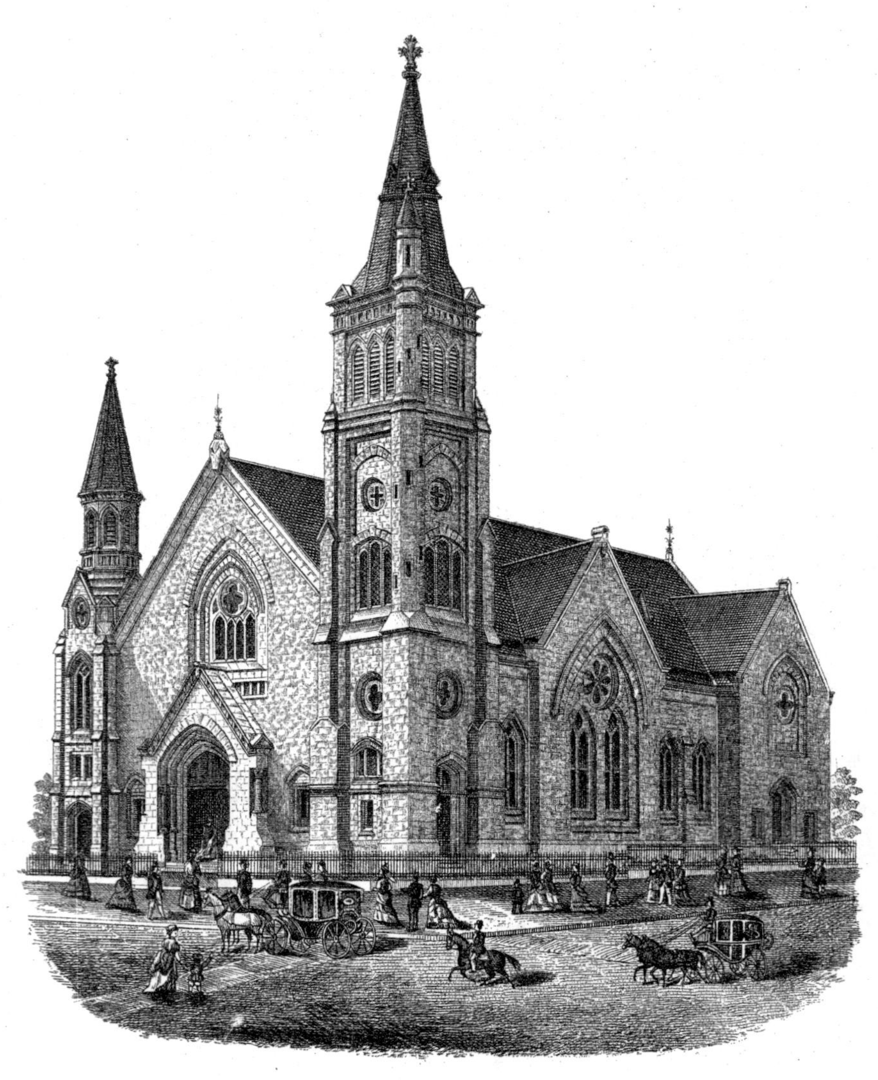

The Brown Memorial Presbyterian Church.

BROWN MEMORIAL CHURCH.

On page 436 we give a handsome cut of Brown Memorial (Presbyterian) Church. It is built of Baltimore County Marble, in the gothic style, and is one of the most elegant church edifices in the city.

It was erected and completely furnished at the cost of one hundred and fifty thousand dollars, by Mrs. Isabella Brown, the widow of the late George Brown, Esq., of Alexander Brown & Sons, who, by her liberal benefactions and noble deeds has endeared herself to our citizens, and whose name is associated in the public mind with all that is true and elevated in religion and lovely in woman.

It is "in memoriam" of her husband, as expressed on a marble tablet in the rear of the pulpit. This is an appropriate monument to him who regarded religion as preeminent above all other things, and loved his church with all the ardor of his noble nature. It perpetuates his memory and extends the cause he supremely loved. This is a pleasing connection in which to refer to the financial house of which he was the head for many years. Alexander Brown, the father of William, George, John A. and James, emigrated to Baltimore with William the eldest son, from the North of Ireland in 1800. With a small capital he began to import Irish Linens, and gradually extended his business to general shipping and commission. In 1810, William went to Liverpool and with his brother James formed a house, which subsequently became Brown, Shipley & Co., a branch of which was created in London. This house soon attained great prominence and power, and William in consideration of his eminent commercial standing and his generous gifts to the people of Liverpool of a Free Library and Building, was made Baronet by the Queen in 1862. In 1811, Mr. Brown organized the firm of Alexander Brown & Sons in Baltimore. In 1818, John A. Brown founded the branch in Philadelphia, as John A. Brown & Co., and in 1825, James Brown established the house of Brown, Brothers & Co., in New York, of which he is still the head. These sons became eminent not only in financial affairs, but also in deeds of benevolence, expressed in the most comprehensive and effective forms. On the retirement of John A. Brown, in 1839, the Philadelphia house took the name of the New York, viz: Brown, Brothers & Co.

During the life of Alexander Brown, the Baltimore house was head-quarters for the others, and it was customary for the brothers to meet here and consult with their father on important matters connected with the operations of the house. Alexander Brown died 1834, and his death made a profound impression through the community, as he had sustained the highest position in public esteem, had exerted a grand influence, and contributed an invaluable part to the welfare as well as a commercial growth of the city. The spirit of the man towards his fellowman, was beautifully illustrated in a remark of his on the occasion of a financial panic. "No merchant in Baltimore should be allowed to fail, who can show he is solvent." His son George Brown having remained with him in the Baltimore house, succeeded him as the head, retaining the original name of Alexander Brown & Sons. He was one of the most valuable citizens Baltimore ever had. He was always foremost in all great and good enterprises. To his comprehensive views, his prophetic vision, his expansive enterprise, the city is greatly indebted for the Baltimore and Ohio Railroad and other important institutions which are now its pride and source of conmercial revenue. To the causes of humanity and christianity he not only gave liberally, but in them was an active worker. Among these the House of Refuge stands, an enduring and useful monument to his munificence and beneficence alike. The inscription on a marble shaft which was erected to his memory by the late Benjamin Deford who was associated with him in this and other benevolent works, well expresses his life. He died in 1859, leaving a large fortune, a name universally honored and an influence which will never fade away.

The firm now consists of his son, George S. Brown, W. H. Graham and W. G. Bowdoin, which maintains the reputation and credit of the house, conducting it on the same principles of high honor and unbending rectitude. They have enlarged and improved their building, which as seen from the cut on page 412, is one of the finest structures on Baltimore street.

The house of Brown, Brothers & Co., sustains a like relation to the cities of New York and Philadelphia that Alexander Brown & Sons does to Baltimore, and it is an occasion of no little gratification, that from our city has sprung institutions which have so honorable a record, and exert the most important influences throughout the commercial world.

THE MONUMENT AT THE HOUSE OF REFUGE.

IN MEMORIAM.
GEORGE BROWN,
ONE OF THE FOUNDERS,
And until his death, the first President of this Institution.

In spirit eminently charitable; cautious in judgment, in action prudent; wise in council, and an earnest helper in all good works.

From his abundant means,
he bestowed his gifts
with an open hand and a cheerful heart,
living, he enjoyed
the consummation of his christian deeds;
dying, it was as a good steward
in humble trust of the Master's acceptance
and the peaceful hope of a
blissful immortality.

THIS STONE
may serve to recall his virtues;
his best monument
is this
House of Refuge.

"*Si monumentum quaeris circumspice.*"

"Faithful unto death."

" He delivered the poor that cried, and the fatherless and him that had no helper. The blessing of him that was ready to perish came upon him, and he caused the widow's heart to sing for joy."

Born in
County Antrim, Ireland,
April 4th, 1785;
A citizen of the United States,
1804.
Died in Baltimore,
August 26th, 1859.

This Monument
was erected by
Benjamin Deford,
one of the Managers of this Institution as a mark of esteem for the
memory of
a venerable colleague.

Dimensions—Height 15 feet.

THE ENVIRONS OF BALTIMORE.

The environs of Baltimore are very attractive, and this is especially the case to the north and west. The ground is beautifully rolling and rises into ridges of sufficient elevation to afford fine views of the surrounding country, the city and river. These features of configuration are very marked upon the line of the Harford Road, an avenue which runs out from about the centre of the city nearly a little east of north, and which crosses the Northern Boundary avenue, having a width of one hundred and fifty feet, and so laid out as to sweep around the city on the three sides not obstructed by the river. This fine avenue is destined to become a very attractive Boulevard, and when laid out in broad walks and roadways, and planted with trees, will afford one of the most splendid drives in the country. Beyond this point the road rises, until some ten miles out it reaches the Gunpowder River and a height of over four hundred feet above tide-water. About two miles from the city lies Clifton, the estate comprising some four hundred and eighty acres, which was devised by the late Johns Hopkins for the great university, the buildings of which, will be there erected. The grounds not required for this use, will, it is understood, be tastefully laid out and devoted to the purposes of a Park. As the university project is in the hands of a Board of Trustees, composed of some of our most intelligent citizens, who will have command of very ample means, we are confident of great results, both of an educational and local value. Facing this property and running northwardly lies the splendid estate of Mr. John W. Garrett of over a thousand acres, and beyond, on the left of the pike, hundreds of workmen are already busy with the excavations for Lake Montebello, for which the City in connection with one of its water supplies, has recently acquired about eighty acres at the cost of a thousand dollars per acre. This will be a very beautiful improvement and will no doubt enhance the value of adjoining property, as well as, add greatly to the picturesque beauty of the neighborhood. We learn that a broad drive will surround this Lake, and as this will be reached by two already popular roads leading from the city, distant less than three miles; as well as a Passenger Railway, and will later be connected directly with Druid Hill Park by a projected avenue of a hundred feet wide; it would seem evident, that many important improvements must follow on this suburban line, facing the lower end of the Lake, and running along Herring Run an affluent of the Patapsco River, is the property of the Hon. J. Morrison Harris, and beyond, the lands belonging to the estate of the late Col. Hall. Beyond the Run the ground continues to rise, and is thickly settled and handsomely improved with the country-seats of many of our most prominent citizens. We have given this detailed description of one of our suburbs, because it offers a number of salient features, but we could justly point with pride to the attractions presented in other directions also, did our space permit.

RANSTEAD'S IMPROVEMENTS AT SPRING GARDENS.

Among the most important improvements now being made in Baltimore is that of Mr. Charles Ranstead.

He purchased of the late James Carroll, the land lying between the Baltimore and Ohio Railroad and Middle Branch of Patapsco River. A large portion of it is admirably situated for business purposes, having perfect facilities by Rail and Water for shipping.

Mr. Ranstead perceiving the prospective value and possibilities of this property as a point for shipping and manufactures, with great energy and expense, has begun to work a transformation there, which is already astonishing.

Where once were only bayous and marshes, are now Wharves, Docks, Squares and Streets. He has built a Bridge over the three pronged branch on the bed of Warner street, and has dredged channels to connect his docks and wharves with the dredged channel of the Middle Branch. This main channel was dredged by the city to a width of 200 feet and depth of 16 feet, and should the improvements in the Middle Branch as recommended in the Port Warden's annual report for 1875, and in the inaugural address of Mayor Latrobe, be carried out, this will constitute one of the most accessible and desirable parts of the harbor of Baltimore.

Bayard street now being graded from Washington Avenue to the head of a dock 100 feet wide and 600 feet long, affords direct communication with the North Western section of the city.

Already some most important enterprises have been established on the premises, such as Swindell Brother's Glass Factory, Biemiller's Ice Houses and others.

Mr. Ranstead's determination is to make this one of the great shipping points of the city, being near to its centre from east to west, and no place offers better inducements to shippers and manufacturers.

Many of the largest industries are situated around and contiguous to the property, which fact, is an indication of the importance of the locality.

THE STEAM MARBLE WORKS

Of Messrs. Hugh Sisson & Son, whose card is on page 242, is one of the important industries of Baltimore, and among the most extensive in the country. They merit special mention in this work as illustrative of our enterprise and advance in the mechanical arts.

Mr. Sisson has for more than twenty-five years been developing this great business, and has come to be recognized at the head of the industry in the United States. Early perceiving the superiority of our Baltimore County Marble for building and ornamental purposes, he began to utilize it, and established his Steam Marble Works, where he employs a large number of skilled workmen, and has prepared the marble work of some of the most important public buildings and business houses in the city, among which we briefly mention: the ornamental and interior work of the City Hall, Franklin Bank, Alexander Brown & Sons' New Banking House, the Counters and inside work of the Custom House, New Safe Deposit Building, Carrollton Hotel, and the Altars and Pulpits of many Churches, the Doorways, Caps and all the interior marble work of the State House of South Carolina, at Columbia, a portion of which was destroyed at the close of the late war.

Possessing every facility in handling and securing the Native and Foreign Marbles, and employing only the most efficient and skilled artisans, they turn out the most perfect and beautiful work.

There was added years ago, what may be termed the department of Art, and their Salesroom in the Rinehart Building, 140 west Baltimore Street, is indeed an Art Gallery. Here every floor is suitably arranged with specimens of exquisite workmanship, of their own and foreign manufacture, Mantels, Monuments, Vases, Tessalated Slabs, Statuary, &c., &c. They make a speciality of their importations which are of the finest sculpture out of Carrara, Sienna, Broccadillo and other Marbles. Among these may be specially mentioned, "Hope," "Remembrance," "the Angel of Peace," "the Sleeping Child," "the Virgin of the Sacred Heart," and "Grief." The Busts are numerous. The salesrooms are among the most attractive places in Baltimore, which should be a favorite resort for all lovers of art.

On January 1st, 1876, Mr. Sisson associated his son, Hugh Sisson, Jr., with him, and the firm is known as Hugh Sisson & Son.

We do not hesitate to claim for them a position in the front rank of this great and important branch of industry. They cannot be surpassed for the quality of work, or the reasonablness of prices, They successfully compete with the great works of New York, and supply largely northern demand. Their reputation has extended into those very sections once controlled by the great dealers of New York and Philadelphia. Mr Sisson is one of our business men, who by his untiring industry and liberal enterprise has contributed so greatly to give us our well earned title, *The Monumental City*, and with pleasure we make this special reference to his establishment

---

Messrs. POOLE & HUNT'S

Union Machine Shops at Woodberry, are among the most celebrated in the country and are specially prominent in one of the leading industries of Baltimore. Their business career began 25 years ago, and they have displayed an energy and attained a success equalled by few. The premises comprise twenty acres of ground on which are the Iron Foundry, Pattern and Machine Shops, Melting House, Brass Foundry, Storage Lofts, &c. The working force is about four hundred hands. Their facilities for making all kinds of machines from a chisel to a locomotive, are not surpassed in the country. Specimens of their work are seen in the iron columns supporting the Dome of the Capitol at Washington and Custom House in New Orleans. They have made several Metal Lighthouses. Their specialty is LEFFEL'S TURBINE WATER-WHEEL, more than seven thousand of which are now in use, it is the best Water-Wheel extant. The Union Works of Messrs. Poole & Hunt have contributed most largely to the growth and manufacturing importance of Baltimore.

[*See page* 207.]

IN THE OYSTER, FRUIT AND VEGETABLE

Interest of Baltimore, our enterprising citizen Mr. Louis McMurray, may be regarded as one of the pioneers. He has wrought up through a long series of years of steady, persistent enterprise an immense business, which is not only creditable to him, but of exceeding importance to our city and State. His mammoth Packing House in this city is situated on the Basin, where it has the most convenient arrangements for receiving and shipping at the lowest cost to the consumer.

He is the proprietor of the Mountain Sugar Corn Factory, established at Frederick City, one of the most complete in all its appointments, and the largest in the world, having a capacity for 75,000 cans per day. He cultivates in Frederick County about 1200 acres, capable of producing 1,500,000 cans of corn annually. Mr. McMurray has thoroughly systematized his business in the factory and field, and gives personal attention to every department, so that he safely guarantees every can of Oysters, Fruits and Vegetables which goes out from his establishment.

BARTLETT, ROBBINS & CO'S

Architectural Iron Works, to which we have at length referred on pages 214 and 215, have contributed as much as any industry to adorn our own city and give us a reputation abroad. We are pleased to record, that during the present unprecedented financial depression, they have erected many large and elegant Iron Buildings, among which we mention as especially deserving of praise, Hamilton Easter & Son's new addition to their grand marble store on Baltimore street, and their Iron structure on German street, Enoch Pratt's stores on the corner Charles and Baltimore streets, L. W. Gunther's warehouses on Gay near Baltimore, J. J. Thomsen's Drug House for Thomsen & Muth on German near Hanover, and the New American Building, one of the finest edifices in the United States. These buildings are all built on a grand scale and have introduced a new era in the architecture and structure of business houses.

This firm also built the stairway and the partition screen of the New Post Office in New York, the screen being 1000 feet long: also, put up the heating and ventilating apparatus of the General Post Office, the New State Department and New Jail in Washington city. Thus they have a national reputation, and we can safely say that for facilities in constructing and furnishing Iron Buildings, they are not surpassed if equalled in the United States.

JAPANNED WARE.

Until recently the manufacture of Japanned Ware was confined to the North, and our dealers were compelled to purchase abroad. In the year 1872, Messrs. MATTHAI, INGRAM & Co. introduced in our city this branch of manufacture, and by the employment of skilled workmen and extreme care to make goods of the first quality, have succeeded in establishing here one of the best factories in the United States, the only one south of Philadelphia, which now commands not only the local and Southern trade, but is supplying to a large extent the Northern and Eastern markets, where the older factories are located. This is due to the enterprise of the firm and the superiority of their goods. They are very careful in the selection of material and use the most tasteful designs in ornamentation.

It is a matter for congratulation that in this important branch of industry Baltimore has in so short a time attained a reputation over that of other cities, and we accord to the above mentioned House its meed of praise for contributing so large a share in producing it.

HOTELS.

THE CARROLLTON, R. B. Coleman & Co.

See Page 252.

R. B. COLEMAN. A. G. SMITH.

GUY'S MONUMENT HOUSE, S. C. Little.

See Pages 251 and 253.

Mansion House Hotel, I. Albertson.

See Page 253.

R. S. DODSON,
PROPRIETOR.

Fine resort for both Summer and Winter—within 6 miles of Atlantic Ocean—Fishing and Hunting unsurpassed.

Board, $2.50 and $3.00 per day, and liberal arrangements for Parties by the week or month.

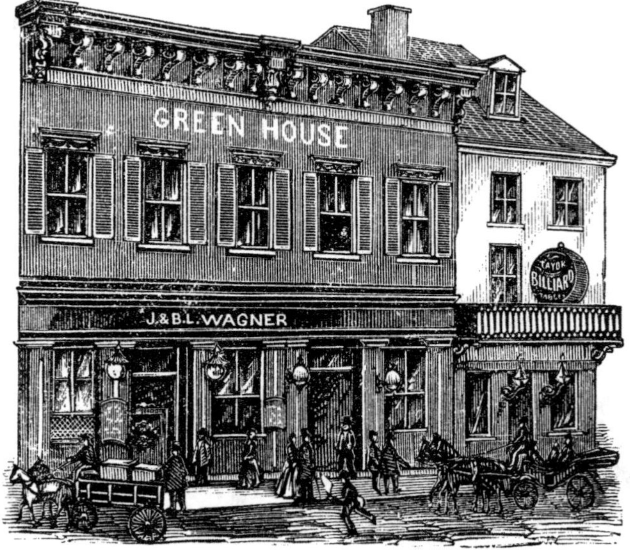

WAGNER'S
GREEN HOUSE RESTAURANT & BILLIARD PARLORS,
186, 188 and 190 WEST PRATT STREET.

The oldest and most extensive in Baltimore. Is conveniently located for business men, especially for travellers stopping for a few hours in the city.

The POPULAR RESORT of gentlemen from the counties, and visitors by steamboat or rail. The BAR is supplied with all kinds of LIQUORS, and the TABLE furnished with every delicacy

BIRDS, GAME, FISH, FRUITS AND VEGETABLES.

Prices Moderate, and Entire Satisfaction Given to Guests.

J. & B. L. WAGNER, Proprietors.

THE NORTHERN CENTRAL RAILWAY.

Having given on pages 291-300 an extended, illustrated description of this grand corporation, in which its importance and valuable relations to Baltimore were shown, we refer to it again in view of the new developments in its recent history, and the great enterprises that it has undertaken, which will contribute even more largely to our growth and importance as a commercial and manufacturing city.

The Extensive Workshops of the Company have been established here, which are among the most complete in the country, and employ hundreds of hands, and maintain a large number of families, that otherwise might be in idleness and destitution.

The Company has erected an elegant building on the corner of Calvert and Centre streets, for the accommodation of its offices, which in point of style and proportion, is one of the handsomest in our city, built by the enterprising firm of Messrs. S. H. & J. F. Adams.

Large purchases of Real Estate have been made on Monument, Madison, North and Buren Streets, and on the Falls, which are being improved with Depots and Tracks; thus the Company is adding largely to the taxable basis of the city. These purchases and improvements will amount to about $700.000. This is independent of its improvements at Canton, the value and results of which, to the city, cannot be estimated. These consist of extensive Grain Elevators, Freight Sheds, Wharves, Warehouses, Docks, Trestle Piers for Coal, and every possible facility for shipment and transfer of all kinds of freight. There will also be Special Warehouses to be used exclusively for Coffee, Sugar and Flour.

By the arrangements made with the Western Maryland Railroad, the Company secures the great and growing traffic of that road, especially in Cumberland and other soft coals, and in connection with the Union Railroad through the Union Tunnel, gives us at Canton, terminal facilities to which nothing in the other Atlantic Cities can compare.

The citizens of Baltimore and Maryland cannot too highly esteem this Road, which sustains such relations to their City and State, and closely connects them with the greatest and richest sections of the country, and has added incalculably to their solid wealth and commercial prominence. The success of this road means the welfare of Baltimore The prosperity of the one is identical with that of the other.

At the last election the following officers were chosen, who constitute its present efficient administration:

President, THOMAS A. SCOTT; Vice President, A. J. CASSATT; Secretary, ROBERT S. HOLLINS; Treasurer, JOHN S. LEIB, Auditor, JOHN CROWE; General Counsel, WAYNE MCVEAGH; General Manager, FRANK THOMSON.

THE BALTIMORE AND POTOMAC RAILROAD

Forms with the Northern Central Railway a main trunk line between the South and the North West and North. Under the efficient management of its administration great improvements have been made, and arrangements perfected, whereby it is a most desirable route of travel. The NEW SIXTH STREET DEPOT in Washington City, (built by S. H. & J. F. Adams, of our city, on whom it reflects great credit,) is an evidence of the prosperity and popularity of the Road, and of the purpose of its managers to consider the comfort and convenience of the travelling public. It is built of pressed brick and free stone, and is a very handsome specimen of the Renaissance in architecture, possessing some novel and pleasing features, and is one of the ornaments of Washington. The interior arrangements are complete, comprising large sitting rooms for ladies and gentlemen, a spacious and pleasant restaurant and dining rooms. The Ladies' Parlor is handsomely furnished and conveniently situated, both to the street and cars. The main saloon is very large and airy, with perfect ventilation, being, as it were, an inside court with handsome galleries on each floor, upon which the offices and rooms of the Company open.

The entrance to the cars and platforms are protected from the weather, and the police regulations are most perfect, so that this may be considered as to the building itself and all of its appointments and management, a Model Depot.

Its nearness to all of the principal hotels, public buildings and lines of city railways, makes it most convenient and desirable, and proves the wisdom and foresight which located it there.

CANTON COMPANY.

The account given on pages 281–285 of Canton is most authentic and complete, and forcibly presents the immense importance which it and its allied interests sustain to Baltimore.

The CANTON COMPANY, who originated this great enterprise, and during long years of undaunted energy and patient waiting, developed it to its present proportions, deserves the gratitude and praise of all Baltimoreans who desire the advancement of their city. Early prospecting the growth and possibilities of Baltimore as a manufacturing and commercial city, the company selected that section so admirably adapted to manufactures and shipping; and by affording the greatest facilities, encouraging enterprise, and liberally providing for the accommodation of the industrial class, it has, in the face of gigantic competition at home and elsewhere, constituted Canton one of the greatest business localities in the United States. We do not propose traversing the same ground as in our former article, but only to make prominent mention of this company as suggested to our own mind by the last annual report of the President and Directors.

As a report of operations during a year of unprecedented commercial depression, it must be very gratifying and assuring to the stockholders. There is scarcely a financial corporation in the country which has not materially suffered from the general distress, either in the falling off of demand or shrinkage of values; especially has this been the case with real estate corporations and investments, and railway interests. Yet, the prosperity of the Canton Company has been maintained, though its capital consists most largely in real estate. It has always pursued the most judicious course, never having established prices that were either speculative or excessive. The policy has ever been to sell at prices which would encourage investment, either for homes or business purposes, and yet be fairly remunerative to the company. Thus proceeding only on a real and legitimate basis in its operations, its landed estate has not been subject to fluctuations which obtain in ordinary real estate investments; and there has been even during these untoward times no decline in prices. Indeed on account of increased railroad and terminal facilities much of the property has appreciated in value. A number of leases has been effected for manufacturing purposes, which will greatly add to the population as well as the capital employed.

We gather from the report that by the sale of certain ground rents to the Trustees of the Union Railroad Company, a considerable portion of the bonded debt has been redeemed and cancelled. The income of the company was increased over that of the previous year and the expenses reduced over $13,000.00.

The receipts for the year ending May 31, 1876, are in excess of those of any year since 1870, while the expenses have been materially diminished, leaving a large cash balance.

For the security of the debt, the Company has its large landed estate consisting of 18,000 building lots and 900 acres of farm and wood land, and over three miles of water front on the deep water of the harbor, and other valuable securities, such as the Union Railroad, &c., of nearly $3,500,000.

The proposed extension of Patterson Park eastward, in view of which the Directors have made the liberal offer of 9¼ acres, will greatly enhance the value of the lots in that portion of the property.

The improvements begun by the Northern Central Railway Company, in the way of wharves, warehouses, elevators and other shipping and terminal facilities, will greatly increase the receipts of grain and other commodities from this country and from Europe.

This brief survey of the condition and prospects of the company must convince all, of its strength and importance, and the substantial character of its property and stock. With its past record of able and judicious management, and the character and standing of its present Officers and Board, it needs nothing more to commend it to capital seeking investment, either in real estate or industrial enterprises.

Officers—CHAS. J. BAKER, President; GEO. S. BROWN, Vice President; W. W. JANNEY, Secretary and Treasurer.

Directors—CHAS. J. BAKER, GEO. S. BROWN, WM. G. HARRISON, CHAS. WEBER, S. SPRIGG BELT, of Baltimore; ABM. B. BAYLIS, WM. MERTENS, JAS. B. COLGATE, GEO. F. STONE, of New York City.

See Pages 161, 162 and 165.

See page 265.

THE HOUSE OF ROBERT LAWSON & CO.

No. 277 W. Baltimore street, (see page 167,) is one of those characteristic establishments which have given Baltimore prominence among the great manufacturing cities of America. The senior Mr. Robert Lawson through a period of more than thirty years, by indomitable enterprise, has, against the powerful competition of northern manufacturers, built up his house which is now one of the first in the trade.

They manufacture Saddles, Harness, Trunks, and import and sell Saddlery Hardware, Whips, Horse-blankets and all goods pertaining to their department. They have three establishments in the city—the Factory No. 16 McClellan's Alley, Warehouse 16 S. Sharp Street, and the Sales and Warerooms 277 W. Baltimore street.

The Factory is the largest and most complete South of New York. It is supplied with the most improved machinery and employs a large number of skilled workmen.

The cellar and first two floors are devoted to the manufacture of Trunks of every description, the best material being employed, and in style and durability they cannot be surpassed by those of any factory North. The upper stories comprise the Harness and Saddlery Factory—this department has attained a wide reputation. The very best of leather is used and the finish of the work is of the highest order. The display of stock in their Warerooms is very attractive.

The House may well be congratulated on its success and untarnished reputation, and we take pride in citing it as one of the signal instances of the result of untiring industry and honorable dealing.

ESTABLISHED 1857.

THOMAS SHANKS,

PRACTICAL MACHINIST,

DEALER IN

New and Second Hand Machines, Iron and Wood,

AND

BOILERS and ENGINES, PRINTING PRESSES, SEWING MACHINES, &c.

If you have any Machines for Sale, send me a list with lowest price.

N. B.—No Charge for Storage, except the goods are removed.

SHANKS'S BUILDING, S. W. COR. SHARP & LOMBARD STS.,

Price, 4 Horse Power, $330, to 15 Horse Power, $850. BALTO.

FRANCIS ALBERT, (Late of Penniman & Bro.)

FREDERICK ALBERT. (Late with Schwerdtman & Co.)

ALBERT BROTHERS,

IMPORTERS AND DEALERS IN

Foreign and Domestic Hardware,

4 N. HOWARD STREET,

BALTIMORE.

SPECIAL ATTENTION GIVEN TO ORDERS.

See page 155.

See page 170.

JOSHUA REGESTER & SONS.

See page 204.

BURNS & SLOAN, LUMBER DEALERS,

132 LIGHT STREET WHARF.

See pages 188 and 246.

ST. PETER'S P. E. CHURCH,

At the corner of Druid Hill Avenue and Lanvale Street,

Is one of the most beautiful church edifices in the city. It was built in 1871, of white marble in the Norman Gothic style, surmounted by a graceful spire and castellated tower. The original structure, on the lot at the corner of Sharp and German streets, was built in 1802, which Mr. Andrew B. McCreery, formerly of this city, and now of Paris, France, purchased and where he has erected, at great cost, an iron fire-proof building, called the "McCreery Building," which is one of the handsomest and most massive business edifices in the city and occupied by some of our leading importing and commission merchants, who have made it the centre of a very large trade.

The Church has enjoyed the ministry of eminent Rectors, three of whom were elevated to the Episcopate—Bishops Henshaw, Atkinson and Cummins. The congregation has always been largely composed of influential and valuable citizens, and among the present number we mention one of our most honored merchants, Wm. Woodward, Esq., who has been superintendent of the Sunday School for over fifty years. Under the present Rector, Rev. Julius E. Grammer, D. D., the congregation has greatly enlarged and extended the sphere of its operations.

FRIENDS' MEETING HOUSE AND SCHOOL HOUSE,
(ORTHODOX,)
N. E. Corner Eutaw and Monument Streets.

THE KELSO HOME,

For Orphan Children of the M. E. Church.

On page 51 we briefly alluded to the munificent appropriation of our venerable citizen Mr. Thomas Kelso for an Orphan Home. Under his own supervision it is now in successful operation. He has in charge of it a matron who is admirably fitted for the position.

The children are all dressed differently, so that the sombre appearance of an Orphan Asylum is absent from this. They receive their education by special arrangement with the Public Schools, and at the Colvin Institute of which Mr. Kelso is president, and which he largely sustains. Thus this institution is in every possible aspect a *home* and the children are as happy in it, as orphaned childhood can be.

Mr. Kelso has himself invested the fund in ground rents, and it now has a revenue ample for all its needs, and secure against those contingencies which attach to *post mortem* benevolence. In this he has shown his wisdom, and shall receive the greater reward.

"It is more blessed to give than to receive."

THE WESTERN AND SOUTHWESTERN SUBURBS.

Notwithstanding the fact that the region of country lying immediately west and southwest of Baltimore has never been so thickly settled as the suburbs in the northwestern and northern direction, its peculiar beauty of scenery and superior natural advantages have not by any means escaped attention. Indeed, it is certain that but for the interposition of "Gwynn's Falls," the territory to which we refer would, long ago, have been dotted with villas and the streets of the city would have extended that way a mile or two beyond their present limits. The picturesque appearance of the valley through which the stream referred to flows, has always made it a favorite resort of those who sought to ride or drive from the city through the most attractive district and purest atmosphere. The whole area, from the line of the falls as far back as the high and rolling lands in Howard county, which drain to the Patapsco river, has always been regarded as one of the healthiest and most productive portions of the State, and was very early settled by wealthy and refined people. In more recent years, as Baltimore has grown and the demand for suburban residences correspondingly increased, efforts have, from time to time, been made to overcome the obstacles which seemed to prevent direct and rapid communication with this region. The Frederick Road, which was once the great highway of the famous wagon trade with the West, has become entirely inadequate to the accommodation of the daily local travel to and from the city in that direction. While along its borders, as far as the village of Catonsville, a thrifty and industrious population has rapidly accumulated and a line of horse railway is in active and successful operation, still, the development of the country more remote from it, on both sides, has rendered the opening of new avenues and the construction of new bridges indispensably necessary. A very large number of elegant and comfortable places border on the Frederick Road; some of which we enumerate: Wm. Wilkens & Co., page 184; Charles Shipley, Mary's Choice; Dutchess of Leeds' estate; Mount Olivet, (see article;) McTavish estate; Loudon Park Cemetery; C. Irving Ditty; Lewis Seldner; Dr. Schwartz; G. A. Schlens; H. H. Graue, Airy Hill; Charles J. Baker, Athol; William Baker, Tremont; Alexander Rieman, Aqua Vista; Hermon Simon; John Q. Hewlett's estate; Dr. H. P. C. Wilson, Idle High; John Cummings; John Stellman, Markland; Benjamin Whiteley, Herndon; Asa Needham's estate, Montrose; Henry James, Tower Hill; Talbot J. Taylor, Cloud Cap; John B. Phillips; D. C. Howell; Hon. William J. Albert, Belmont; H. K. Hoffman, Winston; Thomas M. Johnson; John Gill; Alexander Gould; William W. Taylor, Craigie-Burn; T. L. Tinsley, Paradise; Dunmore; Hon. John Wethered; Dr. James Armitage; Robert Lawson, Mount Herbert; Dr. Charles G. W. Magill, Eureka; St. Timothy's; Henry J. Farber; James A. Gary, The Summit; E. Livezey, Elton Park; Charles Keidel; Rev. Dr. Ebeling, Overlea Home School; Three Flour Mills, James E. Tyson, Samuel Hazlehurst, Frederic Tyson, owners.

WILKENS AVENUE, which is to run nearly parallel with the Frederick Road to the south of it, was projected some years ago and is now in a fair way of completion. Notwithstanding the indomitable energy and public spirit of the wealthy gentleman after whom it was named and of other citizens, who were equally interested in the enterprise, the construction of this avenue has been long delayed by litigation now happily ended. The questions at issue have been settled, and under the terms of a special act of the last Legislature, the work is being rapidly pushed forward. This road, which is of excellent width and regular and easy grades, will extend from the city limits for a distance of about six miles to intersect the old "Rolling Road" leading from the Relay House, on the Baltimore and Ohio Railroad, to Catonsville. It will open up a most beautiful country and bring many splendid estates into direct communication with the city. Several of the most important public institutions will be reached in this way, and among them we may mention particularly the St. Mary's Industrial School, the Protestant Manual Labor School, St. Agnes' Hospital, and the Maryland Insane Asylum. The residences and country seats of many prominent and wealthy persons are also located on the line of this avenue—William Wilkens & Co., page 184; George F. Webb, page 136, Millington Mill; Clairmont Company; J. B. Brinkley; Mrs. Caldwell; Joseph Judik; A. Seemuller's estate, Linden; Robert Fowler's estate, Harvest Home; John Fowler; Robert W. Rasin, Athol Grasslands; G. S. Watts, Beverly; David Carson, Homewood; Prof. N. R. Smith; Thomas C. Yearly; Capt. E. K. Cooper; Spring Grove Asylum, see page 48; Mrs. Lurman, Farmlands; C. Morton Stewart, Bellevue, see page 228; Dr. J. P. Thom, Manor Vale; John Glenn's estate; George Richstine, Foxhall. Directly at the city limits an extensive area of ground belonging to Mr. William Wilkens is being built upon and improved with great taste.

North of the Frederick Road and south of the Franklin turnpike, there is also being constructed another avenue, to be called "EDMONDSON AVENUE." This work is being done under the provisions of the street law for Baltimore county—George H. Carman, Lewis Lehman and John Cole, commissioners; William H. Shipley, engineer—the commissioners having laid it out and made the assessments for benefits and damages, upon the petition of property owners along the line. This new avenue is one hundred feet wide and of uniform easy grade, extending from the city limits a distance of two and a half miles to a point where it will intersect the old Frederick road, and from which there is already direct communication with Catonsville. This work will develope a remarkably beautiful country hitherto almost cut off from the city by the obstacles to which we have before alluded. The range of hills over which the road will pass, known as "Hunting Ridge," has advantages of landscape and water view not excelled anywhere in the State. From almost all the building sites in the neighborhood, as from every portion of this western section, the view extends over the city and all its environs and across the Chesapeake Bay to its Eastern Shore. From the upper rooms of the houses, the State House steeple at Annapolis, distant forty miles, can plainly be seen. This avenue, after passing on the eastern side of the falls, through the extensive property of Mr. A. S. Abell and Mr. Charles Shipley, and what was part of the old almshouse farm, enters on the western side of the stream and passes through the extensive estates of the late Captain Richard B. Fitzgerald, William Heald, Hugh Gelston, and Hon. Reverdy Johnson, Lindhurst. On or near its line are the Cathedral Cemetery, and the beautiful country seats, residences and property of Charles M. Heald, Allendale; James A. Wilson, Bonnie Brae; John Swan, Hunting Ridge; Thomas Winans; William F. Frick; P. S. Chappell's estate; William Wilkens, Villa Wilkens; Arthur H. Mann, Laurel Hill; George F. Page; Mt. De Sales; S. S. Boggs, Prospect Hill; George R. Granger, Oak Lawn; Ross Campbell's estate; Mr. Crosby's estate; George J. Appold, Glenwild, three hundred and twenty acres, see page 163; Miss Gibson, Ingleside Seminary; A. W. Stehman. Near the eastern section of the avenue are situated the properties of John Hurst, Poplar Grove; Thomas L. Berry's estate, Woodland Grove; Gen. John S. Berry, Dukeland; Cary McClelland; E. A. Tinker; Hiram Kaufman; Rev. Franklin Wilson; Francis White; James Broumel; Wm. S. Rayner; Thomas G. Scharf; Hebrew Orphan Asylum. The completion of this avenue, which will certainly be accomplished during the present season, will produce a wonderful change in all this country. In a few years it will doubtless be covered with cottages and intersected with new roads, for its elevated position and delightful atmosphere cannot fail to commend it, at once, to all who are seeking suburban locations. The scenery along this road, and particularly the wild beauty of the banks of Gwynn's Falls, will always make it a popular thoroughfare. The Bridge now being constructed over the falls, four hundred and fifty feet in length, will be a very fine work and reflect great credit upon our skillful and enterprising citizen, Wendell Bollman, (see page 218.) The substantial masonry was done by Haffer & Pilert. The entire improvement cost over $1[illegible],000. The general direction and supervision of the whole improvement have been chiefly in the hands of George H. Carman, one of the commissioners. While his faithful discharge of duty has been duly appreciated, his display of good taste and judgment has been also recognized.

The country is being intersected with avenues running north and south, chief of which are ATHOL and BEECHFIELD. The former has been constructed at great expense by Charles J. Baker and C. Irving Ditty; beginning on the Frederick turnpike and running to the old Frederick road, west of Loudon Park Cemetery, and which has been extended by James A. Wilson through his property, Bonnie Brae, to Edmondson Avenue, near the late Reverdy Johnson's estate. This avenue binds on Athol, the beautiful property of Charles J. Baker, from which it derives its name. A large portion of this has been laid off and handsomely enclosed in building lots and villa sites, that for healthfulness and beauty of situation are unsurpassed. It also binds on Irvington, the handsome improvement of C. Irving Ditty, a group of graceful cottages, which are unusually attractive as suburban residences.

Athol Avenue connects with Beechfield, a little to the west on the turnpike, and by it forms a direct communication with Wilkens Avenue. Thus a continuous connection is made between Edmondson and Wilkens Avenues, and over the choicest portion of this western section.

Too much praise cannot be accorded to the public spirit and liberal enterprise of the gentlemen who are thus developing one of the most charming and attractive sections of Baltimore county.

MOUNT OLIVET CEMETERY.

On the Frederick road, two and a half miles from the city, is located Mount Olivet Cemetery, a noted burial place for the ministers of the M. E. Church. The idea of such a Cemetery originated with the late Rev. George C. M. Roberts, M. D., D. D., founder of the Methodist Historical Society and an eminent local preacher, who prevailed with the Board of Trustees "of the M. E. City Church in the city and precincts of Baltimore," to purchase a ground for the above purpose. It includes thirty-three acres, and commands a fine view of the Patapsco river to its entrance into the Chesapeake bay. Some of the most illustrious men, both of the clergy and laity of this church, sleep here. What is unusual, and a feature of special interest, a certain part of the cemetery is appropriated for the itinerant ministers who may not have provided a burial place here or elsewhere. In this *preachers' lot*, as it is called, repose the remains of many of the great men of the church whose devotion to Christ and zeal for His cause make up the most interesting portion of the History of Methodism in the United States. Four of the Bishops are buried in this lot, all of whom were national men, for the system of Methodist Episcopacy, being a general superintendency, extends the supervision of these officers of the church over every part of our great country; it especially deserves to be mentioned that the Father of American Methodism, Bishop Asbury, is buried here. For many years his remains rested under the pulpit of one of the city churches, but soon after the opening of the cemetery, they were removed to the preachers' lot. On either side of him lie the remains of Bishops George and Emory. Within the same enclosure Bishop Waugh is buried. A handsome monument has been erected by the Trustees, who hold the ground; on each of the four sides of which is inscribed a fitting epitaph, in honor of these distinguished men. For many years Bishop Waugh's home was Baltimore, where he exerted a wide-reaching influence, and was universally respected. Under his ministry, long before he was called to the duties of the Episcopal office, the father of the author of this work, Mr. Samuel Howard, joined himself to the Methodist Episcopal Church, of which he continued an honored member for sixty-five years; he died April 27, 1876, at his residence, Clifton Farm, Muskingum County, near Zanesville, O., in his 92nd year. East and West of the Alleghany Mountains, he was well known and distinguished for the voluntary and powerful exhortations he would frequently deliver at the close of the sermon by the minister. As his life was a beautiful example of piety, his death was a scene of holy triumph.

To this preachers' lot have been brought the remains of Robert Strawbridge, who, it is believed, was the first Methodist preacher that organized a society in America. Next to his, is the grave of Jesse Lee, and near by lies the Saint of "Pilgrim's Rest," Henry Smith. Others of the fathers, together with many of their brilliant sons, might be added to the list if we had the space to sparefor such a record. The Local Preachers' Association of Baltimore have purchased a portion for the interment of their members, and here lie the remains of faithful men who have done a work whose results may not be measured by time.

It is very natural that this Cemetery should possess a special interest to the clergy of the M. E. Church. During the Session of the Centennial General Conference held in this city in May last, the delegation of the New England Conference learning that Jesse Lee, who planted Methodism in New England, was buried there, visited his grave, and within a few weeks afterward a beautiful monument arrived from Boston—which, with appropriate ceremonies, was unveiled July 11th, 1876—in commemoration of the Eighty-sixth Anniversary of the first sermon preached by this christian hero from Virginia under the famous old Elm Tree on Boston Common. To Methodists, from all parts of the country, who visit Baltimore, there will be much to interest them at Mount Olivet.

LOUDON PARK CEMETERY.

One of the distinctive and most attractive features of this western section is Loudon Park Cemetery. It is situated about three miles from the city, on an elevated and undulating plateau between the Frederick Road and Wilkens Avenue; having a handsome and spacious entrance on the former, built in the Roman style of architecture. A massive gateway, designed for an opening to Wilkens Avenue, which affords a more beautiful approach to the cemetery, will, when completed, constitute the main entrance.

Loudon Park was formerly a private residence and one of the most elegant estates on the Frederick Road, containing 110 acres, whose surpassing beauty and admirable adaptation to its present use were readily appreciated by the incorporators of the cemetery, and soon after its purchase the Directors of the Company, who were gentlemen of taste and energy, put into execution those plans and improvements which have made it one of the loveliest of our "Cities of the Dead."

The Cemetery was incorporated on the 22nd of February, 1853, and consecrated July 14th of the same year with appropriate and imposing ceremonies.

Owing to the felt necessity for a new burying place for our rapidly growing city, and the superior situation and attractions of Loudon Park, it soon commanded general attention and favor; and was selected by many citizens, churches and corporate institutions as the resting place for their dead.

Many of the remains from the old cemeteries that have given way before the march of improvement, are deposited here, and which, owing to the situation and franchises of the cemetery, will in all probability lie undisturbed until the resurrection.

Here "rest in peace" the remains of the departed of old St. Peter's, Whatcoat and Mount Zion Grave Yards; here as the chosen cemetery of many present congregations, rest their dead; and here the soldiers of the federal and confederate armies who fell in deadly combat, "sleep their last sleep" beneath the same sod, and within the same enclosure, two separate portions having been consecrated as their burial place. Their graves are carefully watched and tended, and annually decorated with flowers and a tribute paid to their memory and their devotion to the cause in which they fell.

The place has been admirably chosen—containing within itself every feature and advantage which fit it for a cemetery; the variety of its surface beauty giving unlimited scope to landscape adornment; its perfect drainage; its magnificient old forest trees, that bestow a solemn grandeur which art could not impart. Its situation is beautiful beyond description. From its elevation, the eye ranges a country which for quiet beauty is not excelled anywhere; diversified with hills and valleys in the highest state of cultivation, and adorned with beautiful villas and cottages.

It commands the most extensive view of the Chesapeake bay whose marvellous waters, like an immense mirror reflect the golden glory of the sun, and gild the scene o'er which the funereal associations of Loudon Park shed a sadness, to many a gloom.

To the native beauty, the skilled hands of the landscape gardener and the artisan, have added greatly. The avenues and terraces; the grouping of evergreens and shrubbery; the monuments and curbings of the lots underneath towering trees—remnants of a forest long since passed away—make it unique and unusually attractive.

Among the multitude of elegant and artistic monuments, we mention only the grand Mausoleum erected at the cost of $15,000, a work unsurpassed in any cemetery we have seen.

The monument to the late Capt. Rich'd B. Fitzgerald of the distinguished firm of Fitzgerald, Booth & Co. It consists of a vault with statues and vases, costing $16,000. The statues represent respectively the Saviour and the angel Gabriel; on the vases are carved figures of the three Marys at the tomb, and Mary Magdalene meeting Jesus on the morn of the resurrection. It is an exquisite work of art, wrought by Rhinehart, in Rome, 1865.

The Officers and Directors by whom this cemetery has become so enriched and beautified deserve commendation for so judicious a selection, and for their liberal enterprise which has brought it to its present attitude among the great cemeteries of this country.

The Board of Officers and Directors consist of

HENRY A. THOMPSON, President; W. F. PRIMROSE, Secretary and Treasurer.

Directors—HENRY A. THOMPSON, WM. F. BURNS, JOHN A. WHITRIDGE, JOHN Q. GINNODO, JACOB H. TAYLOR, W. F. PRIMROSE.

THE MARYLAND LIFE INSURANCE COMPANY,

Peculiarly a Baltimore institution, shows a gratifying growth, and has become thoroughly established in public confidence. Its ratio of profits to expenses is greater than that of any other first-class company in America of the same age. Identified as it is with us, and having its funds invested largely in our city and State, it is incumbent on our citizens and to their interest to sustain it by their patronage. See page 429.

SOME OF THE OLD BUSINESS HOUSES OF BALTIMORE.

In the quick haste and absorbing pursuit after prosperity, communities too soon forget those who have preceded them. The question is natural and often asked, what have we to do with the old men? they belong to a past age. Yet they had a great deal to do with the present; they laid the foundations of the present prosperity and proportions of our city. They did a work, exerted influences, started movements, developed resources, pointed out possibilities, on which their successors have erected a grand city and commonwealth.

There are those living who recall the old *Signs*, that were not only sign-boards, but truly Signs of men and merchants who are worthy to live in memory, and in the commercial history of Baltimore.

It is impossible for us to name all of these; those shipping, commission and jobbing houses that made Baltimore renowned on the seas, and known throughout the country for commercial enterprise. We only recall a few of the Grocery and Commission firms, as their houses were the headquarters for all the different departments of the trade, and are obliged for want of space to omit many others worthy of mention.

Among the eminent firms were Bohn & Slingluff, who commenced in 1798. The house was continued through a number of firms successively and successfully, closing with C. D. Slingluff & Sons, 1870. Mr. Bohn was for many years President of the Commercial and Farmers Bank. Mr. Slingluff removed in 1814 to Frederick, now Carroll County, and for a long period was President of the Bank of Westminster. Jesse Slingluff, Esq., his son is now and has been for twenty-four years President of the Commercial and Farmers National Bank. Among his numerous grandsons are John A. and T. Edward Hambleton, of the house of John A. Hambleton & Co., who transact a successful banking business as seen on page 266 of this book.

Their cotemporaries were Elder & Taylor, who commenced in 1810 and continued until 1828, then dissolved and formed Basil S. Elder (whose fifth son is now the R. C. Bishop, of Natchez, Miss.) & Son and Joseph Taylor & Son, maintaining the highest reputation throughout. Talbot Jones & Co., whose successors, at their old stand, are Wilson, Burns & Co., one of the most prominent and successful houses of Baltimore, (page 119;) McDonald & Ridgeley; Erskine & Eichelberger; Dinsmore & Kyle; Andrew Gregg & Co.; Robert Garrett, the founder of Robert Garrett & Sons; Wm. W. Taylor & Co. Mr. Taylor was for a long period President of the Commercial and Farmers' Bank, and was the grandfather of the present esteemed President of the National Union Bank of Maryland, (page 264); Young & Pochon; Gerard T. Hopkins & Co.; Hopkins Bros. & Co., founded by Johns Hopkins; Hopkins & Moore; Abner Webb, who began in 1809; having come hither from Savannah, Georgia, conducted a successful business for over forty years, and is now the oldest surviving merchant of Baltimore, being in his 94th year; he has enjoyed uninterruptedly the esteem and confidence of the community, is blessed in his old age with the devotion of a large family circle, and has the gratification of seeing his sons prosperously and honorably established in business. These were some of the heavy grocery firms, who sold to the towns and country of the South and West.

The Groceries were securely packed and loaded, together with the dry goods, hardware and the assortment usually bought for country stores, into wagons of six horse teams, the freights varying of course according to the distance. To the Ohio river, the rates ranged from 1½ to 2½ cents per lb. to Pittsburg, and 25 cents per 100 more to Wheeling; and to distant points in Ohio and Tennessee from 3½ to 4½ and 5 cents per lb.; the teams generally hauling 4 to 5,000 lbs.

Besides the grocery business Elder & Taylor and their succeeding firms were large forwarders of dry goods and other wares bought in Philadelphia, New York and Boston, and brought here by sailing vessels from those points, hauled up town where they were weighed by 56 lb. weights, (before the days of platform scales and steelyards,) and loaded into wagons. Besides dry goods, shoes, hats and bonnets, and especially Yankee clocks, made up a large portion of their assorted cargoes.

The produce of the West composed the return cargoes of these wagons; tobacco, ginseng, snakeroot, butter, lard, beans, beeswax, feathers, hemp, linen, wool, &c., and they were brought in at a rate of freight generally one-third and sometimes one-half less than the outward rates.

The excellent turnpike to Cumberland, built mainly by our Banks, at an expense of nearly $500,000, which was extended by the National Government to Wheeling, and that to Westminster, Bedford and Pittsburg, aided largely by our *merchants*, presented great inducements to trade with Baltimore.

The time occupied by these teams to Wheeling, was 16 to 18 days and to Pittsburg 14 to 16 days—so that the merchants of the present day may appreciate the change that has come over the face of things within the last forty-five years. The freight on a pound of coffee then to Columbus, O., was considered reasonable at four cents, with three weeks for delivery, whereas, to-day the average rate is ¼ cent per lb. to Cincinnati and Chicago in about three days for delivery. In 1832 and 1833, when the Baltimore and Ohio Railroad was completed as far as Frederick, the goods generally were sent that far by rail and then hauled in the wagons, and a few years later this transfer took place at Cumberland.

SAMUEL JONES, JR.

Good and useful men are a city's greatest treasure, they are her most fertile resources whence she must derive her material and moral wealth. Among the many great and good men who have been identified with the commercial history of Baltimore, Samuel Jones, Jr. deserves honorable mention. Justice to his useful career among us, and the gratification of his cotemporaries in the trade, induce us to record in our work a tribute to his memory, as a representative Baltimore merchant.

He was the junior member of the old and distinguished firm of Talbot Jones & Co., established by Talbot Jones, who emigrated here from Ireland during the rebellion in 1796-98, and became one of our most important merchants and estimable citizens, was one of the originators and Directors of the Commercial and Farmers' Bank, the Water Works, B & Ohio Railroad and other valuable corporations. His son, the subject of our sketch, became early associated in the house, and evinced those qualities of moral and commercial character for which he was universally respected.

Peculiarly gifted in mental power, which he trained and cultivated to a degree that constituted him an authority among his cotemporaries and enabled him to guide opinion upon subjects of great importance in civil and commercial matters; a correct reasoner, a fluent speaker, an eloquent writer and judicious counsellor, he became necessarily prominent in every relation which he sustained to the community.

In the several relations of life—he was in business indefatigable, in society invariably courteous and kind, in the church zealous and consistent, in his official position dignified and scrupulously polite.

He came upon the stage of action at an important era in the history of Baltimore. It was the period of the inception and rise of many institutions and movements which have determined largely the commercial strength of the city.

From the confidence reposed in his judgment and ability, he was honored with prominent positions. He was a Director of the Commercial and Farmers' Bank, Savings Bank of Baltimore, Baltimore and Ohio Railroad, Merchants' Bank and other Corporations.

He was the first President of the Western Bank of Baltimore, and acting President of the Baltimore and Ohio Railroad during the absence of the Hon. Lewis McLane, the then President, to Europe on a special mission for the United States Government.

He was a member of the City Council; State Senator and in connection with Judge Buchanan of Washington County and General Emory of Eastern Shore, was appointed by the General Assembly to negotiate the $8,000,000 loan in Europe. Though declining the appointment, his jealous regard for the credit of the city and state showed itself in the zeal with which he, together with Osmond C. Tiffany, Thos. W. Hall and other valuable citizens pursued the matter, resulting in the appointment of George Peabody, then a Dry Goods Merchant, residing in London as the representative of the Baltimore house of Peabody, Riggs & Co. The effect of this upon the subsequent career of Mr. Peabody and the commercial credit and future of Baltimore no one could then forsee; but at this day, the *agency* of Mr. Jones *appears* in that event which made the honor of Maryland and Baltimore conspicuous, and humanly speaking greatly influenced the remarkable career of the noble philanthropist.

Mr. Jones was deeply devoted to the interests of Baltimore. The spirit of his enterprise was not satisfied with individual results; it took a broader scope and meditated the welfare of his fellow citizens. It was his ambition to see Baltimore in the advance of the commercial cities of America. Thus he writes on the 8th of January, 1874, from New Orleans, to the author of this book:

"I rejoice with you in the continued and constantly increasing prosperity of Baltimore; it is only what the projectors of the Baltimore and Ohio Railroad anticipated for it upon the completion of the Road," &c.

After the reverses of the house of Talbot Jones & Co., feeling keenly the force of that unrighteous disposition which exists in all communities to animadvert upon those who suffer financial reverse, he sought another home, and emigrated to New Orleans, contrary to the expressed wishes of many of our most influential citizens.

It was not long before the citizens of New Orleans discovered that they had received a valuable accession in him. He went there, not as some have said, "to begin a new life," but to start afresh, a business career, in the exercise of the same noble qualities and virtues which characterized his life here; and to the end, *that life* was sending out its same pure streams, only *more abundant* and refreshing, enriching all that came within its boundaries.

After merchandising for several years, he became the Treasurer and Manager of the New Orleans Savings Institution, which position he held over eighteen years, to the day of his decease.

The universal regard for him, appears from the extracts we make from the resolutions of the Board of Trustees and the press of the city.

IN MEMORIAM.

Be it Resolved, That in the death of Samuel Jones, Jr., our late efficient and worthy Treasurer, this Institution has lost a faithful and competent officer and friend; one who has filled the office of Secretary and Treasurer for more than eighteen successive years, and during that time, he has always enjoyed the fullest and unstinted confidence of the Board of Trustees.

He was a man of singular purity of character, of rare intelligence, of great and winning modesty. Never was there an office of trust held with a fuller, clearer sense of duty, and never was that duty discharged with firmer rectitude, with a deeper religious obligation to God and man. We shall long miss him at his daily toil, we shall miss his peculiar smile, his gentle manners, his quick pleasing address. We would praise him for his general information, his uniform civility, his peculiar trust in man, were it not for the more praiseworthy traits of his character in his desire to fill the largest measure of duty, his aims to live that no shadow of wrong should rest upon his life. We tender to his family the assurance of our sincere sympathy, mingle our sorrows with theirs; and that we may be aided in cherishing his memory and connecting it with this institution, we recommend that the President obtain a copy of the best portrait of him that may be procured, and hang it on the walls of the bank.

W. N. MERCER,
JHO. ALLEN CLARK,
THOS. A. ADAMS,
Committee.

New Orleans Daily Picayune, April 24th, 1874.

A few days ago we met that venerable and most amiable gentleman, Mr. Samuel Jones, Jr., the Treasurer and Manager of the New Orleans Savings Institution, in apparently good health for a septuagenarian; yesterday morning his death was announced, and this evening his remains will be followed to the grave by a large number of old friends. Mr. Jones was a native of Baltimore, and has resided in this city for many years, respected by everybody and beloved by many. He possessed in a large degree the characteristics of the Baltimore gentleman, of a high sense of honor, of dignity and purity of life and character combined with a genial love of society, and of good company, and of all the rational enjoyments of life. Mr. Jones was the cherished friend and fellow countryman of that venerable patriot and philanthropist, Dr. W. N. Mercer.

Extract from a letter of Rev. B. M. Palmer, D. D., of New Orleans.

"I knew Mr. Jones intimately, and there were few in my church to whom I was more tenderly attached, * * * * There was no office in the church, to which he could be elevated, which would not have been conferred upon him, if he could have been induced to accept it. * * * * He was pre-eminently a good man, and his death filled the community with sorrow."

SAMUEL HOFFMAN.

No city in the United States can boast of a richer legacy in her record of noble and upright merchants than Baltimore. We have been false to their memory and indifferent to their example in not having preserved in a conspicuous form a history of their lives.

Samuel Hoffman was one of the noblest of the noble merchants who have given Baltimore its reputation. He was the seventh son of Peter Hoffman, who emigrated to Maryland from Frankfort on the Main about 1765, and a few years after established in this city the House of Peter Hoffman & Sons, which became one of the leading houses in the country, and his family one of the most influential in Maryland.

After the death of his father, Samuel for some time carried on the Dry Goods business in Philadelphia; but subsequently formed a copartnership with his nephew S. Owings Hoffman in this city; a man of like character with himself, who became prominent in the community and Director of the Merchants' Bank, the Baltimore and Ohio Railroad and State Senator from the city, and was possessed of a high degree of literary and aesthetic culture.

At this period the auction and commission business began to assume an important relation to the trade. They acted upon the auspicious indications, and opened the Auction House of Hoffman & Co., which soon became famous in all this portion of the country.

In order to give additional attraction to their sales, they had a resident partner in Europe to purchase the *finest* goods in that market; consequently their auction rooms were crowded with buyers.

At one of these sales a circumstance occurred which illustrates the inflexible rectitude of Mr. Hoffman's House; a party who had made a notoriously dishonorable failure and in the settlement defrauded his creditors, was buying. Mr. Hoffman being informed of the case, requested him to desist, when he replied "I am buying for *cash* sir." Mr. H. with dignified disdain, said "we do not want your money sir, we demand *principle* in this house," and upon his exclusion, Mr. H. was loudly cheered by the crowd present.

To his rectitude and nobleness, was added a genial and sunny spirit, which made his presence animating and encouraging. During the financial pressure of 1837, caused by the removal of government deposits, Mr. Hoffman often visited the counting rooms of his fellow-merchants, speaking words of encouragement and hope, accompanying them with offers of necessary aid, and freely extending it, without additional interest or commission, which enabled a number to weather the storm, who probably without that, would have been overthrown. It is not strange that he was honored and loved by all. That he was elevated to positions of responsibility and trust, as a Director of the Baltimore Branch of the United States Bank, Baltimore and Ohio Railroad Company, Merchants' Bank and other useful corporations.

The esteem in which he was held, and the appreciation of his value to the trade were illustrated, at a meeting of the Wholesale Dry Goods Merchants, who presented him with a handsome piece of silver, accompanied with feeling expressions of regard. His implicit confidence in the merchants of the city was never betrayed; when public confidence was almost entirely destroyed, when men were losing faith in each other and in the State, he stood firm, never doubting the ultimate triumph of the honor and ability of his State and her citizens.

Such men as Samuel Hoffman are truly gifts of God, and their lives serve to elevate the standard of commercial dealing, and strengthen public virtue. May Baltimore never be without ensamples of his kind.

OSMOND C. TIFFANY.

The war of 1812 had made Baltimore famous. The indomitable spirit of her enterprise which sent her "Clippers" to the ports of every sea, took the lead in the strife, and her Privateers became the terror of British commerce. At the close of the war, her reputation attracted attention in all parts of the Union, and numbers of energetic men sought it as the field of their industry and fortune. Among these was Osmond C. Tiffany, a young man of energy and honor, trained in the business of domestic manufacturing at Pawtucket, R. I. He arrived in 1815, and soon formed a partnership with his friend William C. Shaw who had preceded him hither; a gentleman of refined character, and retiring disposition, who stood before the community as representative of all that is elevating in manhood, in whose association Mr. Tiffany always took pride.

They introduced a new era in the history of the trade. At first they did strictly a domestic commission business on Baltimore street, between Howard and Liberty, but in order to profit by the advantages which they perceived Baltimore to possess as a distributing market for the South and West, they added to their stock every variety of manufactured goods, straw goods, boots, shoes, wool hats, cotton and wool hand cards, &c., and began to sell by the package to wholesale dealers, thus creating the first *Great Jobbing House*, and originating that system which has given wealth and renown to Baltimore. The House soon became the leading one in the city, and its reputation extended to all parts of the country. This was prior to the days of Rail Roads, and Mr. Tiffany appreciating the advantages of Baltimore over the other Atlantic cities for communication with the West, determined to seek its growing trade.

His brother Comfort Tiffany, then merchandising in St. Louis, was taken into the firm, 1824, which became Shaw, Tiffany & Co.; bringing to it his large custom and valuable influence, their expectations were more than realized. Thus Shaw, Tiffany & Co. was the first house that *considerably* extended the trade of Baltimore beyond its adjacient country and across the mountains.

While thus assiduous in his attention to the business of the house, Mr. Tiffany was not unmindful of the community in which he resided. There was nothing narrow about him. It seemed a ruling purpose of his heart to benefit his city and his fellow citizens. He made his own success a channel through which to enrich others. He scorned that inexpressibly mean spirit which seeks to monopolize every customer, and prevent a neighboring house from having access to him. Although the house was able largely to control the western trade, through Mr. Tiffany mainly, a wagon line to Wheeling was established, with a joint stock company and a uniform tariff, which greatly advantaged the general trade of the city, while it was a loss to the individual stockholders of which Shaw, Tiffany & Co. were the largest.

At this period the city began to make giant strides towards the future; she had regained her foreign commerce; an immense accession was made to her tonnage; the West was being laid under tribute; the future began to loom grandly up; the day was propitious for enterprise; yet it demanded men of prophetic ken, courageous spirit and judicious action. Mr. Tiffany was such; he comprehended the situation and took his position in the fore-front; sustained by an unshrinking faith in the God of this nation, and in its unbounded resources, he stepped boldly forth and led in the march of trade from this locality. He became necessarily one of the most conspicuous men in business matters. He felt the responsibility of his position, and sought always to provide for the security, honor and prosperity of his city.

When the closing of the United States Bank put the trade in great jeopardy, he came to the rescue; was among the first to propose the organization of the *Merchants' Bank*, and labored earnestly and successfully to effect the proper legislation, by which the banking policy of the state was established to the satisfaction of the whole community, and which resulted in the organization of the other Banks, and a large increase of the banking capital of the city. He was prominently connected with the Merchants' and Union Banks.

Knowing the value of manufactures to the wealth and elevation of a community, his generous spirit of enterprise set itself to work, and suceeeded in the establishment of the Baltimore Cotton Factory on the Gunpowder River, and Laurel Factory on the Patuxent, which created an additional inducement to dealers to trade in our city.

In every movement which directly or indirectly enhanced the welfare of the state and city, he was an active leader, whether it was of a commercial, civil or benevolent character.

He prominently aided in the erection of the Eutaw House to meet the want of a first-class hotel in that section. To his efforts more than any other, is due the Baltimore Athenæum on St. Paul and Saratoga streets, for which he raised most of the money used in its erection.

It is partially due to his agency that Baltimore has become closely identified with the name of a man, whom a stricken humanity love, who was blessed of God in his life, honored by kings in his death, and whose memory will be hailed by the marching generations till the closing day, when those whom he has blessed, shall "rise up and call *him* blessed." We refer to the appointment of George Peabody as the agent of Maryland in Europe, to negotiate the $8,000,000 loan.

Deeply sensitive to the honor and credit of his state, when it seemed trembling in the scales of public opinion, when repudiation was advocated and justified even in high places, Mr. Tiffany gave himself no rest; with Samuel Jones, Jr., and other noble men, he frequently visited Annapolis and besought the legislature to maintain the credit of Maryland, and proposed the only practicable measure to avoid the threatened disgrace. He entertained the joint committees of the House and Senate at his residence, where in company with other leading citizens, the proposed measure was discussed and arrangements fixed for the payment of the past and future interest on the bonds.

He died suddenly on June 11th, 1851, universally lamented, having lived a truly representative life, which may serve as a guide to those who are threading the perilous paths of a commercial career.

GEN. WILLIAM McDONALD.

This gentleman may be considered the pioneer in establishing the local shipping trade of Baltimore. Having emigrated to this country during the existance of the colonies, he espoused their cause in the revolution, and distinguished himself by his bravery. At the close of the war, he was honorably discharged at the "head of Elk," and soon came to Baltimore, where he was engaged as a "hand" in the sloop trade between this city and Elk river. He rapidly advanced, becoming mate and at last master and owner; having accumulated a small amount of money, began business in an humble way at Fell's Point, which soon developed into importance in connection with his sloop trade.

From this arose the Packet business with Philadelphia, by sloops to Frenchtown, thence across the Peninsula to New Castle on the Delaware, thence by sloop to Philadelphia.

The *Fulton* Steamers having now proved a success, Mr. McDonald was quick to perceive the advantages of *rapid transportation*, and established the first line of Steamers on the Chesapeake Bay.

Steamers between Baltimore and Philadelphia soon displaced the Sloop Line; which carried nearly all the trade between the two cities until the Rail Road Lines were established.

General McDonald was one of the projectors of the "Bay Line of Steamers," and largely interested in it to the day of his death. He was owner in part and actively engaged in nearly all of the Steam Lines that were originated and conducted during his active life, and had the first Steamboat built in this city in 1813, which was named *Chesapeake*, to run between Baltimore and Frenchtown.

The shipping business between this City and Philadelphia, is now chiefly carried on by the Baltimore and Philadelphia Steamboat Company of which J. Alexander Shriver is Vice President.

Mr. McDonald's active commercial career began about 1790, and he developed a large trade with the farmers of Maryland and Virginia, supplying them with groceries, and acting Commission Merchant for their produce. In 1810 he associated his son Samuel with him as the firm of William McDonald & Son, under which the business greatly increased. In 1832 Geo. W. Richardson became a partner, and the firm was then Wm. McDonald & Co. In 1845 Gen. McDonald died and Samuel retired, and the business was sustained by Mr. Richardson and two former clerks. Mr. Richardson died in 1846 and was succeeded by the junior members, James McConky and Israel M. Parr, who became the clerks of Gen. McDonald in 1838. In 1865 Mr. McConky retired and Mr. Parr continued, since associating with him his son Henry A. Parr, and the firm is now Israel M. Parr & Son, see page 133; thus the house is one of the very oldest in the City, having had no interruptions or suspensions in its history, and has sustained throughout, the highest credit and a most valuable part in the commercial growth of Baltimore. Mr. Israel M. Parr is one of our most important and enterprising merchants; was an originator of the Corn and Flour Exchange of which he has been president, and is always in the advance in the advocacy of those measures which meditate the welfare and improvement of the City.

WILLIAM WILSON & SONS.

No house ever established in Baltimore has had a more honorable history; none has exerted a greater influence than this. They were one of the eminent shipping firms of their day, and owned a large number of vessels, which carried on an extensive trade with Calcutta and other East India ports, Holland, England, Brazil, West Coast of South America and China The spirit of their enterprise led them upon every sea and to every available port, and they brought our city into commercial communication with every part of the habitable globe.

The head of the house, William Wilson, came to Baltimore from Limerick, Ireland, 1770, and by indomitable energy and strict integrity increased his limited means to such an extent that at the conclusion of the war, when our commerce was revived and extended, he became interested in a number of ships, and largely imported foreign goods under the firm of Wilson & Maris in 1790. He subsequently took his sons James and Thomas into business and the firm became William Wilson & Sons. This was established about 1802 and continued to carry on a prosperous shipping trade until 1862. During its entire history it enjoyed the highest credit, and its members universal respect and confidence as merchants and men.

William Wilson was one of the noblest and best of men. He was distinguished for his urbanity, his uprightness and beneficence. He was ever ready to encourage every enterprise of benevolence, and was a most liberal supporter of the Baptist Church, of which he was an active member, having been one of the founders of the First Baptist Church and contributed nearly all the means for the erection of the edifice on the corner of Sharp and Lombard streets, (as seen on page 75,) of which Rev. Dr. J. W. M. Williams has been the efficient and loved pastor for over twenty-five years; a church whose history has been closely identified with the progress of Baltimore in civil and religious matters. The original edifice and parsonage stood, until 1818, at the corner of Front and Pitt (now Fayette) streets, on the present site of the Merchants' Shot Tower. His public spirit was evinced in 1814, when no funds could be obtained from Washington to meet the obligations of the Government; he tendered the Navy Agent, James Beatty, a loan of $50,000, and thus sustained the honor of the Government and then refused to accept any interest, saying that "he did not wish to profit by the necessities of his country." His sons James and Thomas were men of like character and well maintained the credit of the house and reputation of his name.

Mr. Wilson raised a family which became one of the most cultivated and influential in the State, and widely and honorably connected. His descendants worthily maintain his name and reputation. Though the firm has ceased to do an active business, its name is still retained by the senior members, David S. and Thomas J. Wilson; the junior members having embarked in other pursuits. One of them, James G. Wilson, with another great grandson, Wm. B., is partner in the successful banking house of Wilson, Colston & Co., (see page 267.) His great nephew is our distinguished Banker and Philanthropist, William Wilson Corcoran, who is named after him. Mr. Wilson occupied a number of important stations of responsibility and trust, which he filled to the satisfaction of all interested. He was the second President of the Bank of Baltimore for seventeen years, and a prominent member of other leading corporations. He has left a record of which his family are legitimately proud, and to which Baltimore may point as an honorable chapter in the history of her commercial men.

THE SAVINGS BANKS.

Among the most useful and important institutions in a community are Savings Banks. Those of Baltimore have demonstrated their benefit to the people, and enjoy, as they certainly merit, universal confidence. In each of the institutions here mentioned it appears that the Officers and Directors are chosen from the most prominent and successful business men of the city, who are characterized for their high position and judicious enterprise.

THE SAVINGS BANK OF BALTIMORE,

As seen by reference to pages 260 and 261, is the oldest, and has an honorable history. Its success has been uninterrupted, and it has long been regarded as one of the strongest and best savings institutions in the country.

Its depositors have increased from 734 in 1826 to 32,500, and the deposits from $126,911 to over $12,500,000, which could have been largely increased had the Board so desired.

Its worthy President, Mr. Archibald Stirling, who is universally esteemed among us, has been connected with it for fifty years, twenty-four of which he has been President. He is ably and worthily surrounded by Officers and Directors, who maintain its character and reputation.

Officers—Archibald Stirling, President; David Baldwin, Treasurer; S. McD. Richardson, Assistant Treasurer.

Directors—Archibald Stirling, Michael Warner, Chauncey Brooks, Deeter Bargar, Edward Kurtz, Galloway Cheston, William McKim, James I. Fisher, Joseph Cushing, Jr., Thomas C. Jenkins, N. Popplein, Samuel Kirby, George S. Brown, Thomas Whitridge, Solomon Corner, Austin Jenkins, Thomas M. Smith, William Lamping, Laurence Thomsen, Enoch Pratt, Henry James, George B. Coale, Werner Dresel, B. F. Newcomer, A. H. Stump.

THE EUTAW SAVINGS BANK,

Of which a correct and concise account is given on page 262, has well fulfilled the designs of its founders, and, by strict adherence to the provisions and conditions of its charter, has established a character which is gratifying to its friends. Its usefulness is being demonstrated from year to year, and its depositors have steadily increased, as far as the Board deemed advisable. They numbered January 1st, 1876, 13,833, and its deposits $5,346,089.15.

Officers—William F. Burns, President; Robert D. Brown, Treasurer.

Directors—William F. Burns, James Harvey, John Cushing, Francis Burns, Matthew S. Clark, William Devries, Henry R. Lauderman, Daniel M. Thomas, Aaron Fenton,

Elisha H. Perkins, William J. Rieman, John Gregg, Samuel R. Smith, George P. Thomas, Francis Dawes, J. Harman Brown, William Wilson, Jr., William H. Perkins, Nicholas G. Penniman, Henry Snyder, John L. Weeks, John R. Seemuller, G. A. Von Lingen, Walter B. Brooks, William H. Graham.

THE CENTRAL SAVINGS BANK.

(See page 259.)

This comparatively young institution, under its efficient administration, shows a most gratifying growth, having more than doubled its deposits during the last two years. The number of depositors the first of July, 1876, were 6,436, and deposits $1,030,649.

Officers—Francis T. King, President; John Curlett, Vice President; William E. Coale, Treasurer.

Directors—Frederick W. Brune, Geo. W. Corner, W. B. Canfield, J. B. Seidenstricker, William Bridges, Edward Roberts, George Sanders, Charles J. Baker, Robert Turner, William Numsen, Thomas J. Wilson, William Woodward, James Carey, Jesse Tyson, German H. Hunt, Daniel J. Foley, J. F. Monmonier, M. D., D. L. Bartlett, Henry C. Smith, Christian Ax, Samuel Appold, Hamilton Easter.

THE NATIONAL BANK OF BALTIMORE,

To whose advertisement we refer, (on page 271,) has a history which is peculiarly interesting among our financial institutions. From it we gather the fact that, during its entire course of eighty years, it has never failed to declare its regular semi-annual dividend.

Its Capital is $1,210,700 *with a Surplus of* $400,000.

PRESIDENT—HENRY A. THOMPSON.
CASHIER—J. THOMAS SMITH.

DIRECTORS.

Henry A. Thompson, Thomas M. Smith,
David S. Wilson, Alexander F. Murdock,
C. Morton Stewart, Christian Devries,
William M. Boone.

MARYLAND WHITE LEAD COMPANY

OF THE CITY OF BALTIMORE.

(See page 226.)

PRESIDENT—JOHN CURLETT.
SECRETARY—W. R. FLUHARTY.

DIRECTORS.

Charles J. Baker, Thomas M. Smith,
James E. Tyson, John Gregg.

All the modern improvements in the manufacture of Lead have been adopted by this Company. The popularity of their Lead has greatly increased, especially in New York, Philadelphia, Boston, and other Eastern makets.

THE JOHNS HOPKINS UNIVERSITY.

Since our first article on the munificent appropriation of Mr. Hopkins for a University was published on pages 51-54, which met his approval, he has passed away, and the efficient Board of Trustees have put into active execution the provisions of his bequest.

They elected Professor Daniel C. Gilman, late professor in Yale College, and President of the University of California, to the Presidency, who had acquired the highest reputation as an organizer of Universities. He entered upon his duties May 1, 1875, and spent several weeks of the following summer in visiting the great educational institutions of Europe and this country. He has received the most cordial co-operation from the Trustees, and the University may be regarded as thoroughly organized. A portion of the faculty has been elected, composed of scholars of the highest attainments and reputation as teachers.

The Academic Staff consists of: 1. The PRESIDENT and PROFESSORS. 2. LECTURERS. 3. ASSOCIATES. 4. FELLOWS.

Pending the construction of the permanent buildings at Clifton, the fine accommodations will be used on Howard street, next to the Baltimore City College. In a few weeks this great University will be opened for the reception of students, and fairly launched on the sea of knowledge and discovery that knows no bounds. We bid the President and Trustees good speed and a prosperous voyage, hoping for them a favoring Providence, and a renown for the University that will place it beside the ancient seats of learning in the old and new world.

SAFE DEPOSIT AND TRUST COMPANY
OF BALTIMORE.

This company, the cut of whose elegant building is seen on page 451, may well be gratified with its history since its organization. Its building is altogether the handsomest and most complete in the United States. In its appointments, and construction of its walls, safes and vaults, it is confessedly superior to any other known. Perfection of work characterizes every department. So far as human ingenuity and mechanical skill could contrive, this building is absolutely safe from fire and burglary.

The Building Committee consists of the President and Board of Directors, Mr. H. S. Shryock, chairman. They have adopted the most approved features hitherto known, and added new ones, which were the result of their own careful study and examination. It is a work in which they may take a just pride, and for which they are entitled to the praise of the community.

[The origin of Safe Deposit Companies is accredited to F. H. Jenks, Esq., formerly an esteemed merchant of our city, now a resident of New York, who first appreciated the necessity and utility of a place for the deposit of securities and valuables, other than the expedient of Bank vaults, and after much effort succeeded in inducing others to unite with him in establishing a place of Deposit in New York.]

NEWSPAPERS.

THE BALTIMORE DAILY NEWS

Is the only afternoon paper in the city, and is in a most flourishing condition. It was started by E. V. Hermange on the fourth day of November, 1872, as a penny evening paper. On the 9th day of February, 1874, James R. Brewer, Esq., purchased a half interest in the paper and the firm became and still remains Hermange & Brewer. On the 9th of February, 1875, the NEWS was enlarged to contain twenty-eight columns, eight columns to a page, and the subscription price raised to two cents per copy or ten cents per week. On the fourth day of October, 1874, the same firm started the Baltimore SUNDAY NEWS, which is the only Sunday paper published in Baltimore. The NEWS, both Daily and Sunday, has become a popular institution, and will represent the energy, enterprise and progress of Baltimore.

THE BALTIMOREAN,

A first-class Literary Journal, is published every Saturday, and although its first issue dates back but five years, it has long since secured a hold upon the public support and confidence, which may be received as a sure guarantee of permanency. It is the only illustrated journal published in this city, the familiar face of some prominent citizen, or a perfect representation of some one of the many handsome public buildings, (religious, benevolent or municipal,) which adorn the city; being a distinguishing feature of every issue. THE BALTIMOREAN is thoroughly and unreservedly devoted to every movement and enterprise which can tend to the physical and moral advancement of the great City of Monuments, but its columns always contain reading that cannot fail to interest all lovers of a pure morality and a pure literature, while at the same time it aids in the enlightenment and the improvement of mankind generally.

A new daily morning paper, price one cent, the only one cent paper in Baltimore, has a large and steadily increasing circulation. It is especially devoted to Reform principles and the interests of the working people, but is read by all classes.

THE GAZETTE.

In December, 1875, Mr. Wm. H. Welsh, one of the former proprietors, purchased the interest of Mr. Charles. J. Baker and on the 1st of January, 1876, changed the whole basis of the journal, inaugurating a new policy; announced its independence in politics and reduced the price of the Daily to two cents a copy or six dollars a year and the *Weekly* to one dollar. Under the new regime, it has continued to grow in popular favor, has received the highest encomiums of the press and the reading community, and is now regarded as one of the ablest and most interesting Journals of the country.

THE BALTIMORE WECKER,

A German paper, was established in the year 1850, and is published as a Daily, Weekly and Sunday Journal. It has a very large circulation and is one of the best German papers issued in the country.

SINCE THE PUBLICATION of the article on the Baltimore Press, some changes have occurred, prominent among which are the completion and occupancy of the *New American Building*, one of the largest and most complete in the country. For an account of the American, Sun, German Correspondent and other journals the reader is referred to pages 54—62.

THE McSHANE BELL FOUNDRY.

No department of Manufacture in Baltimore has exhibited a greater increase and improvement than that of Bells. It is not long since this was a comparatively small interest with us. Messrs. Henry McShane & Co., perceiving the importance of this branch of business, with their characteristic enterprise added to their already large establishment a Bell Foundry, with all the facilities for casting Bells of every size, and secured among other skilled moulders, an educated German trained from his youth in one of the celebrated Bell founderies of Europe, who is exclusively employed on their Bells. They are thus enabled to give perfection of finish and tone to their bells, which are not surpassed in this country or abroad. The special superintendent of the Bell department is Mr. Marcus R. Jones, whose experience in the renowned Troy Bell Foundry eminently qualifies him for this responsible post. As a consequence of the expense and care thus bestowed, the reputation of the McShane Bells extends to all parts of the world, and their clear tones are heard from Maine to California, in Europe, Asia and South America, from the belfries of Churches, Cathedrals, Mission Chapels, Fire Stations, Factories. Schools, Steam Boats, &c. Messrs. McShane & Co. have not only the satisfaction which arises from indivdual success, but also of having built up an establishment which is of immense importance to Baltimore and is heralding throughout the world its name. They are literally ringing the Bells which call attention to us from near and afar, inviting the world "to come to us and buy."

They deserve the thanks of our citizens, for giving Maryland the honor of making the greatest single exhibit at the Centennial Exposition, and of being the first to proclaim the joyous tidings of the grand opening on the anniversary of the day when Charles Carroll, of Carrollton, signed with his compatriots the immortal Declaration of Independence. Their *great chime* consisting of *Thirteen Bells* (to represent the original thirteen States of the Union) was placed in position ready for the signal, and when given, their mighty peal thrilled the immense multitude with indescribable emotion.

This chime, the first ever cast in Baltimore, is pronounced by competent examiners, perfect in every respect. They range in weight from 300 to 4,000 lbs., aggregating 21,000 lbs. They comprise a full octave and a third, with a *flat seventh* and a *sharp fourth*, whose even vibrations give a richness and resonance of tone, which is perfectly sustained until they die away. The Bells are hung in the Main Tower, or the N. E. angle of the Machinery Hall, and are operated upon by Prof. Widdows, the chime ringer of the Metropolitan M. E. Church, Washington City. Their cost is $10,000.00 and constitute one of the principal features in the Centennial Exhibition.

The foundry and shops of this firm, are among the great forces of our city, to which we give this prominent notice, not only because it is due to McShane & Co., but our work, aiming to exhibit those forces, would be incomplete without it.

The demands of their business, have necessitated the establishing of a Branch in New York. See pages 203 and 478.

BALTIMORE RETORT AND FIRE BRICK WORKS.

As an example of the rapid and substantial growth of Baltimore's manufactures, we cite the Factory of Geo. C. Hicks & Co., at Locust Point—the centre of many other great interests—the engraving of which is on *page* 406. "The Baltimore Retort and Fire Brick Works," of which they are proprietors, under their energetic management are among the largest in the country. The superiority of the clay they use, which is found within a thousand feet of the factory, and the employment of the best workmen, enable them to make perfect articles. Their facilities in manufacturing and shipping; having coal brought fresh from the mines to their Kilns by the B. & O. R. R., and loading vessels at their own Wharves, give them decided advantages. They ship by vessel to Boston and other New England and Eastern Ports at a cost of freight, not exceeding the drayage to the Northern and Western limits of our own city. The varied character of the articles they manufacture may be seen by reference to page 247. The success and importance of the establishment are evident from the extent of their trade. They supply a large number of cities all over the country North, East, South and West, with Sewer and Drain Pipes; the Gas Companies with Gas Retorts, Fire Brick, &c. From the fact that they make better articles at a less cost than can be manufactured elsewhere, they are filling orders from the very quarters which formerly supplied this market. They were awarded the contract for furnishing the sewer pipe for the Centennial grounds at Philadelphia, which is a very sure indication of their superiority. In the short period of eight years they have built up one of the great industries, in our city, which is a source of support to a large laboring population, and is daily contributing to our manufacturing and commercial importance.

R. Q. TAYLOR,

(Page 158,)

Has erected for his business at the old stand an establishment which for elegance and completeness is not surpassed anywhere. It is truly a model in its architectural beauty and proportions. The fixtures and interior decorations are finished with exquisite taste, excelling anything we have hitherto had in Baltimore in his department. It is a complete success, for which he is to be congratulated. He deserves the thanks of the community for such an improvement as this, as it is a grand step in that species of advance which Baltimore greatly needs, and which we hope to see extensively imitated. For his house we have only the highest encomiums. He commenced in April, 1843, and has established a business and a reputation which are gratifying to himself and our citizens.

COMMERCIAL AND FARMERS' NATIONAL BANK

OF BALTIMORE,

Corner of Howard and German Streets.

Chartered by the State of Maryland 1810. Organized as a National Bank 1865.
Capital, $512,560—Surplus, $114,000.

President, JESSE SLINGLUFF; Vice President, JOSEPH H. RIEMAN,
Cashier, JOHN D. EARLY.

DIRECTORS.

Jesse Slingluff,	Augustus J. Albert,	William Carmichael,
Joseph H. Rieman,	William Devries,	W. G. Bansemer,
G. A. Von Lingen,	John Cushing,	W. J. H. Watters.

EXECUTIVE OFFICERS SINCE ITS ORGANIZATION IN 1810.

Presidents.

Joseph H. Nicholson,	1810.
Isaac Burneston,	1817.
Wm. W. Taylor,	1821.
Charles Bohn,	1832.
Jacob Albert,	1836.
Eli Clagett,	1846.
Thos. Meredith,	1848.
Jesse Slingluff,	1854.

Cashiers.

Geo. T. Dunbar,	1810.
Trueman Cross,*	1842.
John D. Early,	1876.

*Connected with the Bank for more than fifty-one years.

THE FIRST NATIONAL BANK OF BALTIMORE,

No. 8 South Gay Street.

J. S. NORRIS, President. THOMAS KELSO, Vice President.
E. K. HOLTZMAN, Cashier.

DIRECTORS.

W. E. Hooper,	George Small,	Horace Abbott,
J. S. Norris,	S. M. Shoemaker,	Joseph Friedenwald,
William J. Albert,	Thomas Kelso,	John G. Cockey.

See page 261.

Maryland Britannia and Gold and Silver Plate Works,

ESTABLISHED 1850.

HOLMES BROS. & CO., Successors of William Holmes,

OFFICE AND FACTORY:

Nos. 50 & 52 N. HOLLIDAY ST., BALTIMORE.

Orders left at No. 3 N. Charles street will receive prompt attention. See page 200.

YORK RIVER LINE.

See page 447.

Daily Line in effect on this Route on and after August 22d, 1876.

THE WESTERN MARYLAND RAILROAD.

In our special article on this road, pages 344-5, we stated that its two great necessities were proper terminal facilities and a centrally located depot. Under its energetic management these have been secured. A handsome and spacious depot with every accommodation for freight and passengers has been erected on Hillen and Exeter streets, and permanent arrangements made with the Baltimore and Potomac and Union Railroads, for the use of the two tunnels, giving it a tide-water terminus at Canton. The road, with these increased facilities, has shown rapid improvement and gives promise of fulfilling the expectations of its founders. The Western connections to which allusion was made in the former article are in a fair way of being effected, and other important ones are to be made with the Shenandoah Valley Railroad, to a junction with the Chesapeake and Ohio Railroad, at Staunton, Va; the Harrisburg and Potomac Railroad, running the entire length of the Cumberland Valley, from Harrisburg to the line of the Western Maryland Railroad, and the Hanover Branch, opening a new short line from Harrisburg via Hanover and Reisterstown to Baltimore, thus making an all rail route for the Reading coal to Baltimore and tide-water. These routes are being surveyed and graded as rapidly as the enterprise and judgment of the gentlemen in charge approve, and we may expect ere long to see them in full operation. The President, J. M. Hood, Esq., and the other Officers and Directors have accomplished a great work for Baltimore in their successful administration of this road.

See page 203.

THE CALVERT SUGAR REFINERY.

Reference to page 113 shows the engraving of this celebrated Refinery. In regard to its size and the completeness of the machinery and facilities for refining and shipping, it has no superior in the United States. The troubles through which it has passed have been rectified by the reorganization of the company, comprising some of our most prominent and judicious business men, with a capital of $500,000. The Directors, fully appreciating the situation and needs of the Refinery, are managing it with great care and judgment. They have appointed efficient officers, who are placing it upon the best basis for utilizing its vast capabilities. This concern is of immense importance to Baltimore, and in its thorough reorganization every citizen is interested; and the whole trade of the city should encourage and contribute to its success. It is one of our giant forces which we cannot spare. Officers—Samuel P. Thompson, President; William Cunningham, Secretary and Treasurer. Directors—Saml. P. Thompson, Enoch Pratt, Jos. H. Rieman, Henry James, John E. Hurst, Henry Janes, Thomas Deford. Office—56 S. Gay street.

THE BALTIMORE STEAM SUGAR REFINERY
OF MESSRS. WOODS, WEEKS & CO.,

Whose engraving is on page 112, is one of those characteristic enterprises which are the pride of our city. It has made a most honorable record in the commercial history of Baltimore, and through all the changes and vicissitudes of its contemporary trade, the firm has maintained the highest reputation and credit. They manufacture all grades of Refined Sugars and Syrups, and their facilities for supplying the trade of the country are not surpassed by any other Refinery. They offer inducements in quality and price to dealers to trade with Baltimore in sugars and syrups at least equal to Philadelphia, New York and other markets. This is one of the houses which have extended the high character of Baltimore, and whose correspondence has greatly awakened public attention and drawn to us a large custom from distant quarters.

TO THE YOUNG BUSINESS MEN OF BALTIMORE.

Though my work has an interest for the general reader, it has a peculiar fitness for your use. Realizing, from a long business experience, the difficulties with which we have to contend in our competition for the trade of the country, I have endeavored to compile the information and present it in such a combination and form, as to constitute it a valuable, and I trust it may prove a necessary aid to you, upon whom the future of Baltimore largely depends. The exhibition of the facts, the short mementoes of some of our noble men and merchants who have passed away, I hope may contribute to the development of your business character, and give you a more comprehensive knowledge of the great resources and forces of your own city, by which you may more successfully urge its claims upon the country. A *complete* business man not only thoroughly understands his own special department, but acquaints himself with all the facts, resources, advantages and capabilities which his city possesses; knows what forces are being employed, what results produced, what others are doing, what they are contributing to the general character of his city as a trading centre; knowledge of this sort is not only expansive of character, but makes an immediate return. To a young man soliciting custom in his particular branch, thorough understanding of the market in all departments is of paramount importance. Buyers cannot be brought to a city to any great extent by the inducements of a single house or branch of the trade. Salesmen and solicitors must be intelligently informed of all the industries and resources of the city, so that they may forcibly and convincingly represent its commercial importance and secure the patronag of the *general* trade. If a young man confines his view and knowledge to his own special line, he will attain but a stunted growth and be a narrow man, without that influence and respect which are the prerogative of every good business man to enjoy.

You, who are now the young men of the city, must soon occupy the posts of importance in its affairs and take the reins into your hands. It becomes you therefore to fit yourselves for the responsibility which awaits you.

I am confident that this book in your possession will greatly assist you in attaining the necessary knowledge of our city, and success in your immediate efforts in behalf of the houses in whose employ you are and whom you represent abroad. Such information as is here presented in detail and in combination, cannot fail to make your services vastly more valuable to them as well as to yourselves.

Respectfully, GEO. W. HOWARD.

CONCLUSION.

The labor connected with such a work as this none can fully appreciate but those who have performed it. Hence we do not propose to recite the months of incessant toil in gathering facts and information from sources near and remote, many of which were at first inaccessible. The utmost care has been exercised in the collation and presentation of the matter in the work, especially that relating to the commercial situation of Baltimore; and no expense has been spared to make it not only acceptable to the general reader, but in the highest degree valuable to our tradesmen, manufacturers and financial institutions. The book is mainly designed to furnish the most authentic information concerning the facilities and resources of our city, which will awaken a more comprehensive spirit of enterprise at home, and increase patronage and favor from abroad. It also aims to direct attention to our vast capabilities and resources, many of which are as yet undeveloped, and to *utilize* more thoroughly the facts which demonstrate our superiority as a commercial and manufacturing city.

No city in the United States of similar proportions to Baltimore is as little known and understood, as every one who has traveled much can testify. A very low estimate is placed on her capabilities, compared with New York and other cities, by the country at large. This is due to our *neglect* of the *proper utilization* of facts. Impelled by a just motive of commercial gain, they have availed themselves of every channel, especially the *printing press*, through which to secure the notice and patronage of the country; we, resting unwisely on the supposition, that others would *seek* our hidden possibilities, have neglected to inform the world of our resources and advantages, even where we may *justly* claim superiority.

Among the great difficulties which obtained in the prosecution of this undertaking, not the least was the inability of many, and the unwillingness of others, to recognize or accept those facts which lie beyond their narrow range of observation. Perched on the mole-hills which their *terrene efforts* have raised, conceited with the idea that their view embraced the whole horizon, they could not be induced to ascend the altitudes from which they might observe the magnitude and grandeur of the true economy of things, and to understand the relations existing throughout the whole. The wheels of commerce would run more smoothly, the hammers of mechanics beat without intermission, the social and civil economy present fewer disorders, if all men would appreciate the relations they sustain to each other and freely discharge the obligations which inhere in those relations. No one man is unrelated to the rest; it is the combination of interests and enterprise that gives strength and proportions to communities. The author emphatically expresses his gratefulness to those who have encouraged him with their sympathy and influence, and especially to his patrons who compose so valuable a portion of our business men, and are contributing most largely to the growth and importance of Baltimore.

REMOVALS.

Methodist Episcopal Book Depository, to 168 W. Baltimore street.
L. W. Gunther, to "Gunther Building," S. Gay street.
Gambril, Sons & Co., to "Gunther Building," S. Gay street.
A. Schumacher & Co., to "Gunther Building," S. Gay street.
H. Sanders & Co., (Sanders & Stayman,) to 15 N. Charles street.
Stickney Iron Company, (office,) to 11 S. Gay street.
Troxell, Handy & Greer, to 237 W. Pratt street.
Baltimore American, to new building, corner of Baltimore and South streets.
Stewart & Co., to 46 S. Howard street.
Geo. P. Thomas & Co., to 387 W. Baltimore street, corner of Paca.
Johnson, Sutton & Co., to "Slingluff Block," N. E. corner Baltimore and Howard streets.
Henry Bogue & Son, to 244 W. Baltimore street.
E. M. Lazurus & Co., to corner of Holliday street and Exchange Place.
Seim & Emory, to 40 and 42 German street.
The Safe Deposit and Trust Company, to new building, South street, (page 451.)
J. D. Kremelberg & Co., *Austrian Consulate*, to 31 German street.

CHANGES IN FIRMS.

Jno. J. & S. J. Hurst, dissolved; continued by Hurst, Miller & Co., 252 W. Baltimore st.
Perry, Clark & Co., succeeded by Clark, Perry & Hohman, 9 N. Charles street.
David W. Glass & Co., dissolved. D. W. Glass & Co., at 19 S. Charles street; Marcus Wolf at old stand, 7, 9 and 11 Sharp street.
Wheelwright, Mudge & Co., succeeded by Dobler, Mudge & Chapman, S. E. corner of Lombard and Sharp streets.
Cushing & Medairy, succeeded by Medairy & Bowers, 6 N. Howard street.
A. Werker & Krug, dissolved; succeeded by Gustav Krug, S.W. cor. Saratoga and Jasper sts.
George & Jenkins, dissolved; Philip T. George & Son, Samuel E. George, continue in the same line at 94 W. Lombard street, as P. T. George & Co. T. Robt. Jenkins & Son, Frank X. Jenkins, continue at 48 South street.
Drakeley & Fenton, dissolved; succeeded by Hinman & Newcomb, 1 and 3 S. Paca street, corner of German.
Lamb & Kemp, dissolved; succeeded by George M. Lamb & Bro., 57 South street.
John Gill & Co., continued as Gill & Fisher, 29 South street.
Chas. A. Gambrill & Co., composed of R. G. Macgill, P. H. Macgill, A. Gambrill, H. C. Corner, G. C. Hilt. See page 132.
Robt. Moore & Bro., now Robert Moore, Hughes & Co., 233 W. Baltimore street.
Mackenzie Bros., dissolved. Geo. N. Mackenzie & Co., 18 S. Charles street; C. T. & C. B. Mackenzie, 338 W. Baltimore street.
Poultney, Trimble & Co., continued by Trimble & Kleibacker, 200 W. Baltimore street.
Brown, Lancaster & Co., dissolved, continued by Brown & Lowndes, 17 German street.
John H. Haskell associates his son J. H. H., Jr., as John H. Haskell & Son.
Pitcher & Wilson dissolved. Wm. H. Pitcher and son, 4 S. Paca street; Young O. Wilson, 1 N. Paca street.
Keith & Kelso dissolved. John R. Kelso, Jr., 23 S. Charles street; Edward M. Keith, 25 S. Charles street.
Ammidon & Co. succeeded by D. F. Haynes & Co., at old stand.
Russell & Alger succeeded by Benjamin Russell at old stand.
Sam'l. G. B. Cook associates J. Glenn Cook, Chas. H. Wier and John K. Wilson as Sam'l G. B. Cook & Co., 5 and 7 German street.
Wilson, Burns & Co., present partners Francis Burns, Jr., F. H. Burns, Joseph S. West.
James W. Geddes; now James W. Geddes & Co., (William Mentzel.)

THE LORDS PROPRIETARY OF MARYLAND.

George Calvert, (see page 7,) First Lord Baltimore.
Cecilius Calvert, Second Lord Baltimore, - 1632
Charles Calvert, Third Lord Baltimore, - 1675
Benedict Leonard Calvert, Fourth Lord Baltimore, - - - - - - - - - - 1715
Charles Calvert, Fifth Lord Baltimore, - 1715
Frederick Calvert, Sixth and last Lord Baltimore, - - - - - - - - - 1751
Henry Harford, Esq., Last Proprietary, 1771-1776

THE COLONIAL GOVERNORS.

Proprietary Governors.

1633—Leonard Calvert.
1647—Thomas Green.
1649—William Stone.
1654—Commissioners under Parliament.
1658—Josiah Fendall.
1661—Philip Calvert.
1662—Charles Calvert.
1667—Charles, Lord Baltimore.
1678—Thomas Notely.
1681—Charles, Lord Baltimore.
1685—William Joseph, Pres. of Deputies.
1689—Convention of Protestant Association.

Royal Governors.

1692—Sir Lionel Copley.
1693—Sir Edmond Andros.
1694—Francis Nicholson.
1699—Nathaniel Blackistone.
1703—Thomas Tench, Pres.
1704—John Leymour.
1709—Edward Lloyd, Pres.
1714—John Hart.

Proprietary Governors.

1715—John Hart.
1720—Charles Calvert.
1727—Benedict Leonard Calvert.
1732—Samuel Ogle.
1733—Charles, Lord Baltimore.
1735—Samuel Ogle.
1742—Thomas Bladen.
1747—Samuel Ogle.
1752—Benjamin Tasker, Pres.
1753—Horatio Sharpe.
1769—Robert Eden.

COLONIAL POPULATION OF MARYLAND.

Year	Population	Year	Population	Year	Population
1634	about 200	1671	20,000	1748	130,000
1660	12,000	1701	30,000	1756	154,188
1665	16,000	1715	50,200	1776	about 200,000

GOVERNORS OF THE STATE OF MARYLAND.

When Elected.

Name	Year	Name	Year	Name	Year
Thomas Johnson,	1777	Chas. Ridgeley of Hampton,	1815	E. Louis Lowe,	1850
Thomas Sim Lee,	1779	Charles Goldsborough,	1818	T. Watkins Ligon,	1854
William Paca,	1782	Samuel Sprigg,	1819	T. Holliday Hicks,	1857
William Smallwood,	1785	Samuel Stevens, Jr.,	1822	Augustus W. Bradford,	1861
John Eager Howard,	1788	Joseph Kent,	1825	Thomas Swann,	1865
George Plater,	1791	Daniel Martin,	1828	Oden Bowie,	1867
John H. Stone,	1794	Thomas King Carroll,	1829	William Pinkney Whyte,*	1871
John Henry,	1797	Daniel Martin,	1830	James B. Groome,	1871
Benjamin Ogle,	1798	George Howard,	1831	John Lee Carroll,	1875
John Francis Mercer,	1801	James Thomas,	1832		
Robert Bowie,	1803	Thomas W. Veazey,	1835		
Robert Wright,	1806	William Grason,	1838		
Edward Lloyd,	1809	Francis Thomas'	1841		
Robert Bowie,	1811	Thomas G. Pratt,	1844		
Levin Winder,	1812	Philip Francis Thomas,	1847		

*Governor Whyte, having been elected to the U. S. Senate, resigned the Gubernatorial office, March 4, 1874, when Gov. Groome was elected to fill the vacancy.

MAYORS OF THE CITY OF BALTIMORE.

When Elected.

Name	Year	Name	Year	Name	Year
James Calhoun,	1797	Samuel Smith,	1835	John Smith Hollins,	1852
Thorowgood Smith,	1804	Sheppard C. Leakin,	1838	Samuel Hinks,	1854
Edward Johnson,	1808	Samuel Brady,	1840	Thomas Swann,	1856
George Stiles,	1816	Solomon Hillen,	1842	Geo. Wm. Brown,	1860
John Montgomery,	1820	James O. Law,	1843	John Lee Chapman,	1861
Jacob Small,	1826	Jacob G. Davies,	1844	Robert T. Banks,	1867
William Steuart,	1830	Elijah Stansbury,	1848	Joshua Vansant,	1871
Jesse Hunt,	1832	John H. T. Jerome,	1850	Ferdinand C. Latrobe,	1875

INDEX TO ADVERTISEMENTS.

FINAL INDEX.

(See other Index pages.)

Extracts from the Press and Correspondence

CONCERNING THE FIRST EDITION.

Hon. Reverdy Johnson.

That a publication like yours cannot fail to be advantageous is evident from the information it gives the public.

The advantages belonging to our city are strikingly illustrated and must attract the attention of the people of other States and of Foreigners. The scope of this attraction will be increased in proportion as the work is distributed.

Bishop E. R. Ames, D. D., M. E. Church.

Your exhibition of our city must commend itself to every one as complete and attractive, and will gratify a lawful pride in every citizen who reads it.

While it would be difficult to specify any portion more interesting than the rest, I especially commend your portrayal of our immense commercial and mechanical resources, proving conclusively to the country that Baltimore is not surpassed by any city on the Atlantic coast in the advantages she offers to the trade. Our resources have too long been neglected, and as a city we have failed properly to utilize them. I believe that your book will awaken a higher appreciation at home, and develope a better estimation abroad, of our city.

Archbishop J. Roosevelt Bayley.

It deserves all that has been said in its praise by so many good judges, and I trust that it may be widely circulated, to the honor and advantage of our good city.

House of Representatives,

WASHINGTON, D. C., Feb. 10th, 1875.

GEO. W. HOWARD, ESQ.

Dear Sir:—Your book, "The Monumental City," &c., is not only an interesting and instructive description of the city of Baltimore, but it is a most comprehensive exhibition of her trade and vast capabilities.

The generous circulation of the Book abroad would satisfy the whole country, South and West, that Baltimore is their natural and most valuable centre of trade; and in the hands of the Members of Congress, it would by its truthful portrayal of her increasing greatness, facilitate any measures before them looking to her interests.

Yours truly,

THOS. SWANN,
WM. J. O'BRIEN,
STEVENSON ARCHER,
LLOYD LOWNDES, JR.
GEO. R. DENNIS, U. S. Senator,
E. K. WILSON,
WM. J. ALBERT,

Rev. Richard Fuller, D. D., Eutaw Place Baptist Church.

Your elaborate work will surprise even the people in Baltimore, who have too long been ignorant the real wealth, enterprise and true mercantile and moral greatness of their city. And yet I venture predict that the author of such a work in the year of our Lord, 1890, will refer to this volume as a hi tory of Baltimore yet in her earliest youth. Again I thank you for this labor of love, the details which must have cost you a great deal of hard toil.

Rev. John Leyburn, D. D.

Your exhibit of the present activities of the city will no doubt excite surprise among our own peop as well as at a distance; but it should prove a source of deep gratification and laudable pride to eve Baltimorean, and at the same time awaken renewed zeal and enterprise to attain the vastly larger pro perity which is evidently so practicable. Not only the heads of business houses, but the young me the prospective leaders of future years, should "read, ponder and inwardly digest" the food for thoug and high purpose which you have so skillfully provided.

If Baltimore is to become the emporium for which her advantages adapt her, *she must take the trou* to let the world know the extent and variety of her resources.

BALTIMORE, Feb, 12, 1874.

GEO. W. HOWARD, ESQ.

Dear Sir :—As representatives respectively of the Union Merchants' Exchange and the grain interest of St. Louis, we are visiting Baltimore for the purpose of effecting more intimate and extensive relations between these two great cities in the trade; and having seen your admirable work, "The Monumental City," &c., in the West, we take the occasion of our visit to express our gratification with it, and to say that its circulation throughout the Western country would greatly contribute to the very object we have in view, and to a much wider expansion of the *general trade* with your noble city.

Yours respectfully, U. J. LIVINGSTON, *Chief Grain Inspector, St. Louis.*
THEO. BARTHOLOW, *Of the firm Nanson, Bartholow & Co.*

Hon. Wm. Pinkney Whyte, of Maryland.

A careful examination of "The Monumental City," &c., satisfies me that great advantage would result to our city, by a free circulation of it in all parts of the country.

A knowledge of the resources and the growing trade of Baltimore, and the enterprise of its manufacturers, and best of all, the great reliability and integrity of its people cannot fail to attract both population and capital.

I am quite sure that no means can be better suited to accomplish this result than the spread of the information contained in this book.

Hon. Joshua Vansant, Mayor.

Viewing the book as a work of art, in its engraved illustrations and fine typography, it reflects credit upon the artists, that contributed to adorn its pages, but much more praise is due him, who conceived the idea of putting forth a work, which as a matter of public utility, is an adjunct to the industrious enterprise of the people of our noble city, and presents the energy, perseverance and capacity, that rendered the measure effective.

The book is substantially and essentially useful, and should be laid upon the parlor table and the business desk of every citizen of Baltimore.

Hon. J. Morrison Harris.

I have examined it with care and am not only greatly interested but astonished to realize from its disclosures and array of carefully compiled statistics, the extent of the business resources and advantages of our city. I had no idea whatever of the completeness of our ability to supply the demands of the most extensive business in the staples of trade, nor of the great development of manufacturing industries in our midst. I think you have rendered all classes of your fellow-citizens a most valuable service by your publication, and that the widest circulation should be given to it, especially throughout the West and South, where its perusal is calculated to have the most beneficial effect in the enlargement of our trade.

Henry C. Smith, of Tucker, Smith & Co., President of the Shoe and Leather Association.

I am fully impressed with its importance as a valuable means of introducing to the American people the unrivalled resources which Baltimore possesses as a manufacturing and commercial city, and it is all important to make the facts known throughout the country in order to induce capital and skilled labor to seek our beautiful, healthful and centrally located city, as a desirable field for their profitable employment.

It has often surprised and annoyed me, to find in traveling South and West such a want of knowledge in regard to these facts, and I have many times thought that we needed just such a Work as yours, in order to present the facts which "The Monumental City" contains.

I. O. O. F. Office Cor. and Rec. Secretary R. W. G. L. U. S

Baltimore owes you a lasting obligation for presenting to the world all such elements of her wealth and power and general prosperity, for the moral elevation of a people is no less an evidence of greatness, than commerce and the arts, agriculture, manufactures, letters and Religion itself; since there can be no true religion without morals as its basis.

Your Book will open the eyes of people abroad, who have very vague and barren opinions of Baltimore, and contribute largely to a general enlightenment, which cannot fail to produce great good for our grand city.

Very respectfully yours,
JAS. L. RIDGELY, Cor. Sec'y.

Wm. Devries, of Wm. Devries & Co.

Your exhibition of Baltimore's industrial and commercial character and relations, is surprising eve to our best informed business men, since their observation has been confined mainly to their own departments; and until the appearance of your Work they had no means of comprehending its entire trade and resources.

A commercial experience in Baltimore of more than forty years, has taught me that the radical error of the past is this, *we as a city* have neglected to make known through appropriate channels our unsurpassed facilities.

John T. Morris, Esq. President of Board of Commissioners of Public Schools,

I have examined the "Monumental City, Its Past History and Present Resources," with great pleasure and cordially commend it to the attention of every citizen of Baltimore.

The past history of our city is full of interest and instruction, and its present resources, as shown by you, indicate what its future may be, if we properly appreciate our position and opportunities. Your work will be of special value to our city, if it can be extensively circulated throughout the country.

Hon. A. M. Waddell, Member of Congress, Third Congressional District, North Carolina.

Accept my thanks for the very interesting account of "The Monumental City," &c., which I found a day or two ago, on my return home.

It is a very interesting contribution to the history of American civilization, and a monument to the enterprise and industry of the author.

Rev. Cyrus Dickson, D. D., Presbyterian Mission House, No. 23 Centre Street, New York.

I have read it carefully, and with a pleasure quickened by the memories of fourteen years' happy residence in Baltimore.

It is a grand compend of the past history, present resources, and future progress of the metropolis of Maryland and Queen of the Chesapeake.

Many things of which I had a very vague knowledge are here put into permanent form, and will furnish a treasury of valuable information to all parts of the conutry.

Hon. Charles E. Phelps.

The sketch of Washington City and its environs is the most successful effort which has come under my notice to present in a popular and attractive style valuable information concerning *all* points of interest in connection with the seat of the National Government. * * * *

In point of style it is a literary gem possessing a vivacity and polish which distinguish it from any work of the kind yet offered to the public.

From the Sentinel, Milwaukee.

We have received a considerable volume entitled "The Monumental City: Its Past History and Present Resources." The author, Mr. Geo. W. Howard, makes an interesting review of the past progress of Baltimore, and indulges in prophecies as to her future with an enthusiasm which the reader must largely share. That city owes much to Mr. Howard for this comprehensive volume.

From the Richmond Dispatch, Virginia.

This is the title of a book which will be interesting to business men and of value to Baltimore. It is the history of one of the most enterprising and prosperous cities in the Union. Baltimore has had a career beset with difficulties. Her example may be studied with benefit by other cities. The history presented in Mr. Howard's book well shows the triumphs of that city.

From the Religious Herald, Richmond.

Baltimore is a great and prosperous city. The volume before us contains not only its early history, but a finely illustrated account of its public buildings and its spacious factories. The volume is highly creditable to its author and to the city which it describes. It is interesting to the general reader and *very valuable to business men*, who desire to be thoroughly informed of the manufactures and trade of the Monumental City.

From the Rural Messenger, Petersburg, Va.

It contains a mass of valuable information in relation to the city of Baltimore, presenting its resources and development in a new and attractive light, naming many of its prominent business houses, and giving at the same time illustrations of the public works and a large map of the city. The writer has done a good work for the city, and deserves the thanks of the public.

From the Wytheville Dispatch, Virginia.

To the citizens of Baltimore we can say that never before have your commercial interests, the extent of your trade and your wonderful business advantages, been so prominently placed before the people of the United States.

From the Sacramento Union, California.

There is nothing in regard to the early history of this noted city that is interesting to know, and nothing in regard to its extended resources, improvements and advantages at this day, but can be found described to the minutest detail in this book, which cannot but be perused with pleasure and instruction to the general reader, as well as by those who have the satisfaction of having been residents of old Baltimore.

Brantz Mayer, Lt. Col. U. S. Army.

[Author of "Mexico as It Was and Is," "Mexico; Aztec, Spanish and Republican," &c., &c.,]

BALTIMORE, July 13th, 1875.

GEORGE W. HOWARD, ESQ.

Dear Sir:—I thank you very much for the handsome volume of Baltimore's "Past History and Present Resources," which you kindly sent to me. I read it with interest and instruction; and as I went over much of the ground some years ago, I can bear witness to your accuracy on the matters with which I am best acquainted.

Having lived for the last four years and a half in California, and observed closely the development of the Pacific States, I am impressed by the great importance to our city of a *broadcast distribution of your Book over the whole Pacific slope, including California, Nevada, Oregon, and even Arizona.* The population of that region is the most eager and energetic I ever dwelt among. It is always striving for wealth, and, of course, is prompt to open fresh and cheap channels of supply, as well as to find markets for its productions. These productions—especially of California and Oregon—are, as you know, marvellous in quantity and variety. One of its favorite modes is "Advertising." It knows the value of the Press. It not only uses the city and country papers, but nowhere do I remember to have seen such quantities books, maps, circulars, pamphlets, prospectuses and handbills, displaying the wares and industries, the prospects and advantages of various cities and States, as cover the tables and desks of Oregon, Nevada and California. These are not mere *puffs*, but mean and actually produce business, and that too just in proportion as they are skillfully prepared to attract and convince the keen readers they address. It is the way in which the attention of such an active society is reached, arrested and controlled. I am sorry to say I do not recollect having seen, anywhere, even a handbill from Baltimore.

Now, it seems to me, knowing these things as I do personally, that just such a publication as yours—serious and not clap-trap—a publication addressing itself authoratively to intelligent business men, must be extremely useful to Baltimore on the Pacific. For instance—cheap, quick transportation between the seaboards of the two sides of the continent is one of the main problems of Californians. Manufacturers, farmers, traders, importers are all alert on the subject.

I believe, (and I have so said and *published* in California,) it is *demonstrated* that Baltimore's *central geographical position*—so skillfully availed of by our own great Railway Company—is *nearer* to the Pacific coast, and certainly to its sea-going steam transportation at Sacramento, Vallejo, and San Francisco, than any other of the great importing cities of the Atlantic coast. This valuable freight-cheapening fact is alone worth the cost of placing thousands of your Books in the hands of business men of all classes on the Pacific. But, short, quick, transportation is not all that is needed. They want clear, truthful information as to what you grow, what you import, what you manufacture, and who sells, and how you sell your commodities.

Cities grow rich by trade, but no cities have ever grown rich *on freights* alone. Freight augments the wealth of the transporter; but, all the facilities and good designs of transportation in the world will never enrich a city *or* the carrier of freight, if the citizens do not second the transporter's efforts by mercantile capital and enterprise. That mercantile enterprise must be brought properly and steadily to the knowledge of purchasers everywhere, especially in a country of eager competition like ours.

I am induced to make these remarks, because, during my long stay and travel on the West coast, I have so often been mortified to see how little Baltimore and its business are known in California and Oregon. One hears very little of any Eastern city but New York. If our business men do not personally push their trade *to* California. give Californians the information of what you have and what you can do, and they will soon begin to push their trade to Baltimore. That would be a victory which I am sure you would be proud to help to achieve. I am, dear sir, very respectfully, your obedient servant,

BRANTZ MAYER.

Brown & Brune, Attorneys and Counsellors at Law.

From your long and great experience as a business man in Baltimore, you are well fitted to comprehend and exhibit its vast and constantly expanding commercial, manufacturing and industrial enterprises, and to present to our attention the energetic men engaged in promoting them. This information you have in your book, very pleasingly connected with a sketch of the past history of our city, and with a very complete account of its many and interesting Religious, Scientific and Charitable Institutions. * *

I am very truly your friend, F. W. BRUNE.

GEO. W. HOWARD, ESQ.

Wm. W. Taylor, President National Union Bank of Maryland.

"The Monumental City," &c, disclosing succinctly, but with remarkable perspicuity and intelligence, the "past history and present resources" of Baltimore, whose progress and popularity cannot be more surely advanced, than by the diffuse circulation of the profitable information compiled by you with such laborious skill and patience.

B. F. Newcomer, President Safe Deposit and Trust Company.

"The Monumental City, Its Past History and Present Resources," which has proven to me a source of much information as well as most agreeable entertainment, and exhibits on your part, in its compilation, a degree of research and persevering energy that I trust may be appreciated by your fellow-citizens, and especially by the Councils of the City in such substantial manner as will not only benefit you, but will enable the whole City to reap the advantages of so valuable a work.

Rev. Julius E. Grammer, D. D., P. E. Church.

No foreign guide-book of a single city surpasses yours, and the contrast between Baltimore of 1752 and Baltimore of to-day is a type of the growth of this country and the spirit of progress among its people, which cannot be more strikingly presented than it has been by you.

Rev. B. Szold, D. D., Rabbi of the Oheb-Shalom (Cong.)

It will induce thousands to whom the wealth and attractions of Baltimore are unknown, to visit and enrich it with new enterprises.

Our city and State would be greatly benefitted if our authorities would give your book—which I consider a monumental work—a wide circulation. It ought to be a household book throughout the city and State. It shows the abundant germs this city has for a great future.

Rev. Samuel D. Alexander, D. D., 73d Street, New York.

NEW YORK, August 23, 1875.

MESSRS. EDITORS:

In looking over the new addition of "The Monumental City," &c., I am deeply impressed with its value to the residents of Baltimore.

It would be a mistake to suppose that it is a mere advertising medium, benefitting the large dealers and manufacturers; I believe that it tends as much to the advancement and best interests of the poorest man in the city; for whatever advances the interests of the city, reaches the every day laborer who is industrious. I can conceive of no better way of helping every man in Baltimore, from the man that sweeps the streets to the Merchant Prince, than by scattering 100,000 copies of this Volume over the whole land.

And then this book places beside Trade and the useful Arts, the Church, the School, and the grand charities for which Baltimore is distinguished. They must all rise together or fall together. There is a power that emanates from the Church and the School that reaches even the channels of Trade and Commerce, and then there is a reflex influence sent back upon these Religious and Moral Institutions. The exhaustive notice of the Peabody Institute which this Book contains will doubtless influence other monied men to follow his noble example.

When I first took up this Book, it appeared to be simply a mere advertising medium; but after reading it, these pages of advertisements proved to be grand testimonies of the wealth, the industry, the morality and the culture of this great city.

Mr. Howard seems to have a genius for making sign-boards speak great historical truths, and may I not say prophecies of what Baltimore shall presently be.

I have placed this Book in my collection of Local Histories, and I predict that it will be a rich storehouse from which the future Historian of Maryland and Baltimore will gladly turn for facts.

Yours, &c., S. D. ALEXANDER.

www.ingramcontent.com/pod-product-compliance
Lightning Source LLC
LaVergne TN
LVHW020916110826
845150LV00004B/693

9781425555283